MISSION HOUSE AND CITY OF KOLAPOOR.

"With 44,000 idolaters under my window, and 120,000 within a few miles of my door, with no other missionary to care for their souls, where, oh! where on the globe can I find a more needy or noble field for Christian effort?" (Page 275.)

MISSION SCHOOLS

IN

INDIA

OF THE

American Board of Commissioners

FOR

FOREIGN MISSIONS,

WITH SKETCHES OF THE MISSIONS AMONG THE NORTH AMERICAN INDIANS, THE SANDWICH ISLANDS, THE ARMENIANS OF TURKEY, AND THE NESTORIANS OF PERSIA.

BY REV. R. G. WILDER,

FIFTEEN YEARS MISSIONARY OF THE BOARD.

"GO YE THEREFORE, AND TEACH ALL NATIONS."—Matt. 18 : 19.
"GATHER THE CHILDREN."—Joel 2 : 16.

PUBLISHED BY SUBSCRIPTION.

New-York:
A. D. F. RANDOLPH, 683 BROADWAY.
BOSTON: CROCKER & BREWSTER.
1861.

JOHN A. GRAY,
Printer, Stereotyper, and Binder,
Corner of Frankfort and Jacob Streets,
FIRE-PROOF BUILDINGS.

TO THE

American Board of Commissioners

FOR

FOREIGN MISSIONS;

THE OBJECT OF UNBOUNDED ADMIRATION IN MY EARLY LIFE,

AND OF

SINCERE AND ABIDING AFFECTION

DURING ALL THE

YEARS OF MY MISSIONARY SERVICE;

THIS WORK IS

RESPECTFULLY DEDICATED BY THE

AUTHOR.

PREFACE.

WHEN I went to India, fifteen years ago, I had no distinct views in regard to the different agencies employed in the missionary work. When I looked down for the first time from the Highlands near the village of Tas, upon the broad and fertile plain of Ahmednuggur dotted with beautiful villages, the morning sun glancing gloriously from the white domes of their numerous temples thronged with idolatrous worshippers, the one passion and purpose of my soul was to win as many of them as possible to Christ. I knew nothing of "mission policy," but our blessed commission.

A joyful welcome awaited us from our elder brethren, and the next day they committed to me the care of the mission seminary at Ahmednuggur. They soon added to my duties the city free schools, and subsequently the free schools in the villages. This system of schools had been devised and prosecuted for many years, and I can claim no credit or responsibility in regard to its origin or adoption. I engaged in such duties as were committed to me. I watched the working and results of these schools with increasing interest and much care. I observed their special power for good, in accomplishing the salvation of souls. I became convinced of the wisdom of my brethren who had devised and adopted them. Hence, when in 1854, I saw their views *wrested* or *disallowed*, and these schools suppressed, I grieved for their loss.

The question involved in the use of these schools is *vital* to the success of our missionary work. My love for this work has led me to prepare this volume, with the earnest hope that by helping to right views, it may contribute to our success, and the more speedy triumph of the Gospel in India and every dark land.

This work is not designed to be controversial, but *historical.* I have spoken freely of our able Deputation to India, and the changes they effected, but only so far as necessary to be true to the facts of history. Should any reader, by a bare possibility, think I have said too much of the Deputation, let him bear in mind that he knows not how much I have left unsaid. Let him also compare this with the larger volume which the Deputation published, embodying and enforcing their views and the changes they effected in India.

This volume does not so much represent my own views as it does the views of my brethren in the foreign field, and of the officers of the American Board. Its chief aim is to gather up the most important *facts*, *incidents*, and *results* in the history of our mission schools. In doing this it sometimes brings to view the discouraging details and patient, persevering toil involved in this work of missions, but it also brings to view the rich and abundant blessing which God has bestowed upon such toil. Many pages will be found to develop the results of our schools, in scenes and events as precious and glorious as those of the day of Pentecost.

In my efforts to let facts and the views of others rest on *their* authority rather than mine, and at the same time avoid cumbering my page with references and foot-notes, I have used frequent quotations. These may have interfered somewhat with a forcible style, but if so, it is hoped the ready authority they carry will furnish ample compensation.

Discrepancies and errors in dates may exist; but so far as a most laborious and patient examination of manuscript and printed reports and letters from the missions, and of the organs of the Board, could avail, all errors have been guarded against with scrupulous care.

On the 20th of last December, I was about to engage an immediate passage to India. Delayed a few months by an event beyond our control, I have sought in this volume to make it accrue to the benefit of the cause we love and to which we have devoted our lives. Impatient of further delay, we now hasten back to our adopted home and field of labor in the dark kingdom of Kolapoor. R. G. WILDER.

New-York, March 4th, 1861.

CONTENTS.

CHAPTER IV.

HISTORY OF OUR BOMBAY MISSION SCHOOLS CONTINUED.

CHAPTER V.

CHARACTER AND RESULTS OF SCHOOLS IN THE AHMEDNUGGUR MISSION.

CHAPTER VI.

SCHOOLS OF THE SATARA AND KOLAPOOR MISSIONS.

SATARA.

KOLAPOOR.

CHAPTER VII.

SCHOOLS OF THE CEYLON MISSION.

INTRODUCTION.

Modern Missions have become a fact and a power in the world. Their results, for the last fifty years, put to shame alike the timid faith of the Church and the scornful predictions of the infidel opposer. A recent vigorous writer in India, with the fruits of Protestant Missions around him there, and looking only at their temporal results, very justly remarks: "We are tired of listening to nonsense about the small results of missionary work, the enormous revenue expended, the inadequate return secured. In the midst of the mighty events now passing over Asia, though every throne is rocking, and every dynasty crumbling into dust, though the Tartar lords are ceasing from the face of the earth, and the great struggle of the North and the South seems rapidly approaching, there is no event more wonderful than the progress of the mission power. Within one poor half-century the unregarded effort of a few fanatics, with a 'visionary cobbler' at their head, has become the strongest of social levers. If a third of the human race are now in internecine struggle among themselves, it is because a missionary instructed a poor Chinese lad sick in his hospital."

This last remark refers to the internal conflict then waging in China, the end of which is not yet.

Our writer might have added, if the degraded islanders of the ocean have been raised from their ignorance and pollution and blessed with a written language, and with all the arts and sciences of civilized life, it is the result of missions. If the vast regions of Central Africa are being opened up to the light of science and civilization, it is because missionary zeal impels the explorer.

India is the great land of idolaters, and in regard to *India*, more frequently than elsewhere, have the missionaries been reproached for their want of success. Such cavillers are well met by the statements and interrogatories of this writer. "Is it nothing," he continues, "that one entire race, shortly to people an entire province, eagerly embraces Christianity, maintains its own pastors, builds its own churches, and when called upon to suffer for the cause, dies calmly with Christ upon its lips? Those who know the *Karens*, know that they have done all this. Is it nothing that at this very moment in the jungles of Chota Nagpore, among a race wild as our painted forefathers, *three thousand men* have declared their eagerness to be baptized; that Government with another wild race to tame, and that race recently in rebellion, can find no civilizers so efficient as Christian Missionaries? Is it nothing that among one of the worst and most degraded populations of Asia, the Pariahs of Lower India, 100,000 men have embraced the faith, and do, so far as the human eye can see, live according to it? It has been evident for years, to all men with eyes, that the old fabric of Hinduism is breaking up. In the Arctic Seas, before the ice cracks, a low steady murmur is heard, never ceasing, springing no one can tell whence, yet always, in the midst of the vague terror it suggests, announcing the approaching deliverance. The ice has not cracked, but the murmur which precedes it is on the air. Who believes in Hinduism? Some few Europeans, the Court of Directors, the British Parliament, but certainly not the Hindus. Sutti and widow celibacy are abolished. Polygamy is doomed, and what Hindu, knowing all this, raises a hand? There is no heart left in the creed, and though it may exist for generations, as the corpse of Roman Paganism did, its downfall is assured."

This utterance was penned in India by an experienced and observant mind shortly before the outbreak of the terrible Sepoy rebellion of 1857. Does not the fact of that rebellion show that he misapprehended in some measure the spirit of the Hindus? I think not. On the contrary, the *result* of that rebellion clearly proves that Hinduism has no elements which can stand before true science and Christianity; and that in its *general* import, this prophetic utterance is finding a rapid fulfillment.

With reference to the agency in effecting this mighty change, our author continues: "This has been accomplished by missionaries, and is not the greatest of their achievements. For years their influence and that of the class which supports them, has been permeating Indian society. That society is consequently utterly changed. The tone of the official world has utterly changed. Is this nothing to have achieved? We have not spoken of souls saved, for we are not writing for religious men who know these things without our guidance. We address those who will look only at the social aspect of the question, and we ask them whether the result does not justify the cost?"

Now, in properly estimating the results of modern missions, we may not, with this writer, limit our vision to the civil and social benefits accruing from them. These, in comparison with the spiritual results, are as time to eternity, earth to heaven. Worldly philanthropists may well rejoice in the civil and social changes effected by missions. These changes are every where such as to challenge their admiration and merit their cordial coöperation in the work. But the crowning glory of missions is, that they are God's appointed agency for saving immortal souls—for despoiling Satan's kingdom and reëstablishing the kingdom of Christ. And when we attempt to estimate these higher and spiritual results, we are constrained to feel that the triumphs of the Gospel in the achievements of modern missions eclipse all that is recorded of Apostolic times.

In confirmation of this view it is sufficient to mention the more than 40,000 converts gathered into the Christian Church within the last thirty years from the degraded idolaters of the Sandwich Islands, or the wonderful reformation now progressing among the Armenians of Turkey and the Nestorians of Persia, or the 50,000 converts won to Christ by the labors of our Wesleyan brethren on the Fejee Islands, or the 25,000 converts gathered into the mission churches, which like so many glorious lights begirt the dark continent of Africa, or the 30,000 or 40,000 natives of India who have broken the adamantine chains of Hindu idolatry and caste, and now gather with us in humble faith and love around the table of the Lord.

It is well to bear on our minds and in our hearts these triumphs of the cross in our own times. They serve to quicken our faith in the purpose and promise of God, and to fill our souls with adoring gratitude to Him through whose word and spirit all has been achieved. "Not unto us, not unto us, O Lord, but unto thy name be all the glory."

But it is not enough to raise peans of thanksgiving for triumphs already achieved. Before "the kingdoms of this world shall become the kingdom of our Lord and of his Christ," far greater victories must be won. While we rejoice over the 30,000 native communicants who have been gathered into the Church of Christ in India, we must remember that some 200,000,000 of idolaters still remain in that land fast bound in the cruel bondage of heathenism—that the true light which has risen upon Western Asia and a few of Ocean's Islands, while gilding the mountain tops with divine radiance, serves at the same time to reveal more clearly the dark regions of heathenism which still cover the slopes and fill up the valleys of islands and continents over three fourths of our habitable globe. So that the true soldier of the cross must regard the brightest triumphs of the past and present only as a faint earnest of greater conquests yet to be achieved. The success of missions hitherto should only nerve the arm of the Church with new faith and courage for more vigorous campaigns, and lead her to consecrate every energy to this work intrusted to her by divine commission, till the last dark corner of earth glow with gospel light, and the heathen be wholly given to Christ as his rightful inheritance.

But, by what *agencies* is the Church to prosecute this warfare? With what *means* is she to bring the truth of God to bear on pagan minds and hearts?

In reply to these inquiries, it would seem to be sufficient to point to the agencies she has hitherto employed. Had past agencies proved ineffective, we might properly discard them and seek for new appliances. But such is not the case. Past missionary efforts have been crowned with success which stirs the deepest gratitude of every sanctified heart.

And how has this success been achieved? "Not by might, nor by power, but by my Spirit, saith the Lord." The word and Spirit of God have achieved it all, and these are our only reliance for the future. And here we might rest the case, assured that no dissenting voice would be heard among the entire band of Christian laborers.

But, doubtless, there have been human agents, and these have applied various instrumentalities. *Oral preaching*, *schools*, *the press*, *itineracies*, *medicine*, and other agencies have been pressed into the service for evangelizing the nations. In all this we might rejoice, leaving Paul to plant and Apollos to water, each according to his own judgment and ability, still rendering all honor to God who alone giveth the increase. But with this, the agents and laborers of some of our missionary societies have not been content. Claiming to be convinced of the superior efficacy of one or more of those agencies, they not only discard the others themselves, but insist that their brethren shall discard them also. Were they willing to make their convictions a rule for themselves only, all might continue to labor harmoniously, having God's glory and the salvation of souls for their object, though seeking tocompass this object by different agencies for making known and applying God's truth.

But with this these well-meaning agents have not been content. They have opposed their convictions to those of their brethren equally conscientious, faithful and laborious. They have sought to enact regulations which should restrict these brethren to the particular agencies which *they* approve.

Now here is a serious evil—one which opposes a new hindrance, and unless speedily overcome can not fail to retard the progress of this blessed work. This evil has recently developed itself in the proceedings of the American Board of Commissioners for Foreign Missions. This Board is the oldest and most successful of any supported by our American churches. Her missionaries are found on the Sandwich Islands, in Micronesia, along the coast of China, on Ceylon, that

> "Fairest isle of the ocean,
> Brightest gem of the sea,"

in Southern and Western India, among the Nestorians of Persia, the Syrians of Mesopotamia, the Arabs of Lebanon, the Armenians of Turkey, the dwellers of classic Greece, and at different points skirting the dark continent of Africa.

For fifty years this Board has conducted missions with a measure of success which has brought new glory to God on earth, and won a good degree of honor to our American Zion. Oral preaching, the press, schools, and itineracies have been generally employed in all her missions. In the use of these appliances, the agents of the Board at home and abroad seem till recently to have been entirely unanimous. Each year the success attending these agencies has developed new cause of praise to God, and frequent formal votes of the Board, commending the wisdom of her missionaries in devising and applying these agencies. In perusing the published records of the Board, it is most gratifying to observe the mutual confidence between the agents at home and abroad, the unanimity and zeal with which these agencies have been applied, and the blessed results which have followed in their train.

But, unhappily, this pleasure was not to be enjoyed without interruption. The published records of the Board, for 1856, develop a painful feeling of distrust and dissatisfaction with one of the agencies hitherto so unanimously and successfully employed in our missions. The value of some of the *schools*, which had been in use from the origin of our missions, is explicitly called in question in these records. A Deputation had been previously sent to our India missions, and in their published Report to the Board, at the special meeting held at Albany, March 4, 1856, we find, in their instructions from the Prudential Committee, the following paragraphs giving utterance to this distrust and dissatisfaction, namely:

"At present, it is the strong persuasion of the Prudential Committee that no *school* can properly be sustained by the funds of the Board, in which the vernacular language is not the grand medium of instruction."

"It is time to inquire more earnestly as to the place which schools ought to hold in the system of missionary efforts among the heathen. And the Deputation is instructed to procure an answer, as far as possible, to the inquiry, whether, in general, missionary schools should not be restricted to converts and stated attendants on preaching, and their children."

The results of this distrust, and the consequent doings of the Deputation, are somewhat known. Mission seminaries were disbanded; common schools with "heathen teachers" were interdicted. In one mission more than *five hundred* children and youth, who were daily enjoying faithful instruction in the saving truths of the Gospel, were "turned out into the great and terrible wilderness of the heathen world," by order of the Deputation.

Now the schools thus interdicted were such as had been in use from the origin of our missions; and the blessing of God has rested largely upon them, as the published records of the Board abundantly show. The Secretaries and Prudential Committee have repeatedly joined with the missionaries in sorrow and lamentations and appeals to the churches, in behalf of just such schools when disbanded for want of funds. (See Annual Report for 1838, pp. 41–43, and Heralds and Reports, *passim*.)

With all deference, then, to the judgment of the Deputation, and the present officers of the American Board, we must be allowed to inquire, should not the propriety of supporting such schools have been investigated and settled at a much earlier date? If they were not worthy of support in 1856, how came they to be worthy of support in 1850, or during the forty years previous to that date? Will it be said that such schools may have been proper at the origin of missions, and not so after years of progress? That agencies may and should be modified and adapted to the progress of the work, in a given mission is readily conceded. But there were *new* missions in 1856, as well as in 1840 or 1820; and if these schools were proper in *new* missions and *old* ones too, previous to 1856, how came they to be unworthy of support in the new and unbroken regions of Hinduism subsequent to that particular date?

These inquiries are propounded as well deserving the candid consideration of the officers and patrons of the American Board. Has there been a grave mistake in the conduct of our missions through all the past history of the Board? Have the funds of the churches been misapplied for the support of schools not worthy of patronage? If the views and doings of our late Deputation were correct, how can we avoid the inference that, for more than forty years, the funds of the Board, so far as used for the support of the different kinds of schools interdicted by the Deputation, have been misapplied?

Nor is it possible to stop here. If the home and foreign agents of the Board have made so great a mistake for more than forty years, what guarantee can the churches have that they are right now? May not the funds of the Board still be misapplied in many other ways at the present time? Nay, may not this very act, suppressing the schools in question, prove to be the greatest error hitherto committed?

These inquiries deserve the prayerful consideration of all who love the cause of missions, and the American Board. We leave them here, and turn to review the agencies in which all have been so happily united, and which have been so richly blessed of God.

In approving and sustaining the various mission schools of the Board, her home and foreign agents have been wonderfully harmonious up to a recent date. Is it not probable that to their harmonious views and action are to be traced, under God, the blessed results of these schools?

It is believed that if the true theory and practice of the officers and missionaries of the Board, in regard to these schools, and the blessed results which have attended them, were thoroughly understood by the Christian public, no place for controversy would remain. That instead of enactments interdicting any of these schools, and consequent division and strife, all would unite in thanksgiving and praise to God for the signal blessing he has bestowed upon this imperfect agency for making known Christ and him crucified to the perishing heathen.

It is the design of the following pages to develop *the educational theory and practice of the American Board*—THE CHARACTER AND RESULTS OF HER VARIOUS MISSION SCHOOLS. May He whose glory among the nations is the great object of the American Board and all her agents, enable us to present the *principles*, *facts*, and *results* connected with this department of mission labor, so that our humble effort may meet with His acceptance and prove serviceable in the great and blessed work of evangelizing the heathen.

MISSION SCHOOLS.

CHAPTER I.

THEORY OF MISSION SCHOOLS.

Origin and Object of the American Board.

THE origin of *the American Board of Commissioners for Foreign Missions* dates from the memorable Association at Bradford, Mass., June 27th, 1810. The large hearts and broad views of its founders are conspicuous in the incipient measures adopted, and in nothing more so than in the comprehensive declaration of their purpose in organizing the Board. Their first formal resolution on the subject stands recorded in the following language, namely: "Voted, that there be instituted by this general Association, a Board of Commissioners for Foreign Missions, for the purpose of devising ways and means, and adopting and prosecuting measures, for promoting the spread of the Gospel in heathen lands."

No attempt was made to limit their proposed efforts to any particular agencies, and none were interdicted. A wide margin was left for all the wisdom and experience that might accrue in the progress of the work.

At a later period, when the "Laws and Regulations of the Board" were more definitely determined, we find their object enunciated in the following terms, namely: "The object of the Board is, to propagate the Gospel among unevangelized nations and communities, by means of *preachers, catechists, schoolmasters, and the press.*" Here *schools* are distinctly recognized as one of the prominent agencies of the Board for propagating the Gospel; and experience has abundantly shown the wise forethought and consideration of the venerable founders of the Board in this respect. They gave no special prominence to one agency over another, but left all to be employed in such proportion as the experience and judgment of their missionaries should determine to be most effective in accomplishing the great work to be achieved.

Schools and Oral Preaching one in Aim.

The possibility of oral preaching and mission schools ever being regarded as antagonistic, seems not to have entered the minds of those large-hearted men. The terms "preaching missionaries," and "educationalists," is an invention of modern times, and no less invidious than unfortunate. The aim of mission schools and of the oral proclamation of the Gospel is ever one and the same. They are never to be viewed as having a different object, but as different ways for accomplishing the same object, each rendering the other more effective in accomplishing the great work of evangelizing the heathen.

Without schools in many parts of the heathen world, the preacher could obtain no stated hearers, and even if obtained, few among them could read his books or understand his message, without frequent and continued repetition—"line upon line," and "precept upon precept"—a continuous course of instruction which is found in every country to be most easily effected by means of a regular system of schools.

I confess to little sympathy with those over-nice exegetical speculations which, on the one hand, would limit our great commission to the *oral proclamation* of the Gospel, or on the other, to *teaching it technically and only in the schoolroom.* The work to be done furnishes a sufficient exegesis of our Lord's intent, whether we translate his words, "Go, *preach* the Gospel to every creature," or, "Go, *teach* all nations"—"*Teaching* them to observe all things whatsoever I have commanded you."

Difficulty of communicating Christian Truth to Heathen Minds.

That much repetition and a continuous course of instruction is necessary to enlighten and convert the heathen, would seem to be obvious from the nature of the human mind and the character of those corrupt systems of false religion which for many centuries have enthralled and debased their intellects and their hearts. Long-cherished views, however erroneous, are not easily eradicated. "Can the leopard change his spots?" Every superstition of the heathen has not only acquired the force of habit, but is entrenched and cherished with all the sanctities of religious faith and feeling. An empty cask may be soon filled by pouring in water; but if it was filled centuries ago with crooked nails and spikes imbedded in cement which both rain and sunshine have indurated ever since, a previous process will be necessary before the water can find entrance.

In regard to the Hindu's state of mind, and the difficulty of communicating Christian ideas to him, I am aware the rash statement has been made, that "you have the same difficulty here [in America] in conveying to one of our people the true idea of sin, before he has been taught by the Spirit of God, that you have there, [in India.]" But this statement stands opposed to the combined experience and testimony of all considerate missionaries ever since the days of the Apostle Paul. Have grossly perverted religious views and most debasing practices, all indorsed with the highest sanctions of the Hindu Shasters and religion, no demoralizing, corrupting, and searing effect upon the conscience and heart of the idolater? Have we indeed no more difficulty in conveying true ideas of God, sin, and holiness to those ignorant and depraved minds, into which *no one right idea* on these momentous subjects has ever yet penetrated, than to the minds of non-professing men in Christendom, who have been trained from childhood under the concentrated light and influence of the Gospel and Christian institutions?

Views of the Secretary, Dr. Anderson, on this Point.

Rev. Dr. Anderson, in his valuable Tract entitled, "Labors and Hindrances of the Missionary," has ably presented some of the facts and features of heathenism, which expose the very grave error of this statement. He says: "Consider, again, in how unfavorable a condition heathen communities are to be operated upon. Generally they are thoroughly sensual, earthly, and selfish; unaccustomed to be influenced by, or to think upon, intellectual or moral subjects, unused to change, without enterprise, with no models of excellence before them, and little inclined and little able to appreciate them when presented; full of prejudice and love of sin. It is difficult to conceive how unlike they are to an active-minded, enterprising, progressive community in such a Christian land as this. Public sentiment there, instead of being a great motive power in favor of religion and morality and social improvement, has become inveterate and consolidated as an almost insurmountable barrier to any reformatory effort.

"Consider, again, how slowly religious truth can be communicated to heathen communities! In addition to their not having been trained to think on moral and religious subjects generally, and their disinclination to take into their minds truths or considerations which interfere with their cherished habits, their superstitions, and their love of sin, there is a difficulty in the very *novelty* and *strangeness* of the truths to be taught, and in presenting them so that they shall be clearly apprehended, in a language not made nor used to convey such ideas. An intelligent missionary states that a Gospel sermon might be preached in the Tamil language, explicit and pointed in every doctrine, and as correct and plain as idiom and style could make it, and yet the uninstructed Hindu would not get one Christian idea from it, but would construe it all in favor of Brahminism. Our theological terms, so brief and expressive to a well-instructed hearer, are of no use there. The same missionary says that with a well-instructed Christian congregation in the

United States, more can be done by a single sermon to communicate new truths, and carry the hearer forward in Christian knowledge, than can be done in a newly-gathered Hindu congregation in three months. It is doubtless substantially so in every heathen community." . .

"What time, then, will be required for the missionary to eradicate the heathenish errors, detect the heathenish sophistries, and rectify the heathenish and perverse ways of thinking which he meets with in his untaught hearers, and which they love and cling to because they countenance their corrupt passions and habits? . . Is this the work of a year, or of any short period of years? In the case of a Christian child, whom, at the age of two or three years, the mother begins to teach the same truths, the object is likely to be more speedily and perfectly accomplished."

Necessity of Schools from the Character of Heathenism, as sketched by various Authors.

That the above view of Dr. Anderson is correct, is obvious from every portrait of heathenism which has ever been sketched by enlightened men. The Rev. Dr. Storrs, in his sermon before the Board, in 1850, drew this portrait in the following language, namely: "Ignorant of God and his law, as well as of their own, and the moral character of the world; content with mental inactivity, and indifferent to moral elevation; untaught in the principles of science, and fast-bound in errors venerated for their antiquity; vicious in their habits, and absorbed in sensual indulgences; accustomed to the profane rites of religions glittering yet grovelling, and degrading yet commanding and terrible—they are unprepared to listen to the annunciation of glory to God in the highest, and to appreciate the Gospel as proclaiming deliverance from the dominion of sin and death. They are strange things which are thus brought to their ears by men of other lands and a purer faith, claiming the authority of that unknown God,

'From whom departing, they are lost, and rove
At random, without honor, hope, or peace;'

and often their thoughts are not to be turned by any amount of testimony or argument from their deep-worn channels, nor their affections diverted from objects of their earliest and devoutest worship. The stupidity of the Hottentot, the sensuality of the Hindu, the prejudice of the Mohammedan, the ancestral pride of the self-styled 'son of heaven,' and the sottishness of the South Sea Islander, alike interpose a wall high as heaven between the Christian teacher and the child of ignorance. . . Paul has described the heathen every where, not more graphically than truthfully. He deals not in fiction when he portrays them as vain in their imaginations, given up to uncleanness, worshipping the creature more than the Creator, full of envy, murder, debate, deceit and malignity. Long and sad experience declares that infernal passions dwell in pagan bosoms, triumphing over even the great law of self-preservation, dealing out death and destruction to parents and children, driving on wars and fightings for purposes of rapine and plunder, shedding the blood of acknowledged benefactors for gain, and devouring enemies with the remorseless fierceness of the tiger or anaconda; and all this in the presence of their gods, and in avowed obedience to their behests. Essentially true is this of the entire pagan world."

If, then, these false views, and cruel and wicked practices of heathenism are to be supplanted by the pure faith and sanctifying power of the Gospel, with what patience and persevering efforts must the missionary be prepared to prosecute his labors, and what an immense vantage-ground must he find in any agency which brings the heathen under stated and systematic instruction, and especially in dealing with youthful minds before they become hopelessly impregnated with the false and debasing teachings of their fathers!

The Annals of the American Board close a dark portraiture of Hinduism, as follows, namely:

"The moral condition of Hindu society is what such influences could not fail to make it. There is an utter destitution of moral principle. The population is thoroughly demoralized; and vice, thus taught and practised for ages, has produced both mental and physical imbecility. . .

"Hinduism has, indeed, a powerful hold upon the great mass of the population. Its philosophy and its ethics, its superstitions and its worships, are wrought into the entire framework of society. The intellect and the heart of every man, woman and child, have been thoroughly steeped in principles and practices which are utterly opposed to the gospel of Christ."

Similar to this is the testimony of almost every missionary. The Rev. Myron Winslow, D.D., after some thirty-five years of labor among the Hindus, says: "The obstacles to the missionary work in India are great. There is a hereditary priesthood, an ancient and extended literature; immemorial and time-indurated custom; the iron and adamantine barrier of caste; a cruel but fascinating superstition, controlling every action; and inconceivable love of sin."

The Rev. Dr. Scudder testifies: "If I were asked to tell in one breath what I thought the mightiest present obstacle to the onward course of the Gospel in India, I should unhesitatingly say *caste.* It is a monster that defies description. Caste has its hold on every sinew of the Hindu. Its bitterness is diffused through every drop of his blood. Its threads are woven into the very texture of his soul. Caste gives form and life and strength to the Hindu religion. Hinduism would soon be shivered to atoms if it were not for caste. This is Satan's masterpiece. The more I look at it, the more I am struck with the cunning of the great Deceiver, in so skillfully forging and so firmly riveting upon this people the fetters of caste. No one can conceive of its universal power and its malignancy until he comes in contact with it. It stands directly in the way of the Gospel, like a mountain with immeasurable base and sky-reaching summit. . . Have I drawn a dark picture? Yes; but it does not approximate to the reality. Gigantic forms of error stalk like spectres through the midnight that wraps this land in dismal darkness. Hindrances to the advancement of the truth are great. The enemies are mighty and subtle. Haughty speech, violent blasphemy, and demoniac laughter, rise from every fortress of idolatry, and mingle in one great shout of defiance."

But we may not pursue this subject further. The reader is requested to reflect on this picture of heathenism; to let his mind dwell for a little on their deep moral debasement, the utter perversion of their intellects and their hearts, and see if he does not find here an invincible argument showing the necessity of a long and patient course of instruction, systematic and persevering efforts to reëducate the heathen mind.

With reference to the peculiar elements of Hinduism, and the result of right education on Hindu minds, it has been well affirmed: "Every person must see that, without necessarily attacking their religious prejudices in the first instance, the mere communication to them of just scientific views in a popular form, accompanied by that rigorous demonstration which the acute Hindu can intelligently appreciate, would eventually involve, along with the demolition of what they deem heaven-revealed science, complete disbelief in the pretended divinity of their worship. Their astronomy and their religion are, in their opinion, equally divine, and they stand or fall together. Show them conclusively the absurdity of the one, and you give an irrevocable death-blow to the other."

The correctness of these sentiments has been tested by long years of missionary experience. The nature of the human mind and its deep debasement under the influence of these corrupt systems of heathenism, furnish abundant proof of the wisdom and necessity of schools, and of their forming a prominent part of mission plans and labors. That the early missionaries and founders of the American Board perceived this necessity so readily and clearly, understood it so well and adapted their plans and measures to it so wisely, is cause for devout gratitude to God.

But we may not dwell longer on the dark features of heathenism. There are other incidental considerations, more or less intimately connected with those already presented, and which combine to show the wisdom and value of these mission schools. We can only glance at a few of them.

Schools are necessary to procure a Stated Audience.

We can not expect the soul-humbling truths of the Gospel to take effect on minds and hearts so utterly debased, unless the heathen can be brought to listen to them, and listen repeatedly, till they gain an intelligent understanding of them. Now, what motive will operate on the mind of a heathen to induce him to listen *continuously and statedly* to the preaching of the Gospel? Can it be a *love* for the *truth?* This he understands not, and the very fact that the missionary comes to teach him a new religion, is a reason why he regards him with suspicion and distrust, and keeps at a distance from him unless some special motive draws him. What possible motive can bring the heathen to listen to the Gospel except *curiosity* or *self-interest?*

Value of Curiosity.

Curiosity operates upon all, but with no *permanent* effect. It leads them to wish to see or hear "some new thing," but it is soon satisfied, and has no power to secure a *stated* audience in a heathen land. It is most serviceable when a missionary travels from village to village on preaching tours. Curiosity to see a white stranger, and hear what new things he may have to say, brings crowds around him in every village. But as soon as this curiosity is satisfied, the missionary finds himself deserted, and passes on to another village. I have no disposition to depreciate this kind of labor. Preaching tours serve somewhat to break up the fallow ground, and make known to the heathen the fact that there is "a more excellent way." But the view already presented, precludes the idea that an intelligent and saving knowledge of Christian truth can be effectively communicated in so short a time. Preaching tours are preëminently a preparatory work, and will bear no comparison with schools for visible and permanent results. But more on this point in the sequel. I mention it here only to illustrate the value of curiosity in gaining the attention of the heathen. It must be evident that this principle can never be relied on in heathen lands for securing *regular* and *stated* hearers of the Gospel.

Self-Interest the only controlling Motive.

The remaining motive is *self-interest*—the moving principle of the unregenerate human heart the world over. But is the Christian missionary to avail himself of this bad motive? Most unquestionably, with proper limitations. To exclude it would be to shut out the heathen from the Gospel forever. Let any one who would condemn such a course, go first and condemn our Saviour for feeding the multitudes with loaves and fishes. We may, as Christ did, condemn their worldly motive, but, like him, we may gladly avail ourselves of the opportunity thus presented for preaching the Gospel.

Why do the heathen attend upon the instruction of the missionary at all? Of spiritual good they can have no appreciation at first. What motive other than self-interest is possible? This motive is developed in different ways and degrees. Some even fancy, at first, that if they will become Christians, they will receive large sums of money. I have known heathen men to come to a missionary and deliberately name their price. It is needless to say that in every such instance they must be rebuked, and the spiritual nature of Christ's kingdom be clearly pointed out. But several ways remain in which this principle may properly be made available for securing *stated* hearers among the heathen.

1. *One way is to furnish employment.* In the family of the missionary, and in his printing-press, if he have one, there is occasion for servants and laborers. Though self-interest is the ruling motive which induces the heathen to accept such service, and come under regulations which require them to attend at stated times on Christian instruction, yet the missionary may properly avail himself of this motive,

and thus secure hearers for his message. But this means of obtaining hearers is extremely limited. If the missionary can regularly preach the Gospel only to those whom he *employs*, what hope can there be for the great mass of the heathen?

2. *Another appliance for securing hearers is medicine.* This, doubtless, is a legitimate agency, and some are disposed to exalt it above all others. It shows a kind regard for the suffering, and imitates the compassion of Christ in caring both for the bodies and souls of men. But of this appliance it is enough to say, *it avails only with the sick and suffering*, and, in India, chiefly with the lower classes of these. The higher castes, however sick, will seldom take our medicine. And shall we restrict our labors to the sick and suffering of the lowest classes?

3. *Alms* is another means of securing hearers, and may be resorted to with the same propriety as the use of medicine. Probably there are few missionaries, certainly in India, who do not distribute *alms* to a large number of lame, blind, and deaf paupers, and thus secure their attention to stated Christian instruction. But will it do for missionaries in heathen lands to confine their labors to paupers?

The Offer of Education appeals to the Worthiest Motives and to the Better Classes.

4. *Schools*, on the other hand, secure hearers from the more intelligent and better classes of the heathen community. Most of the heathen world readily manifest some appreciation of the value of letters. They are aware that a knowledge of the common branches of learning will be serviceable to them in the business of life. They will gladly come to the missionary, and listen to his Christian instruction, of which, at first, they have no just appreciation, if they may only at the same time be gaining that knowledge which they *do* value. In *boarding*-schools self-interest is enlisted still more strongly by means of the food and clothing which are furnished. But of all the forms in which this principle of self-interest develops itself, where is it less ob-

jectionable than when it appears in a pure desire for education? This desire may be rendered available in India to almost any extent. Among the Mahrattas of Western India, if a missionary will impart the rudiments of true science a portion of the time, he may secure any number of intelligent young men, who will attend upon his instruction, commit to memory the Lord's Prayer, Ten Commandments, Catechisms, and all the fundamental truths of the Gospel, and, at his stated preaching services, listen attentively to the plainest exhibitions of Christian truth. From long experience and observation of every agency hitherto employed by Christian missionaries, it is my firm conviction that no agency is more valuable than this—that no motive which can influence the heathen mind is more praiseworthy, or can be more properly rendered available for securing their attention to the claims of the Gospel than this love of education. A thirst for knowledge is commendable in *Christian* lands. It can not be less so among the *heathen*. It is generally the first hopeful indication among the most ignorant and barbarous tribes, and many a missionary longs to awaken this desire in the degraded, sensual, and listless heathen, for whose spiritual good he labors.

As a means of securing a stated audience mission schools avail, not only with the pupils of the schools, but to a good extent with their parents and friends also. These are interested in their children, and having gathered into the school-room, or chapel, to listen to recitations, they not only acquire a knowledge of Christianity very effectively from this exercise, but when once there, they remain through the preaching service, and thus the facilities of the missionary for communicating Christian truth are more than doubled by means of his schools, even if he could get some hearers without them.

Schools remove Ignorance and lay Stable Foundations.

To the above consideration must be added the necessity of schools for removing the *ignorance* of the heathen, and fitting them to become intelligent and useful members of society. If the heathen nations could be brought at once to profess the Christian faith, and then be left in all their present ignorance, how soon would their Christianity degrade into superstitions as vile and debasing as most of those which now hold them in bondage? Instances to illustrate this point are not wanting in countries once blessed with the light of the Gospel, but now requiring missionaries. Most of the Roman Catholic converts in India furnish an illustration on this subject. They have only exchanged one form of superstition and error for another. Unable to read, uninstructed in true knowledge and science, they know nothing of their own faith even, except to worship the images the priest directs. I have often met in India bands of these native Romanists, from the province of Goa, and found them entirely destitute of any correct idea of their own faith. I have asked them why they called themselves *Christian*, and the reply has been, "Because the priest tells us to;" while in regard to the saving truths of the Gospel, or even who Christ was, or what he had done to save them, their minds were a complete blank. Such must not be the case with Protestant converts in heathen lands. That Christianity may be intelligently understood and embraced, and exert an elevating and saving influence on the heart and life, some measure of true knowledge and science must ever accompany it. The Christian faith is *light*, and loves *light*, and out of this element it can not exist.

Schools conciliate the People.

Again, mission schools are valuable to conciliate the favor of the heathen, and convince them that the missionary seeks to benefit them. Influenced only by selfish motives themselves, they think the same motives rule all others. They are slow to appreciate the benevolence of the missionary, or to believe that he seeks their highest good. But when he opens *free schools*, and instructs their children without charge, they have positive evidence that he seeks to do them good. There is no more ready access to the confidence of a parent than by an act of kindness to his child. In all heathen communities the missionary is first received with a measure of distrust, and no means for winning their confidence have been found more effective than mission schools.

Experience in a New Mission.

It became my duty and privilege to commence and carry on a *new* Mission in Western India, in an independent native state, beyond the limits of British territory, in a region of Hinduism quite unbroken, and almost unexplored by missionaries, even on their hasty preaching tours. The result of my experience in this mission may properly find a place in this connection. On my first going among them, I found the fears and prejudices of the people strongly excited against me. They united their influence, and sent to their king an earnest petition praying him to banish me from his kingdom. When this petition proved unavailing, they adopted a plan of rigid non-intercourse. The Brahman priests stood aloof themselves, and admonished the common people that certain defilement would ensue if they went near the missionary, or had any thing to do with him. All efforts to obtain a preaching audience were quite unavailing. At length I attempted to establish schools: here, too, the priests opposed and threatened to expel from caste any who should let their children attend. At length I succeeded in employing a Brahman teacher, and he soon persuaded the parents of two little boys to let them come to our school. The people anxiously watched the result. It soon became known that the priests did not and could not put the parents out of caste for this offense. The school gradually increased in numbers, and the fears and prejudices of the people subsided in like proportion. In the course of six or eight months, from this small beginning, I found myself in a state of friendly intercourse with the people, a good number of pupils in my schools, and these with their adult relatives attending my stated preaching services. At the end of two years, the fears of the people had so far disappeared that my schools were crowded with pupils of all castes and ranks, from the cottage to the palace; five youth attending from the royal family. By means of these schools and the adult hearers thus secured, the saving truths of the Gospel have been preached to thousands of idolaters who but for the schools would never yet have heard them. Besides this, hundreds of youth and children in these schools have committed to memory Christian catechisms, hymns, portions of the word of God, and become thoroughly acquainted with the fundamental and saving doctrines of the Gospel.

Thus my personal experience in mission labor, and a wide field of observation in the other missions of Western India, have convinced me that such schools are a wise and effective agency in prosecuting the missionary work. They communicate true science, and this undermines the errors of heathenism; they inspire and foster a love for true knowledge, and help to overcome the deep debasement of the heathen mind and heart. They communicate an elevating influence, prepare the heathen to understand and intelligently embrace Christianity, help to render native Christian communities stable, to preserve among them the purity of faith and sound doctrine, and a correct Christian practice, conciliate the favorable regards of the heathen, and secure their attention to the Gospel, furnish an opportunity for the uniform and systematic instruction of youth and children in the principles of Christianity, appeal to the worthiest motive in bringing the heathen under our influence, and a motive which operates on the better class of the heathen, and constitute the best and most effective agency of which the Christian missionary can avail himself in heathen lands.

That the great body of Hindu youth in India, are possessed of so strong a desire for education, and by it are so readily brought into mission schools and under Christian teaching, is cause for sincere gratitude to God, and of much encouragement in prosecuting the work of missions among them. Should missionaries in India neglect to avail themselves of this state of things they would prove unfaithful to their high trust.

Practice of European Missionaries.

Well do the missionaries of the Scotch Free Church and most other European societies, understand the vantage-ground furnished by this state of things, and nobly have they availed themselves of it. In the principal cities of the three Presidencies of India, they have established large and flourishing missionary institutions, and in those of the Free Church alone, some five thousand of the better class of Hindu youth are receiving the rudiments of a liberal education, and are constantly brought under the influence of systematic Christian instruction. They are thus laying broad and deep the foundations of the native Church for generations to come, while the number and character of their converts, catechists, and preachers, sufficiently attest the wisdom of their measures, even for those who can be satisfied only with immediate results. What man, in all Christendom or the world, has a nobler, choicer field for usefulness in the service of Christ, than the venerable Dr. Duff, with some fourteen hundred promising Hindu youth daily under his Christian teaching and burning eloquence, in the great metropolis of India?

It is fully believed that the views of the early missionaries and officers of the American Board, were no less comprehensive and correct, in regard to this important agency, than those of the European missionaries. Some views of the present senior Secretary of the American Board, bearing on this subject, have already been quoted. Similar sentiments have been placed on record by other officers of the Board. Rev. D. Greene, late Secretary of this Board, defining what a missionary may properly do to improve the intellectual and social condition of the heathen, well remarks:

"1. He may do whatever will cause Christian truth to be most speedily disseminated, and most intelligently embraced. If the people to whom he is sent *need schools*, he may establish and *teach* them; if they need school-books, he may make them, etc.

"2. The missionary may do what will bring the people

most speedily and steadily under the influence of the means of grace, etc.

"3. The missionary may labor to reform what in the habits and condition of a people tends to immorality, etc.

"4. Those measures which promote the purity and permanent influence of Christianity in a nation, fall within the sphere of a missionary's labors. . . *Who will dare to say that it is not as much a part of God's plan, that science, and literature, and the fine arts, and all the useful inventions for facilitating labor and intercourse, shall be carried to their highest point, and that the human mind shall know all that it is capable of knowing, and discover all which it is capable of discovering, here in this world, as it is that the Gospel shall be every where preached and every where triumphant?*"

These brief quotations are worthy of the comprehensive views and large heart of their author, and are believed faithfully to represent the sentiments of the early missionaries and officers of the American Board on the subject of education in mission schools. How well these sentiments have been brought into practice, in the past history of the Board, will appear in the following pages.

CHAPTER II.

DIFFERENT KINDS OF MISSION SCHOOLS.

Testimony of the Rev. D. O. Allen, D.D.*

IN accordance with the views already expressed, the missionaries of the American Board have found it expedient to establish schools more or less extensively in all their missions. The Rev. Dr. Allen, who labored as a missionary of the American Board some twenty-six years among the Mahrattas of Western India, says: "In commencing their operations, missionaries have generally seen the propriety and importance of establishing schools. One reason for them is to educate the minds of the people, so that they may be more capable of understanding and appreciating the facts and evidences, the doctrines and duties of the Scriptures. Another reason for them is to increase the influence of the missionaries with the people, by communicating some advantage which they can appreciate, and by showing that Christianity rests on an intelligent perception of its doctrines, and contains reasons for the performance of all its duties. And another reason for such an education, is in its procuring means and opening ways of access to the people, and opportunities of preaching to them. One great difficulty which missionaries often experience, is in obtaining access to the people, in circumstances where Christianity can be made the subject of communication or conversation.

"In such circumstances schools become very important, as a means of communication with *different classes of people*, with children and parents, and with men and women. And

* India, Ancient and Modern.

school-houses also become important, as places for becoming acquainted with people, for social intercourse and religious worship. School-houses become chapels under the control of missionaries. Their use for this purpose is often more important than for education. These reasons for making the education of the common people a part of missionary operations, are stronger in some heathen countries than in others, and I believe they can seldom, if ever, be adequately and fully appreciated by persons who have not themselves lived among a heathen population, and so had opportunities for becoming acquainted with their state and character."

These schools have been of different kinds, according to the circumstances and requirements of the case, and the judgment of the missionaries.

Boys' schools have usually been found most practicable, especially at the commencement of a mission, and most effective for accomplishing the objects in view. The heathen more readily appreciate the value of education for their boys, and such schools are most successful in conciliating their favor, and obtaining both the pupils and their parents and friends as hearers at preaching services.

Girls' schools find the strongest prejudices of the heathen to contend with, and hence have usually been established after other schools have succeeded in winning their confidence, and making them understand the true objects of the mission. In most heathen communities, an attempt to establish female schools at the outset of the mission, especially without doing any thing for the education of the boys, would awaken an amount of prejudice and misapprehension which would be needless and quite unwise. In Bombay, the oldest mission of the American Board, girls' schools were not found practicable until some ten years after boys' schools were in operation; and more recently, in one of our new missions, the schools having all been interdicted by the Deputation, and subsequently the girls' schools being allowed to continue temporarily, (in deference to the grief of the lady who had them in charge,) it was found expedient to disband them also.

Girls' schools not only fail, in a new mission, to conciliate favor and secure hearers, but from the low estimation in which women are held in all heathen countries, and from the fact that no education whatever has heretofore been allowed to any of them, except to the *dancing-girls* of the temples, it will be evident at once that any attempt to limit our schools to the female sex, would expose a mission to much obloquy and misapprehension.

But it must be admitted that this perverted sentiment and practice of the heathen constitutes itself a strong argument for including girls' schools among the agencies for their moral elevation. Never will any heathen people be evangelized till their women are morally and intellectually elevated. Well has it been said that: "Vain will be the attempt to rescue man from the ruin and desolation which Hinduism creates, if woman is still left to her cruel charities." "Where there exists a low estimate of the female character, there will man himself ever be low. Where the female, with all her softening influence, so beautifully fitted for the humanizing of man, and for rendering him a social being, is in a degraded condition, and not viewed as the companion of her lord, there will man himself be in a low, vile, degraded, and uncivilized state." "It is only *Christian education* which can make woman in India what woman is in Christian America and Christian Britain. Only *Christian education* can take the Hindu female out of the lowest depths of degradation and sorrow which the human mind and heart can know, and elevate her to that dignified and blissful sphere for which God created her."

This subject has been appreciated to a good extent by missionaries, and female schools of some kind constitute a part of the evangelizing agencies in every well-regulated mission.

Schools for Heathen Youth.

A second distinction in mission schools is that which divides them into schools for *heathen* children, and schools limited to the children of *native Christians*. Strange to say, the propriety of the former has, by some, been called in question. But of such we would ask, Is it not for the *heathen* that the missionary is to labor? Is it not the favorable regard of the *heathen* which he wishes to conciliate? and *heathen* men, women and children, whom he desires to win as hearers, and bring under the stated teaching and influence of the Gospel?

At the commencement of a mission, if heathen children are excluded, there can be no schools, for there are none but heathen children to attend them. The wisdom of such exclusion would be much like that of the Greek simpleton, who gravely resolved never to touch the water again till he had learned to swim. There is no stage in the progress of a mission in which schools are so indispensable as at its origin. Hence, in many missions, such schools have uniformly been established, and their value has become one of the plainest facts of missionary experience. In the progress of the work, when a native church and Christian community have been gathered, the propriety of educating the *Christian* children no one calls in question. It is hardly possible to over-estimate its importance, in properly laying the foundations of Christian society in a heathen land.

But if such schools are sustained, shall the heathen be excluded from them? On this point there is an honest difference of opinion. There are some reasons for isolating the children of native Christians in separate schools, but far stronger reasons, I think, for educating them in the same schools with *heathen* children. If we maintain separate schools for *Christian* children, we can not keep them secluded from heathen influences at other times, nor is it desirable. We are to seek, not to "take them out of the world" of heathenism, but to fortify their moral natures with Christian principle, so that they may be able to resist the influences of heathenism. Besides, if we exclude heathen children, we thus far put the light of the native Christians "under a bushel," and exclude the heathen from the very teaching and influence which they *must* have, if they are ever to be evangelized. Often the admission of heathen children into such schools would involve no additional expense. The house, once provided, may as well be full; and the teacher, once employed, may as well have full occupation. The exclusion of heathen children would limit the facilities of the missionary for accomplishing his appropriate work.

Employment of "Heathen Teachers."

A third distinction in mission schools is indicated by the character of the teachers. *Heathen* or *unevangelized teachers* have been employed in most or all of our missions. Of late much exception has been taken, in certain quarters, to such teachers. The exception is plausible, and perhaps finds sympathy, at first thought, with many who love and support missions. Some are ready to exclaim: "What, employ *heathen* to teach *Christianity!*" The very proposition brings odium. But the reader will kindly bear in mind, that the wisest and most devoted officers and missionaries of the American Board have sanctioned and employed such teachers from the very origin of their missions among the heathen. This fact may not be regarded as conclusive evidence of the propriety of employing such teachers, but it will at least lead candid minds to apprehend that there may be some good reasons for so doing, and dispose them to give these reasons due consideration. The sound judgments, large hearts, and devoted piety of the early officers of the Board furnish a strong presumption that they could not have sanctioned the employment of such teachers without deliberately weighing all the arguments in the case; and the same may be said of the successive missionaries who have employed them. The advice of the present senior Secretary of the Board on this last point is considerate and well expressed. He says:

"Let the friends of Christ also be exhorted to presume, when the missionary comes to a decision or adopts a course of measures different from what to them seems to be right, that he has done it honestly and prayerfully, and in view of what seem to him to be good and sufficient reasons; and let them consider whether it is strange that the opinions of a missionary, formed in the field, with all the facts and relations of the case before him, should sometimes differ from theirs, unacquainted, as they must be, with the facts which influenced him, and separated, as they are, from those states of society and those scenes, by half the circumference of the globe; and let them also consider whether opinions formed by wise and good men at home, relative to the internal affairs of the several missions, are, on the whole, more likely to be right, than those formed in heathen lands by men equally pious, learned, and discreet, having the same New Testament to guide them."

This is well stated, and in the spirit of this paragraph will the reader kindly weigh a few of the considerations in favor of this class of teachers?

1. *At the origin of a mission none but* HEATHEN *teachers are procurable.* If it be said that Christian teachers should be sent with the missionary, my reply is, that hitherto enough such have not been sent to meet the wants of our higher institutions. Any attempt to supply from Christendom the requisite number of teachers for common schools is entirely out of the question. Besides, the necessary support of one American teacher would be sufficient to supply a dozen or more heathen teachers; so that where one American teacher or missionary is employed, it becomes the truest economy to limit his time and labor mainly to the communication of Christian instruction, and for the secular instruction to employ heathen teachers.

2. HEATHEN *teachers are more successful in bringing pupils and adult hearers under missionary influence and teaching.* It must ever be borne in mind that one great object of schools in a new mission is to remove prejudice, conciliate favor, and obtain a hearing for the Gospel. For this purpose a Christian teacher would have no advantage over the missionary. Even a *native* Christian teacher is regarded as having become defiled by breaking his caste, and hence is usually looked upon with as much prejudice and dislike as the missionary himself. Even in missions of long standing, efforts to bring heathen children into schools taught by Christian

teachers have often failed entirely; and whenever heathen parents become willing to send their children to such Christian teachers, it is properly regarded as an indication of marked progress in our work.

Much odium has been cast on the employment of *heathen teachers* by a wrong use of terms. The idea which has been held up as so preposterous is, the employment of *heathen* to teach *Christianity!* This is by no means a proper statement of the case. They are employed to teach the secular branches, mainly for the purpose of bringing the pupils, parents, and teachers themselves under the Christian instruction and influence of the missionary. They are required to see that specified catechisms and portions of Scripture are committed to memory by their pupils; but for explaining and impressing divine truth upon the minds and hearts of both pupils and teachers, the missionary holds himself or his Christian assistants responsible; and daily thanks God for the precious opportunity afforded by these schools for this kind of labor.

And pray what possible objection to the employment of heathen for the purpose here specified? Why not as proper to employ a Brahman to teach heathen children arithmetic, as to teach the missionary the language, to copy his MSS. for the press, or to set type for printing the Bible? What means for bringing the heathen under the influence of the Gospel is safer? What appeals to and fosters better motives in the unsanctified heart? Nay more, on what agency has the blessing of God hitherto more manifestly rested? Let all missionary experience bear testimony.

Occasionally a heathen man comes to a missionary, claiming to be an inquirer, and asks for support, that he may attend on Christian instruction, and better understand the character and claims of the Gospel. Some missionaries have thought it proper to support such a man for a time, from mission funds, until his character and motives are developed. This course *may* be right, but how much better in such case to say to the applicant: "Go into such a village or part of the city and gather a school, and I will pay you wages." If a worthy character, he will gladly avail himself of such an opportunity to earn a support, bring his pupils and come himself to the preaching services of the missionary, gain a rapid knowledge of Christian truth, and at the same time furnish the missionary an opportunity to communicate Christian instruction more widely among the people by means of his school; and gradually his knowledge will increase, and his convictions ripen, until he avows his faith in Christ. If, on the other hand, he is a worthless character, he will decline such a proposition, or perhaps make some puny efforts to gather a school, and soon develop his inefficiency and selfish motives. In either event the missionary is saved from imposition and a useless expenditure of money. That such cases of imposition occur should be matter of no surprise. There are too many unworthy characters in Christian lands to allow duplicity among the heathen to be any great marvel.

3. HEATHEN *teachers while thus employed are often converted.* It is obvious that teachers, while listening day after day to the catechetical and Scripture lessons of their pupils, must be in favorable circumstances to gain a knowledge of Christianity; and then to this must be added the regular Christian instruction which they receive from the missionary. The opinion has been expressed that heathen teachers, if employed, should have nothing whatever to do with the Scripture lessons of their pupils. My experience has led to a different view. I would have such teachers take all the appointed lessons, and be as responsible for the progress of their pupils in the required Scripture lessons, as for their progress in secular studies. Enough will still remain for the missionary or Christian assistant to do in the way of examining, explaining, and enforcing the truth thus taught, while there is much to be hoped for from the constant repetition of these lessons, and the daily action of the truth upon the mind of the teacher. I know of many instances in which these lessons have resulted, with God's blessing, in the conversion of the teachers. The oldest and ablest native pastors in the Ahmednuggur Mission were thus converted, and I

shall not soon forget the impression upon my mind, as I listened to the touching narratives of their Christian experience at the time of their ordination. The senior pastor described in detail his successful efforts each night after returning to his Hindu friends, to throw off his serious impressions, which had been induced by these lessons, and the increased force with which the same lessons revived those impressions the succeeding day, until they became resistless, and led him to profess his faith in Christ.

The objection has been urged to heathen teachers that they counteract the Christian instruction of the missionary. Such has not been my experience. Among many there may be one occasionally thus reckless of his own interest and the wishes of his employer, but it is easy to dismiss such an one, and employ only those who will be faithful to their duty. Strong motives operate upon such teachers, leading them to do all they can to please the missionary, and the very acceptance of such service is generally regarded by other heathen as evidence that the said teachers are throwing off their stricter prejudices, and becoming favorable to Christianity.

But the large number and stable character of the converts from this class of teachers is our best argument on this point, and no less so as to the propriety of their employment. In our Ceylon Mission the conversion of sixty-two pupils and eighty teachers is traced directly to these schools, and the recent testimony of the Ahmednuggur Mission is: "*Our native pastors*" and "*most efficient laborers were originally heathen school-teachers, and in this way were brought under the influence of the truth and converted.*"

Native Christian Teachers.

The employment of *native Christians as teachers* admits of but one opinion. Such teachers can not be had at the commencement of a mission unless brought from abroad, and hitherto this has been generally found impracticable, the older missions still requiring their educated Christian teachers in their own service.

Besides, it must be borne in mind, that if such teachers could be procured and taken with the missionary when he goes into unexplored regions to commence a new mission, the heathen would regard them with no less prejudice and dislike than they do the missionary himself; often, indeed, they view them with peculiar hatred as having brought reproach upon the religion they have forsaken, and contracted deeper defilement than adheres to the foreigner; so that in a new mission the heathen are found less ready to send their children to such teachers than to the missionary himself.

But in the progress of a mission, when a native Christian community has been gathered with baptized children to educate, or the prejudices of some of their heathen neighbors have so far given way that they become willing to send their children to such teachers, then surely they should be employed. There is a two-fold advantage in so doing. It secures their most effective assistance in prosecuting the mission work, and at the same time proves a means of support and of valuable discipline to the native convert. Their assistance in the work is the first object, and all other considerations should yield to this. With equal education, and with pupils who will attend their schools, they are much to be preferred to heathen teachers from their comparative fitness to explain and enforce Christian truth.

And then, most natives on becoming Christians have no means of support—not perhaps because they are deprived of their inheritance, for in India the civil rights of native converts are now secured by legal enactments—but because they are generally from the poorer classes of the people, and if dependent on heathen relatives are cast off, and if prosecuting some little business, are often obliged to abandon it or do acts which violate their enlightened consciences. So that it often becomes desirable to furnish such converts some means of support, and in most missions they can be rendered serviceable in no way so well as in teaching schools.

Again, if brought into regular habits and active service as teachers, the discipline is very valuable in rendering them stable, active, and useful members of the native church, in giving them character and fitting them for higher posts of usefulness in the mission. It is a question whether native converts should be employed as assistants unless they have education and capacity sufficient to teach at least the rudiments of their own language. When this is not the case, and they are employed only to converse with people at large on the subject of Christianity, their active habits seldom improve, and their office is soon looked upon as a sinecure by their heathen neighbors, and often by the other native Christians. Whereas, teaching is visible and actual service, and in my own experience and observation native converts thus brought into regular and active habits as teachers will effect more to make known the truth to others by voluntary efforts out of school-hours, than those above alluded to who do not teach at all.

It is evident, then, that there are many and valid reasons for the employment of native converts as teachers. The points to be vigilantly guarded by the missionary are, that no convert be employed *merely* for giving him a support; no one who is wanting in education or capacity; and that no one when employed have too light duty—too few pupils to occupy his time and tax his abilities. This last danger is most common when such teachers are employed in villages at a distance from the missionary, for the sake of two or three Christian families whose children become irregular in attendance, or are kept at home by their parents for months together, it may be, as in harvest-time, the teacher still receiving his pay while he performs no actual service.

Vernacular and English Schools.

A fourth distinction in mission schools classifies them as *vernacular* and *English schools.* By vernacular are generally meant the *free* schools which missionaries have found it expedient to establish for teaching the common branches of study, and imparting Christian instruction in the language of the different heathen people among whom they labor.

For these schools all the arguments apply which can be urged in favor of a good system of common schools in a

Christian land, and to these must be superadded their value in removing heathen prejudices, scientific errors and debasing ignorance, in conciliating the heathen, and bringing them to listen to the Gospel, and, in fine, all those considerations mentioned above in speaking of heathen and Christian teachers.

But vernacular teaching is not confined to this class of schools. Vernacular studies form a prominent department in most of the higher schools and seminaries in which English also is taught; and doubtless this characteristic obtains in all our most valuable missionary institutions.

By *English schools*, then, are not meant those only in which all study and teaching are restricted to the English language. A few such there may be; but most English schools have a vernacular department, and some only teach English as one branch of study, in the same manner as Latin or Greek is taught in European and American institutions. Such was the case in the late Mission Seminary at Ahmednuggur. As to the utility and expediency of these English schools in our missions, time and space will here allow but a brief reference to a few of the considerations which have influenced the minds of those who have established and conducted them.

1. They have found in heathen youth an earnest desire to acquire a knowledge of English, and hence English schools have proved most effective in bringing the higher and better classes under the influence of the missionary and of the Gospel.

2. The English language unlocks the treasures of Western science, and thus becomes a most effective agent in overthrowing the false systems of heathenism which always combine scientific and theological errors in their sacred books.

3. The English language unlocks the treasures of theology and scripture exegesis, and is very desirable and useful in training a native ministry.

4. Native preachers should have access to the English language and all its Christian science and literature, and

avail themselves of these in Christianizing their own language and creating a vernacular Christian literature.

5. In India and some other countries, so strong is the desire for a knowledge of English that such institutions become necessary in a mission in order to retain its more intelligent and valuable converts in service, who otherwise seek connections with other missions where they can enjoy the advantage of such institutions, or resort to government schools with great risk to their Christian character and usefulness. These and other considerations have usually been found sufficiently cogent to lead to the establishment of English schools in most or all the missions of the American Board.

Among missionaries in India there is almost a universal opinion that such schools are one of the most efficient means for bringing the higher castes under the influence of the Gospel and leading to their conversion.

Experience of European Missionaries.

The results of such schools in the Scotch Free Church Mission furnish very satisfactory evidence on this point. In their mission at Madras were recently reported 2250 pupils in their English schools—the pupils being of every caste from the highest to the lowest. In giving a summary of results the missionaries say: "The native Christian congregation at Madras is mainly the fruit of teaching and preaching in the schools. . . . It has increased since 1841 from three Hindu young men, as first fruits, to upwards of one hundred converts, male and female, of whom more than sixty are communicants. A large proportion of this number were brought into the church from respectable caste families at Madras and the branch schools. . . . Many of the converts are well educated, some of them highly so, and maintain themselves as teachers, catechists, writers, and medical pupils. They are almost all able, as well males as females, to speak English, and to read and understand books and discourses in it, in addition to knowing their own tongues. . . . Besides the three ordained native mis sionaries, a band of ten students are preparing for the ministry."

Mention is also made of some ten students who had received their first impressions and convictions of the truth in those English schools, and who had subsequently been baptized in other missions.

In mentioning other collateral results it is further stated that "the mission has been honored to give a great impulse to native education, male and female. It has sent forth not a few well-educated young men to conduct and assist in Christian schools, and to set agoing among the Hindu community schools of their own, both for males and females. Above all, it has been privileged to imbue with the leaven of God's word many thousands of Hindu youths, and hundreds of Mohammedans, and has thus been paving the way for greater triumphs of the Gospel in the day of the Lord's power."

The experience of the London Missionary Society is much in point. They commenced a vernacular seminary at Bangalore for training native converts for the ministry, and for many years restricted all their labors very much to the native languages. But failing to secure a well-qualified native ministry, they have lately established an English High School at Madras which now contains more than four hundred youths. They have also English schools at Bellary, Belgaum, and all their larger stations.

The results in the Scotch Missions at Calcutta and Bombay are much the same as at Madras.

Experience of American Missionaries.

Rev. Dr. Winslow, speaking of the schools of his own Mission at Madras, very appropriately remarks: "Four young men, baptized while in the *English* school, in which three of them are now teaching, the other being an assistant catechist, and four more, at least, who received in it good impressions and have since been baptized elsewhere, are witnesses that the great Master does not wholly disapprove of this form of labor."

During the six years the English Seminary at Ahmednuggur was under my supervision, ten young men of its most promising students were hopefully converted and brought into the Church. Eight or ten more have been brought in since.

The results of English schools in the Ceylon Mission are equally conclusive, as will appear in the sequel. So that from the widest observation of the facts, as well as from the arguments of the case, we are constrained to feel that these schools bear the seal of God's approval; that in his Providence they become a very effective agency for bringing Christian truth in contact with the minds and hearts of the better classes of the heathen, and leading to their conversion —an agency valuable also in training an efficient native ministry, and one which missionaries, especially in India, can not neglect to use without proving unfaithful to their sacred trust.

Boarding-Schools.

Boarding-schools have been found expedient and useful in most or all the missions of the American Board. Such schools are found desirable in Christian lands, and in addition to the arguments in favor of them here, some of the considerations which have led to their use in the missions are as follows:

1. Boarding-schools isolate children and youth from the constant influence of heathen parents and friends.

2. They relieve the pupils from the necessity of daily performing idol worship, and from the interruptions caused by frequent heathen festivals, pilgrimages, etc., so that their progress in study and Christian knowledge becomes more rapid and hopeful.

3. Boarding-schools furnish the best facilities for training native teachers, catechists, and preachers, who generally can not give their time to study unless supported.

4. The food and clothing furnished operates as an additional inducement for bringing pupils under Christian instruction. This argument is valid only so far as the bare offer of instruction fails to draw pupils in sufficient numbers, or those of the class desired.

5. When the pupils of different castes are required to sit and eat together, these schools become a very effective agency in breaking up caste distinctions.

6. They furnish facilities for educating orphans and indigent pupils, when desirable, and an asylum for young converts when obliged to seek protection from the persecution of heathen relatives. Each of these arguments admits of indefinite expansion and a large induction of facts and results.

In one such school for girls in our Ceylon Mission, out of 222 girls—the whole number received into the school up to a given date—175 became members of the church. In the principal male boarding-school of the same mission, out of 670 pupils, (the whole number,) 352 were hopefully converted and received into the Christian church. From facts like these, it would seem that these schools prove very useful and effective, even if viewed only as converting agencies.

Of *all* the various schools here described it should be remarked:

1. They have been in general use in the missions of the American Board from its origin.

2. The boarding character of some, the use of the English language, and the employment of *heathen* teachers, have been with the full knowledge and sanction of the officers of the Board.

3. In regard to those missions in which boarding-schools, English schools, and heathen teachers have been most extensively employed, frequent reports and resolutions have been adopted at the annual meetings of the Board, approving these schools, and complimenting the missionaries for their wisdom in devising and adopting, and their efficiency in conducting them. So that if these schools have proved a failure and entail discredit, this must be shared in common by the Board, its officers, and missionaries. But if results show that they bear the seal of God's approval and blessing, then we will all unite in ascribing glory to Him who condescends to use such imperfect human agencies in effecting results so lasting and glorious.

In attempting to bring to view the results of these schools

it must be borne in mind that they have a collateral and far-reaching influence, securing results which can never be correctly estimated in this world. But there are other more immediate results, particularly the conversion of pupils and teachers, and the training of native helpers and preachers, which are more visible, and admit of little or no difference of opinion. These results it will be the object of the following pages to present with all possible accuracy and brevity.

CHAPTER III.

CHARACTER AND RESULTS OF MISSION SCHOOLS IN OUR BOMBAY MISSION.

Origin of the American Mission in Bombay.

THE attempts of the first missionaries of the American Board to establish missions in India, their arrival in Calcutta, their prohibition and banishment by the government of the Hon. East India Company, their dispersion to Burmah, Ceylon, and the Isle of France, where still rest the remains of the beloved Harriet Newell, the first martyr in modern missions, their heroic courage and endurance in "hoping against hope," and persisting in efforts despite opposition and defeat, their subsequent arrival in Bombay, and the renewed order of government for transportation to England, their escape to Cochin, their arrest, reconveyance to Bombay, and long detention under government surveillance, their earnest and touching appeals to be allowed to remain and preach the Gospel to his heathen subjects, and their ultimate success in gaining a foothold there—these facts must ever form a memorable page in the annals of modern missions, and especially of the American Board.

Gordon Hall's Appeal to the Governor of Bombay.

Their final appeal to Sir Evan Napean, then Governor of Bombay, is worthy of the most devoted martyrs who have ever lived, suffered, or died in the cause of Christ. It closes in the following language, namely:

"We most earnestly entreat you not to send us away from these heathen. We entreat you by the high probability that an official permission from the supreme government, for us to remain here, will shortly be received, and that something more general, and to the same effect, will soon arrive from England; we entreat you by the time and money already expended on our mission, and by the Christian hopes and prayers attending it, not utterly to defeat its pious object by sending us from the country. We entreat you by the spiritual miseries of the heathen, who are daily perishing before your eyes, and under your Excellency's government, not to prevent us from preaching Christ to them. We entreat you by the blood of Jesus, which he shed to redeem them; as ministers of Him who has all power in heaven and on earth, and who, with his farewell and ascending voice, commanded his ministers to *go and teach all nations*, we entreat you not to prohibit us from teaching these heathens. By all the principles of our holy religion, by which you hope to be saved, we entreat you not to hinder us from preaching this same religion to these perishing idolaters. By all the solemnities of the judgment-day, when your Excellency must meet your heathen subjects before God's tribunal, we entreat you not to hinder us from preaching to them that Gospel which is able to prepare them as well as you for that awful day. By all the dread of being found in the catalogue of those who persecute the Church of God, and resist the salvation of men, we entreat your Excellency not to oppose the prayers and efforts of the Church, by sending back those whom the Church has sent forth in the name of the Lord, to preach his Gospel among the heathen; and we earnestly beseech Almighty God to prevent such an act, and now and ever to guide your Excellency in that way which shall be most pleasing in his sight.

"But should your Excellency finally disregard the considerations we have presented, should we be compelled to leave this land, we can only say, Adieu, till we meet you face to face at God's tribunal."

Here breathed the spirit of earnest, devoted, and God-fearing men, and well has it been remarked, that: "Nothing but the consciousness of the high spirituality of their object, and the impossibility of connecting it with questions of a secular nature, imparted boldness to our brethren to make this appeal, and gave it favor and efficiency in the high places of power."

Oral Preaching Unsatisfactory.

And it should be further remarked that these were the men, thus deeply impressed with the high spirituality of their object and labors, who first found it necessary to resort to schools for heathen children, and employed "*heathen teachers*" in prosecuting their work.

Messrs. Hall and Nott arrived at Bombay on the 11th of February, 1813, and from this time dates the origin of the Bombay Mission, the first and oldest mission of the American Board. Mr. Newell joined them on the 7th of March, 1814. From ignorance of the language, and the peculiar embarrassments arising from the opposition and restraints of government, it is evident little missionary labor can have been effected in those first years of the mission.

Near the close of 1814, we find on record that they preached in English every Sabbath, in the quarters which had been assigned them by government, "and also at another place a short distance from the town," and they "had opened a *school*, which they hoped would in the end become a boarding-school of considerable importance to the mission."

Of their labor sin 1815 we find the following record:

"They had acquired such familiarity with the Mahratta language that they were able to commence their great work of preaching the Gospel to the heathen. But the reader must not imagine that the heathen came by hundreds on the Sabbath to hear them, and listened attentively, like a Christian congregation, to sermons half an hour or an hour long. Instead of this, they had no stated congregation of heathen hearers. They were obliged to go to the temples, the markets, and other places of public resort, and converse with such as would hear them."

Necessary Resort to Schools.

This impossibility of gathering a stated audience by preaching, forced upon the attention of these devoted men the expediency and *necessity* of schools as a means of coming in contact with the people, and gaining their attention to the truth. Hence, in the same paragraph with the above extract we find recorded: " They made such efforts as their means allowed for the education of heathen children, and strongly recommend this department of labor to the Board."

At this stage of the mission their schools were wholly for *heathen children*, and they could employ none but *heathen teachers*. That they became so strongly impressed with the value of these schools is deserving of special notice, as also the reasons for this impression. That they were earnest and persevering in efforts to preach to the people in their temples, streets, bazaars, and elsewhere, is abundantly evident from the history of their labors, and especially from their private journals. The following brief extracts from the journal of Gordon Hall illustrate this point, and serve to show that their estimate of these schools arose from no pre-formed theory, but from their daily experience:

"*November* 19, 1815, *Lord's day.*—In the morning I spoke in four different places, to about seventy persons. In one of the places, where I had not been before, read a tract and addressed about twenty. At Boleshwur, a famous temple, a Brahman expressed great indignation, threatened, and told me I should not come there. In the afternoon I spoke in another place, where I had not before been, to about twenty; also in four other places. At Momadave, a place celebrated for temples, and the resort of Hindu worshippers, I held a long discussion with some Brahmans, in the midst of sixty or seventy people. . . Have spoken in all to about two hundred this day."

"*Monday*, 20.—I have spoken in six different places, and in all to more than one hundred persons to-day. . . Part of the time a few mocked and were noisy. It is one part of a missionary's trials, rightly to bear the impertinence contradictions, insolence and reproaches of men who are sunk to the lowest degradation, both mental and moral."

"*Tuesday*, 21.—To-day I have spoken in several places to about one hundred persons. Six or eight of them were Jews. In one place I addressed a considerable number in front of a large temple, where a woman was fulfilling a vow to her idol, by giving it half-a dozen small lamps, ghee, cocoa-nuts, rice and flowers, etc. . . As I proceeded, some agitation arose among the people; and one or two cried out: 'Come away from him; come away.' . . One, blustering up, said to me: 'How many months have you been preaching to these people, and nobody has regarded you?'"

"*Wednesday*, 22.—Walked out as usual at four o'clock P.M., and spoke to about one hundred and twenty people; . . At another place where I addressed the people, there were several hundreds of wooden gods under one small shed, which served as a temple. Here scores of sheep are at some seasons offered in sacrifice to these wooden gods."

"*Thursday*, 23.—To-day have spoken in five or six places to about one hundred of the heathen. I saw a man dragging out of a house a woman by her hair, whom I supposed to be his wife. Similar instances of abuse almost daily occur."

"*Friday*, 24.—To-day have spoken in several places, to more than one hundred people."

"*Saturday*, 25.—This day addressed about seventy persons, and in the course of the past week have spoken to more than eight hundred persons. Blessed be God for the privilege! . . But alas! when I fix my eyes only on the people, all is dark as night. . . Thousands have heard from our lips the tidings of the Gospel, and many more are still hearing them from day to day. But alas! so far as we can see, all seems to be as the seed that fell by the wayside."

Here is a week's experience of one of the first and most devoted missionaries of the American Board, in efforts to bring heathen under the influence of the Gospel without schools. He was in the populous city of Bombay, where by going to different localities he might seldom or never fail of an irregular audience. But such hearers did not satisfy him. He saw no clear and permanent impression made on their minds and hearts. He saw that the more frequently he went among them, the more were they inclined to disregard and abuse him; and though ready to persevere in this kind of labor, and endure any amount of contradiction, insolence and abuse, yet he *longed* to bring some under *stated* and *regular* Christian instruction. Hence originated the *schools* with *heathen teachers*, as the only effective agency for securing this object.

1816.—At the close of 1816, "their journal states that during the greater part of the year, nearly three hundred heathen boys had been receiving instruction under their care."

1817.—In the annals of this mission for 1817, we find that "two new schools had been opened, making six in all, having four hundred pupils on their lists."

In 1818 two new schools were established on the continent, and "the schools on the island of Bombay continued to increase. In April there were eleven, having six hundred regular attendants, and as many more who attended irregularly. At the end of the year the number of schools was fourteen. . . Though the teachers were all *heathen*, the mission prescribed the course of study, so that instruction in heathenism was excluded, and much scriptural truth and morality inculcated. Thus they were raising up a generation who would not be the slaves of Hindu habits of thought, and who could better appreciate the claims of a pure morality and of evangelical truth."

Gordon Hall's Estimate of these Schools.

Deeply devoted as Hall was to the spiritual object of the mission, experience soon taught him that these schools were his most effective agency. He therefore devoted time to the preparation of school-books. There is still extant and much in use in Western India, a volume prepared by him to assist natives in acquiring the English language. Thus did he seek, in every proper way, to bring the heathen under his influence. It was after seven years' experience that he wrote to his much venerated teacher, the Rev. Dr. Porter, of Andover, as follows, namely:

"Native schools and the School-Book Society are among the most promising objects in that region, [Madras.] Those books which the Society is now translating and printing, in the rudiments of general science, will prove a powerful auxiliary in the propagation of gospel truth. Our mission, without any very great expense, might do much in the same way. All our exertions in the way of schools and school-books, are attended with much encouragement." And again he writes: "The schools continue to prosper. Our funds for the last six months have not allowed us to open any new ones, though we have had many pressing calls to do so. This is greatly to be lamented. The business of schooling among the natives is every day becoming more and more interesting, promising and popular."

Such became the experience and conviction of this devoted missionary, of whom it has been fitly testified: "But few men have possessed minds more comprehensive and better balanced in regard to the great work of evangelizing the world than Mr. Hall."

1819.—"In August five new schools had been established. During the remainder of the year they received frequent applications from the natives to establish schools, but they could not be opened for the want of funds. The education of native children in the families of the missionaries, to any considerable extent, proved impracticable, from the impossibility of procuring pupils."

1820.—"At the close of this year the mission had twenty-one schools, containing about 1050 scholars, who were learning to understand and respect Christianity."

So much had these schools extended, and so effective were they in making known Christian truth, that the Hon. Mountstuart Elphinstone, then Governor of Bombay, though approving the general object of the schools, "feared that too rapid advances would be made against the prejudices of the natives."

These schools became centres of light, not only to the pupils, but through them to their parents and adult friends; for the acquisitions at school were sure to be repeated at home, and furnish subjects for much conversation among the people. Besides, many of the parents and friends were attracted to the school - rooms, and there listened to the Christian lessons of the pupils, and the preaching of the missionary.

Testimony of Mr. Hall's Biographer.

In regard to these schools, we find Gordon Hall's intelligent biographer and fellow-laborer giving testimony as follows: "The opportunity which these schools afford the missionaries of communicating religious instruction not only to the children, but to their parents and friends, is worthy of special attention. The school-rooms are, in fact, chapels, where the missionaries preach the Gospel to the whole neighborhood, who usually assemble whenever the school is visited by the missionary. Besides, not only the scholars, but their parents and friends manifest a warm attachment to the mission; and in this way the mission acquires an influence which it could obtain by no other means. Several years may indeed elapse before we shall hear much of the good effects of these schools; but it is impossible that children thus educated, should ever become bigoted pagans; and there is reason to hope that the Gospel, in which they are so fully instructed, will by and by take hold of their hearts. It is but reasonable to expect that when these boys, thus educated, shall become men, and take an active part on the stage of life, their influence will be extensively felt as teachers of schools, and in other departments of life."

I am happy to bear witness that this expectation has not been disappointed. Thirty years have passed away since the above was placed on record. A manifest change has come over India in the vicinity of all mission stations—a change which is commanding the attention of the most indifferent and faithless. And among the agencies which have been employed in bringing about this change, none have been more effective than mission schools.

Practice of the Missionaries.

So thoroughly did the missionaries become convinced of the value of these schools, that they continued to increase them to the extent of their means, and when these failed it became a cause of much grief. Thus the history of their labors for 1821, after mentioning the return of Mr. Bardwell to America, from failure of health, and the death of Mr. Newell, adds:

1821.—"This mission had other afflictions. The deficiency of the treasury at home curtailed its means of usefulness. Their joint letter, dated July 1st, states that of the 25 schools under their care, the want of funds had compelled them to discontinue 10; thus abandoning 500 children, at least for the present, to the uncounteracted influences of heathenism."

In this emergency, they drew encouragement from the fact, that Mr. Hall had succeeded in bringing into his family "ten or twelve native children as boarding scholars," and Messrs. Nichols and Graves each of them four more. They now began to hope that the plan of boarding-schools, an object of much desire with them and the officers of the Board, would at length succeed.

1822.—This year "the number of schools, which had been reduced to 15, was increased to 18. The number of children received into mission families for education was greatly increased."

1823.—The estimate of these schools, by European Christians living on the ground and observing their character and influence, is well worthy of notice. This estimate may be inferred from their frequent and generous contributions for the special support of the schools. These appear in successive years, and such as meet the eye will suggest the proper inference. The amount contributed this year was "about

$1300." "The whole number of the schools, at the end of the year, was 26. The number of scholars was 1454."

1824.—So generous had been the contributions received for schools from the Governor and other European Christians, that the mission now "resolved to increase the number of schools to 34," and before the year closed they increased them to 39. This year the mission commenced a school for girls, the first ever known in Western India. It was broken up in a short time by the death of the teacher, but it was resumed the following year, and others commenced.

"In October, Manuel Antonio, a superintendent of schools in the service of the mission, requested admission to the church."

In 1825, was formed "the Bombay Missionary Union," "for promoting Christian fellowship," and "advancing the kingdom of Christ in that country." With reference to this Union, and the change he had witnessed during his residence in Bombay, Gordon Hall writes: "What a contrast with the trials of 1813 and 1814 did it present! Instead of being a prisoner under sentence of transportation from the land, I found myself among the representatives of five Christian missions, now carrying on, without molestation, their various and extensive operations in this immense field, where then there was not a single mission established. I was the patriarch among the little missionary brotherhood—none around me so old in years and missionary labors, and not one with so many gray hairs. I was affectingly admonished but greatly encouraged." One of the chief grounds of his encouragement and joy is thus expressed in his own language: "Four of these missions have in operation about 60 schools, in which are more than 3000 children reading, or daily learning to read, the word of God, and receiving catechetical instruction."

The schools continued to prosper, and at the close of this year the girls' schools had 75 pupils.

In 1826, the devoted Gordon Hall was attacked with cholera while on a preaching tour, and sweetly rested from his labors amidst the people for whom he had come to toil and die. Thus weakened, the mission was "obliged to decline pressing invitations to open free schools." Twenty-four such schools were in operation, of which 9 girls' schools contained 466 pupils. The friends of the mission in Bombay contributed 2032 rupees for their support.

I have thus far given the annual statistics of the schools to show their increasing favor with the missionaries and the Board, but as I propose to condense them all in a brief table at the close of Chapter IV., the reader will no longer look for them in the text.

In 1827, a female teacher died, "giving some evidence of piety." The contributions of English friends for the schools amounted to 1880 rupees.

Moral Courage of Babajee.

In 1828, a rule was adopted "requiring teachers and scholars to stand during prayer." The Brahman teachers combined to resist the rule, and all but one, named Babajee, left the service of the mission. He declared the rule required nothing improper or contrary to the Hindu Shasters, and persisted in complying with it. "Council after council was called to condemn him and put him out of caste, at one of which at least a thousand Brahmans were present. He appealed to their common-sense against the absurdity of persecuting him so violently for" such an act, "while there were Brahmans present with whom he had eaten beef and drunken brandy, and caroused for whole nights together, and no censure had been inflicted on them. They, however, imposed such humiliating penances upon him, and were so resolute in their wrath, that it was thought best for him to retire awhile to the Deccan." But "other teachers soon came forward, eager to be employed by the mission; and many of the Brahmans who had left, soon came back and resumed their places, submitting to the offensive rule without further contest. After a while Babajee came back, and was permitted to pursue his business unmolested; but these events did much to cure him of his regard for Brahmanism."

This case brings to view some of the benefits of these schools. They secured to the missionaries a hold upon the teachers and scholars, and an influence over the community which they had no other means of gaining. The schools diffused light and knowledge among the people, which alarmed the Brahmans and led them to fear any farther concessions; and which now agitated their whole body, and doubtless did more to make known the objects and doctrines of Christianity, during this discussion and excitement, than could have been effected without schools in many long years. The ultimate result on the mind of Babajee will soon appear.

In 1829, "The superiority of the mission schools was acknowledged by parents and children of all classes, and contributions in Bombay, for their support, amounted to 1500 rupees."

The organs of the Board testify this year as follows: "The Brahmans are said to be evidently losing their hold on that portion of the people which has been taught, and is beginning to read, to reason, and to reflect." "There are adult females connected with some of the schools who give pleasing attention to religious instruction."

This last quotation reveals the very close connection and strong influence of the schools in the conversion even of the adult converts.

The records of the Board, and of the missions every where abound in testimony, facts and incidents showing the great value of these schools. Take a few specimens, as follows:

"Mr. Stone found every where in his tour most gratifying evidence that the school system is producing a change highly favorable to the introduction of the Gospel." "It is manifest to the children and the parents, that the pupils of the mission schools learn more and better things, than they were able to learn from any other quarter."

What wonder that we hear this missionary exclaiming:

"Oh! that I had the thousandth part of the resources of the American churches: then would I establish schools in all these pagan villages, which like so many springs of living water, breaking out in a desert, would soon, by the blessing of God, change this vast moral waste into the garden of the Lord." "At one place Mr. Stone found several of the larger scholars had a good understanding of the Christian religion. They acknowledged their belief in its truth, and said it was wrong to worship idols."

In 1830, the records of the Board say: "These schools exert a favorable influence on the character of the villages where they are situated, and the missionaries justly regard them as so many lights burning amidst the deep spiritual gloom which covers the country. . Nowhere is there found such a disposition to receive and read the publications of the missionaries, as among those who have been instructed in the mission schools. These are also most forward to listen to the preaching of the Gospel, which, owing to their acquaintance with Christian books, they understand better than the other natives." "The number of attendants on public worship at the chapel was considerably increased by the influence of the schools."

Conversion of three Heathen Teachers.

1831.—This year the missionaries began to realize more fully their hopes from these schools and the employment of *heathen teachers*. For eighteen years from the origin of the mission they had found it impracticable to employ any Christian teachers. During these years a few persons had been hopefully converted and gathered into a Christian Church, mostly in connection with the schools, and their labors in English. These were three Europeans, (two of them being a *school-master* and his wife,) one American, one Dane, a Portuguese and his wife, a Malay woman, a Mussulman, and one low-caste Hindoo. Of the whole number, only *three* were natives of India, two of whom, and also the Portuguese and Malay, were connected with the *schools*, and thus became acquainted with saving truth. There is also mention made of three other persons, two of whom were *teachers*, who became acquainted with Christian truth in the schools, and gave good evidence of conversion on their death-beds. But the brightest event in the history of this mission thus far, was the conversion, this year, of three *heathen teachers* of high caste. These were the Brahman, Babajee, mentioned already in 1828, and two others, named Dajeeba and Moroba. The conversion of these intelligent and educated high-caste teachers marks an era in the history of the mission. It brought fresh hope and courage and joy to the hearts of the toil-worn missionaries, while at the same time it roused the native community to a sense of their danger from these mission schools. The Brahmans held council after council—all Bombay was in commotion, and petitions were sent to the British Government, praying that these schools of the American missionaries might be interdicted by legal enactment. Could we have more positive proof of the wisdom of employing such *heathen teachers?*

1832.—Referring to the records of this year we find: "Female education in Bombay is gradually assuming a more encouraging appearance." Of their preaching tours, the missionaries say: "We have been well received by the people generally; and especially in the villages where we have *schools* established, a desire for books is rapidly increasing, and a preparation of mind, to read them with profit, and to attend on the preaching of the Gospel to advantage, was manifest. We may hope that the *schools* will have no small share of influence in increasing, as they have had in producing, this state of things. Many families are now blessed with the reading of the Scriptures and tracts, in consequence of these *schools*, which otherwise would not have been the case."

1833.—The missionaries say: "There is every reason to believe that the children who are receiving instruction in these schools, will by no means be so tenacious of their idolatrous and superstitious rites as their fathers are. It is ours to sow the seed, water it with our prayers and tears, and look to God for the blessing and the final accomplishment of all his purposes of grace towards the heathen."

Death of Gungah.

This year died Gungah, a pupil of one of the girls' schools, who had for some time been regarded as hopefully pious. Miss Farrar, who had taken her into her own family, says of her manifest piety: "It did not seem to matter whom she met, or where; if there appeared a suitable opportunity for her to speak of the love of Jesus, and his blessed cause, she was not backward to do so. She manifested a realizing sense of her depravity, and of her desert for sin, and of gratitude for the great goodness of God to her, in blessing the means for bringing her to the knowledge of the truth, and for her hope of glory through a crucified Saviour. Her mind was remarkably clear and rational to the last. Her last words were, 'I am looking for the coming of Jesus,' and she sunk into his blessed embrace, as I trust, without a sigh."

Death of Babajee.

This year died Babajee also, and the record concerning him is a permanent testimony to the value of such educated *heathen teachers*, when once converted, in making known the Gospel to others. A few sentences of this record are as follows:

"His death is a very great loss, not only to the particular mission to which he belonged, but to the cause of Christ in general. Though he was not permitted to labor in the service of his divine Master above eighteen months, still he was enabled to accomplish more in this short period than can ordinarily be expected of a foreigner during twice that time. He addressed his own people in their vernacular tongue. He knew their prejudices and superstitions, their rites, and their sacred books. His appeals to the corrupt priesthood, from which he came out, were as pointed arrows, prepared, not in the spirit of rancorous bitterness, but in the spirit of divine love. Since his conversion he had been a most ardent, persevering helper in the work, and a most sincere, conscientious Christian."

In reviewing their past labors, the missionaries this year found that the effective years of labor by all, from the origin of the mission, amounted to the same as one man forty-nine years; and very fitly represent that if any thought little or nothing had been accomplished by that mission, he would, on the same principle, consider the 183,600 men, who left their homes and went to the mountains and forests to prepare materials for the temple, as having effected nothing by all their labor towards building that magnificent structure at Jerusalem.

Estimate of the Schools by the Board and the Missionaries.

1834.—The estimation in which the schools were held by the Board at this date, may be inferred from the following resolution, adopted at their annual meeting, namely:

"*Resolved*, That in view of the great deficiency of missionaries, the Board esteem the establishment of *high-schools* and *seminaries* for educating native catechists and preachers, as highly important; and that it be recommended to the Prudential Committee to foster those seminaries already in operation, and to found others as there may be opportunity, with the hope of supplying in part the deficiency of Christian teachers from this country."

The estimate of the English language by the natives had long before led the missionaries to avail themselves of it to some extent, and some young Brahmans had been taught English in private classes. The Report of this year says:

"A school for teaching the English language has been commenced at Ahmednuggur, and another at Bombay, with the hope that each of them will grow into an institution of more importance. Their average attendance may be about 25. It has not yet been found possible to get up *boarding-schools* on the plan of those in the Ceylon mission."

So much were the home-officers of the Board impressed with the value of schools among the Mahrattas, that this year six more teachers were sent out from America, namely: Messrs. Hubbard and Abbott, with their wives, and Miss Kimball and Miss Graves, to assist in teaching and superintending them. Miss Farrar continued to prosecute her zealous labors in this department, as she has done to the present time, and the other ladies of the mission all seem to have borne a part in the teaching and care of schools, to the extent of their health and strength. "An asylum or charity school was opened at Bombay in the summer of 1834, for the reception of native orphan girls, and for other poor female children." "The estimated expense of feeding, clothing, washing, and instructing one of these girls, is about a dollar a month. Ten girls have been received and promise well."

1835.—This year the English school at Bombay reports 50 scholars, and another English school was commenced at Mahim. The report brings to view the earnest desire of the Board to see boarding-schools in operation in Bombay, and the great hindrance to them from caste; hopes Miss Farrar will yet succeed, and mentions with encouragement that Mrs. Graves had "collected 40 girls at Satara."

1836.—Of the free schools the missionaries say: "One reason of supporting these schools is, they furnish a medium of communication with the inhabitants of the villages." "In addition to the advantages which these schools afford the children in the way of education and religious instruction, they furnish a medium of communication with the inhabitants of the villages, and thus open the way for imparting Christian instruction." "To raise them from this state of ignorance, to remove those prejudices which keep them morally and intellectually degraded, and, above all, to make them acquainted with Christianity, so that they may feel the force of its great truths on their hearts, and may become wise unto salvation, is the end we aim to accomplish, in our efforts in the cause of education."

The schools were still the principal reliance for preaching audiences. Of the *stated* audience in Bombay, it is said: "The assembly consists principally of the larger children from the boys' and girls' schools, of the teachers of the schools, of the men employed in the printing establishment, and of other persons connected with the mission, or belonging to the families composing it." "Curiosity will sometimes induce people to attend for one or two Sabbaths," but for a stated audience it was found of no avail.

The English school which had been established in 1834 was of brief continuance. The Annual Report of this year says: "The school for teaching the English language has been relinquished, at the suggestion of the committee," [in Boston.] The intelligent reader will hardly be able to avoid the reflection that this "suggestion of the Committee" was a departure from the broad and liberal views of the early officers and missionaries of the Board, and illy accords with the views of the Secretary at a still later date, (see p. 22.) Who can avoid the conviction that had this English school been allowed to continue, and grow into a large and valuable institution, similar to that of our brethren of the Scotch Free Church, the success of our Bombay Mission would have been far greater, and its present position and prospects much more hopeful than they now are?

Two or three who had long been instructed in the schools were this year received into the church.

1837.—In this year of financial distress, "the extension of the Mahratta missions was checked for want of funds." The reductions necessitated caused a voice of general lamentation to come up from all the missions; and in the statement of the Secretaries at the annual meeting, they say: "The effects of the curtailment were first felt in the free schools and seminaries connected with the missions, and they were disastrous and painful nearly in proportion to the extent and success with which they had before been conducted." "The schools among the Mahrattas suffered much from the curtailment, and would have been wholly broken up, had not timely aid been furnished by friends of the mission, residing in that quarter."

The Secretaries' estimate of these schools may be inferred from their opinion of the disastrous results of suspending them. On this point they testify as follows:

"The mere suspension of the schools constitutes but a small part of the calamity which the missions are suffering, in this respect. There is the difficulty of collecting those pupils again when the missions shall have the means to receive and instruct them, requiring perhaps not less time and labor than were necessary at first. Then there is the retarding of the education of native preachers and other helpers, who are so much needed, in addition to the loss of most of the labor and expense which had been bestowed upon those candidates for such employments, who have been turned away. Then there is the diminished number at the word preached on the Sabbath, and on other occasions. The schools are the preaching places; and the masters and pupils, and their friends, who all felt that they were receiving favors from the missions, were the most constant and the most interested hearers. This retrograde movement has, in some instances, exerted a most unhappy influence upon a whole heathen community."

The inquiry is respectfully proposed, Why this lamentation for schools necessarily disbanded for want of funds in 1837, and the forcible suppression by the Deputation of precisely the same kind of schools in new missions in 1854?—schools too, which, in the latter instance, never cost the Board a farthing!

1838.—In this financial emergency, "The schools at Bombay received important aid from European Christians, who gave liberally to sustain them through the season of pecuniary embarrassment."

Opposition of the Hindus to the Schools.

1839.—This year is memorable in the history of the Bombay missions for the opposition of the native community. This opposition was excited by the conversion and baptism of two *Parsee* students in the *English Institution* of the Scotch Free Church Mission—a case forcibly illustrating the value of such schools. If there is any other agency which could have so extensively and intensely excited the native population of Bombay, and led to so wide an extension of the knowledge of Christianity, it certainly remains to be discovered. However much missionary societies may undervalue these schools, those among the heathen who most resolutely oppose our efforts, show that *they* understand their character and influence. To no department of our labors was more vigorous opposition manifested on this occasion, than to our mission schools of every grade. In narrating some of the circumstances of this opposition to the Secretaries of the Board, our missionaries say:

"The people whose children attended our schools were told to withdraw them immediately, and that fearful consequences would follow if their children should continue to attend. A tract was prepared, printed and freely circulated in Bombay, entreating all classes of the native population to withdraw their children from the mission schools. It was not easy for parents and teachers to withstand such influence and obloquy. The boys' and girls' schools both suffered; the latter suffered most. Female education was represented as an innovation attempted by missionaries upon the good old ways, and so was the subject of special obloquy."

A "Society for Protecting Hinduism" was formed, and "all the Hindus were called upon to subscribe liberally to the funds of the Society, and to exert their influence for the support of their own religion, now in great danger from the *schools*, and other operations of the missionaries." Some leading natives got up a petition to Government, in which, among other things, "they request that a law may be passed which shall allow no missionary *schools* to be established in the interior, without the express sanction of Government."

Approval of Schools by the Board.

1840.—Some of the papers read this year by the Secretaries at the annual meeting, and approved by the Board, express sentiments which show the high estimation in which they held this department of mission labor, as follows:

"Probably not less than 60,000 or 70,000 persons have had portions of the Bible put in their hands, and been taught to read them by the missionaries which this Board has sent forth. How far the missionaries may properly go beyond the elementary education which is requisite for reading the Scriptures, and aim to introduce a Christian literature among a heathen people, it is not necessary now to determine. But one thing is evident, that wherever the Gospel enters with power, and the Scriptures are translated and distributed, and Christian *schools* are established to train up readers, and the mind is awakened from its listlessness, or called off from sensual and grovelling to more intellectual employments, there the foundation is laid for a pure national literature. And it must further be admitted that the object of the missionary will not be fully accomplished, and heathen people become what they are certainly destined to become, under the influence of the Gospel, until such a literature shall be brought into existence. Nor is the object beneath the care of a Christian missionary. To pour such treasures of thought, and science, and refined sentiments as the English language contains into the language of one of the great Asiatic nations, imbuing them at the same time with the Christian spirit, is, except preaching Christ crucified to the sinner, (with which this may have no slight connection,) second to no work in which men can engage.

"If, by giving the missionary *schools*, you can add the power of another man, it is right that he should have this increase of ability."

These sentiments met the cordial approval of the Board, and no doubt encouraged the missionaries in sustaining these schools.

Facts and Conversions in the History of the Schools.

1841.—Four *pupils* from the schools were this year received into the church. One of the missionaries, discoursing on the error of idol-worship, and urging the duty of loving, serving, and worshipping the true God, a boy among the hearers confirmed his remark, saying: "True, and there is only one Saviour, and that is Jesus Christ." The missionary says: "Surprised at this remark, from such a source, I looked closely at the boy, for it was twilight, and recognized him as one who belonged to our school in that neighborhood. Here he had learned the great and important truth which may yet be blessed to his salvation." How many hundreds and thousands of heathen children and youth have learned this same blessed truth in these mission schools!

1842.—While preaching in the villages on the continent this year, Mr. Hume found many persons "who had acquired a knowledge of the fundamental truths of the Gospel," to such an extent that he was quite surprised till he ascertained that "they had been in some of the *mission schools*." The only admission to the church this year was one more girl from the *boarding-school.*

1843.—Mr. Hume writes: "Our boys' schools are now in a flourishing state. All who are able to read assemble with their teachers as a Sabbath-school, and also attend the preaching services. The girls' schools have not yet recovered from the shock which they received at the time of the baptisms in January." The persons here alluded to as having been baptized were two (till then) *heathen teachers.* Of one of them the missionary wrote: "Nantcheny is an intelligent young woman, who, for several years, has been connected with the family boarding-school, first as a scholar, then as a teacher. She has for a long time been fully persuaded of the truth of Christianity, and she has often been deeply interested in the subject of personal religion."

It is worthy of notice that though several pupils and teachers had been received into the church, none of them could yet be successfully employed as teachers of free schools, subsequent to their baptism. Such was the panic among the people that they feared to send their children to such teachers, and in case of most or all of them, other important service was given to them as native helpers. Such had been the case with Babajee and Dajeeba, who were received into the church in 1831, and were soon transferred to Ahmednuggur as helpers. The result of the baptisms this year was much as usual. The missionaries say:

"Considerable excitement has been produced in our vicinity by these baptisms. The most interesting of our girls' schools has been broken up entirely. The teacher was a female, who had received much instruction, who had felt something of the power of truth, and whom we hoped soon to see numbered with the people of God. Her friends have been so much alarmed in regard to her as to prevent her coming to us any more. The parents of the children in her school were, for the most part, of the same caste as Nantcheny, and they have become alarmed lest their children also should be converted. Two of our boys' schools have likewise suffered from the same excitement. The teacher of one of the schools, a promising young man, who desires baptism, has been urged to relinquish his present employment; he has received the promise of a large school with increased pay."

Thus did these schools for *heathen children*, and taught by *heathen teachers*, continue to bring hopeful converts into the Church of Christ, and to arouse the fears and opposition of the heathen.

It is much to be regretted that the reports of the mission do not mention explicitly the immediate influence blessed to conversion in each instance. In most cases there is presumptive evidence that the converts were connected with the schools, but as the strictest accuracy is desirable, no convert is classified in connection with the schools unless it is so stated in the reports or letters of the missionaries.

It should also be noted that in case of the great majority of the converts who were not either pupils or teachers before their conversion, the influence of the schools is manifest in first bringing them to the missionaries, and under Christian instruction.

The teacher who was this year received into the Church continued to be employed as a teacher in the boarding-school two or three months, and was the first *native Christian* teacher employed in the entire history of the mission, so far as recorded. She soon relinquished her useful position as a Christian teacher to become the wife of a converted Brahman, a catechist of the church-mission at Nassick. Mr. Hume writes of her: "She is perhaps the best educated female in the Mahratta country, and one in whose piety we have entire confidence. We were much attached to her, and we doubt not she will be very useful in her new relation."

1844.—Of the Christian teaching in the schools the missionaries say:

"Most of these children have as much historical and doctrinal knowledge of the Bible as children of their age generally in our own country. How far this knowledge is accompanied with a conviction of the truth of Christianity, it is impossible to know, but they can not follow idolatry, and its superstitious and unmeaning rites, without recollecting that these things are forbidden, and, we believe, without often feeling a repugnance to them." "The teachers of these schools are intelligent men, and have acquired much historical and doctrinal knowledge of the Scriptures. They have at times shown that they felt strong convictions of the truth of Christianity, and we have hoped to see these convictions strengthened, till they should experience the renewing influence of the Holy Spirit, and profess their faith in Christ."

Of Mrs. Hume's girls' boarding-school it is said: "The divine blessing has rested upon it, and *seven* of its inmates have given such evidence of having experienced the enlightening and renewing influence of the Holy Spirit, that they have been baptized. Two others, who have not been baptized, have died, leaving evidence that the instruction given them had not been in vain."

Of Mrs. Graves' girls' boarding-school the fact is mentioned in the reports of this year, that it had been mostly supported by English friends from the first.

1845.—Again we find of Mrs. Graves' school, "its entire expense is defrayed by special donations." Of Mrs. Hume's, also: "This, likewise, is mainly supported by special donations, and by work done in the school. For several years past the divine blessing has manifestly attended the labor bestowed upon it."

1846.—Of both these schools it is again stated: "Their expense continues to be defrayed mostly by special donations received in India. The one in Bombay has been more interesting the past year than usual. The scholars not only made good progress in their studies, but some of them have manifested a pleasing solicitude in regard to their spiritual welfare." One had been welcomed to the church, and others were asking to be received.

1847.—Nearly all the fruit of labor in the mission seems to be in connection with the schools. Hence we read: "Only three persons were admitted to the church in 1847, and these were all from the *female boarding-school.* They all gave gratifying evidence that the labor bestowed upon them had not been in vain." "Several children in the boarding-school have exhibited an inquiring state of mind, and three more of them express the hope that they have passed from death unto life."

Up to this date no *native Christian* appears to have been employed as a teacher, in the whole history of the mission, except Nantcheny, as already mentioned, who was soon married, and removed to Nassick. This fact is worthy of notice, in connection with the manifest blessing which rested upon these schools, with heathen teachers, and in connection with the following paragraph in the report of the Committee on the Mahratta missions this year, namely:

"It is delightful to observe the tokens of divine favor granted to this oldest of the missions under the care of this Board. The establishment of the Bombay mission, associated as it is with the labors and faith of the late Gordon Hall, one of the brightest lights in the firmament of missions, illustrate the special providence of God in a peculiar manner."

1848.—Three more pupils from Mrs. Hume's school were this year admitted to the church, and of others it is stated: "We can not but hope that a saving change has been experienced. One of the older girls, who for more than a year has been a consistent member of the church, has been removed by death, leaving the gratifying assurance that she has been called to a better home."

In Mrs. Graves' school, also, "some have been under deep conviction, and some have asked for baptism."

1849.—"Religious interest" continues in *the schools.* "Three more girls have been admitted to the Church." The choice clusters of fruit come only from the schools.

1850.—"Two persons were received into the Church"—one of them a young man who had been educated in the mission school at Ahmednuggur, and the other a pupil in the girls' school.

Of the teachers this year, Mr. Hume writes: "Two *native Christians*, a male and a female, assist in giving instruction to the scholars."

Here is the first notice we find on record of *native Christian teachers* in the Bombay mission, except Nantcheny a month or two, as before mentioned. Let those who doubt the wisdom of employing heathen teachers review the history of this mission, *without a native Christian teacher for* 36 *years*, and yet almost all its converts, during these years, coming from the *heathen teachers and pupils* of these schools.

Influence of the Mission Schools in changing Public Sentiment.

The incidents of 1850 make it an era in the progress of Christian evangelization in India. In April was passed the memorable act of Government securing civil rights and liberty to native converts. The very general progress of enlightened sentiments, and the increase of true knowledge among the native population, became more than ever manifest. Particularly was this evident on the subject of *female education.*

From the statements of the missionaries, take the following: "One of the most encouraging indications of the times in India is the change which is gradually taking place in the feelings of the people, in regard to female education. Hitherto, nothing or next to nothing has been done to elevate the Hindu female, except what has been accomplished by the missionaries. They, wherever located, have addressed themselves more or less to this work. And considering the apathy, incredulity, and even active opposition so generally manifested by the native community, these efforts have been attended with a large measure of success. A gradual change has been wrought in the feelings of the community, so that the more wealthy natives have of late begun to educate their daughters in private. And the way has been prepared for the establishment of female schools, by the natives themselves, and by the Government."

The influence of the mission schools in inducing this enlightened state of feeling and sentiment could scarcely have been more manifest than it is. The influence of the female schools in modifying Hindu prejudices and preparing for a general change of views on the subject, is manifest from their first origin, in 1824. There had now arisen a class of educated natives, not to be restrained and fettered by the foolish and puerile superstitions of their fathers. The students of the Elphinstone College resolved to engage in these praiseworthy efforts to diffuse the benefits of education, and very soon established eight girls' schools in Bombay. Similar schools were established in Calcutta and elsewhere, and now, also, the Government began to give direct countenance and patronage to female schools. Intelligent Hindus became conscious that a great intellectual and moral change was being effected in the native community. One of our missionaries at Bombay wrote as follows:

"Educated natives tell me that there has been, during the last few years, a great change in the religious views of this community, and especially in the younger and educated portion of it. One who has good opportunities for observation, and who is himself speculatively convinced of the truth of Christianity, said to me the other day: 'Our community has gone half-way to your opinions; do not despair of the other half. I am firmly convinced that they will fully embrace your faith before many years.'"

Striking testimony to the progress of enlightened views and the influence of the schools in effecting it, is given this year in the *Prubhakur*, a native newspaper published in Bombay. The editor says: "I can not refrain from acknowledging, and with lively gratitude, that the missionaries who have come to our country, have exerted themselves with praiseworthy diligence to destroy sinful customs and practices. They have done us great favors. See! They have come thousands of miles from their native land, and have taught our people many arts, and the whole round of useful sciences. *They are the men who first established schools, and convinced the Government that this people is not averse to being taught*, but is rather anxious for the knowledge possessed by enlightened countries. Afterwards the Government followed their example, and began to establish schools. We must be grateful for what the missionaries have done for us, in establishing schools in so many places for instructing hundreds of boys and girls, even giving something for the support of such poor children as have no means, and thus instructing them."

In view of such honest testimony from an enlightened heathen editor, no wonder the missionaries also testify:

"The native mind is becoming more and more excited and distracted. Many of the Hindus are dissatisfied with their religious and social state, with the galling bondage of caste, and the degraded condition and character of their females."

1851.—Of Mrs. Hume's girls' school, the testimony this year is: "On no part of our missionary operations has the blessing of God so manifestly rested, as on this school. The behavior and progress of the pupils has been very satisfactory. One of them, an interesting girl, was received into the Church near the close of 1851."

The Annual Report of the Board this year says of these missions: "The laborers at the several stations are pursuing their work with energy and good results. The station at Bombay is evidently one of peculiar importance."

1852.—"The girls' boarding-school continues to enjoy the divine favor." The death of one of the girls is thus mentioned:

"She was, as we fully believe, a true child of God. She had an amiable disposition, a serious, well-balanced mind, and had received an excellent education both in English and Mahratta. We had hoped that she would be very useful, as an example and a guide to other native females, and that she might long be an ornament to the Church of Christ in India. But the Lord, who doeth all things well, hath ordered otherwise, and hath early removed her from the

Church on earth to the company of the redeemed in heaven. We were greatly attached to this dear girl; but it is not for us to murmur at this dispensation. Rather would we praise God that his grace was so clearly manifested in and towards her, and that at the last there was hope in her death. Her memory is precious; and we feel that she has not lived in vain."

This girl had been supported by a pious lady in Scotland. Can benevolent Christians feel that such examples of youthful piety and hopeful deaths on heathen ground, are purchased at too dear a price in the support of schools? And when we see the divine blessing so manifestly resting on these schools, can we doubt that the Lord approves them? In the special report of the Board on the Mahratta missions this year, we read:

"These missions, being in the first field ever occupied by the Board, awaken many interesting reflections. No mission undertaken by this organization has been attended by so many embarrassments as the one at Bombay. But God was pleased to provide for the exigency men of faith and prayer. The names of Gordon Hall and Samuel Newell will stand as memorials of missionary steadfastness and energy for generations to come. The Mahratta missions are exerting an extended influence, far beyond the neighborhood of the several stations. Much interest has been excited *through the schools* and the press. The spirit of inquiry and discussion which has been awakened in the Mahratta mind in regard to caste, and the concessions of the Brahmans, that Christianity is gradually undermining the religion of the Shasters, furnish evidence of the progress of the Gospel, and give promise of still greater success. Your committee think there has never been a time when the aspect of these missions has been so favorable as the present; and they commend this first field of the Board to its continued and increased support."

Statistics of Mission Schools in India, in 1851.

This year were collected and published general statistics of all the Protestant missions in India; and the number of their schools and pupils is doubtless a good indication of their estimate of this department of labor. These statistics give 1347 vernacular schools for boys, with 47,504 pupils.

347 day-schools for girls, with 11,519 pupils.

126 English schools, with 14,560 boys and young men.

93 boarding-schools, with 2414 boys, and

102 boarding-schools, with 2779 girls.

Here we have 64,480 boys and young men, and 14,298 females, under a regular systematic course of Christian instruction. What a fact to cheer the heart of every lover of Zion who is hoping and praying for the evangelization of India! And how forcibly does it witness to the judgment and experience of the whole band of Protestant missionaries in India, in favor of this agency for evangelizing the Hindus!

1853.—The *Missionary Herald* in its annual survey of this year, says of Mrs. Hume's girls' school: "The blessing of God has been manifestly upon it, and a goodly number of its inmates have from time to time been brought, as we trust, to a saving knowledge of the truth."

Of the labors and results of this year in the Bombay mission, the Board says: "The examples of the wise and good men and excellent women connected with this mission, the success of their labors, through the divine presence and blessing, and the evident preparation made for the rapid spread of the Gospel in a near approaching period, all give an interest and importance to this earliest mission of the American Board."

Disastrous Change.

1854–5.—But this bright and blessed prospect was suddenly overcast. Notwithstanding the evident and precious blessing that had rested on the schools through all their history, the frequent conversion of pupils and teachers, and the bright prospect of "the rapid spread of the Gospel in a near approaching period," a sudden change was enforced which has rendered the mission comparatively desolate and barren ever since.

The statistics of this mission for 1854–5 are few, and very little is said of it in the periodicals of the Board. In the Annual Report of 1855 it is stated that: "Owing in part, doubtless, to the broken state of the mission, and in part, it may be, to the visit of the Deputation to India, no report has been received from Bombay, and no communications which enable the committee to go into details."

The mission had been weakened by the return of the Rev. Dr. Allen to America, and the death of Rev. R. W. Hume, on his voyage to this country, and also by *the action of the Deputation in disbanding all the schools taught by heathen teachers, the girls' boarding-school and the English high-school.* This swept overboard nearly every thing of interest in the mission. With all these schools broken up, and but one missionary there, we are not surprised to read in the special report, at the annual meeting of the Board, in 1855, as follows, namely:

"The condition of the Bombay mission is less encouraging than we should all desire," etc.

This sudden change in the special report, from the bright and cheering prospect presented on the last page, is worthy of a permanent record and of prayerful reflection by all who love the cause of missions.

As no allusion has been before made to the *English High-school at Bombay*, some acount of it is here necessary to a full history of the educational operations of the missions. Scarcely any thing appears in regard to it in the regular periodicals of the Board, although the letters of the missionaries were many, and long, and earnest. Its history will be best brought to view in connection with the doings of the *Deputation*, in the next chapter.

CHAPTER IV.

HISTORY OF OUR BOMBAY MISSION SCHOOLS CONTINUED.

Bombay High School and the Late Deputation.

IT is fresh in the memory of pastors and churches, that a Deputation of the A.B.C.F.M., consisting of Rev. R. Anderson, D.D., Senior Secretary, and Rev. A. C. Thompson, visited our India missions, in 1854–6. The doings of that Deputation caused much agitation, both in this country and in India; and a feeling of dissatisfaction still exists very widely in the hearts of our pastors and intelligent laymen. And yet it is doubtful whether the real occasion of the Deputation, and the extent and character of the changes effected by them, have been properly understood by the Christian public.

Since returning from India I have often been asked, "What was the necessity of a Deputation? Why were not our intelligent missionaries there on the ground as well fitted to judge of the best agencies for carrying on this work, as any of our brethren here at home? What less confidence could we have had in the members of the Deputation if they themselves had been laboring a dozen or twenty years in India, and thus come in possession of *experience* as well as *theories* in this great work?" These are questions which the reader can answer as well as a missionary. But there are *facts*, in regard to which eye-witnesses may speak with more confidence than others.

Cause of the Deputation.

The immediate cause of the Deputation was the *High-school* at Bombay, and the earnest appeals of the brethren in its behalf. This is brought to view with sufficient clearness in the Report of the Deputation, published in 1856. In that report it is stated as follows, namely : "In the early part of the year 1854, letters were received from the Bombay Mission, earnestly requesting permission to institute a high-school on the model of certain Scotch and English schools existing in the large cities of India. The proposal was seconded by the Ahmednuggur Mission. . . . The school was urged upon the Committee as a matter of necessity, to save the Bombay mission from extinction," etc.

The true issue is here stated. It may not have been fully appreciated by the Christian public, but it is unmistakable. *The missionaries were united and earnest in asking what the Secretary was unwilling they should have.*

The reader will bear in mind that an English school had been established in our Bombay mission, so long ago as 1834, and that it was disbanded in 1836, "at the suggestion of the Committee," in Boston. But the mission had continued to feel the need of such an institution. For the want of it they had seen their most promising converts attracted to other missions, and after *forty years'* labor, they found their native church still small and weak, with no well-educated and efficient catechists and preachers. They found, too, that the desire for education, and especially for English education, was daily becoming more earnest, irresistible and universal among Hindu youth; and when the English Seminary of our Ahmednuggur mission was disbanded, in 1851, by positive instructions from Boston, they found that several of our most promising converts and inquirers left us and came to Bombay, to secure the advantages offered in the mission institutions of our Scotch and English brethren at the presidency.

The American missionaries in Bombay felt exceedingly grieved and tried at this state of things, and so strong became their convictions that an English institution was necessary to the best interests and success of the mission, that they sent representations to the Secretary and Committee in Boston, urging the measure in the strongest possible language, and using the most convincing arguments. Of these arguments, the following extracts will enable the reader to judge for himself:

Rev. R. W. Hume's Plea for Schools.

"BOMBAY, 25 May, 1853.

"Rev. RUFUS ANDERSON, D.D.,

"Secretary to the A.B.C.F.M.:

"DEAR SIR: . . After a careful and earnest consideration of the character of the field, and our present position, I have come to a settled conviction that we are now, in the providence of God, *clearly called to add an educational institution to the operations of the mission.* None of us have been 'Educationists,' in the popular acceptation of that term. We have resisted the idea that missionaries must become schoolmasters. We each and all came to India to be preaching missionaries; and we have sought to be a preaching mission. We have no wish to relinquish the work of preaching, nor any intention of doing so. But we are satisfied that the mission can not properly accomplish its work, and reap the fruit of its labors, without a superior educational institution. The present character of the field, and our peculiar circumstances with reference to the other missions, require it. The providence of God is shutting us up to this course, and the Board and the mission must submit to the necessity that is laid upon them. Among the better classes in Bombay, and to a less extent in the larger towns and villages, there is now a great desire for education. The most hopeful and important class is the young men; and among these there is not merely a desire for education, but a passion, so to speak, for English education. . . The easiest, nay almost the only way, to bring this important class, for any length of time, under the influence of the mission, is by means of a superior institution, in which English shall be taught. This is the plan adopted by the other missions in Bombay, and at nearly or quite all the mission stations in this country. Without such an institution your missionaries must be more and more cut off from this most interesting and hopeful class, who will naturally be drawn towards those missions which fall in with their feelings and aspirations.

"Again, the *converts* naturally, and very properly too, share in the prevalent desire for education. Those who are parents will insist on the education of their children. And do what we will, the young men of spirit will not be kept back from an education. We have no institution for imparting such an education as they desire. The other missions are ready to receive them, and do for them what we can not. And the sure result must be that the best families, and the most efficient, interesting young men, will be drawn away from us; and thus our labors, in a good measure, must go to build up other mission churches. And will the American Board and the American churches consent to perpetuate such a state of things? Are they willing that their missionaries should thus be made hewers of wood and drawers of water to the other missions?

"We may preach the Gospel in season and out of season; we may prepare, and print, and circulate tracts and books; we may be exceedingly useful in many ways; but it is as certain as the law of gravitation that, are we not allowed to occupy a different position, the best fruits of our labors will be gathered up by others—a state of things which we feel assured the churches which sustain the American Board will not knowingly and willfully tolerate for an hour.

"The evil of which I am now speaking principally concerns us in Bombay. But your missions in the Deccan must also be affected by it, and that in an increasing degree from year to year. Already they are having some bitter experience of what is abundantly in store for them in years to come, unless a suitable remedy is provided. Not long since you announced to the American churches the baptism of Vyenkutrao, a Brahman convert at Ahmednuggur. He is now a student of theology in the Free Church Institution here. More recently you announced the baptism of Krishna, an interesting young Brahman at Satara. He, too, has just been transferred to the Free Church Institution and the Free Church Mission, in the expectation of being there trained for the Gospel ministry. When the Seminary at Ahmednuggur was finally relinquished, an interesting young man, Ramchunder, having studied there for some time, had become convinced of the truth of Christianity, and was thought to be a hopeful inquirer. He wished to remain and pursue his studies in connection with the American mission, but as that could not be, [the Seminary being abandoned] he soon found his way to the Free Church Institution, where a few weeks since he was baptized. Ramaji, a promising convert of the Ahmednuggur mission, and Tukeram, a son of one of the native assistants of that mission, are at present studying here in the Free Church Institution. And in most such cases the sure result must be that the young men are lost to us. Their sympathies and their home are naturally with the mission in which they are trained; and instead of strengthening us, they are likely to draw away others after them. Nothing could be more natural than such a result. The best scholars of our schools, the children of the converts —sometimes those on whom much labor has been bestowed— come to us asking that we should secure their admission into one of the other mission institutions. Inquirers, too, after coming for a time to us, often find attractions at those Institutions which we can not offer; and after getting enrolled in them as students, naturally receive religious instruction there. This state of things has long cost us much anxiety, and the evil is increasing from year to year. I now wonder that we have borne it so long; but there is a limit to endurance, and that limit has at length been reached.

"The proposal to establish a superior institution in connection with the Bombay mission, may not be in accordance with the cherished plans and hopes, either of the missionaries or of the Board. But a necessity is laid upon us which we can no longer escape from. We may regret that there is such a passion for English education on the part of the rising generation; we may regret that your missionaries can not retain their converts, and build up the native Church, without yielding to the current that has set in so strongly; but Providence has settled this matter for us, and regrets are vain—nay, if persisted in, they are wicked.

"God has a high purpose to fulfill in regard to India. And in this passion for English education, and in all the peculiar circumstances of this people, we must discern his workings. His hand is in it. The way in which he has chosen to accomplish his purposes, may be different from what we expected, and different from what we desired. But we must fall in with his plans, when once indicated, or we must suffer the penalty. We may kick against the pricks, if we will; we may row against wind and tide till we are weary; but our blind obstinacy will avail us nothing. God has, in a most remarkable manner, given India into the hands of England; and the English language and literature have here a high destiny to fulfill. Let us be wise enough to take things as they are, instead of wasting our time and our strength in wishing they were otherwise.

"I have long resisted some of the convictions to which utterance has just been given. But I now submit to what I regard a Heaven-ordained necessity. And I am satisfied, too, that God's plan is the best. Your missionaries have not been disposed to come up to the necessities of the occasion in the matter of an educated native ministry. They have been too ready to work through partially educated and imperfectly qualified agents. No where is this a greater error than in India; and God is shutting us up to better things. The Government institutions are yearly sending out men thoroughly trained, a large part of whom are Deists and Infidels. Their influence must be immense. Such educated young men must be the leading spirits of the nation. They will guide and mould public opinion. They must give character and form to the views and feelings of the multitude. Under such circumstances we want, and we *must have*, native preachers of the Gospel thoroughly trained; men who can stand up unabashed before educated revilers, and manfully contend for the faith as it is in Jesus. For us to aim at any thing less than this would be unworthy of the cause to which we are devoted. And we may be assured that if we neglect this high duty, God will raise up men of greater faith, of more expanded views, and of a higher, holier ambition, to do a work which we refuse to perform. . . The *expense* of the Institution, aside from the salaries of those connected with it, need not be very great. A special effort will sooner or later be required to provide a suitable building, etc. But the necessary sum can be raised, we feel assured, without interfering with the ordinary income of the Board. Many would give liberally for this object, who ordinarily give little to foreign missions. We have faith in the churches with reference to this matter. They are neither less able nor less spirited than the churches of other lands, who supply the funds for similar institutions to be devoted to the service of Christ in various parts of India. If you have any misgivings in regard to this point, give us a commission to raise the money, and leave us free to make the necessary arrangements, and to present the requisite appeals. We have no fear but that the claim for funds, if properly set forth and understood, will be recognized and regarded.

"It should, I think, be understood that the proposal now made to the Prudential Committee, is one which involves, not merely the prosperity of the mission, but eventually its very existence. It is a question of life and death. We have no proper provision for bringing under our influence, for any length of time, the most important and hopeful class in the community—the young men. We have no provision for educating the children of the converts, nor for training native preachers and other assistants. They must look to other missions for what we are not in a position to give, and must, of course, be drawn away from us. In such circumstances, the mission may endure for a season, and may do very much to advance the cause of Christ; but it can not reap the fruits of its labors; and consequently it must in the end be given up in discouragement and despair. The great battle with superstition and error will continue to be waged until it is brought to a successful termination. But if you remain in the field, and continue to occupy your present position, you and your missionaries, instead of leading the van, must be content to act the useful but ignoble part of baggage-bearers to the rest of the army. . .

"But if the Bombay mission can not be properly sustained without so much labor and expense, then is it not better to retire and leave the field to other sections of the Church? To such a proposal our heart and our judgment alike answer NO! Let Bombay, the first-born of your missions, be abandoned, and it will strike a cold chill through the American churches. The announcement would tend to dampen the hopes and the feelings of the friends of missions in every land. The heathen, from one end of India to the other, would rejoice and take courage. The enemies of the Gospel on all sides would say, Aha! aha! The friends of the American Board as they, generation after generation, read the history of its origin and first struggles—the hopes, aspirations, and efforts of those venerated men, who, amidst prayers, tears, and rejoicing, planted this mission; would not their feelings be shocked? Would not their hearts heave a heavy sigh if required to read a few pages further on, that after forty years of prayer and effort, the Bombay mission was abandoned, and the fruit of its labors left for others to gather? And would they not make inquisition regarding the reasons for such a procedure? To abandon such a field as this—one of the most important, interesting, and hopeful in all the heathen world—would it not be treason against Christ? Besides, it would be a suicidal measure. It would, to a certain extent, destroy the prestige of the Board—a thing of which some may think lightly, but which is in fact, a serious matter; it would weaken your hold upon the confidence of the churches, so that, in the end, you would lose far more, even in a pecuniary point of view, than would have been required to carry on the mission on the largest scale of expenditure. Let the Board abandon the Bombay mission, and it voluntarily assumes the position of a bereaved mother laying her first-born in the dust. And the vivid impression made on many minds must be, that the remaining children may in like manner, one after the other, soon pass away.

"And what would be gained by abandoning Bombay? You would, indeed, for the present, escape the necessity of establishing a superior educational institution. But will not a like necessity soon arise in any other field which you may occupy?—one which others will recognize, if you do not? And then you might again withdraw, leaving to others the field so long cultivated. But I do not believe the American Board and the American churches are prepared thus to play 'the squatter' in the wide wastes of heathenism.

"The American churches were the first to plant the standard of the cross in Bombay. For forty years they have nobly maintained the warfare with the prevalent systems of error; and now, when these systems are ready to perish, a proposal to abandon the field would be monstrous. God forbid that the churches and the Board should be left to any such course as this. I never should have thought to speak of such a thing as abandoning Bombay, had not such a proposal been made by a sub-committee of the Board a few years since.

"The absolute necessity for a superior institution for the training of native preachers, etc. etc., has latterly pressed more and more upon my mind. . .

"We hope that the subject now brought before you may be considered at an early day, and that God may guide you to a wise decision. You will see how important the question to be decided is in our view; and we earnestly hope that your estimate of the subject may correspond with ours. We shall look with some anxiety for your reply, which we hope may authorize us to take steps for carrying the plan into execution. With kindest regards to your associates at the mission-house, in which Mrs. Hume unites, believe me, in the service of Christ,

"Yours, very sincerely,

"R. W. Hume."

This noble and earnest plea requires no comment. It does credit alike to the head and the heart—to the manly and Christian and missionary spirit of the author. How could its arguments be set aside, except by *authority?*

This plea was virtually indorsed by all the other American missionaries in Western India, and each added remarks from which we present a few extracts. The two other missionaries at that time in Bombay were Rev. Messrs. Fairbank and Bowen.

Rev. S. B. Fairbank's Plea for Schools.

"May 25, 1853.

"Rev. R. Anderson, D.D.,

"Secretary A.B.C.F.M.:

"Reverend and Dear Sir: There is an important subject on which I, as well as my brethren of the Bombay mission, believe it a duty to address you. It has been to me a source of much regret that our missions in this presidency are losing their promising young men. I will give you some facts for illustration of my meaning, and then present the conclusion to which my mind, in revolving this and connected subjects, has arrived."

Mentioning the case of Krishna, the Brahman convert at Satara, Mr. F. says: "I was pleased with his appearance, and embraced an opportunity for free conversation with him. He conversed with ease and propriety in English. In the course of the conversation, he gave me the reasons that had decided him to leave the Satara mission and go to Bombay. He said he wished to be well qualified for the ministry. He had much discussion with educated young men who were versed in infidel objections, who had learned to scout Christianity, and felt proud of their deistical theology. He felt the need of a more thorough training, and of much more study and knowledge, and had determined to have it. The mission at Satara was dear to him. He preferred to labor in *his own* (the American) mission. But there was a fitness for his work demanded which he could not get there, and must have. I need not recapitulate the arguments I used to persuade him to continue his work as assistant, and by reading, and the help of the missionaries, to make up his deficiencies. He said he had tried it, but could not improve much in that way. It was only in an institution, connected with others, inspirited by discussion and fired by emulation, that he could hope for satisfactory progress. Two days after, he left Satara and proceeded to Bombay." . .

"In close connection with this case, I am reminded of that of Ramchunder Powar, who was baptized in Bombay the 29th ult., by Rev. J. M. Mitchell of the Free Church of Scotland's mission, and is now studying in the Free Church Institution. On the first excursion I made in the villages after I reached Ahmednuggur, I visited Kadambe, where one of the mission schools was located. I examined the school and spent a Sabbath there, intensely interested with the company that kept around me for conversation respecting Christianity, though I could only stammer a little in Mahrathi. . . I noticed three boys in the highest class in the school, in whom I afterwards became much interested. They were the sons of the head men (Patils) of the two divisions of the village. Two bore the family name of Powar, and one of Takte. They then expressed a desire to enter the Seminary at Ahmednuggur, and a year before I left A. for Bombay they had all three become members of the Seminary. Whenever their parents came to Ahmednuggur, they used to call on me, and I enjoyed talking with them very much.

"After coming to Bombay I lost sight of these, my friends, and had not thought of them for a long time, till Ramchunder Powar, the eldest of the boys, came to Bombay, in company with Ramaji Bhore, and like him, desirous of continuing his studies. We could offer them no such means of education as they were seeking, and they both became connected with the

Free Church Institution. Soon it became known that Ramchunder was desirous of baptism, and as his conduct seemed to accord with his profession, his Christian friends felt that if, after suitable probation, he should remain firm, the seal of baptism should be granted him. Soon his uncle came to try to change his decision, then his father, then his mother. They used all the means which Hindus know so well to use, to shake his purpose, but were unsuccessful. We approved his baptism, but he was not baptized by us, his foster-parents and his guides to the Saviour. As he naturally would be, he was baptized by those with whom he is now connected, and from whom he expects a liberal education. He will probably remain with, and labor in connection with that mission. I trust and pray that he may become, as he appears likely to, a useful assistant in the missionary work. But I could wish that he had remained with the American mission, and that the fruits he may be privileged to gather had also been given to us.

"I feel sad when I think of Ramchunder, and Krishna, and Vyenkutrao,* etc., and when I think that this is but the beginning of the exodus of the promising young men we may be privileged to lead to Christ. I feel sad that Ramaji Bhore should have left Ahmednuggur, though I can not condemn the reason as wholly censurable. Would I not have done the same in similar circumstances? I hear that Sidu Sonar is somewhat inclined to follow in the same course. The current sets strong, and I feel convinced that the best young men who are brought into the churches of the American missions, as they learn their necessities, and see the privileges of others, will leave us, and become connected with other missions, where they can prosecute to better advantage the study of English, etc., namely, those studies thought necessary to a liberal education, and to fit them for licensure and ordination. If these young men would go but for a time, and then come back and labor with us, it were a less calamity. But until the numbers of such persons become vastly greater than now, they will be retained where they have gone, and we shall not have their aid nor reap the harvest they will cultivate.

"There is a class of young men in Bombay who are interested

* These all left us when the Mission Seminary was broken up by a positive order from Dr. Anderson.

in learning of Christ. Such have frequently come to us for conversation, but no such young man thinks of becoming permanently connected with us. He would naturally prefer to go where he finds a band of similarly-minded youth eager for knowledge, and under the instruction of missionaries, who are heart and soul engaged in supplying the mental as well as spiritual hunger of such inquirers. *We* may gather such young men to a discussion. We may spend frequent hours in conversing with and instructing them. They may look to us as, in a great measure, their spiritual guides. But for reasons I have stated we can not hope to number them among our own people, and to encourage the hearts of Christians in America by telling them of the good they have been instrumental of doing in India, in helping to raise up such champions for Christianity. I have earnestly sought, while endeavoring to sow the seed beside all waters, and to spread as widely as possible the knowledge of the principles, and practice, and spirit of Christianity, to discover also the best way of *gathering converts* from among the heathen. Our relations to you and the American churches require that we should not be content with sowing the seed. We must also reap, and garner, and preserve. How shall we get the attention of the vast multitudes that throng Bombay? How draw men aside out of the tide of business and the current of public sentiment, into some eddy where they shall examine their position and course? How secure an earnest and pleased study of those things which pertain to their salvation? How persuade them to break their fetters, and join with the people of God? How lead them forth, and bring them in, and foster them, as good shepherds of the flock of God? Perhaps we have paid too little attention to gathering together and training a native church. Not that it lies in man to convert the soul, and supply the continual oil of divine grace; but some modes of operating are better fitted than others to the gathering a church. The church towards which inquiring souls shall look, and into which they shall flee for refuge, must have a character, and what shall go to form that character is matter for grave consideration.

"We have expended much time and strength in the publication of Christian books and tracts, and in securing their sale. This will remain a good department of labor. It must be persevered in with a still greater earnestness, and will require a greater and greater amount of labor. But the results of such work are as it were comminuted and disseminated through the entire country around us, and the direct results, in adding to our church of those who shall be saved, is yet to be realized. . .

"How feebly, in comparison with what he might do, does that missionary war against the empire of Satan, who has dropped from his quiver all his polished shafts, and relies on his clumsy weapons and untutored skill of the (intellectually considered) *children* that follow with him! That we may do the work set before us in providence, and perform our part in providing a Christian literature for the infant church and the inquiring community of this presidency, we can not act to good purpose, (comparatively,) but with the aid of well-trained, liberally-educated assistants, who recognize in us their pastors and teachers, and whose efforts it is ours to guide and control.

"I would say in this connection, that there are causes operating, which are waking up the *whole* community, and it will not do for us to attempt quarrying another and lower stratum, trying to ignore the 'enlightened' body of young men who are now foremost in religious discussions, and whose sentiment, and feelings, and spirit must necessarily tinge and leaven the whole mass of Hindu society. The rigid strata of Hinduism are being broken up and pressed together, and this process must go on till they disappear in the volcanic melting, and mingling, and re-moulding of society into its future condition. Who shall bind the strong man, and take from him the armor wherein he trusts? The battle may be set in array, but the hosts wait till the champion finds his equal and his conqueror."

The following extract from Mr. Fairbank's plea may properly be considered in close connection with his testimony on the platform at the special meeting in Albany, March, 1856. Doubtless many at that meeting regarded his testimony as strongly in favor of bazaar or street-preaching. Such seems not to be the view expressed in this carefully written letter. In this Mr. F. writes:

"So far as Bombay is concerned, I would not advocate the expenditure of much mission strength in what is called 'bazaar-preaching,' for the expenditure of strength and spirit is too great, and the result generally is that some 'fellow of the baser sort' raises an uproar, and the only good accomplished by the missionary, who is unable amid the noise and confusion to declare his message, is that he can show an example of suffering patience under abuse. Is not our Saviour's injunction, that we cast not our pearls before swine, applicable to such efforts? . .

"In all such efforts [namely, preaching in our school-houses and chapels] there is a necessity for a *nucleus.* The missionary must have with him those who constitute a small audience, or he will often fail of drawing hearers from out-doors, and also of keeping them when drawn in. The mission, also, which has its nucleus, stands on a vantage-ground. That nucleus is attractive in many respects. There is society, sympathy, aid, standing, and indeed all those *facts* of social and religious life, which are so necessary to a man, and specially to a Hindu, and which now bind him in almost inseparable connection with *his own caste.* . . . There is a grand defect in our present system. Not that any course of effort in which we have engaged should be given up as unsatisfactory. We may and do modify as occasion offers. But there is a desideratum. There is a heart wanted to this body of means, which would send the healthy life-blood coursing through all its arteries. There is a manufactory needed in which the weapons and munitions of war shall be prepared. *We need a first-rate educational institution*, under the charge of, and in vital connection with, the American Missions in Western India. This, it is true, would be but a means in the hand of God; but it would be, among other means, *as the heart is in the body.* . .

"That such an institution be made available to others than Christians; it has the example of the colleges of Christian lands in its favor. It would bring many thinking young men under Christian instruction, whom God might see fit to choose for his service. It would require no greater expenditure of missionary strength than ought to be devoted to teaching the Christian young men. It would give, in itself, to the missionary teacher the most hopeful audience he could at present possibly collect. It would form a magnet of attraction to those without, bringing them to hear him with attention and candor. . . . I see no objection to allowing other young men to put themselves under so healthy an influence. I should hope their conversion in many cases, and should expect that in most they would become theoretically Christianized. I think, too, that the best interests of the converts taught would require larger classes, etc., than they alone would constitute.

"Such an institution seems a prime necessity to the American missions in the Bombay presidency—to conserve, to attract, to elevate, to energize, to put us in our proper position, so that we may become not merely what we are now considered, an industrious corps of sappers and miners, but also a body of occupation. . . . I have thus briefly sketched the course of thought in some of its phases, which has convinced me of the expediency and necessity of a first-class literary and theological institution in Bombay. I am not considered an educationist, in the sense that our Scotch brethren in Bombay are so. But I have seen and deplored a great want of our missions. I believe the necessity will become more and more palpable and imperative, till that want is supplied. I would urge on the Prudential Committee the establishment of such an institution at the earliest opportunity, and on a broad basis. The times demand great efforts, and if we heed not the signs of the times, if we shut our eyes to the providences of God, we are recreant to the charge committed to us. . .

"In the work of the Lord,

"Yours, faithfully,

"S. B. FAIRBANK."

The Rev. George Bowen's Plea for Schools.

Omitting the preface, Mr. Bowen says:

"1. Among the young men of this country, the desire for education is very strong, and is daily becoming stronger. What they principally seek is an English education. They regard it as the avenue of success and influence. We may find fault with that desire; we may prefer to see them cling to their vernaculars; we may exert ourselves to make them do so: the fact remains. We can not overcome it. We should incur odium by attempting to do so. And having the appearance of being something providential, it commands our respect.

"2. Young men connected with our missions in Western India have their full share of this desire for what is termed a liberal education. And they are drawn to institutions superintended by other missionaries, and the consequence is, that they join other missions. This, though not a great evil, is still, I think, not the most desirable state of things. It is a reproach to our missions in the public estimation that they should be parting with their converts in this way. . .

"3. If missionaries have not a mind to preach, (that is, to make this their principal business,) you can not make them preach by shutting up their schools, or withholding the liberty to found an educational institution. If missionaries have a mind to preach, the fact of their being engaged in teaching some hours in the middle of every day will not hinder them from preaching. Taking the year round, I doubt if there be in India a missionary who preaches (in the technical sense) on an average, two hours a day. No missionary connected with the educational institutions of Bombay is actually employed in them more than twenty-four hours in the week.

"4. I believe, as I have always believed, that the greatest results of missionary effort shall eventually be seen in connection with the preaching of the Gospel. I look for no great and splendid spiritual results from educational efforts. As things now are, they seem to be expedient; they seem to be necessary. A day is coming, doubtless, when the preaching of the Gospel will be attended by such displays of the power of God, as have never yet been witnessed. That day may be at hand. But at present street-preaching is little else than street-quarrelling. Wherever you go in Bombay, men present themselves armed with infidel objections against Christianity, or with obscene descriptions of its origin, or with a treasury of personal insults, or with an overwhelming volume of voice, or in default of all, with handfuls of sand. And the most complete refutation of their objections, though repeated a hundred times, never induces them to relinquish a single one of those objections. . . . I would not have any thing as a substitute for preaching. But I see not why an educational institution, where any native of any caste may come and learn Natural History, Natural and Mental Philosophy, Natural Theology, History, English, the grammar of his own language, Geography, Logic, the Evidences of Christianity, the Bible—why such an institution, particularly cared for by two missionaries, with native assistants, may not exist in conjunction with all the preaching of the Gospel that now is in Bombay.

"5. If young men are not afforded the means of getting an education such as I have just indicated, they will go to the government schools, and get an education from which the more beneficent features of the above list are excluded. They will thus become infidels.

"6. I believe this mission is possessed of the pecuniary means of commencing such an establishment. The fund, in my opinion, should be used; and I see no better way than this.

"7. I am willing to aid in such an institution to any extent that may be thought desirable. I am also willing to remain disconnected with it. . . In all faithfulness,

"Yours,

"GEO. BOWEN."

These impartial views of Mr. Bowen are the more valuable, as he went to India with views and feelings strongly in favor of oral preaching, as the only proper agency. A few years' experience led him to the views here expressed.

In the statements of these three brethren, we have the honest convictions of the whole Bombay mission on the question at issue. But those brethren did not rest here. They knew that their convictions were opposed to the views and wishes of Dr. Anderson. For this reason, and to give him and the Committee the benefit of all our united views, the brethren in Bombay forwarded their own appeals to Boston, and immediately sent copies of them to Ahmednuggur, Satara and Kolapoor, with the following

"Circular.

"To the Rev. H. BALLANTINE, Rev. A. HAZEN, Rev. L. BISSELL, Rev. E. BURGESS, Rev. W. WOOD, Rev. R. G. WILDER:

"DEAR BRETHREN: We forward herewith for your perusal copies of letters which were dispatched by us to the Rev. Dr. Anderson, by the mail of yesterday. It was our wish to forward with these letters an expression of your views regarding our proposal to commence an educational institution in Bombay. Want of time necessarily prevented this, and as there is no other mail for a considerable time, we thought it best not to detain the letters. The subject is one in which you will feel much interest, and it is proper that the Prudential Committee should know your feelings and views in regard to it. We wish to furnish them with all the light which can be obtained, so that they may fully understand the merits of the question. If you will kindly peruse these letters, and favor us with an expression of your views, we will forward them to the Prudential Committee by the first overland mail. . .

"Yours, very faithfully,
"R. W. HUME,
"S. B. FAIRBANK,
"GEO. BOWEN."

Rev. Henry Ballantine's Plea for Schools.

This "circular" elicited a reply from Mr. Ballantine, signed also by the other brethren at Ahmednuggur, from which we present the following extracts, namely:

"In reference to the proposed plan of the Bombay brethren for the establishment of an educational institution in connection with that mission, I have only a few remarks to make, as I concur generally in the views expressed by the Bombay brethren.

"1. I believe, with Mr. Hume, that the existence of the Bombay mission is at stake. Very few missionaries would be willing to work under the circumstances of discouragement and humiliation to which our Bombay brethren have been long subjected. . . . They are not permitted to reap any of the fruits of their labors themselves, because those individuals who are favorably affected by these means, are at once drawn to other missions, where they receive religious instruction, and when baptized are of course received into those mission churches. Now who will be willing to go and labor in Bombay under such discouraging circumstances? . . . I do not believe that any missionaries will be found willing to supply the place of the Bombay brethren after they are removed, and that that mission must therefore become extinct, unless there be a change of mission policy—and I see no other plan at present than that proposed by the brethren there. *It is the only way they can obtain an audience* of persons most likely to be affected by the truth, under favorable circumstances for making a lasting impression on their minds and hearts. . . .

"2. Shall the Bombay mission be given up? I hope this alternative will not be thought of. I know not what we should do in the Deccan without the Bombay mission. That mission is absolutely necessary to the best working of our missions in the interior. Besides the remarks which Mr. Hume has made on this point, in which I fully concur, I would add that the abandonment of our printing-press at Bombay would be, in my opinion, of immense detriment to the cause of Christ.* Even should it pass into the hands of another mission, this would be the case. But especially would the interests of our missions in the Deccan suffer from giving up our mission in Bombay with its efficient native press. We should feel crippled in all our operations. . . .

"3. I approve of the plan which the Bombay brethren propose. . . . They have not the privilege of *using* the capacity of instructing, which they have with great labor acquired, under circumstances where it will turn to the best account. They have no means of bringing around them that class of minds which they are best prepared to influence, *and which are the minds* which in a few years will influence the great mass of the native community. Until they have this educational institution which they desire to see established, they are shut out from that class of young men entirely, except as opportunities of casual intercourse occur. To a zealous missionary this is extremely tantalizing and discouraging. . . . An institution there, will be of great use to us, as things are at present. Our young men will be saved from running to other missions, and even some of those who have left us to attend the institutions in Bombay may be brought back. As for the future we know not what is before us, and it is useless to speculate on what may be our necessities before long. The face of society is now undergoing great and rapid changes in the community around us. Large classes of educated young men are coming forth on the stage, who have been trained in the government schools, and who are exerting very great influence on the masses around them, for they are able to penetrate those masses and to diffuse their infidel and atheistic opinions with very great success. We see this process going on, on every

* The Deputation crippled this press, when in India, and it has since been entirely given up.

side. Now we must have the means of reaching these educated young men, of commanding their respect, and of bringing them around us to hear lectures on science and morals and religion. We can not do without these means in Bombay; the only way of accomplishing the object is that, I believe, which the brethren there have proposed. . . . We must be prepared to use the most effective means for reaching the class of mind that is to influence the community here for years to come.

"I am glad to see that the brethren in Bombay have come boldly up and faced the difficulty before them, and devised a plan for overcoming it. *It is indeed a question of life or death with them.* . . .

"H. BALLANTINE,
"A. HAZEN,
"AHMEDNUGGUR, June 4, 1853. "L. BISSELL."

Rev. A. Hazen, in addition to the above plea, sent a separate letter to the Bombay brethren, of which the following is an extract:

"The question of giving up *Bombay* is the question of giving up *all Western India*, and I can regard it in no other light. I should be very unwilling to labor here and no one in Bombay, unless circumstances be very different from what I conceive them to be. I feel that *all* the brethren on this side of India will enter an emphatic protest against any such step. This proposal [for the institution] brings to mind the *oneness* in *interest* of all our missions, and I am very glad to see it is so. May the present feeling of *fraternity* never be interfered with. May we all be ready to stand by each other, shoulder to shoulder in this great work. I feel that there is no doubt of a unanimous expression of feeling going home in regard to this subject, and hence, I trust, great good will result. I am very glad you have thought out your plans so successfully."

Writing on another occasion with express reference to Dr. Anderson's views, Mr. Hazen says: "I can not go with Dr. Anderson. . . . I have never advocated such a plan for schools as Dr. A. makes," etc.

The Rev. L. Bissell, also, besides signing the document

given above, prepared by Mr. Ballantine, sent to Mr. Hume the following earnest approval of the proposed institution:

"I like the plan proposed, and am glad to see it presented to the Committee in so strong a light. I trust it will receive a candid consideration and a prompt response. It seems to me that any doubt of the expediency and immediate necessity of an institution of the kind asked for, can no longer remain."

Rev. Messrs. Burgess and Wood's Plea for Schools.

From the response of these brethren at Satara, take the following extract:

"The arguments advanced by the brethren of the Bombay mission in favor of an educational department of a high order, we think sound and *conclusive*, and we can not see how the Prudential Committee can fail to be convinced of the *absolute necessity* of such a department in our Western India missions.

"The letters of the Bombay brethren, together with the communication from the Ahmednuggur mission, have gone so fully into the whole subject that little more remains to be said. To write our own views would be repeating what they have already written. We remark therefore that we concur in general with the views expressed in these letters, and we think the Prudential Committee should accede to their request.

"The reason why the Committee have of late *not been* so favorably inclined to educational labors, in their Western India missions, appears to be that they wish to have as much time and strength as possible given to the work of *preaching the Gospel.* The work of *preaching*, technically so called, we consider an important work. We would not have less of preaching, but we would have more of teaching. And we believe that a mission with an educational department, such as the Bombay brethren propose, would *not do less of preaching*, with such a department. . . We believe that in such a country as this, were the entire field left to us, *the best and the only true mission policy* would be for our missions to have schools of a high order.

"Wm. Wood,

"Satara, June 16, 1853. "E. Burgess."

Again brother Wood writes: "Our views are similar to those expressed in the Bombay documents; and it seems to me there can be but one view by any missionary who has had any experience in the field. I can not but feel that our present plan of operations is very defective. We ought to have a good school in all our missions. . . I have no doubt that could you commence a good school, [at Kolapoor,] you would in this way gain a more ready access to minds, and preach the Gospel more effectively than in any other way."

Rev. S. B. Munger's Plea for Schools.

At the time of these earnest pleadings for our schools, Mr. Munger was making his second visit to America. But as he was still a member of the missions, and having *changed* his views, was hastened back to India, overland, in time to be present with the Deputation, it is proper to give his honest convictions a place in this connection. He had made a permanent record of them and the results of his missionary experience, a few years before, in the following language, namely:

"The hope, therefore, of India's emancipation from the thraldom of Hinduism, and of her exaltation to the social and moral dignity and blessedness which the Gospel of the Son of God has power to confer, looks for its most ample realization to the *Christian education of the children and the youth of the nation. . . The use of the Western sciences is as really a means of reëducating the Hindu mind, as is the use of the Christian Bible and any system of Christian ethics. . .* The Puranas are alike the source of knowledge in religion and science. And, therefore, the endeavor to supplant Hindu science by the introduction of Western sciences, will most surely prove the subversion of the Hindu religion."

These deep convictions and emphatic statements of Mr. Munger are found scattered through the history of the Ahmednuggur mission, and more of them will find their appropriate record in developing the facts of that mission.

Of the whole band of American missionaries then in Western India, the only one remaining, whose views have not been given, was myself, in the little new mission at Kolapoor. My views are so well known that it is hardly necessary to state them here. From the statements sent to the Committee at the time, with those of the other brethren, the following brief extracts are sufficient:

"The valid argument in favor of such an institution is that it will bring talented young men under the influence of the mission and of Christian truth. . . I regard it the wisest policy to have an educational institution of high character connected with each and all our Mahratta missions, *from their origin.*" "I am glad to see your strong position in favor of English. It is impregnable. If you can get up such an institution in Bombay, I shall rejoice to see it prosper."

As the need of such a school at Kolapoor has been mentioned in the foregoing paragraph, it may be well to say just here, that I was allowed to employ an assistant, a pious Indo-Briton, at an expense of some $500 a year. With him already in service, such a high-school at K. would have involved little or no additional expense. In such a school his service would have been invaluable. With no such *regular* duty, the benefit of his assistance was scarcely appreciable, and I dismissed him from an unavoidable feeling that his support was not a proper expenditure of mission funds. But this in passing.

The reader has now before him the unanimous views and earnest pleadings of all the American missionaries then in Western India, in behalf of schools, and especially of a high-school in Bombay. There was not one dissenting voice in our whole number. What was the result? Did our senior Secretary remember his own considerate advice, namely: "Let the friends of missions consider whether opinions formed by wise and good men here at home, relative to the internal affairs of the missions, are, on the whole, more likely to be right, than those formed in heathen lands by men equally pious, learned, and discreet, having the same New Testament to guide them"? In the spirit of this advice did he say: "Brethren, you are all united in your views. You have been on the ground many years, bearing the burden and heat of the day. You know better about this matter than we do. You shall have your schools." Was this the generous response? Let us see. The historical record runs as follows:

Those earnest appeals from *all the missionaries*, pleading for the school with *all possible haste*, were dispatched from India the last of May, 1853. A prompt reply might have reached them in about four months. A brief acknowledgment of their receipt was penned in Boston, September 9th, but not forwarded till November, and reached India January 9th, 1854! It bore a postscript of November 1st, saying it had been forgotten or mislaid in Dr. A.'s desk. But the most grievous thing about it, to those dear brethren in Bombay, was, that it did not grant their request. They had waited some eight months, as patiently as possible, hoping and expecting permission to put the school in operation and thus find relief from their embarrassing position. But the letter brought no such permission. It recognized the lucid, unanimous and weighty character of their arguments, and the *necessity* of some sort of a school *somewhere*, but doubts were expressed as to its proposed character and locality, and several questions were propounded; as for instance: "Would you have proposed such an institution at Bombay, were you not subjected to the annoyance of the Scotch and English high-schools in that place?" "Would it not be necessary . . that it be every way equal to the English and Scotch schools?" etc. The hopes of those brethren were disappointed by this letter. What could they do?

It is sufficient here to record what they *did* do. Three days after its receipt Mr. Hume penned a long reply, from which the following extracts are taken:

Rev. R. W. Hume's Second Plea for Schools.

"BOMBAY, 12th January, 1854.

"Rev. RUFUS ANDERSON, D.D.,

"Secretary to the A.B.C.F.M.:

"DEAR SIR: Your letter to the brethren of the Bombay mission, dated 9th September, 1853, with its postscript dated November 1st, reached us on the 9th instant. With you we regret the delay that has taken place in forwarding that letter, and hasten to reply to your inquiries. . . Such an institution would present a most important field of missionary labor. (1.) It is needed for converts, the children of converts, and others more or less connected with the mission. (2.) It is needed as a means for bringing the missionaries into contact with young men and youth of respectability and influence—the class which, above all others, is the most hopeful and important. (3.) The rising generation is thirsting for knowledge; there is on all sides a great and growing desire for the acquisition of English; one that can not and will not be repressed. This is a most important fact in reference to our field of labor, and one which we are called on to turn to account. As formerly remarked, we should discern the signs of the times and fall in with the arrangements of an all-wise and holy Providence. If we are to act on the rising generation of young men, if we would bring them under our influence and the influence of the Gospel, then we are in a manner shut up to the course already recommended. (4.) If there are not mission schools of a high order, then the enterprising, influential youth who desire an education, and who are hereafter to guide the destinies of this great country, must go to the government schools, from which Christianity is excluded, and where, almost as a matter of course, they become deists and infidels. And is the Church of Christ to sit down contented, and leave all the leading minds of the rising generation to be trained under such influences? If so, then alas! for India. Alas! for the native churches, and for the cause of Christ in this country. Who are to control the periodical press? Who are to discuss and settle all the religious and social questions which for years to come must agitate native society? Who, during the next half-century, are to mould public opinion, provide books for the people, and, under God, fix the character of succeeding generations?

"All this must, for the most part, be done by those who receive a superior education. It is as true here as elsewhere, that knowledge is power. Here, as elsewhere, educated men will mould the opinions of the people. And if those educated men are generally deists and infidels, bitterly opposed to the Gospel, then what an obstacle must it be to the progress of truth and righteousness!

"If, therefore, we had the whole ground to ourselves, and there were no missionary institution in Bombay, for imparting a superior education, it would be our imperative duty to found one without delay. *If need be*, let the common school be disbanded, let street-preaching and tours be sacrificed, and let the missionaries as a primary duty, address themselves to the work of raising up educated, competent defenders of the truth, and thus raise up a barrier against the rising flood of Deism and Infidelity. They should pray and strive, first of all, that native laborers, workmen who need not be ashamed, may be sent forth into this great vineyard. The soul of the most ignorant and humble individual is indeed of infinite value; but in a missionary point of view, a single individual of education and talents, who can maintain an aggressive warfare with ignorance, error, and superstition, is worth scores and even hundreds of feeble, ignorant converts, who need to be carried and cared for like new-born children.

"In giving a prominent place to education, the other missions in Bombay evince a practical wisdom which is deserving of the highest commendation. They are acting in keeping with the spirit of the times—in keeping with the circumstances in which they are placed, in the midst of a great heathen city. Their plan may not be the best in all its details, but they are wise in giving special prominence to the Christian education of the rising generation. And such is the deep and general conviction of the most judicious and ardent friends of Christ in this country.

"Thus I have given an affirmative answer to your first question. What we *might think*, or what we *might do*, in certain conceivable circumstances, is however, a minor matter. Our duty is to act in view of *actual* circumstances. And to the best of our ability, we have already informed you what those circumstances are. It is scarcely necessary to repeat, (1) that in connection with each of the other missions in Bombay, there is an institution for imparting a superior education; such an education as is desired by the influential and promising young men; (2) that the converts and the children of the converts fully share in the desire for education, and if they can not obtain it in connection with us, they will obtain it elsewhere—as indeed they ought to do; for outcasts as they are, and hated and persecuted by the heathen, they can in no other way secure influence and respect. (3) The converts will naturally come under the influence of, and prefer to be connected with, the mission in which they or their children are educated. Thus the best scholars of our schools, the children of our converts, and inquirers who share in the desire for education, must be drawn away from us to other missions. We are not in a position to gather the fruit of our labor. Justice to the missionaries; justice to the churches which sustain them; and justice to the Society with which they are connected, demands that such a state of things should continue no longer. We enter our deliberate, solemn, and united protest against the policy which places the missionaries of the American churches in such unfavorable and trying circumstances. And we can not believe that either the churches or the Board will for a moment consent that this state of things should be perpetuated. . The times demand that we have an efficient institution, and an all-wise Providence is shutting us up to this course. Nothing else can save the mission from constant depletion and consequent weakness. And why should not the American churches have as much practical wisdom, and be as ready to come up to the exigencies of the case as the churches of other lands?

"You ask what we propose regarding expense. . . At first we should expect to rent premises, the monthly expense of which would probably be from 50 to 100 rupees; and the other expenses ought to be about 200 rupees a month. Probably Rs. 250 (= $113) a month, would cover all this expense. Ere long, an effort to provide a building should be made, the expense of which, land included, should not be less than that of the Free Church Institution; say, about $25,000. If not provided for before, this might be raised during your 'Jubilee Year.' My hope is, that by proper representations to wealthy individuals, the requisite amount may be raised in pretty large sums, or by a special effort in some particular locality, without at all interfering with the general income of the Board."

It is proper to say here, the annual interest of the money spent by the Deputation, if well invested, would, I think, have supported this High-School which they went to suppress, in perpetuo. Or, it would have met nearly half the cost of the building desired, and brother Hume could easily have raised the balance in India, in a twelve-month.

Mr. Hume continues: "I am not unaware of the difficulty of raising money, but the same spirit that is filling our own land with academies, colleges, and theological seminaries, if properly enlightened and called forth, will not fail to provide a suitable institution for the oldest mission of the Board, located as it is in a city of more than half a million of people, and the chief centre of influence to all Western India and the adjacent countries. No part of the heathen world, as we believe, presents a more inviting field for missionary operations. And no where is the call for superior education, in connection with such operations, more unmistakable and imperative. . .

"If this mission is to be doomed to a living death, then all plans for the training of candidates for the ministry is but building castles in the air. I will only add that the almost indispensable necessity for superior educational institutions in connection with missions, especially in large towns, is now all but universally acknowledged by missionaries and the friends of the Gospel in India. And this conviction has been arrived at, not as the result of mere theory, but in spite of all previous theories. It is the result of long and general experience, and an intimate acquaintance with the circumstances of the field. This fact certainly is deserving of some weight in the minds of missionary committees at home; and those who venture to set it at naught, assume a very great responsibility.

"By far the greater portion of the aggressive power of the native churches is the fruit of mission schools, and especially of the institutions for imparting a superior education. Something has been gained through the conversion of pundits, [heathen] teachers of common schools, and others who in various ways have been brought into long-continued and intimate connection with the missionaries. The converts who have been gathered in as the fruit of bazaar preaching and tours—what is sometimes designated evangelistic, in opposition to educational operations—have generally been ignorant and uninfluential; most of them have been from the lower castes, and have added little or nothing to the moral power of the Church. They have generally exerted but little—very little aggressive influence; and too often have hung like a dead weight upon the mission. . . I would advocate educational institutions, not in place of preaching the Gospel, but because in them and through them the Gospel can here be best brought into contact with the mind and the heart of the community. To designate as an educationalist him who labors in an institution, instructing the pupils in the Bible, the evidences of Christianity, and the higher branches of useful learning, and to term him a preacher of the Gospel who labors in the bazaars and villages, is simply an abuse of terms. The former preaches the Gospel as truly and as much as the latter; and in far more favorable circumstances.

"Such are my present convictions, with which those of the other members of the mission fully agree. Such has been the experience of the India missions, as a whole; and such are the well-known opinions of the great majority of the missionaries in this country. . .

"Praying that you and the Committee may be guided in this and all other matters with wisdom from on high, I remain, in the service of Christ, Yours very faithfully,

"R. W. HUME."

Rev. S. B. Fairbank's Second Plea for Schools.

Mr. Fairbank approved of Mr. Hume's letter, and sent to Dr. Anderson additional remarks, of which the following extracts speak for themselves:

"Your disappointment and grief on account of your letter's being delayed so long, have found abundant sympathy in my own feelings. I regret the necessity laid on me of writing at this time, . . but my views and feelings when I glance at the urgent necessities of the case, impel me to write by this first mail, however briefly. . .

"The necessity, in any case, of a good school, and of such an one substantially as we look for, appears to me undoubted. I look on it as a calamity too great to be measured, that this mission did not, from its origin, sustain a first-rate school, one which by this time should have come to have its graduates in places of trust and influence, not only as religious teachers, and helpers to the missionary in his peculiar work of proclaiming the Gospel, but also as government servants, and as schoolmasters, as doctors and as merchants. I would then answer your first question definitely in the affirmative, only omitting the word *just* in the phrase 'just such a school.' I confidently expect that the Bombay mission will one day have such an institution, and believe that the sooner it is undertaken the better—the better for the cause of Christ here, and especially the better will it be to render visible and tangible the results of the labors of this mission. I do not think our labors are *lost now*, but as we are, their results are and must be *lost sight of*, or appear under forms that *we* can hardly recognize them, much less map them down for you and for the encouragement of the American churches. . . .

"I must be very specific as to the necessity of a school *in Bombay*. A school *somewhere* will do us little good. Each mission must have a high-school, an *academy* perhaps it might be called. I think Bombay should have *its college* as well as its academy. And these should admit, up to a certain limit, those who wish to attend, though not of our converts or their children, at least till we have a larger number of promising youth. There is an interest and a benefit in numbers. Almost no man, (and especially no Hindu,) will develop and grow in *a class alone by himself*, or with one or two others, as he will in a class of twenty. Do I open my mouth wide? I am straitened in saying these things. I would ask more, but fear you would think the plan *too* broad. If we come up towards the necessity of the case, as seen in the vista of the future, we should plant a Yale College, with its feeders, their body of teachers, and its *faculty*, its library, and museum, and apparatus, and all its means of influence. . .

"As a means of training our young men for helpers, and as a means of adding to their ranks from among those who are to mould the mind of this nation, as a means of leavening the community with truth, and as a place for the *dwarfed* germ of this mission to root and flourish in, I earnestly look for a first-rate educational institution in Bombay. I am yours in Christ,

"S. B. FAIRBANK."

Rev. George Bowen's Second Plea for Schools.

From Mr. Bowen's second letter we take only the following, namely:

"BOMBAY, Jan. 13, 1854.

"MY DEAR DR. ANDERSON: With reference to yours of Sept. 9th I am glad to see that you appreciate in some measure the difficulty and disadvantage under which we as a mission labor. You say, 'It is clear that you ought not to remain in your present helpless state'—in other words, that some means should be found of placing our mission on a footing equal to others, with respect to the ability of presenting attractions to Christian young men who are desirous of obtaining an education. You are unwilling, however, that we should enter into competition with other educational institutions, or become too prominently educational. You suggest that a seminary at Ahmednuggur would answer the purpose. I do not think this would obviate the difficulty. The town of Bombay is swallowing up the presidency. It is the metropolis of India in a different sense from that in which our great cities are metropolises. The current sets more and more strongly hitherward. I could not do more than repeat, so I will only refer to our letters, written in May and June past, upon this subject, and upon the strong desire possessed by the younger portion of the community for an education. India is awaking, and like a Casper Hauser, needs to be taught every thing. The younger men, who are likely to be withdrawn from us, wish to know not only Western theology but every thing Western. To run the gauntlet of merely secular instruction in government schools, is a more dangerous thing here than it is in our country.

"I do not wonder that you shrink from encouraging us to launch ourselves into an educational sea. You feel that while education is a great want of India, we are here to supply a greater want. But would the Gospel be less preached under the proposed circumstances than it is now? I do not think so. I believe the contrary would be the case. . .

"I continue to preach in the streets, and wherever the people so congregate that I can quietly talk to them. . . Occasionally I am maltreated or am mobbed. But I do not suffer my mind to dwell on these occasional unpleasantnesses. . . I have never forgotten what you said to me upon my embarkation, namely, that I should consider myself rather the servant of the Lord Jesus Christ than of the Board. Upon this I have acted, feeling that the highest interests, indeed that the only interest of the American Board, is that I should fulfill my course, and hear from my heavenly Master, 'Hail! well done.' To this end pray for me, etc. I am, faithfully,

"GEO. BOWEN."

This second series of pleadings for their school, by the three Bombay brethren, was sent to all their brethren in the Deccan, as was the first, and elicited a second series of remarks, from which we can afford space for only very brief extracts, as follows:

Rev. H. Ballantine's Second Plea for Schools.

"1. In reference to the first inquiry, I have no hesitation in saying, that were there no educational institutions in operation in the other missions at Bombay, it would, in one point of view, be much more important than it is now, that our brethren should have such an institution as they propose. Were our mission the only mission in Bombay, and were the government institutions there turning out deists and infidels yearly upon the community, as they now are, all would acknowledge the necessity of a Christian institution to exert a counteracting influence, and to raise up young men, who should be prepared to maintain the cause of truth and religion.

"The want has been *to some extent* supplied by the educational institutions established by the other missions. At the same time, the very existence of those institutions renders it very important that our brethren should have their institution also; for unless they do their part with the other missions in counteracting the influence of the educated young infidels, and in raising up young men to do battle for the truth, our mission will fall behind the other missions in character and influence, and gradually be more and more shut out from all access to the influential classes of the native community.

"There is, then, an independent argument for such an institution as is desired at Bombay, apart from the educational institutions of the other missions, and there is an additional reason, from the very existence of those institutions, why we should have one there, and this last reason is perhaps the most important one in the present circumstances of our Bombay brethren. If other missionaries in Bombay were allowed to preach the Gospel, and the mouths of American missionaries were shut by the government, it would be thought at once that we had not the means of exerting our appropriate influence for the diffusion of the truth, and therefore it would be best for us to go somewhere else. And in very much the same light do I view the question of teaching the young men of Bombay.

"2. In reference to the second inquiry, I think that we ought to be prepared to give as good an education to young men in Bombay as they can obtain in the other mission institutions, so far at least as an academical and collegiate course is concerned. . . I am, therefore, of opinion, that the brethren in Bombay should be allowed their institution, and it appears to me that an expenditure of Rs. 250 a month, or Rs. 3000 (=some $1350) a year, (which, I have no doubt, will be sufficient for the support of such a school,) could not be incurred for a more important object. I do not think that there would be any necessity for purchasing premises or erecting buildings for some time to come, and perhaps not at all. . .

"Could the Prudential Committee see the facts as we see them here, I have no doubt they would urge us to do far more than we are now doing in this department of labor, and would readily grant us all that we ask.

"H. Ballantine.

"Ahmednuggur, Jan. 19, 1854."

Rev. L. Bissell's Second Plea for Schools.

Mr. Bissell indorsed the views of our Bombay brethren and of Mr. Ballantine in the following language:

"I concur in the statements of the brethren at Bombay, in reply to Dr. Anderson's letter of inquiry respecting an educational institution, and in the remarks of Mr. Ballantine. I believe in the validity of the reasons assigned for the immediate establishment of such an institution at Bombay. A single institution of the kind at *one* of the Mahratta missions would doubtless be a great advance upon our present position, and might save us many valuable laborers, but only a small part of its advantages could be received by more than one mission.

Lemuel Bissell."

Rev. A. Hazen's Second Plea for Schools.

"I concur in the statements of the brethren at Bombay in reply to the inquiries of Dr. Anderson, and in the remarks made by brother Ballantine. In addition I would remark, that there seems to be a *local* demand for an educational institution of a high order in the vicinity of the present operations of our mission. None of the existing institutions are in that part of the city. A school in the neighborhood of the mission press would afford advantages to a dense population now unsupplied with such privileges. The common-schools in connection with our mission are in that vicinity. The Grant Medical College is also near the press. There should seem to be room enough in any part of that city of half-a-million inhabitants for another institution, but all the eastern part of the city is unoccupied ground.

"I earnestly hope the requisite permission for opening a high-school may be granted without delay.

"A. HAZEN."

The letters of our Bombay brethren, in their journey around the missions, came next to Satara. Brother Burgess had left for America, but brother Wood was there and added a second series of remarks, from which we take extracts, as follows:

Rev. W. Wood's Second Plea for Schools.

"Much more might be said in urging the importance of having a higher order of schools than now exist in the missions of the American Board in Western India. . . With the best reports we can give, the ablest, clearest statements we can make, it must be very difficult, not to say impossible, for the Committee at such a distance to look at things here as they really exist. When we tell them that their four Western India missions of Bombay, Ahmednuggur, Satara, and Kolapoor are located in the midst of a population half as large as that of the United States, do they fully comprehend the fact? Do they realize that Ahmednuggur is as far from Bombay as Boston is from New-York? That Satara is as far from Bombay and Ahmednuggur as Albany is from New-York and Boston? and that Kolapoor is 80 miles south of Satara? Do they realize that while they can travel from Boston to New-York or Albany in ten hours, it takes us as many days to travel the same distance? Do they realize that the population of the Satara state *alone* (*my field!*) exceeds the population of Maine, New Hampshire, and Vermont? Certainly we can not believe that they do when they gravely ask the question, *if one school located at Ahmednuggur will not answer for us all.* Well has brother Hume remarked that a school at Ahmednuggur would be of little use to the mission at Bombay; and we may with equal propriety add, *vice versa*, a school in Bombay would be of little use to any of the other missions in the Deccan.

"But let us come to a few facts. The brethren have said, and with truth, that the rising generation of this land, educated in the Government schools, are *educated infidels.* The highest Government educational institutions in Western India, are the Elphinstone College in Bombay, and the Poona College in Poona. These institutions furnish all, or nearly all, the teachers of the government schools scattered throughout the land. And, so far as I know, these teachers are thoroughly infidel in sentiment; and they are assiduous in their efforts to instill their infidel sentiments into the minds of their pupils. Such a teacher was appointed at the head of the Government school in Satara, a little more than a year ago, and as a fruit of his efforts, in less than six months the young men of his school came into our meetings for religious discussion, and boldly affirmed that 'there is no God.' Just such men are being scattered all about the country, filling all the offices of government. Such a man is at Wai, a large town of 10,000 souls to the northwest of this. He is well educated, well read in infidel books, and has made his boast of turning away Christians from the faith, and of his intentions of turning away others. Another such man is at Kurrad, 30 miles to the south of this, with a population of 10,000. And such are scattered about in all the larger towns. . . They gather around them the youth, and instill their infidel sentiments into their minds. And what have we to oppose this tide of influence? Scarcely nothing. True we have books. We have schools of a certain kind. We preach on the Sabbath, and on week-days. We make tours in the villages. This is all well; but this is not all we want. We want another weapon of attack; and I believe each mission must have it to fight successfully. That weapon is a good school. With such a school in active operation, I should expect during my missionary life to effect fourfold more than without one. WM. WOOD.

"SATARA, January 24, 1854."

What peculiar force do these last words gather from the subsequent history of that mission? Only one or two converts gathered in for six years, and from the lowest caste.

Rev. R. G. Wilder's Second Plea for Schools.

These letters and remarks of all the brethren came last of all to me at Kolapoor, and again I joined my feeble testimony, with that of the other brethren, in favor of the school for which they were pleading. My views will be sufficiently understood from the following brief extracts:

"I have perused these papers with interest, and am glad to see the necessity of a good institution in connection with *each* of our missions so generally conceded and ably urged. I need not repeat my conviction, that I regard it the wisest policy to have an educational institution of high character, in which English shall be taught to some extent, connected with each and all our Mahratta missions *from their origin*. . .

"I fully concur in the views expressed, that *one* institution can not supply the wants of all our Mahratta missions. All the interests involved, and more especially *all past experience*, is sternly opposed to such an arrangement.

"The Prudential Committee can have little idea of the pains-taking, strength-consuming labor involved in getting up and sustaining such institutions as we ask for, or they would never subject their missionaries to the painful necessity of pleading for them in this manner. It is really pleading for permission to engage in the most trying, toilsome, life-consuming labor, only because of our thorough conviction that it is our most effective means of bringing these precious souls to a knowledge and belief of the truth."

Here we have extracts from a *second* series of arguments and pleadings from *every* American missionary then in Western India, showing their deep, unanimous, and abiding convictions in favor of schools, and of this particular institution.

Commencement and Success of the Institution.

After forwarding these pleadings to Boston, and waiting some four or five months longer for a reply, the Bombay brethren, with the cordial approval of those at Ahmednuggur, decided that *then* was the most favorable time to commence the Institution, and to wait no longer. Accordingly, the school was opened, and to their great gratification, in less than two months, it gathered in 150 young men of the very class they desired to bring under their teaching and influence. The missionaries thanked God and took courage—their hearts animated with fresh hopes for the success of their labors.

The number soon increased to 175, who were allowed to study English; and the vernacular department, in which there was no English allowed, embraced 100 more. The time of special favor to this mission seemed to have come.

Result of these Second Pleas in Boston.

But how were these repeated and earnest arguments and pleadings of the missionaries received in Boston? Did the Secretary and Committee feel that they ought not and could not oppose the united views and earnest convictions of *all* their missionaries, and cheerfully grant their request? Far otherwise. Their brief reply, dated April 10th, 1854, says:

> "The very grave import of your statements . . has decided the minds of the Prudential Committee in favor of sending a Deputation to India. . . I ought to say that I have no expectation whatever, that the Board and the churches of this country will be willing to prosecute missions in India, on what we understand to be the views of our friend Dr. Duff," etc.

That the Secretary and Committee felt the force of our united, earnest, and repeated arguments and appeals, is sufficiently evident from the Report of the Deputation. In that, it is stated, page 5: "They did not know what to do; nor did it seem possible to solve the problem except on the ground."

Whence arose this embarrassment? Was it from any recusancy on the part of the missionaries? This is impossible, for in this matter of schools, as in all others, they had ever shown themselves ready to obey instructions, however much against their convictions.

Was there any doubt what the combined experience, convictions, and unbiased judgments of the missionaries dictated in the present instance? This is not possible, for it was the letters and arguments of all the Bombay brethren united, and these warmly seconded by every other American missionary in Western India, which so embarrassed the Committee. Was it not safe to leave such a question to so large a body of missionaries on the ground, and knowing all the circumstances of the case? (see Dr. Anderson's views, page 40.) And if these unbiased convictions of the missionaries were to be set aside and the Institution disallowed, if this was fully decided upon, then what was the necessity of a Deputation at all? Why not have sent by letter the frank disapproval of the Committee—based either on their judgment merely, or on the want of funds? If the latter was the true reason, would not the missionaries have felt it more forcibly *if sent by letter at the expense of* 30 *cents, than when sent by a Deputation at the expense of ten or twelve thousand dollars?* And who can doubt that they would have yielded to the Committee no less submissively?

The result would have been the same if the refusal of the Committee had been sent by letter. And it is respectfully submitted, if the avowed cause of the Deputation to India is not an unhappy one? Taking the facts given in their Report, and the reason there assigned for their visit, and how is it possible to avoid the plain issue that the Deputation went to India and managed to oppose a measure which had been urged upon the Committee in voluminous and repeated letters, with many and strong arguments, from *every one* of their missionaries then in Western India?

How did the Deputation effect their Object?

The impression has been studiously and widely circulated among the patrons of the Board, that all action and changes effected, while the Deputation was in India, were effected, not by the Deputation, but by the spontaneous votes of the missionaries. Is this impression correct? Let us examine this point. The quotations already given from the two series of letters from *all* the missionaries, represent their experience and convictions decidedly in favor of the schools. The quotations from Dr. Anderson are equally conclusive that *his* views were directly opposed to the convictions of the missionaries; and that he felt embarrassed by them to such an extent, that he made the journey to India on purpose to oppose and thwart their views there "on the ground."

I know it has been affirmed that the Deputation went out with no *settled* views or theories, and only to see what was best to be done. But this statement is opposed to the plain facts of the case. The emergency which occasioned the Deputation contradicts this statement. The terms of their instructions show clearly a wish and purpose "to dispense with the pioneering and preparatory influence of schools, and especially of schools in which the use of the English language is a prominent and characteristic feature." Those instructions expressly say:

"It is the strong persuasion of the Prudential Committee, that no school can properly be sustained by the funds of the Board, in which the vernacular language is not the grand medium of instruction."

It is unmistakable, then, that the Deputation went to India with a "settled theory," and a definite object in view; and that object was to subvert the united and repeatedly expressed views of *all* their missionaries there on the ground. How did they accomplish this object?

Absolute Authority of the Deputation.

The first instrument employed in accomplishing this object is found in their *Instructions.* The Deputation was clothed by the Prudential Committee "with full power and authority" to do what they should think best, irrespective of the experience and convictions of any or all their missionaries in the field. Every man of us knew that he could not oppose such "full power and authority" without incurring displeasure. It became the part of prudence either to yield our convictions entirely, or hold them in strict abeyance to this authority, or resign our connection with the Board. There seemed no other alternative, and each of these three alternatives was ultimately taken by one or more of our number, according to each man's views of prudence and duty. This absolute authority, committed to the Deputation, speaks for itself. Does it not show unmistakably the Committee's estimate of the emergency of the case, and also the object which they had in view?

This *absolute authority* was the first instrument brought to bear in accomplishing the object of the Deputation.

General Meeting at Ahmednuggur.

The second step in this process was to secure a general meeting of all the missionaries. A call was issued, and we all met at Ahmednuggur, Dec. 6, 1854, and continued our sessions till Dec. 26—twenty-one days.

It is an item worth mentioning here, that three of our strongest men, namely, Rev. Messrs. Allen, Hume and Burgess, had left the missions just before the coming of the Deputation. The convictions of all three of these brethren in favor of the schools were deep and abiding, and there is good reason to believe they would not have changed them under any pressure. Brother Hume died on his voyage home, and the other two retain their convictions unchanged.

And let me here guard against an impression that such an interview with a deputation of our brethren from America, *on common terms of Christian brotherhood*, would not always be most welcome to every missionary. There is not a missionary of the American Board in India who would not look forward to such a meeting with joy, and count its opportunities for social and religious intercourse as among the choicest seasons of Christian fellowship on earth. But for such a blessed result this "full power and authority" must be left out of the instructions; the parity of God's ministers and the rights of conscience must be recognized.

The special object of this general meeting at Ahmednuggur was not the communion of saints, nor to take friendly counsel from each other in regard to the great work of converting the heathen. Its true object was *to secure action by the missionaries themselves, which should subvert their own views and convictions, previously recorded.*

The Deputation have taken to themselves credit for not having *voted* in this meeting, and urged this fact to show that the action was wholly by the missionaries. Had they placed themselves on common ground, and been satisfied to urge their arguments and cast their votes with the rest of us, well indeed would it have been for us and for the cause. But they well understood that *two* votes would be of little avail against *nine.* They rightly judged that their *authority* would effect more than their *votes.* Hence the plan for bringing the missionaries themselves to take action right in the teeth of their own experience and practice, and the arguments and convictions they had so persistently and repeatedly urged with the Committee. Did they succeed in this? Let us see.

Dr. Anderson's Address at the Opening Session.

The third step in this process was the written address of Dr. Anderson at the beginning of our meeting. He first had his instructions read, showing clearly his purpose to abolish the schools, and their "full power and authority" to execute this purpose. Then came an exposition of the policy of the Board—a document which occupied Dr. Anderson *fifty minutes* in the reading. This document was in the terms of positive and absolute authority, purporting to utter the fixed views and principles of the Committee, which *must* be carried into effect. This document was intended to give character, and *did* give character, to all the doings of the meeting. This document has never been published, and Dr. Anderson says it never shall be. We asked for a copy of it to put on the records of the meeting, but were refused. I asked Dr. A. for it myself only a short time ago, and was again refused, with the remark added: "*It was never meant to be published, and never will be.*"

W. "But why not, Dr. Anderson? Are you unwilling

the churches should know what means you used to make your influence felt in securing that action?"

Dr. A. "I expect to have influence when I visit the missions."

W. "Yes, you ought to have. But ought not your *responsibility* to be coëqual with your *influence?*"

Dr. A. "What do you mean?"

W. "I mean just what my question implies. You ought to be willing to let the public and the patrons of the Board read that document, and be responsible to them for just the amount of influence you brought to bear on the missionaries."

Dr. A. "That document had its use and importance at the time; but the public has no right to it. One brother in the Madura mission borrowed it to look over, and took the liberty to copy an extract, but I wouldn't let him keep the extract he had copied. It was never meant for the public."

W. "How can you reconcile your course in that matter with your representation to the public that the action of the missionaries was unconstrained and free?"

Dr. A. "The Board sent me to India that I might have influence. It was because the views of the missionaries were wrong, that a deputation was needed. We went *on purpose* to change their views."

W. "Then why not let the churches and friends of the Board know just how great your influence was, and how you managed to secure it?"

Dr. A. "That document will never be published."

I will only add, a written application to the Prudential Committee has failed to elicit the document in question, and it is proper that the churches and pastors should know that such a document was read by Dr. Anderson at the opening of our meeting, and its pressure brought to bear in securing action—a document which has been kept from the public to the present time, not even a copied extract of it being allowed to remain in the hands of a missionary. The moral significance of this fact I leave to the friends of the Board.

I could put on record some of the sentiments of this document, repeated in the subsequent declarations of Dr. Anderson; for instance—"If you can't carry on your operations without such schools as you ask for, then we will give up our missions in Western India, and send our men and money to China, or some other field:" but the studious care and fixed purpose with which that document is withheld even from the missionaries, is sufficiently significant.

Manner in which Action was secured.

The plan adopted for securing the action of the missionaries was on this wise. A specified subject was called up and placed in the hands of a committee. The chairman of said committee was required to bring in a written report. The chairman of the meeting through all its sessions was brother Ballantine, who had plead so earnestly for schools, and especially for the proposed high-school, as vital to the very existence of the Bombay mission. But we soon found, to our surprise, that he ignored his deep and repeated convictions, and at once adopted the views of the Deputation. Although he had again and again declared his belief "that that mission must become extinct, unless there be a change of mission policy, and the Committee grant them the high-school they ask;" although he had declared, "It is the only way they can obtain an audience," yet now he at once joins the Deputation and helps to abolish it. It is an item of some significance that this brother was chairman of our meeting, and had the appointment of the committees.

In case of each subject reported upon, there was a discussion first, which put the writer thereof in full possession again of the views of Dr. Anderson, and in preparing his report he had before him *two certain facts:* 1. That the views of the Deputation *must*, and *would be insisted on and carried out,* whether he embodied them or not. 2. That if he did not embody them, he would come under disfavor.

If any one feels inclined to blame the missionaries for so readily changing the views and convictions so earnestly and repeatedly avowed and placed on record, let him bear in mind that it is no trifling matter to incur the displeasure of one or two men who have the character, happiness and usefulness, not only of yourself, but of your wife and children, greatly in their keeping. Every missionary of the American Board knows that if he wants to visit his native land, the favor must come through the Secretary. If he wants an extra grant of money, he must apply to Dr. A. If he wants his children, far away from him in America, cared and provided for, it is all important that he be on good terms with Dr. A. If he wishes to stand fair in reputation before the churches at home, he must beware of any whisperings from the Mission-House in Boston that he is "an impracticable man."

But all these considerations failed to secure, on first trial, such reports as were desired. Take, for instance, the report on this High-School at Bombay. It was known to us all that our convictions and pleadings for it had brought the Deputation to India; and that they had come with a fixed purpose to suppress it. After discussion, the subject was referred to Rev. Messrs. Bowen and Fairbank, as a committee, to draw up a report which should disallow that High-School.

Report of Mr. Bowen on the Bombay Institution.

Rev. Geo. Bowen was the chairman of this committee, and prepared the report, in substance as follows:

"The English school in connection with the American mission in Bombay was opened about the 1st of June last. It is known as the American Mission Institution. At the commencement of the present month (Dec.) there were about 175 pupils in it, chiefly Hindus; . . . Instruction is given in the word of God, daily, to all classes, by the missionary and the three assistants. . . .

"In the upper classes, English is the principal medium of instruction. In the lower classes the Marathí.

"Connected with the school are two vernacular schools, in which no English is taught. In these are about 100 scholars.

"The reasons which led to the establishment of this school, are the following:

"1. A very great desire has sprung up among the natives of this country to obtain a knowledge of the English language, literature and science. That which sprang up in Europe, just before the dawn of the Reformation, for the classical tongues and classical lore, was not more eager or more general. We need not now inquire minutely into the origin of this desire for English learning on the part of the people of this presidency. Neither need we discuss the propriety or otherwise of such a desire. We may just remark that there is no mystery about its existence. It is perfectly natural under the circumstances. Hindus find themselves brought, in the providence of God, into contact with a race who exhibit not only great military superiority, but a wisdom and ingenuity, an acquaintance with undreamt of powers of nature, an extent of knowledge, a command of resources, a height of civilization, immeasurably above any thing that they were ever in contact with before. One of two things could not but result from a meeting of two races so very different. Either the inferior race must become disheartened and paralyzed by the thought of the unapproachable superiority of the other, lose its energy and perhaps dwindle away as the aborigines of America and the natives of the Pacific Islands are doing; or it must be stimulated into a desire to obtain those things which seem to be most intimately connected with the superiority of the other race. The latter is the case in India. The inhabitants of this country admit the fact of their inferiority in the scale of civilization, but are not disposed to submit to it as a thing that must inevitably continue to be. They have been seized with the spirit of progress. This manifests itself, of course, more among some classes than others; more in the cities than in the interior; more among the young than the aged; more among the middling and higher castes, than among those which are reputed the lowest.

"What we make use of in our argument is the simple fact. The desire exists. It will not be suppressed. It is clearly destined to wax stronger and stronger. It just as much demands our attention as any other fact in the providence of God. The young men of Bombay are ready to flock to educational institutions where they may obtain a knowledge of the English language and the things connected with it; and they are not deterred by the fact that the word of God is there taught and the claims of Christianity urged upon them. Shall the missionary avail himself of this readiness on their part, and embrace this as one mode of fulfilling the command to preach the Gospel to every creature?"

But I need not reproduce this able report. Mr. Bowen condensed, as well as he could in brief space, the arguments for this school already brought to view in the pleadings of *all* the missionaries, and closed his report without one word to prepare the way for its abandonment.

Report committed to another Chairman and changed to suit the Deputation.

Of course Mr. B.'s report was not satisfactory to the Deputation. A significant pause ensued. Each looked at the others. Dr. Anderson was the first to break the silence. "Oh! that won't do—that won't do. You have not embodied our views at all."

Mr. Bowen mildly but firmly replied:

"Brethren: I know this is not what is wanted. But these are my honest views, and such as we have all put on record in pleading for this Institution. It is utterly impossible for me to embody the views of the Deputation and call them mine; but there is one thing you can do—I will resign as chairman of the committee, and you can put in some other brother, who *will* embody the views of the Deputation."

Brother Bissell was accordingly made chairman of said committee, and embodied the views which Mr. Bowen's conscience forbade him to do. Brother Bissell's previous views will be remembered, (p. 104.) How ably he now represented the views of the Secretary may be seen from his report as published by the Deputation.

How was the Report Accepted?

But if the report was against the honest convictions of the missionaries, how came they to accept it?

The Rev. Myron Winslow, D.D., of Madras, writes: "The Deputation, acting under instructions, no doubt enlightened the mission in regard to the general policy and plans of the Board as unfavorable to such a school, and this must have greatly aided the decision." Not a bad guess for one at Dr. Winslow's distance from the scene.

The manner in which the views of the Deputation came into the report has been stated above. When it was ready, the question was put as to its acceptance.

I did not retain a memorandum of the votes on this question, but a large majority, I think, did not vote at all. Having fully expressed their views *against* the report, they now waived their privilege of voting, in deference to the Deputation. But the report *was* accepted. To reconcile this action with those spirit-stirring appeals and arguments which those same brethren had drawn up and sent to Boston in favor of this very school, only a few months before—*hic labor, hoc opus est.*

Some may wonder that the brethren in the opposition were not more careful to have their negative votes recorded. On this point the following considerations may be mentioned:

1. After a faithful exposition of views and arguments, each felt, I have done my duty. The Deputation know my honest convictions, and if they press their views against the known experience and convictions of my whole missionary life, *they* must be responsible. *My* duty and responsibility cease with my avowed convictions and arguments.

2. Only *two* of all our number had any *personal* interest and connection with the Bombay institution. The rest, in all their pleadings, had acted most disinterestedly, and had opposed their views to those of the Secretary most reluctantly, and with feelings of much pain and regret that such a necessity had arisen. Is it strange if some felt, Why risk displeasure which may affect my happiness and usefulness, by pressing my views so far as to *vote*, and especially when the question involved does not affect my *own* labors?

3. It was an item of no little importance to most of us that the Deputation assured us again and again, that our reports would have *no authority*. I did not suppose they were to be *printed* even, and no intimation of this kind was given

until near the close of our sessions. Other brethren have told me of their surprise at this result, and at the use subsequently made of these reports. I think none of us had any idea that there was a purpose ultimately to indorse them and invest them with the authority of the Prudential Committee. On this last point, however, I speak only for myself and some six of my associates, who unhesitatingly expressed their surprise as soon as the result was known.

But all the brethren will remember the frequency and emphasis with which the Secretary assured us that our reports would have no authority.

These considerations may not be sufficient to justify the brethren in the opposition for not recording their negative votes, but, probably, most amiable men, longing for Christian harmony, would have felt their influence, and waived the privilege of voting, as they did.

Votes for the Employment of "Heathen Teachers."

And yet, even with these considerations pressing upon our minds, we sometimes did feel constrained to record our votes against the wishes of the Secretary. On the subject of employing "*heathen teachers*," after discussion, in which the Deputation always engaged without limitation, when the question was finally put to vote: "*Is it well to employ heathen teachers?*"

Two brethren, Messrs. Hazen and Munger, said: "*No.*" The remaining *seven* of us said: "*Yes.*"

And yet, with these votes on record, brother Hazen drew up his report on this subject, in accordance with the wishes of the Deputation, and the next morning the Secretary read a brief statement, saying that *no schools with heathen teachers will be any longer tolerated in any of the missions!* The interdict was unqualified, allowing *not one single exception.*

But this question is introduced here only to show the manner in which action was secured. It is time that we return to the history of the Bombay mission and its high-school.

Suppression of the Bombay Institution.

After brother Bissell had embodied the views of the Deputation, as above mentioned, and his report had been accepted by the assent of a few, the rest remaining silent, Dr. Anderson took action, and the days of this promising institution were numbered. He allowed it to complete one year of its existence, and it then ceased to be. Thus issued the earnest and repeated arguments and pleadings of every missionary in behalf of this institution!

Can we wonder that the special committee on this mission, the next year, 1856, spoke of the "peculiar embarrassments under which it had labored," and reported that "the condition of the Bombay mission is less encouraging than we should all desire"?

Its present condition is far from encouraging. Not only was this English institution disbanded, by the action of the Deputation, but its *girls' boarding-school*, and the *day-schools* taught by heathen teachers, were also interdicted. Their hundreds of interesting children and youth were sent away, "from the missionary, from the Bible-class, from the Sabbath-school, from the house of prayer, to feed on the mountains of heathenism."*

The little native church in the Bombay mission is weak in numbers, talents and graces. I am aware of but two additions to it since the action of our Deputation in 1854; and instead of being a witnessing church, aggressive in its character, it is hardly able to maintain its own position and numbers. Only one missionary (Rev. A. Hazen) remained to watch over the remnant of that mission when I left India in 1857; and although just before the coming of the Deputation he had plead for this mission so earnestly, affirming that, "The question of giving up *Bombay* is the question of giving up *all Western India*," (see page 103,) yet he was now so dis-

* General lamentation for precisely the same class of pupils and schools which were dismissed in the financial crisis of 1837 for want of funds. Annual Report, 1838, page 42, etc.

couraged with its prospects, that almost the last remark I heard from him was, that he would not turn his hand over to prevent the abandonment of that mission. He has since returned to America, and a young brother temporarily fills his place and prolongs the feeble existence of the mission.

It will be remembered that the Rev. R. W. Hume, in pleading for the English school at Bombay, urged that it was necessary to the "*very existence*" of the mission, saying: "*It is a question of life and death.*" Mr. Ballantine fully indorsed this view, saying: "*I believe with Mr. Hume that the existence of the Bombay mission is at stake.*" Were they right on this point?

The history of the schools in our Bombay mission here comes to a close. From its origin, it has been preëminently a *preaching* mission. In no mission has the experiment of faithful vernacular preaching been more extensively and thoroughly tried. Hall, Nott and Newell, those earliest, able and most devoted missionaries of the American Board, who laid the foundation of this mission in many prayers and tears, were eminently *preaching* missionaries. They used to visit the temples, markets and streets of Bombay daily, and often many times a day, for successive years, to preach Christ to those degraded idolaters. But what was their experience? After the most faithful and persevering efforts of this kind, we hear them exclaim: "But alas! when we fix our eyes on the people, all is dark as night." "So far as man can see, all seems to be as the seed that fell by the wayside." And though they still persevered in preaching efforts, yet they felt forced to resort to schools as the only agency which would bring the most hopeful class of the heathen under their stated instruction and influence.

Results of Schools in our Bombay Mission.

This agency proved effective, and they rejoiced, thanked God and took courage. They employed it to the extent of their means. A long line of worthy successors has entered into their labors, confirmed the wisdom of their plans, and kept in operation these valuable schools. We have seen these schools increased at times to more than thirty, acting as so many glorious lights in dark centres of heathenism, and diffusing an elevating and benign influence through large masses of the community. We have seen the entire native population of Bombay thoroughly aroused by means of these schools, engaging in various forms of opposition, and sending petitions to government, entreating it to interfere and prevent these schools from diffusing a knowledge of the Christian religion. We have seen the influence of these schools extending wider and wider, resulting in an earnest and almost universal desire among intelligent Hindus for a knowledge of the Western arts and sciences and a liberal education, revolutionizing the sentiments of the people in regard to female education, and many other subjects closely connected with their well-being, and producing very marked progress in intellectual and moral improvement. We have seen "*heathen teachers*" and pupils yielding to the influence of this stated Christian instruction, rendered effective by the spirit of God, and they at length brought to confess their faith in Christ, and admitted to the holy ordinances of the Christian Church.

The vision which, in prospect, so cheered the hearts of those first devoted missionaries, when, toil-worn and weary, and sighing over the indifferent, noisy and insolent hearers which they found in the streets and the temples, they were wisely led to resort to these schools—the vision of their ultimate influence on the native community, has been more than realized. India is no longer what she then was. Those early missionaries foresaw that children and youth educated in these schools, *could not* believe in idols and the thousand foolish superstitions of their fathers. It is even so. In the vicinity of all the older missionary stations in India, a generation has already arisen who discard many of the errors and superstitions of their ancestors, and have adopted views and practices which lead the old orthodox Hindus to despair of their faith, and to predict the speedy downfall of the whole fabric of Hinduism. A blessed result has accrued from these mission schools in Bombay which can not be estimated in time. And yet the fruit has not been garnered up in our own mission. Our native church there is weak and almost without influence. It is not a living, active, aggressive church. Of the fifty-seven adults received to its communion from its origin, I can learn of only eight or nine now constituting its entire membership. Why is this? Why have so few converts been gathered in? Why have the results become so sadly dissipated?

To such inquiries let no one attempt a reply without much deliberation. I will only suggest,

1. HIGH-SCHOOLS *have not been allowed in this mission.* These high-schools in India are specially successful in gathering intelligent and promising young Hindus under Christian teaching and influence.

2. The primary and boarding-schools, to which most of the converts are traceable, have been more and more restricted for several years past, and the interesting boarding-school of Mrs. Hume, so largely blessed of God, was interdicted by the Deputation. Of the two converts admitted to the Church in Bombay, during the six years since the Deputation disbanded the schools, one was for years a pupil in our seminary at Ahmednuggur, and there gained a good knowledge of Christian truth from daily stated instruction.

Results of Schools in the Scotch Free Church Mission in Bombay.

Let those who would test the propriety of these two suggestions, contrast the history, agencies, and results of the mission of the American Board in Bombay, with the history, agencies, and results of the Scotch Free Church mission in Bombay, which was commenced some fifteen or twenty years later than ours. In the Scotch Free Church mission there have been in operation, not only the primary schools in large numbers, but a high-school, with its college department, has constantly brought under Christian instruction from 100 to 300 of the most intelligent and promising native youth. Their latest report (1859) gives 1075 pupils in their schools, 279 of whom are in their collegiate institution. God has blessed these schools, and they have now a living and aggressive church of some 80 or 100 members, many of whom are young men of good education, high attainments, and earnest piety, fitted to be pastors, preachers, and helpers in prosecuting this work of God.

This contrast between the two missions is all the more striking from the fact that both are in the same heathen city, and the American mission was commenced fully six teen years before the other.

Appeal from the Action of the Deputation.

One of the missionaries, feeling deeply grieved by the loss of his schools, sent to the Prudential Committee of the Board an earnest *appeal* from the action of the Deputation while they were in India. Some extracts from that appeal may properly find a place here. After speaking of the pain it gave him to oppose his "convictions to those of the wise and good whom we respect and love," he assures the Committee that he should excuse himself from this unpleasant duty "but for the painful apprehension that the corporate members of the Board, and the Christian public in America, will not understand the true state of the case, but will infer that the missionaries are responsible for these changes, or at all events, fully acquiesced in them. This apprehension arises mainly from the fact, that our worthy Deputation so frequently and studiously represent, that all action in the general meeting was by the *missionaries alone*, they (the Deputation) never voting." [See p. 124.] The appeal continues:

"Now, to give up our dearest and fondly-cherished views and plans of labor, and yield to the wishes of the Deputation the sternest convictions of our judgments derived from and fortified by long years of missionary toil; this of itself is sufficiently painful. But after having done so with the best grace possible, it would seem, in common justice, that the responsibility of the *new* measures should no longer rest with us; that the Deputation, whose views have been conceded, because coming with *authority*, should cheerfully bear the entire responsibility of these changes.

"Now, I shall greatly rejoice if I find my apprehensions on

this point unfounded, if the result shows that the Board and Christian public in America *do* understand that these changes were conceded to the wishes and *authority* of the Deputation, *against* the experience and convictions of a majority of the missionaries. I have no wish to speak for any of my brethren. If *any one* of them acquiesced, from convictions of judgment, in *all*, or the *larger part* of the changes made in our Mahratta missions, at the instance of the Deputation, I shall be glad to know it.

"Perhaps it is sufficient for me to express my honest belief, that in *most* cases of change, *every* brother yielded his own convictions to the wishes or authority of the Deputation, and I think there is evidence which should convince you and the Christian public that this belief is correct.

"1. *The previous convictions of the missionaries.* These have been *repeatedly*, and *fully*, and *persistently* stated in correspondence with you. The secretaries will bear us witness that the convictions of a *majority* of us have ever been strongly urged in favor of schools as our most efficient agency in prosecuting our work. Representations of our stern convictions on this subject were sent to them, bearing the signature of every missionary then in the field, and only a short time previous to the visit of the Deputation. Is not this evidence that, in assenting to the changes made, the missionaries yielded their own convictions to the wishes and authority of the Deputation?

"2. *The* NECESSITY *of a Deputation to secure these changes.* Why was a Deputation sent to us with *such* authority? Do not regard me as opposed to Deputations. No; send us all you can. The more the better. But let them be clothed with authority only to do us *good not harm*, to *help not hinder* the work; and let it not be thought invidious if I add, If they must come at the expense of the Board, and its funds are limited, let us have *missionaries* rather than *Deputations.* Send us your secretaries and bishops, your best and your biggest men; but let them stop here and labor with us, shoulder to shoulder, in this work, and after a dozen or twenty years, if they retain the views of our present Deputation, why, we'll tell them they are richly entitled to them, and to labor on in accordance with them all the rest of their days. We won't try to controvert them, and if any inexperienced Deputations come out from Boston, and require them to surrender these views, we'll hold up both hands, and solemnly protest against such violence.

"But why did you clothe this Deputation with such full power and authority? Was it not to effect changes which you had found you could not otherwise effect? Was it not because our convictions from experience were too strong to be changed by correspondence? Your Secretary had already exhausted every argument. What remained but the direct *authority* of a Deputation? Will it be said that from the interviews and verbal arguments of the Deputation our convictions were suddenly changed? If this were a fact, what reliance could you or the Christian public place upon us? If our strongest convictions, arising from the experience of ten, fifteen, or twenty years of personal labor among the heathen, and from the experience of all who have labored before us, can be wholly changed *in so short a time*, then what security can you have that they will not change again *as quickly?*

"3. *The discussions incident to those changes.* There *might* have been discussion ending in mutual agreement. But this was not the case. Convictions *unchanged* were yielded to the Deputation. In case of the Report on the English Institution at Bombay, [p. 129,] why did the chairman resign, and another brother take his place, and embody the views of Dr. Anderson?

"On the question of schools with *heathen teachers*, [p. 131,] why does the report condemn them entirely, when *seven* out of nine (our whole number) voted for them? But on these points we must appeal to the Deputation to bear witness for us; and I fully believe they will testify that some of us plead for these schools, and opposed their suppression to the full extent of our ability, and finally yielded only to the *authority* of the Deputation, *against* our experience and the strongest convictions of our judgments.

"4. *The actual votes of the missionaries on some questions.* The result of our votes does not appear in the printed minutes, but my interest in some questions led me to take notes, with the names and votes of brethren. On the question of heathen teachers our votes stood *two* negative, and *seven* affirmative. Now, to this large majority here on the ground, in favor of such teachers in new missions when others can not be had, add the votes of our five brethren who were absent, namely, Messrs. Allen, Abbott, Hume, French, and Burgess, all known to have very strong convictions in favor of such schools, and can stronger evidence be necessary that the responsibility of suppressing these schools must rest *entirely* with the Deputation?

"5. *The authority used by the Deputation.* I need only mention this, as I doubt not our Deputation will cheerfully testify to the fact that they used the full authority intrusted to them. When they affirmed that the Committee would no longer employ heathen teachers, that the experiment had been tried and proved a failure, they will remember that we urged with all earnestness that it had not proved a failure, that these schools had proved a most efficient agency in the Ahmednuggur mission, and though they could now be dispensed with there, yet the necessity for them in the *new* missions was still imperative. When they urged that we could not point to a single conversion in these schools, they will remember our reply, that we *could* point to *many* who had first become acquainted with Christian truth in those schools, and when transferred to the seminary, or boarding-schools, had been converted and gathered into the Church. They will remember that we pointed to our ordained native preachers and most valuable helpers as the direct fruits of these schools, they having, in almost every instance, been brought to a knowledge of the truth while employed as heathen teachers. They will remember our *unanimous* statement, that with one single exception, *every* convert in our mission, formerly of good caste, was converted in connection with our schools; and they will remember the frequently-expressed opinion, that our schools had more influence in bringing in the *Mahar* (low caste) converts, than any and all other agencies combined. When we pressed our arguments and convictions, as they may have thought, too earnestly, they will remember their repeated affirmation, that '*no strength of argument, no force of reasoning will ever change the views of the Board on that subject.*' When our arguments still pressed hard, they will remember the alternative they frequently presented, namely: 'If it be so, then the Board will give up their Mahratta missions, and send their men and funds to China or some other field.'

"But I need not enlarge. Our worthy Deputation will *not* decline bearing the full responsibility of these changes. They can not forget the persistent earnestness with which we opposed them. Surely they will not wish the Board or the Christian public to think *we made* them, or *acquiesced* in them, in any other sense than as yielding our convictions to their wishes and authority. For yielding in this way with so good a grace as we did, they will doubtless give us all due credit.

"I might mention some other considerations — some action in regard to which we were not at all consulted, as the appointing of a printing committee. I might mention some very important action that was effected while in private session, with only *five* of our number, the remaining *four* of us being excluded—such as the division of the Ahmednuggur church, and the ordination of the native pastors over churches in the city instead of in the Northern field, etc. They excluded four of us because we did not belong to that particular mission. But why was it not as proper for us to express our opinions, and give our votes on the changes effected in that mission, as for the Ahmednuggur brethren to give their opinions and votes on the changes about to be *enforced* in *our* missions? And in this connection it should be put on record, that of our whole number, *nine*, *the only two* brethren who voted against heathen teachers in all circumstances, were then members of the Ahmednuggur mission. I might mention the fact that the Deputation did not visit Kolapoor; that they spent only a few hours at Satara, and did not inform themselves as to the peculiar difficulties under which we labor in these *new* fields; that as to all their action affecting these *new missions*, they might as well have sent it from Boston by letter, and saved the fatigue and expense of their long journey. I might go on with such specifications, but it is not necessary. We wish to yield respectfully to all due authority, and neither the Board nor the Deputation will hold us responsible for results, when we thus yield against our own convictions.

"Still, the more I reflect on the subject, the more I fear there is danger that you and the Board, in the absence of any explanation, *may* receive the printed reports of our general meeting, as expressing the sentiments of at least a majority of us. And yet I do not suppose that *one* of us is willing to subscribe to all the principles and details of those reports—no, not even the respective individuals who drew them up as chairmen of the committees.

"Though every report contains much that has my unqualified approval, yet there is something in every one, to which I could not consent, only as coming with the authority of the Deputation.

"The first report (on preaching) embodies much that accords with the experience and conviction of every missionary. But, not to mention some less important items, the single sentence at the bottom of the 29th page, beginning, 'In doing this it will not probably be found necessary to make use of schools in order to collect a congregation,' prevents the possibility of my assent to it. My whole experience and my strongest convictions are directly opposed to this statement. I have never yet seen a permanent or stated congregation [of heathen] obtained in this country without schools, except in the case of workmen, as in a printing-press, or paupers or invalids. Nor have I ever heard of such a congregation, and a challenge in presence of the Deputation, to adduce such a case, failed of being met. So the probability is all on the other side. What accords with all past and present experience, is probable — what is entirely opposed to all experience is *not* probable.

"The report on the printing establishment will perhaps illustrate most of the others. I was appointed with brother Fairbank, a committee to report in favor of having it reduced and a part of the presses sold. I knew brother F. was opposed to the measure, for he had told me so. He had had much debate with the Deputation, and found Dr. A. fully determined to reduce the press. We had no further consultation on the subject. Br. Fairbank prepared the report to suit Dr. A., and the thing was done. He allowed his own hand to perform the act, and then bore the pain as well as he could. How keenly he felt it, may be inferred from the following quotations from one of his letters, while reducing the press: 'It is trying to give the office workmen their discharge. I discharged 25 last week. *It cuts me to the heart,*' etc. He felt, to use his own language, that 'the Deputation have come to do it, and it *must* be done.'

"In the third report (controlling object in missions) there is much that meets the cordial approval of every missionary. But the idea advanced, that the last commission of our Lord stands in the way of our establishing schools among the heathen, to teach them the Gospel, is simply absurd, and a great mistake. The great commission is just as much against the use of the art of printing, as the use of schools. So, too, the attempt to bring odium upon schools, by calling them 'speculations and experiments.' What has stood the test of fifty years, and proved successful, is no longer an *experiment.* When a new mission is organized, and prosecuted among the heathen *without schools*, then shall we have an *experiment*, and shall watch the result with interest. Would it not have been well for the Deputation to commission Messrs. Munger and Hazen, the only brethren who voted against these schools with heathen teachers, to commence some *new mission without schools*, and try this experiment a few years, before attempting to *force us* to adopt the plan *against our convictions?*

"The fourth report (on common schools) has many statements that are objectionable. It says: 'We can not point to a single case of conversion among all this number.' This doubtless means, *while in those primary schools.* Now a closer examination reveals many such conversions, and many more have been converted after being transferred to the higher schools. The seed sown in those primary schools *has* taken root, and afterwards sprung up to eternal life. And then, what agency has proved so mighty as these same schools in breaking up their vile superstitions, and training the present thousands of Hindu youth who discard all confidence in Hinduism?

"This report says: 'A few instances of conversion have occurred among the superintendents and teachers of these schools,' etc. A *few* instances! Such as Hurripunt, Ramkrishnapunt, Narayan, Marooti, Dajeeba, Ramchunder, Dajeeba of Seroor.—*Every* convert, originally of good caste, in all our missions, with one single exception, was brought in through these schools or the seminary. Even this one exception was a teacher in a native girls' school, and hence sprung up his acquaintance and connection with the mission.

"The report says, 'The result seems to show that these schools have failed, etc.' *Not at all.* The result shows the *very reverse*, namely, that these schools have been our *only* means for gaining a stated hearing for the Gospel among the better class of Hindus—the only means, with God's blessing, of securing converts among them The result abundantly shows that our schools have been more effective than any and all other agencies, in making known Christ and winning souls to him.

"I might go on with specifications of this kind through all the reports, but it would require too much time and labor, and is not necessary to my object. I only wish to impress your minds with the fact that we did not assent from conviction, to the principles and statements of these reports; that they were drawn up with express reference to the views and wishes of the Deputation, and embody the views of the individual writers and their brethen only so far as they found their views accorded with those of the Deputation.

"Hence I was surprised and grieved to observe that the responsibility of the views expressed in these reports was so wholly thrown upon us in the general letter of the Deputation. How is this? thought I. In yielding to our Deputation, against our own convictions, have we really incurred the responsibility of these changes which we so much deprecate? It is not possible. The Deputation comes 'clothed with authority.' They tell us there *must* be certain changes. Our English schools *must* be broken up, and our vernacular schools taught by heathen teachers *must* be disbanded. They find us strong in the convictions we have always sent them by letter. But after long and earnest discussions — after doing our best to change or modify views and theories imported from Boston, we respectfully yield to *authority*. *Can* we be regarded as responsible for these changes? Pray do not regard *me* so, for most of them are directly opposed to all my missionary experience and the sternest convictions of my judgment.

"The changes in the printing-press reduce it, from being a most efficient and valuable agency, to one which, in my humble opinion, had better be given up entirely.* In its proper working state, it was able *promptly* to execute all our mission printing, and by filling up the intervals with other work, it not only met all its own expenses, but also the expense of the whole Bombay mission. Now our printing is done with great

* The correctness of this opinion has been verified. The press *has* since been entirely given up.

delay, and the press, if not already a tax upon the funds of the Board, must very soon become so. Our 'printing committee,' with all deference to our Deputation, is not what we want. It only clogs machinery which was before working well. Previous to the appointment of this committee, all works for printing needed only the approval of a majority of the missionaries, and it could be executed at once. Now a MS. must have the approval of this committee of *three*, representing only *two* missions out of *four*, and disturbing the previous equitable balance of influence and power.

"The allowance for building a mission-house is fixed at 2500 rupees. A temporary house, built of mud and covered with grass, may be built for this sum, and even less. But is it true economy to build such houses at permanent central stations? Is there one business man in a hundred that will think so? A brother, [Rev. S. B. Munger,] whose house cost some 5000 rupees, and who now foresees the possibility of its being sold, and he being obliged to build again, said to me the other day: '2500 rupees is not enough. I shall never attempt to build a house with that allowance. I'll go back to America first!' Now this brother made no opposition to our report on building in our meeting. He felt no *personal* interest in the subject at that time; and he and the other brethren who were living in houses which cost from *five* to *ten* thousand rupees each, *may* have thought it desirable to yield to the views of the Deputation on this subject. But let them have to build anew, and we shall better know their feelings. If any brother now in these missions will build a house at a permanent central station, for 2500 rupees, I'll gladly acknowledge myself mistaken.

"My poor schools in Kolapoor — *their* loss will deprive me of my most precious opportunities for preaching Christ in that great idolatrous city. Many will be the weary days when I shall wait with heavy heart and all in vain, for *any* to listen to my message. Hitherto I have had audiences which have gladdened our hearts and awakened fond hopes. From one to two hundred youth have constituted a nucleus around which have been accustomed to gather their parents and friends, often filling our entire chapel. These youth are instructed in the truths of the Gospel every day, from the moment they are able to read. The Sabbath-school exercise of catechising these youth has been more attractive, and done more, I verily believe, to communicate Christian truth to our *adult* hearers, than my more formal preaching. Besides, it is my only means of attracting those adult hearers. Many of them are interested in their children, and will come to hear their prompt replies to my questions. Others are attracted by the gathering, and come in also. And once in the chapel, most of them remain, not only through the Sabbath-school exercise, but through the whole preaching service. I thus secure an attentive hearing for my message from such an audience as I could obtain in no other way.

"And then the result of all this Christian truth on the minds of those youth. It is committed to memory and impressed upon their minds by frequent reviews and repetitions, till it becomes as familiar as the letters of their alphabet. Is it to lose its effect because it has been learned in school? Who *can* believe it? No, if I *must* be deprived of this most efficient means of preaching Christ, I shall not cease to thank God that I enjoyed it so long, that these blessed and saving truths have been so deeply impressed on so many of those youthful minds and hearts.

"Some entertain the idea that any labor in schools detracts so much from direct oral preaching. Oh! what a mistake! I yield to no man in my estimate of the importance of oral preaching. I yield to no man in the amount of time and strength to be devoted to it. Let me not be thought to boast of any toil or sacrifice in the cause of Christ. But my brethren will bear me witness that I fall behind no one in the amount of time and strength devoted to oral preaching of the Gospel. They know that I shrink from no toil or exposure to come in contact with the people. They know that I used to traverse that 'Northern field' of the Ahmednuggur mission *in the hot season and rains*, as no other missionary ever did. They know I have prosecuted this work in Kolapoor amidst the ravages of cholera, passing daily among the dead and dying for successive weeks, till my only attendant was struck down by the disease, and died under my care, and a severe attack prostrated myself, and a malignant dysentery followed for months, working ravages in my system, from which I am still suffering.

"To preach Christ to these perishing heathen is the only work for which we have come to this land. 'Yea, woe is me if I preach not the Gospel.' But it is *in order* to preach that I want my schools. It is that I may make known that precious Name which is above every name, that I plead in their behalf. Gentlemen of the Prudential Committee, it is to you I make this *last* appeal. *Is there no reprieve for these schools?*

"And let me remind you, they ask not your funds. *They have never cost your Board a farthing.* Benevolent Europeans who *see* and *know* their value, have sent in money for their support sufficient to leave a balance each year in your treasury. They ask only the bare favor of *life. May they not live to bless these perishiug idolaters of Kolapoor?* . . .

"My health is precarious. Should what I have here said in regard to the great subjects of mission policy, and the changes I deprecate, prove to be my last testimony, you will kindly receive it as originating in the deep convictions of my judgment and my heart. Do not regard me as in any wise hostile in my feelings towards the Deputation. They are good men, and I expect soon to meet them in heaven, and to rejoice with them over all the good the Lord has effected through such unworthy instrumentalities in this dark land. But both we and they are erring men; and they have not had the facilities for judging of the tendencies and results of the different missionary agencies here in India, that some missionaries in the field have enjoyed.

"I have spoken freely of the changes I deprecate—if too freely, you will excuse it. I can not think it is your wish to prevent the utterance of our honest convictions. '*Give me the liberty to know, to utter, and to argue freely, according to conscience, above all liberties.*' You will see that I am conscientiously opposed to nearly all the changes which the Deputation effected. *But in practice I respectfully yield to authority.* Though deprived of half our strength and means of usefulness, what remains but to toil on, and do what we can? 'We are perplexed, but not in despair—cast down, but not destroyed.' If we may be 'enlarged through your liberality,' we will thank God on your behalf. But if we *must* remain 'straitened on every side,' the *Lord* will help us, and strengthen our fainting hearts. In the bonds of the Gospel, and the service of our common Lord and Master, believe me, very respectfully and sincerely yours, R. G. W."

This appeal speaks plainly to the Committee of the unhappy changes enforced by the Deputation, but avows unqualified submission to authority. If honest convictions thus held in abeyance incur the displeasure of the officers of our Missionary Boards, and lead to the impeachment and excision of earnest and laborious missionaries, is it not an omen of evil which may well elicit the prayers and anxious consideration of all who love the cause of missions?

Unhappy Results of the Change.

It is not my purpose to gather up here all these results. The breaking up of the English high-school, boarding-school, and common schools, in Bombay; the crippling of the Bombay printing-press so that it has since been found necessary to give it up entirely; the suppression of the schools with some 500 pupils in Kolapoor; the suppression of the schools in Satara, and some in Ahmednuggur; the abandonment of the printing-press, the Batticotta seminary, and other schools in Ceylon—these changes, and some like them in Madura and Madras—do they not present sad returns for the heavy expenditure of time and money involved in sending the Deputation to India? But these reveal only a *part* of the disaster attending this change of policy. Among other unhappy results, there are a few which ought to be placed on record for the benefit of those who are to come after us. And these which I mention are limited to my own knowledge, and to our Mahratta missions in Western India. There may be others like them in Ceylon and the other missions, but of those I do not speak. Of the unhappy effects in Western India, which are not generally known to the Christian public, I mention:

1. *The loss to the Board of able and devoted missionaries.*

That I may give no wrong impression on this point, I will mention brief details, sufficient to put the candid reader in possession of facts. My brethren will kindly excuse me for using their initials, which will identify them only where their views and positions are already known.

(1.) Brother B—— joined the missions in 1839, and left India in broken health early in 1854. His estimate of the schools may be inferred from the fact, that when Dr. Anderson and the Committee abolished the Ahmednuggur seminary, boarding-schools, and schools with heathen teachers—all by one order, they detached Brother B—— from that mission at once, and sent him to commence a *new* mission at *Satara.* In the letter of May 10th, 1851, which brought that order to India, the Secretary writes:

"We infer from some of Mr. B——'s letters, that the considerable changes now to be made in the *educational* system of the Ahmednuggur mission, will not accord with his present views. . . . He will find it more pleasant to work without boarding-schools in a new mission at Satara, than to continue to labor where this class of schools has been relinquished after long use."

Brother B—— was allowed to have primary schools with heathen teachers at *Satara*, and continued to labor there till he came to America, just before the Deputation went to India. As to his views of the action of the Deputation, and his principal reason for not returning to India, the following extracts from his letters are quite conclusive:

"I will not attempt to characterize the policy which would not permit you to keep your schools at Kolapoor." "*The policy now inaugurated is a powerful reason for my not returning to India.* Could they have admitted such a liberal policy as to permit your schools at Kolapoor, and ours at Satara, to go on, even this would have made the case different. But no, all must be cut down to one measure. This is enough. I have had enough of such legislation, and shall not again be entangled in that yoke of bondage." April 29, 1856.

Brother B—— resigned his connection with the Board, and has continued to labor in pastoral duties to the present time. With his excellent knowledge of the Mahratta language, his long experience and many facilities for missionary labor, he is lost to the Board and to the work of missions in India.

(2.) Brother A—— labored in India some twenty-six years, and proved himself a most efficient and valuable missionary. He came to America just as the Deputation went to India. His views were decidedly opposed to their doings. Some will remember his testimony on this point, at the special meeting of the Board at Albany in 1856. He, too, resigned, and has been engaged in pastoral duties, or writing for the press, ever since. I suppose he would gladly have returned to his mission duties in India, but for the unwise policy which he saw and *felt* would impede his labors and usefulness there.

In March, 1859, he wrote to a brother whose mission had just been abandoned by the Prudential Committee, much to his grief, as follows:

"The question of your return to India will soon come before you for consideration, and a trying question it will be. The deep interest you feel in that country, your strong attachment to the missionary cause, and your desire to live and labor and die in it; your experience in this good work, your thorough knowledge and ready use of the native language, the extensive acquaintance you have there formed, and the influence and good-will you have acquired among the European and native population; all these are reasons—strong reasons—for you to return to India, for you might hope to accomplish as much in two or three years as any new missionary could accomplish in five or six years. . .

"There is one circumstance in your missionary life, which I know not how far may affect your return to India. When the Deputation of the A.B.C.F.M. visited their missions in India some three or four years ago, you differed from them in opinion in respect to some changes which they wished to make, and you felt it your duty to express your opinions freely to them, and also to communicate your views to the Committee appointed at the special meeting of the Board in Albany.

"Now an honest and conscientious difference of opinion—the result of long observation and experience, and expressed with Christian courtesy, certainly ought not to be to your prejudice. Had I been in India when the Deputation was there, *I should have had the same views of those changes which you had, I should have been as much opposed to their measures as you were*, and I doubt not I should have expressed my views as freely to them, and to the Committee in this country, as you did. And we should have had the satisfaction of knowing that the chaplains, the missionaries, the missionary committees, the presbyteries, etc., in India, generally agreed with us in their opinions and missionary operations."

(3.) Brother H—— was a most laborious and devoted missionary. He labored in India with great zeal and fidelity some sixteen years. His health suddenly failed, and being sent away from Bombay by his brethren a few weeks before the Deputation arrived, he died at sea on his voyage to America. All who knew him will remember the strength of his feelings and convictions on the great subject at issue, and his intense anxiety lest the Deputation should persist in their unwise policy. This anxiety taxed his feelings unceasingly, and led him to exert himself beyond his strength in writing to the brethren and to Dr. Anderson, deprecating with all his soul the changes he was coming to enforce. This anxiety led him to labor too hard, and hold on to his work too long, that he might be at his post when the Deputation should arrive. From the severe prostration which followed he never rallied.

(4.) Brother G—— B—— is a man of tender conscience and a loving heart. He deprecated alike the changes effected by the Deputation and the manner in which they were compassed. The following quotations from this brother are sufficiently conclusive:

"Had rather a warm controversy with the Deputation the very last hour of their stay."

"Dr. Duff says he knows our Deputation went quite beyond the limits of their authority." "I was more dissatisfied with those dear brethren [the Deputation] the last hour or two spent with them," etc.

This brother foresaw the friction and trouble which threatened all who did not repudiate their own views and adopt those of Dr. Anderson, and quietly handed in his resignation. It was accepted, and his connection with the American Board was thus dissolved. Alluding to this act of resignation some time after, in a letter to a brother missionary, he wrote:

"I have done all that I needed to do for myself." "I cheerfully wash my hands of the whole business."

I might mention other similar instances. Some will recall the facts associated with the names of Rev. Messrs. I. N. H——, C. T. M——, and others.

But I forbear. The personal vindication of any one is not the object of this volume. Let us rather keep an eye closely to the interests of the Board and the dear cause of missions. But with these interests in view, and the fact of these noble men—able and devoted missionaries as they were—thus lost to the Board, may we not solemnly ask, *Can we afford it?* can the Board afford it? can the Church afford it? With the harvest *so* great, and her laborers *so* few, can she afford to see them sacrificed in this way? With millions of heathen perishing for want of the Gospel, and the cry for help coming over the seas from every dark corner of the pagan world, can she afford to lose her most faithful laborers—men rich in the treasured resources of long experience, possessing a knowledge of the language and of the people, and rare facilities for effective labor—can she afford to lose *such* men for *such* a reason?

2. Another result of the Deputation was the unhappy *alienation of brethren.*

United as we all were in those earnest pleadings for our schools, and "embarrassed" as they felt themselves by our united front, they could succeed in their undertaking only by acting on the old Roman principle, "divide and conquer." This they did act upon, and we have seen with what success.

The position of those of us who maintained our previous convictions not only incurred the displeasure of the Deputation, but reflected on those brethren who *changed*, and incurred their displeasure also. Here is a most unhappy result of the Deputation. "Behold how good and how pleasant it is for brethren to dwell together in unity!" That a large measure of this blessed unity existed among us, previous to the coming of the Deputation, requires no confirmation.

Those two series of letters from every one of us, pleading for our schools, evinces a complete unanimity of sentiment—a remarkable unity of feeling and views, even among missionaries; and the hundreds of letters in my possession from all in our mission band, develop facts in Christian intercourse and communion, show a strength of attachment and sympathy, and breathe a spirit of Christian love, very rare in the brotherhood of saints on earth.

But this precious "fraternity of feeling," (p. 103,) previously existing, was suddenly broken; and the consequent results are sufficiently evident, both in India and America. Oh! when will Christian men learn to sink their personal differences, agree to disagree, and ceasing to forbid those who cast out devils in the name of Jesus, (Mark 9: 38–40,) join hand and heart in any and all means and measures by which souls can be won to Christ?

The following *Tabular View* of the schools of this mission has been prepared with all possible accuracy from the reports and periodicals of the Board and the letters of the missionaries. It presents the number of schools and pupils each year, from the origin of the mission to 1856, so far as reliable data can be found. When the precise number is not stated in the reports and letters, the best possible estimate is given, and the fact that it *is* an *estimate* is indicated by a *.

Tabular View of the Schools of the Bombay American Mission.

Year.	Boys' Schools with Heathen Teachers: Schools.	Pupils.	Girls' Schools with Heathen Teachers. Schools.	Pupils.	Girl's Boarding Schools. Schools.	Pupils.	English Schools.	Total Number of Pupils.
1816	4	300	....	....	....	....	....	300
1817	6	400	....	....	....	....	....	400
1818	14	900	....	....	....	....	....	900
1819	19	1000*	....	....	....	....	....	1000*
1820	20	1050	....	....	....	....	....	1050
1821	15	750*	....	....	in families	20	....	720
1822	18	900*	....	....	"	40*	....	940
1823	26	1454	....	....	no returns.		....	1454
1824	39	2000*	1	not given.	"		....	2000*
1825	39*	2000*	1	25*		50*	....	2075*
1826	24	1499	9	466	....	....	....	1965
1827	16	1126	10	577	....	....	....	1703
1828	19	1100	10	400	....	....	....	1500
1829	31	1200	10	400	....	....	....	1600
1830	17	1000	18	500	....	....	....	1500
1831	21	1485	12	442	....	....	....	1927
1832	18	1322	12	383	....	....	....	1705
1833	16	1500	12	500	....	....	....	2000
1834	16	1295	12	300	1	10	1 25	1630
1835	17	868	14	330	2	50	2 75	1323
1836	17	868	12	330	2	50	....	1240
1837	10*	550*	6*	200	2	40	....	790
1838	8*	450*	4*	150	2	40	....	640
1839	5*	300*	3*	84	2	44	....	428
1840	8*	317	4*	100	2	42	....	459
1841	6*	300	4*	100	2	42	....	442
1842	6*	300*	4*	100	2	45	....	445
1843	6*	300*	3*	75*	2	45	....	420
1844	5	300	4	95	2	40	....	435
1845	5	298	4	50	2	45	....	393
1846	5	250	4	60	2	48	....	358
1847	5	250	4	60	2	48	....	358
1848	6	300	4*	40	2	50	....	390
1849	6	300	4	80	2	54	....	434
1850	6	300	4	80	2	54	....	434
1851	9	400	4	75	2	54	....	529
1852	8	355	4	75	2	54	....	484
1853	8	350	4	75	2	54	....	479
1854	No reliable statistics.		....	....	....	....	1 275	275
1855			....	....	....	....	....	...
1856			....	....	....	....	....	...

In examining the above Table the reader will bear in mind that no record of native *Christian* teachers appears in the whole history of the Bombay mission, except one for a short time in the girls' boarding-school in 1843, and two more subsequent to 1850. Two native *Christian* teachers and one

Indo-Briton were also employed in 1854, in the English institution which was suppressed by the Deputation.

The above Table shows, therefore, that an average of *twenty heathen* teachers were employed in the Bombay mission schools for *thirty-eight successive years*, with the warm, unhesitating approval of the executive officers of the Board.

Summary of Results.

If the following statistics differ in any respect from the manuscript records of the church, the difference must be attributed to defects in the published reports and documents, not to any want of scrupulous care and patient labor in examining and collating them.

Whole number admitted to church fellowship from the origin of the mission to 1857,		57
Europeans, Americans, and other foreigners converted mostly in connection with labors and preaching in English,	8	
Employed as *teachers* and thus brought under Christian instruction and converted,	8	
Pupils or teachers, ditto ditto,	18	
Parents and friends of pupils and teachers, and thus brought under instruction by means of schools,	10	
Poor persons, subsisting on alms,	9	
Servants, and thus coming under daily instruction,	3	
First awakened by tracts and received after months of daily instruction,	1	
Converted by preaching in streets, markets, and on tours,	0—	57
Of the above conversions, those traceable *directly* to schools,	26	
Conversions traceable *indirectly* to the schools,	10	
Other pupils giving evidence of piety, but dying before baptism,	7	

In view of the facts here presented, the reader is requested to form his own estimate of the value of these schools. What could have been hoped for the Bombay mission without them? And while we grieve that no more have been gathered into the fold of Christ in this mission, let us also thank God that he has condescended to own and bless these agencies so largely as he has.

Tabular View of the Missionaries and Assistant Missionaries in the Bombay Mission, from its origin to the close of 1856.

	Joined the Mission.		Length of Service. Yrs.	Mths.	Dys.
Rev. Gordon Hall,	Feb. 11, 1813.	Died, March 10, 1826.	13	1	0
Rev. Samuel Nott,	"	Returned to Amer., Oct. 7, 1815.	2	7	26
Rev. Samuel Newell,	March 7, 1814.	Died, May 30, 1821.	7	2	23
Rev. Horatio Bardwell,	Nov. 1, 1816.	Returned, Jan. 22, 1821.	4	2	21
Rev. John Nichols,	Feb. 23, 1818.	Died, Dec. 9, 1824.	6	9	16
Rev. Allen Graves,*	"	Died, Dec. 30, 1843.	21	3	16
Rev. Edward Frost,	June 28, 1824.	Died, Oct. 18, 1825.	1	3	20
Rev. D. O. Allen, D.D.,†	Nov. 27, 1827.	Returned to Amer., Feb. 1853.	22	0	0
Rev. Cyrus Stone,	Dec. 28, 1827.	Withdrew, June 20, 1838.	10	5	23
Rev. William Hervey,	March 7, 1831.	Went to N., Dec. 20, 1831.	0	9	13
Rev. Wm. Ramsey,	"	Returned to Amer., July 5, 1834.	3	3	28
Rev. Hollis Read,	"	Went to Nuggur, Dec. 20, 1831.	0	9	13
Rev. S. B. Munger,	Sept. 10, 1834.	Went to Jalna, Feb. 1837.	2	5	0
Rev. Henry Ballantine,	Oct. 10, 1835.	Went to Nuggur, Oct. 20, 1836.	1	0	9
Rev. R. W. Hume,	Aug. 10, 1839.	D. at Sea, left B., Sept. 20, 1854.	15	1	10
Rev. Geo. Bowen,	Jan. 19, 1848.	Withdrew, Jan. 1855.	7	0	0
Rev. William Wood,	"	Went to Satara, June 1, 1849.	1	4	12
Rev. S. B. Fairbank,	Jan. 1850.	Left for Amer., March 1855.	5	2	0
Rev. A. Hazen,	Jan. 1855.	" Jan. 1857.	2	0	0
19.			128	0	20

Assistant Missionaries.

James Garrett,	May 9, 1821.	Died, July 16, 1831.	10	2	7
W. C. Sampson,	Nov. 22, 1833.	Died at Aleppo, Dec. 22, 1835.	2	1	0
Geo. W. Hubbard,	Sept. 10, 1834.	Recalled, June 20, 1837.	2	9	10
Elijah A. Webster,	Oct. 11, 1835.	" 1841.	6	0	0
4.			21	0	17

Female Assistant Missionaries.

	Joined the Mission.		Length of Service. Yrs.	Mths.	Dys.
Mrs. Hall, (Margaret Lewis,)	Dec. 19, 1816.	Retur. to Amer., July 30, 1825.	8	7	11
Mrs. Newell, (Har. Atwood.)		D. at Mauritius, Nov. 30, 1812.	0	0	0
Mrs. Newell, (Phil. Thurston,)	Married Mar. 26, 1818.	Ret. to Amer., Oct. 29, 1831.	13	7	3
Mrs. Garrett, "	Married to Mr. G., Mar. 26, 1822.				
Mrs. Nott,	Feb. 11, 1813.	" Oct. 7, 1815.	2	7	26
Mrs. Bardwell, (Rach. Furbush,)	Nov. 1, 1816.	" Jan. 22, 1821.	4	2	21
Mrs. Nichols, (Eliz. Shaw,)	Feb. 23, 1818.	" Oct. 19, 1826.	8	7	22
Mrs. Graves,‡ (Mary Lee,)	Feb. 23, 1818.	Con. with Satara, Dec. 1851.	27	3	16
Mrs. Frost, (C. Emerson,)	June 28, 1824.	Went to Ceylon, Oct. 12, 1826.	2	3	14
Mrs. Allen, (Myra Wood,)	Nov. 27, 1827.	Died, Feb. 5, 1831.	3	2	8
" (Orpah Graves,)	Sept. 10, 1834. Married, Feb. 22, 1838.	Died, June 6, 1842.	7	8	26
" (A. C. Condit,)	m. Dec. 12, 1843.	Died, June 11, 1844.	0	6	0
Mrs. Stone, (A. Frost,)	Dec. 28, 1827.	Died, Aug. 7, 1833.	5	7	10
" (Abby Kimbal,)	Sept. 10, m. Oct. 26, 1834	Withdrew, June 20, 1838.	4	1	18

* Absent in America, 4 years, 6 months, 21 days.
† Absent in N., 3 years, 3 months.
‡ Absent in America, 6 years, 6 months, 21 days.

	Joined the Mission.		Length of Service. Yrs.	Mths.	Dys.
Mrs. Hervey, (E. H. Smith,)	March 7, 1831.	Died, May 3, 1831.	0	1	26
Mrs. Ramsey, (Mary Wise,)	"	Died, June 11, 1834.	8	3	4
Mrs. Read, (Carol. Hubbell,)	"	Went to Nuggur, Dec. 20, 1831.	0	9	13
Mrs. Munger, (M. L. Andrews,)	Sept. 10, 1834.	Went to Jalna, Feb. 1837.	2	5	0
Mrs. Ballantine, (Eliz. Darling,)	Oct. 11, 1835.	Went to Nuggur, Oct. 20, 1836.	1	0	9
Mrs. Hume, (H. D. Sackett,)	Aug. 10, 1839.	Ret. to Amer., Sept. 20, 1854.	15	1	10
Mrs. Wood, (Lucy Lawrence,)	Jan. 19, 1848.	Went to Satara, June 1, 1849.	1	4	12
Mrs. Fairbank, (Abby Allen,)	Jan. 1850.	Died, Aug. 21, 1852.	2	7	21
Mrs. Hazen, (M. Chapin,)	Jan. 1855.	Came to Amer., Jan. 1857.	2	0	0
Mrs. Sampson, (M. L. Barker,)	Nov. 22, 1833.	Ret. to Amer., June, 1836.	2	6	0
Mrs. Hubbard, (E. Burge,)	Sept. 10, 1834.	" June 20, 1837.	2	9	10
Mrs. Webster, (M. Rawson,)	Oct. 11, 1835.	" 1841.	6	0	0
Miss Cynthia Farrar,	Dec. 28, 1827.	Came to America, 1837.	10	0	0
25 in actual service.			138	6	5

In preparing the above Table, time spent in voyages, and absence in America or elsewhere, is not reckoned.

The existence of the Bombay mission from its origin to the close of 1856,........44 years.

	Yrs.	Mths.	Days.	Yrs.	Yrs.	Mths.	Days.
Labor by 19 missionaries,	128	0	20.	Deduct 2 each, learning language,	90	0	20
" 4 assist. "	21	0	17.	" " "	13	0	17
" 25 fem. assist. miss.,	138	6	5.	" " "	88	6	5
Actual service by all the missionaries and assistant missionaries,					191	7	12

It may interest some to know how many of these laborers died in the field, how many returned etc. Counting Harriet Newell as having died in the service, though not having reached Bombay, and the following Table will show that

	Died in Service.	Returned and Released.	Withdrew.	Transf. to other Missions.	Recalled.	In the Mission in 1856.
Of the 19 missionaries,	6	4	2	6		1
" 4 assist. miss.,	2	–	–	–	2	–
" 26 fem. assist miss.,	8	7	1	7	2	1

From the above facts, it is easy to gather the *average* time of each laborer in the mission, and, deducting two years for learning the language, the average period of effective labor, namely:

	Yrs.	Mths.	Days.	Yrs.			Yrs.	Mths.	Days.
Average time by each miss.,	6	8	26.	less 2	for learning	language,	4	8	26
" " assist. "	5	3	4.	" 2	"	"	3	3	4
" " fem. assist. "	5	6	14.	" 2	"	"	3	6	14
" " of the 6 miss. who died in service,	10	9	19.	" 2	"	"	8	9	19

Of all these laborers, only 4 missionaries, and 3 female assistant missionaries are now (1861) in India.

The reflecting reader will note the very short average period of *effective service* by each laborer, as brought to view in the preceding Table. Is it not worthy of consideration, whether the comparatively small results of labor in this Bombay mission are not owing in part to these very short periods of service and frequent changes among the missionaries? Not only have six missionaries and seven female assistant missionaries been transferred from this to other missions, but some of the laborers in this mission were transferred to it from other missions. Occasional transfers may be desirable, but my experience has led to an abiding conviction, that the more a feeling of individual responsibility can be increased in the members of a mission, by their long labor and personal interest in it, the better will it be for the progress of this work.

Any thing which conflicts with this feeling of personal interest and responsibility is injurious alike to the missionary and the mission. A man who is detached from duties in which his whole soul has become deeply interested, and sent to another field, will find time and effort necessary to make his heart-strings wind so closely around new objects.

And, in like manner, when a missionary is sent to supply the place of another *temporarily*, he will not feel the same responsibility and interest as if he expected the change to be permanent. If the plans and measures he finds in use do not prove effective, he did not originate them. If he changes them he may soon leave, and his successor or predecessor may come and change them again.

Much the same reasoning applies to all dictation and restrictions from abroad. The home Officers of a Society should certainly have authority to limit the funds they will grant to a particular mission and to make grants for particular objects if they choose, but if they put a missionary in a kind of "strait-jacket," interdicting his schools or his preaching in English, there is great danger of destroying this desirable feeling of personal responsibility and interest, and thus degrading a missionary from his high character as a minister of Christ, and rendering his labors to a great extent ineffective.

I have known some unhappy instances which would illustrate these views, but will only commend the subject to the prayerful consideration of the Officers of our Missionary Societies.

CHAPTER V.

CHARACTER AND RESULTS OF SCHOOLS IN THE AHMEDNUGGUR MISSION.

Origin of the Mission.

AHMEDNUGGUR was once the seat of Moslem power in this part of India. It is a city of 28,000 native inhabitants, situated above the *Ghats* or mountains, 175 miles northeast of Bombay, and is now a military station of the British Government. This site for a mission was explored and fixed upon by Rev. Messrs. Allen and Read, in November, 1831, and on the 20th December following, Messrs. Graves, Hervey and Read arrived and commenced their labors.

Among the first notices of this mission, we find mention of schools, and a poor's asylum, in which the missionaries "daily gave instruction." The poor inmates of this asylum were under the stated teaching and influence of the mission, and in this respect it bore a close analogy to a school, and secured much the same results.

The first convert baptized was the wife of Babajee, who had been converted at Bombay, while employed as a "*heathen* teacher." The mother of Dajeeba, another "heathen teacher," who had been converted at Bombay, was soon after baptized, and also several inmates of the poor's asylum.

In the second year of this mission, a *Presbyterian* church was duly organized, consisting of 14 members, 10 of whom were natives. Babajee and Dajeeba were ordained elder and deacon, and the church was connected with the Third Presbytery of New-York. How comes it that all elements of

Presbyterianism have disappeared from this church and mission?

Ahmednuggur was commenced as a *station* of the Bombay mission, but conflicting interests between stations and laborers so far removed from each other caused dissension, and it was separated from Bombay by a positive order of the Prudential Committee, and became an independent mission some years before I went to India.

When Satara and Kolapoor were made distinct missions, Dr. Anderson wrote: "Large territorial missions do not work well any where. . . . It seems, therefore, that nothing would be actually sacrificed, and much probably gained, by making *four* distinct Mahratta missions instead of two."

And yet, by a recent order of the Prudential Committee, Dr. Anderson has reünited all these missions into one, and that too, against the recorded wishes and unanimous votes of *all* the brethren in the Ahmednuggur mission.

Prominence given to Schools.

The missionaries gave great prominence to schools, and as early as 1835, we find 9, and two years later, 17 free schools with *heathen* teachers in operation in Ahmednuggur and the surrounding villages; and though the financial crisis of 1837 enforced temporary retrenchment, yet these schools were so highly valued, that they were resumed as rapidly as possible, and continued to increase and prosper till 1850, at which date there were no less than 21 in operation, most of them still having heathen teachers. Of such teachers, Mr. French fitly says: "We must employ them till it shall please the Head of the Church to give us others." His estimate of the usefulness of these schools may be inferred by his having eight of them under his superintendence at Seroor, and wishing he had means for increasing their number. Of these teachers, the missionaries say: "They are regarded as in the most favorable circumstances for becoming acquainted with the truth and receiving it into their hearts."

As to the character and value of these schools, take the following from the report of 1844:

"We have recently appointed a native superintendent to take charge of all of them, to visit them regularly and see that their Scripture-lessons, as well as their other studies, receive due attention, to assist in teaching the boys of the town schools on the Sabbath, and also to instruct a few young men with the design of preparing them to be school-teachers in the villages. We have long felt the importance of increasing the number of our village-schools, and we can obtain suitable teachers for them only by training them ourselves. The young man whom we have made superintendent, has long been employed as a teacher, originally by Mr. Munger at Jalna, and afterwards by us at this station."

Thus did the missionaries attach so much importance to these schools that they employed *heathen teachers* and *heathen superintendents*, not only in the infancy of the mission, when they had few or no converts, but when *heathen* teachers and superintendents were converted and received into the Church, they found other duties for them, and employed other *heathen* teachers and *heathen* superintendents to conduct these schools.

This page in the history of the Ahmednuggur mission is worthy of careful study, both for the evidence it furnishes of the views and practice of its missionaries, Messrs. Ballantine, Abbott, and French, and also for the signal success of these schools in leading to the conversion of the most intelligent and useful converts in the mission. The life-long and invaluable labors of Miss Cynthia Farrar have been spent in the Christian instruction and care of girls' schools with such *heathen* teachers. They proved a difficult and laborious, but most useful branch of labor. The reports of the mission and of the Board abound in statements as follows: "Miss Farrar is indefatigable in her exertions to make them as efficient as possible. A change is gradually taking place in public opinion as to the importance of female education; but this change is slow, and we fear many years will elapse before the people of this place will desire to avail themselves extensively of the advantages afforded them for the education of their daughters."

Miss Farrar has lived to see this change sufficiently marked to elicit devout thanksgiving from every Christian heart. Her noble pioneer efforts have had much to do in producing this change, and their influence will be felt for good in Western India in all coming time.

English School.

It was early perceived by the missionaries that facilities for acquiring the English language would be effective in bringing a more hopeful class of Hindu youth under their Christian teaching, and hence, in 1835, they commenced an English school, which they "hoped would grow into an important institution."

In 1840 we find this school prospering, under the care of Mr. Burgess, with some thirty students, and the missionaries say: "It seems to be gaining favor with the people, and promises to accomplish much good."

Two years later we find the missionaries rejoicing in the large amount of Christian truth imparted to the young men in this school. They describe the thorough course of Christian instruction, and the frequent visits of the pupils to their houses for books and conversation. "In short," they say, "there are many ways in which the existence of the school affords an opportunity of exerting an influence on a class of people who, comparatively speaking, are not reached by our other operations. It is attended by the sons of some of the first families in the city." . . "But we must not forget that the growth of seminaries and colleges in heathen lands is gradual. The present generation of missionaries must cease from their labors before seeing but little more than a beginning of what will one day, by the divine blessing, be seen in Ahmednuggur."

In full sympathy with this feeling the officers of the Board added: "One important object aimed at in teaching English, is to open to a portion of those great communities the treasures of religious and other useful kinds of knowledge which are stored up in that language."

It was an object of desire to induce the high-caste pupils

of this English school to come into the seminary on the same footing with the middle and low castes. In the infancy of the mission it was impossible to effect this, but as they came to value more the instruction and acquaintance of the missionaries, their prejudices gradually gave way, and in 1843 the two schools were united, English being the inducement which brought and held them under the influence of the missionaries.

Ahmednuggur Mission Seminary.

At the origin of this mission the officers of the Board drew the attention of its missionaries to the prosperous boarding-schools of our brethren on the Island of Ceylon, and earnestly recommended them to adopt the same kind of schools. This they desired to do, but wrote: "The great hindrance to an enterprise of this kind is caste, which makes it almost impossible to obtain boarding-scholars of sufficient promise."

They persisted in their efforts, however, and in 1836 we find them rejoicing "in the success of the boarding-school."

This school was always known as the "AHMEDNUGGUR MISSION SEMINARY," and "was established on the same principle as the BATTICOTTA SEMINARY in Ceylon."

It was not till 1837 that the pupils of this seminary could be persuaded to sleep and eat on the mission premises, and the event marked progress which caused much rejoicing. The two prevailing motives which brought pupils into this school were, the teaching of English, and the allowance for food and clothing. "The course of study embraced several years, and included the acquisition of English." "The annual cost of the institution was about $1000."

This institution was an object of special desire and fostering care with the Board. In the reports of these years we find repeated resolutions recommending "to the Prudential Committee to foster those seminaries already in operation, and to found others as there may be opportunity, with the hope of supplying, in part, the deficiency of Christian teachers from this country." The Committee approved, and the missionaries prosecuted their labors in these seminaries with heathen teachers and pupils, relying on the efficacy of God's truth and Spirit to convert these heathen youth, to whom they were looking as hereafter to supply the deficiency of Christian teachers. And their trust in God was not disappointed. These institutions, in all the different missions, have more than realized all the reasonable hopes that were ever based upon them.

In the fifth year of this seminary we find the missionaries regretting that none of its pupils had been converted; but they add: "We think impressions have been made on the minds of many of them, which will prevent them from ever engaging in 'abominable idolatries' with the sincerity of their fathers," and they express a hope that some of them would soon share in the grace of the Gospel. The missionaries resolved this year, 1840, at their annual meeting, that their "native helpers should be taught the English language, so as to enable them to read and understand the English translation of the Bible, and use English Commentaries." This unbiased estimate of the value of English, on the part of the missionaries, is worthy of permanent record. How strictly the uniform views and practice of the missionaries accord with those earnest pleadings and testimony of *all of us* in 1853 and 1854!

This seminary was specially valued by the missionaries, as being, with the schools having *heathen* teachers, the only connecting link with the people of the higher castes. For the first ten years of its existence, not one of its pupils was baptized, but the missionaries wavered not in their attachment to it, and the officers of the Board resolved that: "From the position which this seminary sustains to the missionary work, it obviously has strong claims to the sympathy and prayers of Christians in this country. . . If the Holy Spirit shall descend from on high, bringing deliverance for these youthful captives of sin, who can estimate the value of the influence which shall go forth from its walls?"

The Holy Spirit did descend upon this interesting school.

After its first ten years its history is marked with frequent seasons of special religious interest, and converts were gathered in who have proved most valuable helpers in the missionary work. Notices of some of these converts will be found in another place, and will be readily understood as constituting an important part of the history of this school.

The Christian teaching and character of this seminary may be inferred from the following extract, taken from the report of the mission for 1848:

"Much religious instruction has been given in the seminary. Mr. Burgess has usually devoted an hour to such instruction every morning, and heard regular classes in Scripture-lessons. Mr. Wilder has heard similar lessons, and during three months of the year gave lectures three times a week on the evidences of Christianity." These lectures were given mainly for the benefit of the native preachers and helpers of the mission.

Speaking of the religious interest in the seminary, the report continues: "Three of the boys, children of Christian parents, asked for admission to the Church, and others were serious. A weekly prayer-meeting was maintained, attended by ten or twelve of the boys. . . I have learned that four of the lads have expressed a determination to be on the Lord's side." But more of this school in the sequel.

Boarding-Schools.

The other *boarding*-schools of this mission, besides the seminary, were, one for girls and a second for boys at Ahmednuggur, one for each sex at Seroor, and the same at Jalna, under the care of Mr. and Mrs. Munger. It was with much difficulty that these schools were started at first, and for four or five years we find the missionaries regretting that "it has not been found possible to get up boarding-schools," and subsequently, as early as 1839, rejoicing that "the *boarding*-schools were found to present inducements sufficiently strong to hold the pupils in the schools despite all the opposition of the Brahmans."

They soon report the presence of some of the highest

native officials of government at the examination of the girls, and rejoice in the increasing favor and promise of the school. Mr. French, expressing a desire to increase the number of his boarding-scholars, adds: "A school of this description should be sustained at every station."

The character of the primary boarding-school for boys at Ahmednuggur, may be inferred from the following report: "As the offspring of native church-members form a large and constantly increasing body of youth, our brethren deem it very desirable to give them a good Christian education. As many of them, moreover, come from other places, and their parents, generally, are too poor to support them away from home, a small sum (usually fifty cents a month) will be appropriated for their food, clothing and stationery. 'We think,' says Mr. Ballantine, 'that money spent in this way will be profitably laid out; and that we may hope for as valuable results from it as from any other expenditure.' The correctness of this opinion the Committee see no reason to call in question." How came they to call it in question three or four years later, and suddenly interdict this very school? And how came this good Brother B. to change his views just as suddenly?

Of the Christian influence brought to bear upon the pupils of these schools, Mr. B. says:

"We might say some of them exhibit evidence that they have experienced the renewing influences of the spirit of God. We have strong hopes in regard to three or four that such is the case, and the number of those who manifest an interest in the subject of religion is much greater.

"The influence of the girls upon each other is decidedly religious, and against the follies of heathenism. Their meeting together for prayer, and their simple, childlike petitions, their desire for pardon and for assistance to resist sin, and their prayers for their friends, exhibit a state of mind which encourages us to hope that they do know something of the evil of sin, and of the importance of forsaking and resisting it, and of seeking divine assistance for this object. And when any one reproaches them with the intention of becoming Christians, they readily own their preference for Christianity and their abhorrence of idolatry. They are free to talk to their parents and friends on the subject, and evidently exert a great influence over them. Their parents frequently ask them to read to them, and are interested in hearing some story from the Bible, or some other good book."

Of one of the girls, Mr. B. wrote: "She often converses with her parents on the subject of religion, and the mother especially, has learned much truth from her, but is afraid to yield to it."

Frequent notices of this kind show the happy influence of these schools on adults as well as the children. It is even added: "The parents themselves, are also brought under religious instruction. Mrs. B. takes the mothers by themselves, and reads to them a portion of Scripture, and converses with them. She thus learns their feelings, which they sometimes express very freely. Some of them tell us they have entirely given up the worship of idols."

Of two little girls who died while in the boarding-school, the hope is expressed that Christian instruction had been blest to their salvation. The elder belonged to the little company of girls who used to meet for prayer, and the missionary writes: "We can not but hope she is now with her Saviour, whom she wished to acknowledge publicly before the world. She had learned from dear Mrs. Burgess' death, how to die, calmly trusting in Jesus, and her death was so peaceful, that even her heathen parents wondered and rejoiced that their daughter could exhibit such peace and joyful trust in the Saviour, on her death-bed.

"Her cousin was very young, but when near death, entreated her mother to lie quiet that she might pray to the true God, and then repeated the first four commandments and the Lord's prayer, and died."

Speaking of the deep impression thus made on young minds by Christian instruction, the missionaries say: "May we not hope that He who said, 'Suffer little children to come unto me, and forbid them not,' will accept as his, this almost infant who had learned to pray the prayer he taught? The circumstances of her death as well as of the other, encourage us to continue to labor for such children." "A larger number than before are now accustomed to meet regularly for prayer, as well as to pray alone. Even the smaller girls soon come under the influence of Christian truth. Some of the mothers, too, seem to be much interested in the subject of religion."

Estimate of the Schools by the Missionaries.

The extracts already quoted furnish abundant evidence of the high estimate of these schools in the views and practice of the missionaries. But as their honest views have been widely misrepresented by some, it is proper to place their testimony on record a little more at length.

Of their village schools, with heathen teachers, the missionaries say, in 1838: "We can not expect to superintend our village schools so closely as those in town, but then they form an important part of our operations. In making tours we always direct our first attention to the villages where our schools are situated, and generally find the people better prepared than in other places for hearing and understanding the word of this salvation. And we can pursue any systematic course we please in visiting and instructing them."

Thus these schools in the villages, least effectively superintended, were regarded as very valuable agencies, notwithstanding their *heathen* teachers, and preaching-tours in such villages were most satisfactory and useful.

When some of this class of schools were broken up by the opposition of the priests, rejoicing in the amount of good already accomplished by them, Mr. Ballantine writes: "Considerable knowledge of divine truth has been communicated by their means, and the impression has been made that Christianity stands on such a foundation that idolatry is in great danger before it. *All that we have given for the support of these schools has, we think, been well bestowed.*"

Of this same class of schools at Jalna, regretting that he could not have more of them, Mr. Munger says: "They have undoubtedly been the means of good. They have communicated some knowledge of the Gospel of salvation to many families, whose prospects at the day of judgment will wear a very different aspect from what they would had not these schools been established among them." "The readiness with which the children study their Christian lessons is particularly gratifying." "I have found both teachers and scholars much interested in the historical parts of the Scriptures."

The impression has been made on some minds that the care of such schools detracts from the preaching time and character of the missionary. The fact is, they increase his facilities for preaching many fold. On this point Mr. Munger writes: "The measure of attention which I give to these schools is far from being any impediment to the higher duties of my calling. On the contrary, they afford the means of gaining a more ready access to the people, and giving an illustration of the beneficial tendencies of the Gospel."

Reporting his Sabbath audience as depending on "the children and teachers of his schools," Mr. Munger says: "Street-preaching, as might be expected, is becoming less popular. It is now more difficult to find people who will listen to the message of a Saviour's love. They even seem to avoid me." This testimony, of one who has spent much time in preaching-tours, illustrates the fact before stated, that alms, medicine, schools, or money direct, must be used as means for gathering a *permanent*, *stated* audience in India. It is well for the Christian public to note how uniformly missionaries have been driven to one of these appliances, and how extensively they have employed schools as the agency which secures the most promising class of hearers, and appeals to the worthiest motives.

The testimony of the whole mission accords with that of Mr. Munger on this point. Of bazaar-preaching the Report for 1840 says: "We found so much angry discussion, and so little apparent desire to become acquainted with the truth, that we were led to think it was better to make use principally of our regular places for preaching on our own premises."

On the other hand, even their preaching-tours led them to value their schools more than ever before. Messrs. Burgess and Ballantine, closing a report of a long preaching-tour, say: "In view of our tour we would remark that, *if possible, we are more than ever before convinced of the great importance of schools among this people.* In those villages where the mission has had schools, we met with the best reception, and found the greatest number of readers. When we came to a village where there were few or no readers, we could not but feel that it was comparatively of but little use to stop and labor."

Messrs. French and Abbott, on a similar tour, wrote: "This village, Sonay, contains some two hundred houses and only eight or ten readers. The reason is, they have had no school for many years. We saw here, as we often do in other places, the importance of schools."

It must be borne in mind that the schools thus spoken of were scattered in the villages, and taught by *heathen* teachers. The mission report goes on to say: "We attach great importance to these schools. The class of men educated in our schools, and soon to appear on the stage of action, will be addressed by the missionary under much more favorable circumstances than their fathers, who grew up in ignorance. Besides, *the school is even now a standing recommendation of the missionary to the people whose children attend it, and to their neighbors. The school-house is a good preaching-place, and the truths taught in the school make an excellent basis for religious instruction.*"

After giving some details of a preaching-tour, Mr. B. says: "From these facts the importance of schools is evident. Even when a school is kept up in a village but a few months, the advantages are probably more than commensurate with the expense. Our elementary books contain the fundamental truths of Christianity, and for thirty or forty children to have committed these truths to memory we regard as a matter of great importance. It is sufficient, with God's blessing, to save the soul. Even if the teachers are *heathen*, and endeavor to teach heathenism, yet they are obliged to teach Christianity or lose their wages. The villagers where our schools are located are far more favorable to us, and more willing to listen to our instruction, and what is perhaps of still greater importance, the teachers themselves are subjected to a course of study of religious truth, which could be secured from them in no other situation. The two Brahman converts of which you have heard were *heathen* teachers, and now, while I am writing, two other teachers, interesting and talented young men, are candidates for baptism, and others still are evidently thinking on the subject of their souls' salvation. Such results, considering the small number of our schools, are exceedingly cheering. Oh! that we had the means of establishing a school in every village within fifty miles of us. Want of funds is now the most prominent obstacle in the way of accomplishing what we would in this department." Again, after having spent a large amount of time and labor in preaching-tours, the missionaries say: "These tours seem to be interesting and useful, especially when made to places where there are out-stations, *schools*, or Christian families."

This seems to be a proper estimate of preaching-tours. I have spent several months nearly every year of my life in India on such tours, sometimes travelling hundreds of miles into the darker regions of heathenism, visiting celebrated shrines, thronged often with a hundred thousand pilgrims, and at other times restricting my labors to the villages in the near vicinity of my own station. I value this kind of labor, but experience has convinced me that its value is very much less than that of schools. It is a department of labor preëminently preparatory. It is well to break up fallow ground, but it yields no immediate fruit, and he who devotes all his time, and money, and labor to this single branch of business will soon find his family starving, and himself a bankrupt. But for schools in the Ahmednuggur mission the results of labor would have been meagre, and mostly confined to the poor-house to the present time.

Estimate of the Schools by the Board.

The missionaries affirm that all these schools originated at the express wish and advice of the home Officers of the Board, and their statement is sustained by good evidence. This is found not only in the manuscript letters of the Secretary through all the first twenty years of the mission, but also in the *Missionary Herald* and the frequent resolutions passed at annual meetings. Some of these resolutions have been incidentally quoted already. We will not repeat them. But of the many others which abound in the reports and organs of the Board take the following, in 1842. Some of the village schools with *heathen* teachers had been broken up by the opposition of the priests, whereupon the *Herald*, grieving for their loss, declares: "Schools of this kind are too important an auxiliary to the missionary to be abandoned." Who can avoid the inquiry, If this was true in 1842, why not equally so in 1852?

For eight subsequent years the testimony is unvarying. In 1848 the Annual Report of the Board says: "Their schools are in a more prosperous and promising condition than at any previous time. The Spirit of God has been present in some of them, manifesting his renewing power in the conversion of some of the pupils."

Again in 1850, "In regard to the mission at Ahmednuggur, your committee particularly notice the prosperous state of the schools." Of the seminary they say: "*This institution seems especially to call for commendation.*"

Why, oh! why the sudden and unaccountable change of feeling in regard to these schools and this promising seminary the very next spring!

But we will not anticipate. The earnest and frequent commendations of all these schools up to 1851, are on record in the organs of the Board, and we need not quote more of them here.

Estimate of the Schools by Europeans.

There is no department of missionary labor in India which has so generally secured the warm approval, interest, and coöperation of European Christians there on the ground as our schools. This fact is deserving of notice by the friends of missions in Christian lands. The judgment of disinterested men on the spot, with an eye to all our operations, ought to be of more value than theories devised by strangers, at the distance of half the circumference of the globe.

The estimate and interest of European Christians in these schools is attested by their generous donations for their support. No other branch of our labors has elicited from them such ready and generous aid. In the infancy of the mission "the girls' schools were supported by the European ladies." When some of the schools were broken up by the financial crisis of 1837, "the European residents subscribed some Rs.5000 for these schools. This enabled the mission to sustain the seminary and some of the other schools." At Jalna, in 1838, Mr. Munger's boarding-school and some of the free schools were supported by the English residents. At a later date, urging the Prudential Committee to send more laborers, Mr. Munger says: "Will you not regard the readiness of the Europeans here to relieve you of the entire expense of native education, as an indication of its being the Lord's will that you sustain these labors? Give us a helper, and I will pledge myself to furnish funds adequate to the educational purposes of the station so long as the great Head of the Church shall continue me here."

The ready liberality of our European friends for the support of these schools will be remembered, as it came to view in the history of the Bombay mission. When our Prudential Committee called for retrenchment in the schools of our Ahmednuggur mission, in 1848, I mentioned our emergency to a dear English friend, the chaplain of the station, and in a few days he brought me some Rs. 1500—enough to support all our schools the balance of the year. In our new mission at Kolapoor, where our Deputation interdicted *all* our schools, those same schools were always supported by our European friends, not a farthing of their expense ever having come from the home funds of the Board. Facts and evidence on this point might be adduced to almost any extent. But it is not necessary. The views of our European friends, and the practice of European missionaries in regard to schools, are becoming pretty well understood in America.

Do Heathen Teachers counteract Christian Instruction?

But some object to these schools that the heathen teachers employed in them counteract the influence of Christian teaching. We might meet this objection as Mr. B. has, by saying, "They are obliged to teach the Christian lessons or they receive no pay," and when divine truth is communicated to the minds and hearts of the pupils and teachers of these schools we my safely leave results to God.

A more conclusive reply to this objection is found in the actual conversions which have resulted from such schools, and this will be noted when we speak of the conversion of *heathen* teachers. But in the mean time, what mean such paragraphs in the mission reports as the following?—

"An interesting fact occurred a few days ago in connection with the teacher of one of our village schools. Hurripunt went out to examine the school, and the teacher returned in company with him. Their time was occupied in conversing on the subject of religion, and the objections of the teacher were all answered one by one, till at length he acknowledged that his course was wrong and the Christian religion was right. A few days after, he called at the house of one of us, bringing with him a friend whom he wished to convince of the truth of Christianity. During the conversation which followed, he would often add his voice on the side of the missionary, and endeavor to show his friend that all idolatry was wrong and the Christian religion true."

May we not trust the truth of God even in the hands of *heathen* teachers when it produces such results? But let us take the testimony of the missionaries themselves on this point. In 1842, Mr. Ballantine writes: "Of some of our [*heathen*] teachers we can say with safety, that their influence over their pupils is *not* in favor of heathenism, . . . but on the contrary much of their instruction goes to the subversion of heathenism. Such being the case, and as we hope that these teachers themselves will be benefited by the truth which they have such good opportunities to learn, we are content to employ them, although still heathen, *especially as the effort to sustain these schools with Christian teachers, in case we had Christian teachers for the purpose, would probably result in the immediate withdrawal of all the scholars under our influence.*"

This testimony of Mr. B. is worthy of permanent record, as also the comment of the officers of the Board, namely: "The foregoing extract shows well how the free primary school patronized by the mission, and that, too, while under the instruction of men who have not yet renounced heathenism, *may be an excellent channel for conveying Christian knowledge to the minds of the pupils, the teachers, the parents, and the friends of all connected with the schools.*"

Now place these statements by the side of those of Mr. B. and the Deputation in their reports and doings in 1854, and whence, oh! whence the sudden and total change!

The School-Girl and the Lord's Prayer.

In this connection, take the following incident which occurred in one of Miss Farrar's girls' schools, taught by heathen teachers. Besides chapters in the Bible, Christian hymns, catechisms, and the like, all the little girls were taught to repeat the Lord's prayer. Many of them learned to do it devoutly, and with a clear understanding of its import. Among these was a sweet little girl of thoughtful brow, who showed special fondness for this prayer. One day her father came to the school and listened long and attentively to the lessons of the girls. When they repeated the Lord's prayer, he asked many questions about it, and told Miss Farrar that his little daughter "every night when she lay down, and every morning when she arose, always covered her face with her blanket and repeated that prayer." He added that at first he did not understand what it meant, and when he asked her, she told him "this was the way to worship the true God."

In giving an account of this incident some months after

it occurred, the missionary wrote: "The little girl still continues to pray. The father also comes to the chapel on the Sabbath, though previous to the establishment of this girls' school he was entirely unknown to us." How happily this case illustrates the influence of those schools both on the tender minds of the children and on the harder hearts of their parents and friends.

Pupils of a Heathen Teacher throw away the Idols.

Of much the same significance is the following incident, which occurred in a school of Mahar boys, taught by a *heathen* teacher. The report of the mission gives it in simple terms as follows:

"The teacher seems to be much engaged in instructing his scholars in the truths of Christianity, and the result is very encouraging. The boys not only refuse to worship idols themselves, but laugh at their parents for their folly in bowing down to wood and stone; and they have actually gone so far as to *pull up and throw away the idol gods in their part of the village*, much to the astonishment and confusion of their elders. Probably none of the boys belonging to the higher castes would be allowed to exhibit so much opposition to long-established customs, without being removed from the school. But here, so far from this being the case, the parents appear more friendly to the truth than ever." The report goes on to state that formerly the native helpers were much abused in that same village, but now the people were conciliated, listened attentively to Christian instruction, and "acknowledged that the word of God is indeed the truth." All this the result of one little school, costing some three dollars a month. Is it any wonder that the missionaries valued such schools, held on to them as long as they could, and plead for them with most forcible arguments and earnest entreaties?

Conversion of Pupils.

We have already seen how the hearts of very young pupils even were affected by the truth, and that, too, in the schools taught by *heathen* teachers. There is sufficient evidence that many of them were truly converted. The weighty charge tabled against these schools by the Deputation was, that no converts had been gathered from them. It is a fact that when pupils in these schools showed much promise and interest in Christian truth, they were taken into the boarding-schools, and thus brought more closely under the influence and protection of the missionaries before their baptism. But to disparage and disallow these training-schools for this reason, would be just as sensible as to disallow all the academies and colleges for training ministers in Christian lands, because none become ministers till they enter the higher seminaries. Besides, our boarding-schools, too, were interdicted by the Deputation, and certainly this plea could not be urged against them. The converts received to the Church from this class of schools are numerous, and still among the brightest lights of our Christian communities in India. Our limits forbid us to specify many of these cases in detail; but take one among the first fruits of our girls' boarding-school.

Ramkore and her Mother.

In the early years of the mission there appeared at Ahmednuggur a lone woman, of good caste, leading by the hand a little girl. Her countenance was sorrowful. She was a widow, and the child fatherless. Left destitute in the distant village where her husband died, she had travelled on foot seventy miles, alternately leading and carrying this little girl, her only child, till she reached the city of Ahmednuggur. Wherefore did she come? She had been told that in this city she had a wealthy uncle, and she hoped he might befriend her and her orphan child. But he received her coldly, and, after subsisting a few days on the charity of strangers, her troubled thoughts reverted to the stinted kindness of some poor neighbors in her distant village at the time of her bereavement, and taking her little girl by the hand, she turned her back upon the city, and started on her weary journey to the village where had been her home.

She could illy conceal her sorrow, and as she was passing

through the city gate, a Hindu who had seen her at her uncle's door, and learned her sad story, felt some movings of pity, and thus addressed her: "Good woman, where are you going?" Choking with grief, she replied: "Back to my village, Maharaj; we can not live here." "But you'll die by the way! where will you get bread?" Bursting into tears, she confessed her only resource was in the charity of those who might feel compassion for her. "Yonder," said the Hindu, pointing to a part of the city where lived the missionaries—"yonder live some white people whom we call '*Padre sahib.*' They are not like the English who come here and rule over us. They are white like them, and talk like them. But they say their country is still farther away, beyond another great sea. And really they are a very good sort of people. They take no money from us, but show great kindness. They establish schools for our children, and teach them to read, and many useful things. In one of their schools they even give the little girls food to eat and clothes to wear. The only trouble is, their *religion* is different from ours, and some of our people have become *defiled* (Christians) like them, and that makes us afraid of them. But really, they are very kind people, and if you are not afraid your little girl will become defiled, you might take her there, and they would take care of her."

The poor woman listened with conflicting feelings. She cast a glance at her child, and then looked in the direction the Hindu had pointed. The act was repeated again and again, and still she hesitated. The thought of her little daughter's becoming defiled was terrible. But after a little, taking the child by the hand, she turned back through the lanes of the city, and they soon appeared at the door of the missionary.

Little Ramkore was welcomed to the school, and maternal affection kept the mother, too, within reach of daily Christian instruction.

Our next notice of this interesting girl is in the language of the missionaries. They say: "Ramkore is now about ten years old, and has long seemed to love the truth. She is naturally of a very mild disposition, and one of the most lovely girls in the school. Some months ago a neighbor came to her mother, and begged this little girl in marriage for her son. The mother consulted the daughter. Ramkore's first question was, 'Is he a Christian?' and when told that he was not, she replied that she would never marry any one that was not a Christian. Her mother reminded her that she would probably never find a Christian husband, when she at once repeated her resolute purpose never to marry an idolater."

A little further on in the reports of this mission, we find an interesting account of this mother's conversion and baptism. Brought thus incidentally under the influence of the Gospel, coming at first with hesitation and trembling, lest her child should become a Christian, that mother's heart is touched and converted; and instead of fearing her little girl will become a Christian, she begins to pray that she may—brings her forward and consecrates her to the true God in baptism. What agency did God employ for bringing this heathen mother to a saving knowledge of the truth? Does the question admit of any doubt? Is not the agency of the school clear and unmistakable?

But let us return to Ramkore. The missionaries soon say of her: "We do hope this little girl is already a child of God. She has long seemed to love the society of Christians, the reading of the word of God, and the exercise of prayer and praise. Still, as she is so young, being only about ten years old, we thought it best that she should be baptized on the faith of her mother. Her influence upon two or three of her companions has been very good, and our hopes have been strongly excited in regard to them."

The very next year we have an account of the admission of this dear girl, and her three companions, to the fellowship of the Church, as the first fruits of the girls' boarding-school. Ramkore still lives to adorn her Christian profession. She presents in that dark land the pattern of a frugal, industrious, intelligent, lovely, Christian wife and mother, training her children in the fear of God, a true helpmeet for her worthy husband—a native pastor, while her winning and elevating influence upon all around her is precious as ointment poured forth. Her aged mother, too, lives with her, and pleasant must be their remembrance of all the way by which the Lord has led them.

In tracing the history of this girls' boarding-school, we find frequent notices like the following:

"One of the girls has been admitted to the Church during the year, and two or three of the present members of the school desire baptism."

"In November one of the girls, and two other young females who were long members of this school, were received into the Church."

"We should not omit to mention that four or five of the largest girls have for some months been asking for baptism." And again: "Four of these converts were girls in the boarding-school."

The records of the mission do not enable us to determine what proportion of the converts were pupils of these schools, but it was very large; and then, in case of adult converts, the influence of the schools was very marked in all of them, and the case of Ramkore's mother would illustrate many of them.

Influence of Schools on Adults.

The facts and testimony of the mission on this point deserve more specific notice. The schools have uniformly proved the main connecting link between the missionaries and the people. The advantages of the boarding-schools became extensively known, and their influence in eliciting interest and attention, and bringing parents and friends in connection with the mission for the sake of placing their children in these schools, became very strong and manifest.

When one of the pupils of the seminary died, giving gratifying evidence that he had become a Christian, we immediately find that his dying testimony in favor of Christianity, led both his parents to come to the mission for instruction. Mr. Abbott writes:

"They determined to come and hear what Christianity is.

They left their homes to come and live with me. They had another son in the seminary, and they immediately put their oldest daughter in the girl's boarding-school. From that time to this, the father has been persevering in learning the way of salvation. He has now *learned to read*, and says that the more he learns of Christianity the more he likes it. He says he thinks he has given his heart to Christ, and is determined to serve him the remainder of his life."

What was the agency blest of God in case of these adults? Again Mr. A. writes:

"Various opportunities occur of giving religious instruction to a great many people who are in some way connected with these boys. Their mothers and sisters usually bring them their food, to whom Mrs. A. reads and converses while the boys are eating. They have lately become much interested in this exercise, and some of them have manifested a good deal of seriousness. Owing to the marriage connections of the boys, people from distant villages are often brought around us, and sometimes stop several days. They often hear from us for the first time the story of Christ." Mr. A.'s lectures and experiments in the natural sciences, drew large audiences, and communicated much valuable instruction, bearing on the truth of Christianity. "These make them feel that if God had made their Shasters, he would not have made so many mistakes on this and many other subjects."

Mrs. Burgess, while in charge of the girls' common schools with heathen teachers, was often heard to say: "I have had a very interesting time to-day. I regard these schools as very important." In her visits to the schools, she often had crowds of women, the mothers and neighbors of the girls, to listen to her instruction, and in this way much Christian truth was extensively communicated in the most winning and effective manner.

Speaking of the "good effected by the girls' boarding-school," and giving an account of a little girl in it who died, leaving good evidence of piety, Mr. Ballantine adds: "We hope both the parents of this little girl are true believers in Christ. Many remarks which they make show us that they have no confidence in the gods of the heathen." And again: "There are many parents of girls now here, and of those who have left, *who owe all their knowledge of Christian truth to being brought into connection with us by means of this school.*"

Doubtless this estimate of the schools is entirely correct. They have ever proved very effective in bringing parents and friends of the pupils under the influence of the mission, and of stated Christian instruction, and then the Lord has condescended to grant his blessing, and gather them into the visible Church.

Reporting hopeful cases of inquiry, Mr. B. says: "Yesterday I had a long conversation with two of them. One is a boy who has been brought up in our *schools*, and is now a *teacher*. He is connected with the principal Brahman families in Ahmednuggur."

These schools have ever been necessary to secure stated audiences, especially in new missions. In the reports of this mission, so recently as 1848 and subsequently, we read: "The majority of our Sabbath congregation are connected with us, or are members of our schools." The same was true at Seroor. "At Bhingar there is no chapel, and no regular congregation. Mr. Munger spends an hour and a half or so, on the Sabbath, giving religious instruction to the children of his school, when more or less of their friends and others, are present." If these schools were necessary to secure a preaching audience in a mission of fifteen or twenty years' growth, how much more necessary must they be in missions newly commenced in unbroken heathenism?

It appears that the officers of the Board early entertained an idea, probably from the large number of Mahar inquirers and converts, that these Mahars, like the Karens of Burmah, were to be converted "en masse," and thus one layer of the community being wholly pervaded by the spirit of Christianity, it would rapidly extend upward through the higher castes. This expectation was probably based upon wrong impressions of the character and influence of this class of the native community.

From the fact, too, that many of the Mahar converts belonged in the villages some distance from Ahmednuggur, it seems to have been inferred that they were mainly the result of preaching-tours. The fact that the *schools* attracted them from their villages to the city, that they came and placed their children in the schools, and generally remained by them, sharing the benefit of stated Christian instruction for years — this seems not to have been sufficiently understood in Boston. Many preaching-tours were performed, and the missionaries very properly say, "Nor do we think all these tours among the villages are vain," and yet they frankly admit, "We have not yet seen much immediate fruit from them in the way of conversion;" and doubtless, in the honest judgment of all the laborers in that mission, these schools had more to do in bringing in the Mahar converts than any and all other agencies combined. The mothers of the pupils were gathered into classes and daily taught to read, and Christian truth impressed upon their minds. The same was done with many of their fathers, and when these adults were converted, as many of them were, they might almost as properly be classified as fruits of the schools, as if they had been pupils, *pro forma*.

Why were they not scholars, and converted through the agency of the schools, as really as their children? The character of the schools into which they were gathered is often and clearly brought to view, in the reports of the missionaries. They say: "Considerable has been done the past year, as well as in previous years, to instruct the *adults* in reading and in the word of God. Each of the ladies of the mission has performed more or less of this kind of work with the native women immediately around her. The Bible is read and explained to them; they are taught the Lord's prayer and ten commandments, and Christian catechism, and commit to memory verses in the Bible. Many have learned to read the Bible intelligently. As one result of these efforts, [or schools,] most of the wives of our Christian converts are desirous of being received into the Church."

The Mahars felt the inducements and influence of the schools far more than the higher castes, and at the same time had no sacrifices to make when they became Christians. On this point the report of the Board says: "A great portion of the converts have hitherto been from the Mahar caste — one of the lowest in the scale. While persons of a higher rank, on becoming Christians, renounced caste, and were consequently disowned by their friends, the Mahars lost no privileges among their own people by taking this step." These facts ought to have impressed the officers of the Board with the importance of increasing the agencies which would strengthen their hold on the higher castes. Had this been done, the interests and prospects of the mission would have been greatly improved. The conversion of heathen teachers and pupils in the seminary had furnished evidence, that when once brought to understand and feel the truth the high castes were readily affected by it, and were not wanting in manly and moral courage, to avow their faith in Christ, even at the risk of losing patrimony, wife, children and all other friends, sacrifices which no Mahar convert was ever called to make.

In view of these circumstances who can fail to see that the suppression of the seminary, of the study of English, and the schools with heathen teachers, unavoidably severed the connection between the mission and the higher castes? Such was the result, and one much to be regretted.

Unwise to limit Efforts to the Low Castes.

All souls are precious, and the lowest in the scale of humanity, are not to be neglected. "To the poor the Gospel is preached," and shall be to the end of time. But it is no disgrace to the Gospel that Saul of Tarsus felt and yielded to its power. And it is no reproach to the missionary, if his heart goes out in earnest longings to gather in Sauls and Luthers and Melancthons, from the ranks of the Brahmans and high castes of India. But to do this he must have appliances to bring these high castes under his teaching and influence. When we weigh the moral power and influence of such converts for the conversion of their countrymen, the value of any appliances which secure them can hardly be over-estimated. The strong desire for English kept some of these high castes in the seminary, and the free schools with heathen teachers availed for the same purpose. But when these were abandoned, the link was broken.

As the Mahar converts increased, the Secretary of the Board seems to have attached increasing importance to labor among them, to the neglect of the higher castes. With reference to this fact, Mr. Abbott, in 1844, wrote :

"Where we formerly had schools, the people listen to the truth with greater interest than elsewhere. From remarks which we sometimes see in the *Herald*, *I apprehend there is a wrong impression in regard to the prospects of missionary labor among the Mahars as compared with other castes.*" Mr. A. thought there was as much hope of the conversion of the higher castes as of the Mahars, if the mission could only have agencies to reach them; though he admitted the fact that the Mahars have nothing to lose and something to gain in reputation, while they run no risk of pecuniary loss; but that the higher castes have "every thing to lose in reputation, and their civil, social, and pecuniary losses are realities, and must continue to be so till they shall become Christians in a body. Besides losing wife and children, they have a prospect of starvation."

It is easy to see why the missionaries attached very great value to the schools which gave them influence with these higher castes. They felt reluctant to see their efforts and the fruits of their labor restricted to the Mahars. The position and proportion of the Mahars in the native community entitle them to no such prominence. In one hundred villages near Ahmednuggur, with an aggregate of 84,000 inhabitants, the number of Mahars is only 7187 — so that considering their small number and little influence, the idea of restricting missionary efforts to the Mahars, would show a very narrow and unwise policy, in efforts to convert India. Many candid and thoughtful men who study this page of missionary history, will be unable to avoid feeling that, at this stage of the mission, while continuing all due attention to Mahars, it would have been true wisdom to have increased as much as possible the effective agencies for influencing the higher castes.

Had this been done at the period now under review, a great advantage would have accrued to the mission. For some years the mission seminary was the only high-school in the city. Had its facilities been increased for teaching the English language and sciences, it might have brought all the intelligent and high-caste youth who wished to prosecute these studies, under the constant influence and Christian teaching of the mission. Neglecting to furnish such facilities, an increasing desire for them among the Hindu youth, eventuated in the establishment of a government English school to meet this demand.

I have no invidious feelings towards government schools. I rejoice in all that government has done, and is doing for the education of Hindu youth, and would gladly see its schools increased tenfold. True, I would gladly see the Bible and Christian instruction introduced into these schools. When true science has exploded the sophisms and errors of Hinduism, and set youthful minds free from the shackles of superstition, I believe that the word of God is the only magnet which can hold them back from the deepest abysses of infidelity, and keep them true to God, to themselves, and to virtue. But if government will not teach the Bible, let it teach true science, and impart the benefits of a sound education, as extensively as possible; and let missionaries and the Christian Church be on the watch to supplement the deficiency as rapidly and widely as possible.

And yet, when there is an opening, like that which existed at Ahmednuggur the first ten years of the mission seminary, with no government institution as a rival, there is a choice opportunity presented for bringing the most promising class of Hindu youth under our instruction—a price put in our hands, which if we do not use most effectively for advancing the cause of Christ, we are verily culpable. By neglecting to enlarge their facilities for teaching English and the sciences, the mission lost this valuable opportunity. A few good caste youth continued to attend —enough to make the seminary one of our most valuable agencies, but our vantage-ground for bringing all the youth, who desired such education, under Christian teaching, was voluntarily relinquished.

Value of a School at Newase.

The happy influence of schools in conciliating the heathen, and overcoming their deep-rooted prejudices and bitter opposition, is forcibly illustrated in the history of the out-station at Newase. This village is situated some thirty-six miles from Ahmednuggur, in the beautiful valley of the Godavery, and the scattered converts and increasing interest in the surrounding villages, rendered it extremely desirable to make it an out-station, by establishing a native assistant there. But the Brahmans long thwarted our most persevering efforts. All our attempts to rent or purchase a house for the native preacher were unavailing; and as they succeeded in foiling our endeavors year after year, their pride and haughty bearing increased, and they boasted that they would never let us have a station in their village.

Brother F., who had the business in charge, first tried to rent a house. He found one owned by a poor widow, who was glad to let it; but just as the contract was being closed the priests heard of it, and their threats soon availed with the poor woman, and she dared not let it. Very soon such a spirit prevailed in the place that no house could be rented for any price. Brother F. was then authorized to *purchase* a house. He at length found one about to be sold at auction, as the owner was insolvent, and we flattered ourselves that success was now secure. The day for the auction came, and brother F. and one of our native preachers were on the spot. The bidding went on till the Hindus reached their highest limit, and then our native preacher bid above them. Thereupon the angry Brahmans raised such a tumult that the judge dared not proceed with the sale, but referred it to the higher magistrate at Ahmednuggur. He decided, very properly, that the sale must go on, and if the priests did not wish a Christian to buy it they must out-bid him, and another day was appointed for the sale.

Brother F. and Hurripunt, a native preacher, went out to N. some days beforehand, to be sure and be in time, and engaging a native to inform them the day before the auction was to take place, they went on to other villages. A few days after, they were awakened one dark and stormy night by their messenger, who came to tell them the auction would take place the next morning. The rain was pouring and the darkness intense, but how could they lose the opportunity to secure the house? They prepared a lighted torch and traced their way back through mud and rain and swollen rivers, fifteen miles, to Newase, as best they could, thankful to reach there a little before the hour for the sale. But what was their chagrin to find that the auction had transpired the day before! Their messenger had been duped or bribed by the wily Brahmans, whose mirth and triumph at our expense were now boisterous and prolonged.

We do not wonder that brother F. closed his account of this event by writing: "What Brahmans can not do openly and according to law, they can do lawlessly and in the dark, making the government officers, in many cases, their tools."

At length brother F. heard of a house at Newase, the Hindu owner of which lived at Poona, one hundred miles distant. Correspondence ensued. The owner came to see us, apparently extremely anxious to sell. He was offered a generous price. He affirmed that it cost more to build it, and dwelt much on the risk he would incur from the angry priests. The offer was increased, and still he delayed to accept it. The case was brought before the mission again and again. Willing to give even more than the house was worth for the sake of gaining so desirable a point, the mission listened to each proposal, and the offer was increased to Rs. 500—600—650—700—800, and finally to Rs. 850. About a year had been consumed in the negotiation, and still the Hindu delayed to accept the offer, feeling, doubtless, that he was making money faster in this way than he could by honest labor.

At this stage of the business, brother F. was obliged to leave the mission by the failing health of his wife. They went to Bombay, and a vote of the mission threw all his duties upon myself, in addition to the heavy burdens I already had. A hasty tour in the valley convinced me that we had better succeed at once in establishing this out-station or abandon it entirely. The protracted efforts and constant triumph of the priests, were resulting only in harm. The native Christians and inquirers were much dispirited by the scorn, persecution and boastful threats to which they were constantly subjected. For some three years the struggle had continued, and we had been foiled at every step. The mission agreed that it was best to end it at once, either by succeeding or totally abandoning the attempt.

The owner of the house was still in Ahmednuggur. He came at my call, ready to resume the negotiation. I reminded him of the many months he had consumed in this way, and told him I did not think he wanted to sell the house at all. He declared he did. I told him Mr. F.'s offers were very generous—altogether too high, and as he had not accepted them they were now all withdrawn. He looked crest-fallen. He declared he would delay no longer, but would accept Mr. F.'s last offer at once. No, said I; his offers are all cancelled, and we'll begin anew. After a little delay he inquired with evident anxiety what I would give. I made him understand that my offer would not be increased, and his decision would be final. I fixed the offer at Rs. 500, striking off Rs. 350 of the former offer. He looked distressed, and began to say he could not take it, when I asked him not to decide too hastily, but to think of it twenty-four hours, and then come and give me his answer, yes or no, and if he declined the offer we would never say another word about it. He wished to talk more, but taking advantage of Eastern etiquette, I bowed a civil *salam*, and he felt constrained to leave. The next morning he appeared, prompt to the hour, and as soon as compliments were passed and he was seated, I asked his decision. He seemed reluctant to give it, and began a preface about the fearful consequences if the Brahmans should put him out of caste for selling us his house. Very well, said I, you don't accept my offer then, and began to bow a parting *salam*. He stopped me with the earnest exclamation, "Oh! yes, yes, I will!" and in fifteen minutes the writings were drawn, signed and delivered!

But the difficulty did not end here. His house was occupied by tenants. How should he get them out and make it over to the mission? This was necessary in order to secure his money. He felt the difficulty. I proposed to go straight to Newase with him, and receive charge of the house. He declared that if seen there with me, the Brahmans would know his purpose, and they would not let him escape alive. I proposed that Ramkrishnapunt, our most courageous native preacher, should go with him. This, he affirmed, would be still worse, for the people would mob them both. "How will *you* do, then? What's your own plan?" said I. He proposed to go alone, remove his tenants, lock up his house, and bring me the key. I assented, and mounting his little pony, he started for Newase.

My thoughts were ill at ease. Suppose he removes his tenants, locks up his house, and comes away; won't every Brahman there watch his movements and divine his motive? And shall I not find the house burned up, or torn down, with no witnesses of the deed? Such musings made me anxious. In an hour or two I got ready my own pony and little tent, and started out on a preaching-tour. I reached Newase the next morning a little before dawn. The unguarded gate was open, and I passed through the silent streets, unnoticed save by a growling dog. I knocked at the gate of the purchased house:—no reply. I knocked again; but could hear no sound. A third and louder knock, and a low, tremulous voice inquired, "Kōn ahā?"—Who is there? I replied, and the heavy bolt slid back; slowly the gate turned on its hinges, and the owner of the house stood before me. He was agitated at seeing me, and his words were few. He gave me the key, mounted his pony, and lost as little time as possible in escaping to Poona. As soon as the day dawned, and the Brahmans learned what had transpired, their chagrin and indignation knew no bounds. They posted horsemen in different directions in pursuit of the flying Hindu, who narrowly escaped their vengeance by taking refuge with a party of police in the service of the British.

But how did they regard the missionary? They soon turned their attention to me, and crowds pressed around my gate. I kindly beckoned them in, till they filled the open court and front verandah, and then closing the gate preached to them on the *Golden Rule* and *Christ's Sermon on the Mount*. After an hour thus spent I asked them to retire and give place to others. Their place was quickly filled with a new audience, and successive crowds kept me thus occupied till long after dark, leaving me no time, "not so much as to eat bread."

At length I dismissed them all, bolted my gate, and after a slight repast, I spread my blanket on the open verandah, threw myself upon it, and was soon asleep. About eleven o'clock a rap at the gate waked me. I called aloud, "Kōn ahā?"—Who is there? There was no reply. The knock and the inquiry were repeated a second and third time, but no reply. I arose, and going to the gate repeated my inquiry. A low voice whispered the name of Wamunrao, the only Hindu in the place who had shown himself friendly to us. I slipped the bolt and let him in. He was much agitated and spoke with difficulty. The amount of his message was, that the Brahmans were in council, had a large mob gathered, and were resolved to attack me, and destroy the house, and my life was in peril unless I escaped at once.

I confided in the friendship of the man, and the case

seemed emergent. What should I do? I thought of home and my dear family, and wished I were out of the danger. I thought of the three long years of persevering efforts to establish that out-station, of the boastful threatenings of the Brahmans, and of the fact that if I fled now it would be a more disastrous defeat than ever. I beckoned to the friendly Hindu to retire, told him to take care of himself, that we missionaries trusted in the living God, and closing the gate after him, I returned to my blanket, committed myself again to God, and lay down. It was some time before I slept, but I *did* sleep—undisturbed till the morning sun shone brightly in my face. A confused vision of the night-scene recurred. Was it a dream? That could not be. What then had become of the council of priests and the excited mob? My first supposition was that it was all a farce, and the friendly Hindu had been bribed to frighten me away, that they might destroy the house in my absence. But the day revealed it. There was no farce—all was real. And the wicked purpose of the excited priests and mob was ripe for execution, when the night post brought dispatches from the British government impeaching several of the Brahman officials who were the ringleaders in exciting this mob! Their opposition to us was entirely unknown to the British officers, but the Lord so ordered it that their other crimes of bribery and oppression should come to the notice of government, and these dispatches should arrive just in time to degrade those ringleaders, and cause confusion in the ranks of our enemies. Thus checked, they desisted from violence, and contented themselves with an appeal to the Governor of Bombay, praying that our mission station might be removed from their village. After such experience why should not a missionary trust in God forever? I occupied the little house myself till our native preacher, Ramkrishnapunt, came out with his family, and was quietly established in it as his permanent home.

It will be readily inferred that the people were in no mood to be profited by our labors. Keen chagrin or sullen anger marked their countenances. The great question that pressed upon us was, How now shall we conciliate the people and bring them under our Christian teaching and influence? The only agency in our power was a school. The native preacher commenced one in the open verandah of his house, and though the people were shy at first, yet gradually their fears subsided, the school furnished facilities for education which they valued, and beginning with two or three boys, it attracted one after another, and despite the indignation and threats of the priests, and the superstitious fears and prejudices of the people, in a few months fifty or sixty youth were gathered in that school, and daily brought under Christian teaching. By means of this school the feelings of the people rapidly changed towards the mission; the daily reports of the pupils told upon the minds and hearts of parents and friends, and thus adults were attracted, and came in increasing numbers to see a Brahman who had become a Christian, and to hear him talk and preach.

The influence of this event was marked and quickly felt throughout the whole valley. The native Christians gained new heart, and the number of inquirers rapidly increased. After some eighteen months of labor in that valley, I appointed a communion season in one of the neighboring villages, and the memory of that delightful Sabbath will remain with me forever. The little band of native Christians gathered around us, and with them came some twenty inquirers asking for baptism. I took for my text those sweet prophetic words of our Saviour: "Fear not, little flock, for it is your Father's good pleasure to give you the kingdom." Never before did their peculiar significance so affect my own heart, as when I addressed them to that little band of Hindu disciples, and baptized and welcomed eleven more to the ordinances of our holy faith. They are still receiving a blessed fulfillment there, for that feeble band has increased in number, till already some two hundred Christian families live in the different villages which adorn that beautiful valley.

That out-station at Newase prospered so long as the school was allowed. What agency *could* have proved so serviceable at the origin of the station as that little school?

What could have been so effective in checking the angry excitement, correcting the false impressions of the people, and leading to a friendly connection with them? What other agency could have enabled that native preacher to communicate so soon and so extensively a knowledge of the saving truths of Christianity? Without this school he might have lived there for years and gained no friendly relations with the people, and no influence over them.

Conversion of "Heathen Teachers."—Hurripunt and Narayan.

Among the early converts of the Ahmednuggur mission were two brothers of the priestly caste, named Hurripunt and Narayan. They had been employed for years by the mission as *heathen* teachers. Hurripunt had been in the service of the mission some four years, first as a teacher and then as a superintendent of all the free schools, though still a heathen priest.

On his first acquaintance with Hurripunt, Mr. Ballantine says: "The most favorable appearance presented in his charcter was his thirst for knowledge. He was constantly inquiring about subjects connected with natural philosophy and natural history, and seemed to love to know the truth, although so often opposed to the Hindu Shasters. *With regard to geography and astronomy, he at once entered into the views presented in our books, and never hesitated one moment to acknowledge the absurdity of the Hindu notions respecting them.*"

It is worthy of notice that the knowledge of true science in contrast with the false and absurd science of the Hindu Shasters, became the starting-point of Hurripunt's doubts in regard to Hinduism, and led eventually to his conversion. The same scientific knowledge was communicated by him to his brother, Narayan, and with like results. Narayan's first earnest question seems to have been, "What proof have you that the world is round, and that it has no such support as is mentioned in the Hindu Shasters?" alluding to the old legend that the earth rests on the head of a huge elephant, the elephant on a tortoise, and the tortoise on an endless snake.

In reply to this question of Narayan, Mr. Ballantine says: "Hurripunt directed him for proof to the sun, moon, and stars, all vast globes like the earth, which evidently had no such support; and on that point his mind was soon satisfied. But he immediately began to make other inquiries on the subject of religion. On learning this account from Hurripunt," Mr. B. continues, "I could not but be struck with the power and grace of God as exhibited in Narayan's state of mind. *His attention had been fixed, and his inquiries directed to these subjects far away from us, and from the usual means of grace.*"

That is, he was a *heathen teacher* in a mission school some twelve miles from any missionary, and even the monthly examination of his school was taken by his brother, a *heathen superintendent* of these schools, and thus, in the good providence of God, these humble schools became the direct means of bringing both these brothers to a knowledge and belief of the truth as it is in Jesus. Both became convinced, resolved to abandon idol-worship and walk according to the truth. And then came the trial. Parents and friends appealed unceasingly to their strong filial and natural affections, and when this proved unavailing they called in the aid of the most influential priests, the heads of their caste. A crowd of Brahmans assembled before the brothers were up, "and stopping them as they came out, began to rebuke them for forsaking the worship of idols." They offered no arguments to prove that the Christian religion was false and the Hindu system true, but asked them whether they alone were wiser than all others, and told them: "When you see us beginning to worship the invisible God, then you may do so, but do not attempt to know more than your betters." They also required them to leave our service immediately, and promised them the same salary we were giving them. They also threatened to expose them to public disgrace unless they returned to their religion. But neither threats nor promises were of any avail.

The Brahmans then appealed to the missionaries, urging them to dismiss Hurripunt and Narayan from their service, and when this failed, they urged that they might be given up to them, and they would convince them in two or three days that it was wrong to forsake Hinduism. When this, too, failed, the indignation of the Brahmans increased. They threatened to take away Hurripunt by force. Night was approaching. Crowds of Brahmans filled the room, and pressed around the doors. Hurripunt saw his danger, stepped out a moment to speak with his mother, sprang up a narrow stone stairway to the upper story of the missionary's dwelling, and thus eluded the grasp of the enemy.

"From this time," says Mr. B., "he always remained the same. And the more we saw of him the more did we feel satisfied that he was indeed a child of God born again of the Spirit. He never seemed to doubt for one moment the propriety of the step which he had taken, nor wish to return to his people and his idols."

In the account of these conversions we have striking evidence of the influence of our schools in the estimation of the priests. Mr. B. goes on to say:

"In consequence of these things the Brahmans held a great council, and decreed that none of their caste should engage in the service of the mission, *or send children to the schools*, or even visit the houses of the missionaries, on pain of expulsion from the order."

Three of the schools were broken up by this decree and opposition, and the Brahman pundits and teachers left the service of the mission. But this wrath of the priests defeated its own object. So many pundits and teachers were obliged to leave good service by these arbitrary decrees that it soon produced a reäction. They complained of the decrees as unwarrantable, and soon effected a division of sentiment, and returned again to their employment.

Hurripunt was baptized on the 14th of April, and Narayan on the 5th of May, 1839, and both are now native preachers in the Ahmednuggur mission, Hurripunt being an ordained pastor of one of the churches. In his own account of his conversion, speaking of the influence upon his mind of the Christian truth he was required to teach in his school, he says:

"When placed over a school I taught the boys those things which they were required to learn from the school-books because it was my business to do so, and not because I thought the instruction entitled to regard. Some things, indeed, I regarded as true, but others as ridiculous. Of the ten commandments the six last I thought excellent, but not so the four first. . . . After some days I began to think that God was without form, as represented in the books which I was teaching, but I thought also that idols partook in some way or other of the divine nature. About that time a wealthy native, of most respectable character, residing near, was accustomed to come to the school-house, and would ask me to read to him some of the stories in the school-books. At different times I read to him the whole story of 'Henry and his Bearer,' and he assented to every thing contained in that book, declaring it was all correct, but that Hindu customs were so different, it was difficult for any one to forsake idolatry. I was not at that time prepared to go so far in giving assent to what I read."

This statement brings to view one happy way in which these schools extend Christian truth, and which I fear is not sufficiently understood. Their utility in communicating Christian knowledge is by no means limited to the pupils and teachers. These repeat the truths they hear and read to their parents, neighbors, and friends, and these truths become the common property of the village, or a circle of villages, and go on extending themselves indefinitely. The influence of true science on Hurripunt's mind is thus attested by himself:

"Many days passed along without any change in my feelings. At length I began to learn something of the principles of geography and astronomy, and soon perceived evident proof that the Hindu writings contain many things false on these subjects. I soon understood that the sun, moon, and stars were no gods, and that all the stories related of them in our Shasters are mere fictions. At that time, leaving the company of pundits and puntojes, (teachers,) I determined to study more of mathematics and natural philosophy, in order to satisfy myself on this subject."

These two brothers still live to bear witness to the blessed and saving results of their being employed in the mission as *heathen* teachers.

Conversion of Radhabae.

The wife of Narayan immediately deserted him on his becoming a Christian, and took with her their little children. Narayan made many and persevering efforts to recover them but in vain. In Hindu law he was dead to her, and his civil rights were at that time all ignored.

But Hurripunt was more successful in gradually enlightening the mind of his wife, Radhabae, before his own baptism, and at length succeeded in leading her to a knowledge and belief of the truth. She was bitterly opposed at first, but the missionaries say: "New circumstances occurred which tended gradually to allay her irritated feelings. *Not the least of these circumstances was her learning to read.* At first the very thought of learning was abhorrent to her, but she found herself thrown in the midst of a circle where most of those around her were capable of reading, and apparently finding a constant source of pleasure in their various studies. After a short time she was induced to begin to learn, and to her praise it should be said, she was remarkably regular in her daily tasks. She soon succeeded in mastering what seemed to her at first great difficulties, and in the course of a few months she was able to read the Bible intelligently."

When she became so far convinced of the truth as to remove the heathen mark from her forehead, her heathen friends immediately gave vent to their anger and contempt. She bore it all meekly, and told them she had laid it aside as she intended to become a Christian. Some one asked her if she was forced to become a Christian, when she replied that she had heard for herself, and believed that salvation was to be found only in Jesus Christ. Her gentle firmness soon silenced all opposition."

Hurripunt, our oldest native pastor, and Radhabae, his worthy Christian wife, with a large and interesting family of children growing up around them, three or four of whom are already members of the Church, are they not a living rebuke to every murmur against the employment of heathen teachers in our mission schools?

Conversion of Marooti.

The conversion of the heathen teachers already mentioned was soon followed by others, among whom, in 1842, was a young Hindu of the cultivator caste named Marooti. In narrating his case Mr. Ballantine says: "He was *at first a scholar in one of our town schools.* He afterwards entered the seminary, and continued there several months. . . Then he became the teacher of a school in a small village about eight miles from here. From the time of his going to take charge of that school he forsook idolatry, and *he taught his boys also that idolatry was wrong.* After a while he began to pray. Still he had no idea of coming out and being baptized. The difficulties in the way appeared too great. But as he learned more he saw that he must acknowledge Jesus before men as well as believe on him in his heart. It was some months after he began to pray before he determined to avow his belief in Jesus Christ before the world. A few weeks ago he came and expressed a desire to be admitted into the Church as soon as circumstances would allow. . . Yesterday, after being baptized, his parents came and exhibited the greatest grief. The poor mother threatened to kill herself."

Marooti had not dared to speak openly in favor of Christianity until he had actually embraced it and publicly renounced idolatry. Mr. B. says: "He feared for his safety in case he should do so. But now he fears no longer. He has come to live in Hurripunt's family, and is employed, as he has been some weeks past, in teaching the girls' boarding-school, where his influence is good."

We need not dwell on the moral of this case. The simple statements of the missionary bring clearly to view the *heathen school* in which he was first a pupil, and his employment as a *heathen* teacher when the Spirit of God led him to a full understanding of the truth, and to avow his faith in Jesus. The following pages show that he was not only a heathen teacher, but also a heathen superintendent of all the free schools. He now ranks among the native preachers of the Ahmednuggur mission.

Conversion of Ramkrishnapunt.

Another heathen teacher converted the same year was Ramkrishnapunt, a young Brahman priest. He had been brought up in the city of Poona, seventy miles from Ahmednuggur, and in early childhood was a playmate of the notorious Nana Sahib, the leader of the late Sepoy rebellion in India. Wishing to employ another heathen teacher, the missionaries at Ahmednuggur wrote to Major Candy, the Superindendent of the Poona Sanscrit College, who sent them Ramkrishnapunt. He came with decided and almost contemptuous dislike of the missionaries, but consented to undertake the service for the sake of the small remuneration. Giving a brief account of him Mr. B. wrote:

"When he first came he appeared very haughty in his manner, and none of us probably thought that his mind would be easily brought under the influence of the truth. But God seeth not as man seeth. This young man was sent out to a large place about twelve miles distant to take charge of a school. He continued there several months, coming in once a month, according to our rule, to receive his pay and attend the Sabbath instructions. While there, away from us, his mind was excited to deep reflection on the things of religion. He was led to think of the folly of worshipping idols by conversation with a Kubeerpunthee, a heretical Hindu, who teaches that all the incarnations and idols of Hinduism are false, and that God alone should be worshipped. Thus he came to see some of the errors of Hinduism, and was convinced that the system of Kubeer was much more correct than that which he had hitherto believed. He then began to compare it with what he read in the Christian school-books which he was daily teaching. He was astonished to find that Christianity agreed with the system of Kubeer, but he also found that it differed from it in some things, and on further reflection he thought Christianity better than either of the other two.

"While in this state of mind Marooti, the other young man, who was superintendent of Mr. A.'s schools as well as teacher of his own school, came along to examine Ramkrishnapunt's school, and began to talk with him about the excellency of the Christian religion. Ramkrishnapunt agreed with him entirely, and said that if Marooti would become a Christian he would follow after soon. Still they both felt difficulties, and they had not courage to speak to any one of us about their own feelings.

"But Ramkrishnapunt's difficulties soon vanished, and he came to Mr. Abbott and told him he wished to become a Christian. He also opened his mind freely to Hurripunt, who was astonished to hear him speak as he did, and thought he could not be in earnest. But he soon learned the truth of the case. Ramkrishnapunt soon began to come to his house, to eat with him, and spend his evenings with him, sitting up often until eleven o'clock reading the Scriptures together, and talking about the things of religion. A short time before Marooti decided to become a Christian openly he met Ramkrishnapunt, and asked him what his feelings were now. Ramkrishnapunt said that all his difficulties had vanished, that he cared not now whether Marooti came with him or not, so far as himself was concerned, that he was determined to be a Christian. He was indeed desirous to obtain his wife before being baptized, as he had no hope of getting her afterwards, and he accordingly went to Poona two or three months ago for this object. But his friends there, learning his intention to become a Christian, confined him, and would not even let him return to Ahmednuggur."

Ramkrishnapunt had been married by his parents to a little girl much younger than himself, and he had never seen her since. He failed of obtaining her on this occasion, and his wish to do so was doubtless more for her sake than his own, as he knew that, child as she was, she would be condemned to perpetual widowhood on his becoming a Christian, with all the attendant servility and disgrace which make the Hindu widow an object of much commiseration. But his efforts to obtain her only resulted in his own confinement, and it was not till he found an opportunity to communicate with the English gentleman who first recommended him to the mission, that he was able to get released. The case was then brought at once to the notice of a magistrate, Ramkrishnapunt released, and a government soldier sent to see him safe from harm on his way to Ahmednuggur.

On reaching the mission again, he came out openly as a Christian and received baptism, counting all things else as worthless, that he might win Christ and be found in him. Persecutions came upon him. When his parents and friends found that they could not reclaim him to Hinduism, they performed his funeral ceremonies and called him dead, and his civil rights were ignored by law. But he had counted the cost, and has remained steadfast ever since. Having failed to obtain his infant wife, his heathen marriage was set aside, and Ramkore, the interesting girl who would have none but a Christian husband, and who, with her mother, had been the first-fruits of the girls' boarding-school, subsequently became his wife. They have several interesting children, and a happy, useful family they are, he being the most able native pastor we have in Western India, and she in every respect a help-meet for her husband.

The spirit of this native pastor may be inferred from the following brief extract from one of his letters. After giving me a lengthy and graphic account of the massacre of native Christians, and the horrors of the mutiny, while in the height of its power and progress, he adds:

"Some of the native soldiers in this presidency, too, are likely to mutiny. We thank God for his mercy in keeping us hitherto in quiet and safety, while our brethren at the north are suffering such horrible persecutions. Yet we do not know what will take place in a few days. Perhaps we also may be called to share the same fate, and we are trying to be prepared for it, if so be the will of our Father in heaven—firmly believing that if *all of us* are sacrificed, it will all result in good to us and to the Church of God. If such is his will, may we be prepared to stand firm in faith, and testify to his Gospel in our death as well as in life."

Let those who are troubled with any apprehensions about the propriety of such mission schools, and of employing heathen teachers, trace again the history of this happy family, from the time that the heathen mother took this little girl by the hand to prosecute their lone wanderings back to their distant village, in the dense darkness of heathenism, and her steps were arrested by hearing of the mission school for little girls. Let them trace the providence of God in the case of the husband—a haughty, self-conceited Brahman, placed in charge of a school twelve miles from the missionaries, and only seeing them once a month, when he visited Ahmednuggur—he a *heathen teacher*, and the monthly examination of his school even being taken by a *heathen superintendent*. If the employment of heathen teachers is ever of doubtful policy, what more hopeless circumstances can be adduced in the whole history of missions? And yet it pleased God to make this agency the means of bringing both teacher and superintendent to a knowledge and belief of the truth—resulting in case of this haughty young priest, in making him one of the brightest lights and most effective laborers among all the native converts connected with the missions of the American Board in Western India. His influence was promptly and signally manifest in the conversion of his own brother, Vishnupunt, the following year.

Conversion of Ramchunder.

Next followed the conversion of Ramchunder, another heathen teacher in the service of the mission at Seroor. In giving some account of him, the missionary, Mr. French, rejoices that the same class of teachers, for whose conversion the divine blessing had been so signally bestowed at the other stations, was affected in like manner by the Christian truth they were required to teach in his schools. Mr. F. writes:

"On the first Sabbath in July [1843] I was permitted to receive into the visible church of Christ, the first convert from heathenism at this station. His name is Ramchunder. He belongs to the Brahman caste, and is about forty years of age. On my occupying this station, I took his school under my care, and he has ever since remained in my employment.

"From his first connection with the mission, he has regularly attended our public services on the Sabbath, *and daily taught our Christian books in his school.* The influence of the truth thus brought before his mind had doubtless an important bearing, though his inquiries were not awakened till about four months since. From that time light began to dawn upon his dark mind; he lost all confidence in Hinduism, threw away the little *pebble* he had formerly worshipped, and began to seek in earnest for a better way. He soon became convinced that Christianity was the only true religion, and Jesus Christ the only Saviour of sinners. As his inquiries advanced his difficulties disappeared, his mind became settled, and he entered upon the practice of Christian duties, at first with much diffidence, but soon with great delight. He was baptized at the chapel on Sabbath morning, in the presence of more people than could get into the house, among whom were some of the principal men of the place."

In the afternoon his three children were baptized, and the missionary and native converts gathered around the table of the Lord. "It was a precious season," says Mr. F.; "in view of what our eyes have beheld, we feel ourselves called upon to rejoice in the Lord, who has remembered us in our feebleness, and visited us with his mercy."

Conversion of Dajeeba, Shiveram, and other Heathen Teachers.

In gathering up the records of heathen teachers converted in this mission, they crowd upon us too numerous for detail. One missionary writes: "The teacher of the boys' boarding-school is anxious to be baptized, and appears remarkably well."

Another reports two heathen teachers baptized and admitted to the Church, one of them a female employed in the girls' boarding-school.

Siddu was baptized and received to church-fellowship at Seroor, while employed as a teacher at an out-station, though he had been educated in the boarding-schools. He is now a native preacher.

Dajeeba, who has been for many years a native assistant, was long employed as a heathen teacher, and thus came to know and believe the truth.

Shiveram was first a pupil, and then the heathen teacher whose pupils threw away the idols, and subsequently pulled down a heathen temple. His meek bearing and persistent affection under the cruel treatment and persecution of his father, a bigoted old priest, finally softened the old man's heart, and led him to feel that the Gospel, which had wrought such a wonderful change in his son, must have elements different from Hinduism. When the old priest first came to me, it was to tell me this conviction, and how Shiveram had meekly borne his abuse for five long years; and he begged to know what there was in the Christian religion which gave it *such* power. He followed me some six months, much of the time travelling with me from village to village, as I went on preaching-tours—always present at my preaching services, and morning and evening prayers; and I shall not soon forget the occasion, after a season of prayer with him, when, bursting into tears, he avowed his faith in the crucified Jesus, and pulling his priestly badge from his neck, begged me to keep it as a memento, alike of his heathen ignorance and superstition, and of the blessed power of the Gospel of Christ. The dear old priest was baptized, and lived and died a Christian. I still keep his old brass badge, and many dear children in our Sabbath-schools will remember it. He, I doubt not, has found a better badge, even the robe of Christ's righteousness, pure and white.

Which case marks most signally the blessing of God on our schools—that of this heathen teacher, or of his old father, the priest? Oh! that dear friends in Christian lands could understand how Heaven's own seal is stamped on these schools! Well and truthfully have our brethren of the Ahmednuggur mission testified, in their Annual Report of 1855: "OUR NATIVE PASTORS AND MOST EFFICIENT LABORERS WERE ORIGINALLY HEATHEN SCHOOL-TEACHERS, AND IN THIS WAY WERE BROUGHT UNDER THE INFLUENCE OF TRUTH, AND CONVERTED."

Schools opposed by the Heathen.

The earnest opposition of the natives to our schools was briefly brought to view in the history of the Bombay mission. The same opposition appears at every stage of progress in the Ahmednuggur mission. When the two Brahman teachers were baptized in 1839, several schools were broken up by this opposition.

In 1843 the priests threatened to put Mr. French's teachers out of caste, if they did not leave his service, and succeeded in breaking up three or four of his schools. Mr. F. says: "The great charge brought against them, was that of teaching the rising generation those books which contained principles at variance with their own religion. I do not wonder that the advocates of Hinduism become alarmed, in view of the tendency of our *schools*."

Regretting the loss of these schools, and the want of funds to establish more, Mr. F. writes: "Nearly 200 youth are thrown beyond the reach of Christian instruction. And not only this, the access which these schools gave us to the people generally of those villages, is closed. The suspension of these schools materially affects my operations, and is an event much to be regretted."

When Ramkore and her three associates in the girls' boarding-school were baptized, it was the signal for a vigorous assault on the schools. Many of the older pupils were removed, and most of the other schools also suffered from this opposition.

Again we read, in the report of the Board: "From the girls' boarding-school two pupils, in respect to whom our brethren have indulged the hope that they would, at no distant day, profess Christ before men, were removed by their parents to prevent their becoming Christians. One of them subsequently returned, begging that she might be allowed to remain with the missionaries, and also asking for baptism. Soon, however, her parents came in pursuit of her, and, by many fair promises, they succeeded in inducing her to accompany them. Having once got her in their power, they were careful not to allow her to return. In a few days we learned that they had beaten her severely, on her returning home, and had immediately sent her to a village fifty or sixty miles distant. We hope, however, that even there the poor girl will be enabled to put her trust in the Saviour."

When Rama and Sudu, pupils of the seminary, were baptized, the Hindus took alarm, and many of the good-caste scholars were withdrawn from that and the other schools. "Some young Brahmans were very reluctant to give up the privileges they enjoyed in the school, but they found themselves unable to resist the efforts made to remove them." The missionaries comfort themselves with the thought: "They have learned enough, perhaps, to make them wise unto salvation."

Through all the history of our missions, no department of our labors has elicited so much opposition from the heathen as our schools. Why is this? The enemy never take trouble to destroy blank cartridge, or spike guns that are already useless.

Converts from the Seminary.

Some account has already been given of the mission seminary at Ahmednuggur — the anxious desire of the home officers to establish it, the votes they passed, and the care with which they fostered it through the first ten years of its existence, without one convert being gathered in from its pupils.

The care of this seminary was the first mission work put

upon me by my brethren—the day after I reached Ahmednuggur in 1846. I entered upon it with deep interest, but interest which constantly increased during all the years of my connection with the school. The religious interest in the seminary was marked, and we were soon permitted to see joyful results of our labors in it.

Conversion of Rama Bhore.

Soon after taking charge of the seminary, I became much interested in a young lad of about 16 years, by the name of Rama. He was foremost among the pupils in showing his disregard of idolatry. I soon selected him as the beneficiary of the "MALONE JUVENILE MISSIONARY SOCIETY" of little girls, who had pledged me $20 a year, to educate a heathen boy. And they fulfilled their promise every year I was in India, some years doubling, and even trebling the amount.

Rama rapidly developed a thorough knowledge and conviction of the truth. His views of the just desert of sin and the way of salvation by Christ were specially clear and satisfactory, and he soon resolved to take his stand on the side of Christ. He was baptized Dec. 13th, 1846, and belonging to a family of Patils, or head men in his village, his baptism caused much excitement. His brothers and widowed mother came in great haste, and tried their utmost to persuade him to return with them. He declined, knowing they would force him to acts of idolatry or keep him in confinement. His poor mother used many entreaties, beseeching him not to destroy himself, and bring perpetual disgrace on his family. In the anguish of her feelings, she beat her head upon the ground, and threatened to destroy herself. It was touching to witness the tenderness with which Rama begged her to refrain from weeping, though his own face was bathed in tears, and affirming his desire to secure the salvation of his own soul, urged her too, to come with him and be a Christian.

The scene soon brought together a large and excited mob, who seemed resolved to take Rama away from our protection by force. We reported the danger to the British magistrate, who came at once with a party of police, and took Rama to his court. None of the missionaries were permitted to accompany him, but some of our native converts followed, and reported to us the public confession of this young disciple, and the noble firmness with which he stood up for Jesus in that heathen court. No questions of the magistrate confused him, no appeal to his affection for his mother even induced him to waver in his purpose; and being of age (16 years) by Hindu law, there was but one decision possible. He was restored to the mission, and the mob dispersed.

For years Rama remained under my immediate direction, as a teacher and native assistant, and never have I known a more industrious, faithful, conscientious young Christian, in any land. It was his fixed purpose, during all those years, to become a native preacher, and aid us in our labors; but when the Secretary and Committee abolished our seminary, Rama felt, with others, that he *must* have a more liberal education; and leaving our mission, he entered the Institution of our Scotch Free Church brethren in Bombay.

Suddu.

The second convert from the pupils of this seminary was Suddu, an interesting young man, originally of the Mahar caste, and still laboring as a native preacher in Western India. Of these two converts the missionaries wrote in their report: "These were the first-fruits of our labors in the seminary in the way of conversion, but we hope they will not be the last."

This hope has been realized. Within six months from the date of these baptisms, we find one of the missionaries writing: "Some of the more promising scholars in the seminary are evidently in an inquiring state of mind. Two or three weeks ago, a Brahman lad came to me and expressed his full conviction of the truth of Christianity, and that Jesus Christ is the only Saviour. He wished to be a Christian, and hoped Jesus would convert his mind. But he has met with the greatest opposition."

Amrooti and his Mother.

One of the early converts of the seminary was Amrooti, a young Hindu, like Rama, of the cultivator caste, and whose case, like that of Ramkore, illustrates the influence of the schools in gathering adult inquirers and converts. Amrooti's mother came to live near her son, and prepare his daily food, and in this way she, too, came to know and believe the Gospel, and was baptized and received to the Church, some time before her son was.

Conversion of Daood, (David.)

This young man was both a student and teacher in the seminary — hearing the lessons of some classes and reciting himself in others. Some account of him at the time of his conversion, is as follows:

"One of the teachers in the seminary, whom we have regarded as one of the most promising young men about us, came to me the other day saying that he had determined to forsake his wicked ways and be a Christian. He is eighteen or twenty years of age, and a Mussulman by birth. From a pretty free conversation closed with prayer in which he took part, he really appeared like a renewed man. He expressed a determination, after some delay, to ask for baptism. The Lord only knows whether he will endure to the end." "Other members of the seminary are evidently in an interesting state of mind. Oh! that we could have a powerful effusion of the Spirit in this school! Will not our friends remember us in their prayers?"

Daood was baptized in the autumn of 1847, and the hearts of all in the mission rejoiced at this event. Some account of him may be found in the *Missionary Herald* for December, 1847. He was a young man of much ability and promise, and we hoped much from his assistance in our work. But Christians will know better how to sympathize with their brethren toiling in heathen lands—tremblingly hoping and praying and striving to encourage such converts—when they learn that the persecution and trials which the friends of this young man brought upon him, were so severe, that he very soon renounced his faith in Christ, and went back to the false prophet. But his conscience had become too much enlightened to give him peace. Sad and sorrowful were the years he passed in this unhappy state; and at length, like Peter, he wept bitterly over his sin, and returned to his Saviour. It is a remarkable circumstance that during the period of his apostasy, the black leprosy developed itself in his system, and marked him for its certain victim. It would probably be impossible to convince the native converts who knew him, that this was not a direct judgment of God upon him for denying Christ. It was with many tears that he eventually sought and obtained restoration to the privileges of the Church, and hearty and unreserved seemed the subsequent consecration of himself to Christ and his service. His last years were full of usefulness. His efforts were untiring to make known Christ, and persuade his countrymen to believe in him. He died about a year since, full of hope and faith, "joyfully looking to Jesus."

Vyenkutrao.

Soon after I took charge of the seminary, in 1846, I noticed one morning, a new pupil. His dress marked him as a Brahman priest, and I soon found that he had come from the city of Mominabad, ninety miles distant in another province. He had heard of our seminary, and had come with a wish to learn English and the sciences. He was welcomed to the school. His progress was rapid, and in a few months his fixed attention, and an occasional tear, hastily brushed away, revealed the effect of Christian truth on his heart.

But the wily Brahmans discovered his state of mind as quickly as I did, and took measures to apprize his distant parents and friends. They came at once, and with mingled affection and authority succeeded in removing him from our influence. We had watched him with increasing interest, hoped and prayed that he might soon become a "chosen vessel," and our disappointment now was keen. But w could not prevent it, and he returned with his friends, t Mominabad.

After some months, however, much to our joy, he ap peared again. His love for study and attachment to th seminary, brought him back. Some love and conviction c the truth, may, even then, have influenced him. Be thi as it may, his convictions rapidly revived, and he develop ed an impressibility to truth and a tenderness of conscienc very rare among the Brahmans of India. Again our hope revived, but again his friends brought their arts and influ ence to bear upon him, and removed him from the school.

He went and came several times, his convictions deepen ing, and the evidence of a work of grace in his heart, be coming more unmistakable. The duty of confessing Chris before men pressed heavily on his heart, and the great hin drance was his affection for his friends. It was a trial t lose caste and inheritance, and subject himself to the scor of all who knew him. But the severest trial was to giv up his mother, and a young wife, between whom and him self there was rare mutual affection. His anxiety to en lighten her mind and win her to Christ was intense. Bu every effort to do this alarmed her fears, when she woul leave him and return to her friends. During this perio my sympathies were so moved that I seldom urged upo him the duty of publicly professing Christ, but as he wa almost daily in my room to read the Bible and pray wit me, I would sometimes turn to Matt. 10 : 32–39. At suc times his troubled look and gushing tears marked the strug gle within, and his feelings would find utterance in th words: "Yes, I must, I *must* give up all for Christ."

The struggle was long and severe, but at length grace tr umphed. Giving an account of his baptism at the time, th missionary says: "He was baptized last Sabbath, and ha thus far witnessed a good confession. A crowd of violen Brahmans assailed him immediately after the morning ser vice, and pressed him so hard that he took refuge in ou house. They again interrupted our communion-service in ıe afternoon, and we were obliged to call in assistance from ıe magistrate to keep them quiet."

"A severer trial is still pending for this young disciple. iis parents will soon hear of his apostasy from Hinduism, nd will hasten, with mingled rage and affection, to tear im from us. They can not restore him to caste; but havıg him once in their power, they can doom him to a life of isgrace and sorrow, and prevent any active efforts by him ı the cause of Christ. Pray for him that he may have race to endure to the end, and may be delivered from the iles of the adversary."

The fears which were foreshadowed in this paragraph ere soon and painfully realized. Vyenkutrao's parents and iends came in great haste, and contrary to the usual policy . such cases, instead of coming directly to us and gathering n excited mob, which would have served to alarm him and ut him on his guard, at the same time enabling us to repel em by aid of the civil magistrates, they encamped at a stance in the city and commenced their weeping and laıentations, sending to their son the most touching entreat-s to come and see them "*once more.*"

Vyenkutrao was much agitated, bursting into tears with ı exhibition of strong filial affection. His natural feelıgs impelled him strongly to go, but after a season of conersation and prayer he seemed strengthened, and resolved avoid the peril. At length his feelings were so wrought pon that with a party of native Christians and some govnment peons, he went and had an interview with his iends. There was much weeping on both sides, and earn-t entreaties were made by the parents and brothers that e would go back with them to Mominabad. After two or ree anxious hours the party returned and we blessed God r the deliverance.

But soon all our anxieties were again painfully aroused. ı the evening his parents sent pressing entreaties for him come and see them "once more." Vyenkutrao wept nd begged to be allowed to go; but after another season f prayer he seemed strengthened and resolute to endure the trial and refuse another interview. But in the morn ing his feelings again overcame him. New messages cam(from his mother, representing that she was sick nigh untc death, and appealing to his affection in most touching terms. Taking two or three Christian friends with him, he hastenec to his mother. The native converts were not allowed t(enter the house with him, and the Hindus, who kept be· tween them and the door, soon increased to hundreds. The converts were alarmed for Vyenkutrao's safety, anc ran back to inform me. I hastened to the magistrate and begged his interference. It was difficult to persuade him that the case demanded his attention, but after some delay, leisurely calling two peons, he bade them go to the localit) indicated and see what was transpiring.

I waited their return with anxiety which I could not re press. They came at length, and very coolly reported tha' the party had taken their horses, and providing one fo) young Vyenkutrao, they hastily departed taking him witl them. This roused the magistrate a little, and calling : party of police he bade them pursue the fugitives and brin; them all back. They started off with much apparent hast and eagerness to execute their orders, but they were Hir dus, and would feel far more sympathy with Vyenkutrao' friends than with him or us.

I will not attempt to describe the intense anxiety and th(many prayers with which our hearts followed that dea: young man. The party of police returned the next day, re porting that they had pursued with all possible haste, bu had been unable to overtake the fugitives till they passec beyond British rule into the territories of a native prince and they did not feel at liberty to pursue further.

Our hearts sank within us. We thought of the dange) lest, under the pressure of trials and persecutions, he shoulc renounce his faith in Christ and return to the idols; or, if he should remain firm, there were the long years of con· finement and persecution till his spirit should be broken and his usefulness, if not his life, be destroyed. In pub· lishing an account of this convert at the time, the editor of the *Missionary Herald* well remarked: "A perusal of the extracts which follow, will enable the friends of missions to understand and appreciate the trials through which many are obliged to pass in heathen lands, on avowing themselves the disciples of the Lord Jesus Christ. Nor is this all. Some will possess a better idea, after reading this communication, of the disappointments and griefs to which missionaries are occasionally subjected."

For three long months we could get no tidings of Vyenkutrao. But the Lord took care of him. He was placed in close confinement by his friends and subjected to much persecution. Idols were placed in his presence and daily efforts made to induce him to deny Christ and return to the faith of his fathers. But young Vyenkutrao remained firm to his faith, trusting in God. At length, under his hard fare and close confinement, his health so gave way that the sympathies of his mother were moved in his behalf, and he was allowed to walk out a few minutes each day in the open air, with a faithful Hindu at his side to keep constant watch of him. On one of these walks he met an Indo-Briton, and exchanged a few words in English which his Hindu attendant could not understand. The next day, on his usual walk, he went to the place assigned, threw off his Brahman dress and put on a suit of English furnished by the Indo-Briton, mounted his horse, and finding other horses posted for him on the road, he escaped as a bird from the snare of the fowler. His Hindu attendant ran to inform his parents and friends, and preparing their horses they pursued with all possible haste; but the few minutes' start and fresh horses on the way gave Vyenkutrao the advantage, and he reached us in safety. Let friends imagine, if they can, the joy of our hearts when this dear convert knocked at our gate at midnight, and sought our protection from his pursuers. The praying band gathered in the house of Mary could scarcely have been more affected when Peter knocked at their gate. (Acts 12 : 13.)

Vyenkutrao has proved a firm, earnest, and devoted Christian. So long as he remained in our mission he manifested a fixed purpose to become a preacher of the Gospel to his countrymen. When our mission seminary was interdicted and broken up, his earnest desire for education detached him from us. He left us with tears and much regret, and joined the institution of the Scotch Free Church mission in Bombay.

Vyenkutrao was the fifth interesting convert from this favored seminary. This school brought him to us, and when it was broken up he left us. My space will not allow me to narrate the conversions of Uma Thorat, Nama Christi, Dhondoo Sonar, Tubba Barsa and Guanoo Powar — five more of its pupils who were converted and baptized during my connection with it—or those of eight or a dozen more of my dear pupils in that school, who have since been baptized and received to the church, either in Ahmednuggur or elsewhere.

Guanoo Powar, the last mentioned, was a young man of much promise, and the second beneficiary of the "MALONE JUVENILE MISSIONARY SOCIETY." If the education and conversion of this one young Hindu were all the good the society had ever accomplished, it would be enough to make glad the hearts of the dear youth and children of that society forever.

Mr. M., reporting his admission to the Church at the time, wrote: "This lad is much loved by us all. No one could say any evil thing of him. The church in Malone, N. Y., has given him the name of their former pastor, and prayed for him. We hope he may some day proclaim to this people the story of the cross."

It was not the church, but this "MALONE JUVENILE MISSIONARY SOCIETY" which educated young Guanoo, and gave him the name of their venerated and much loved pastor, Rev. ASHBEL PARMELEE, D.D., who for fifty-three years has stood on the watch-towers of Zion in Northern New-York, preaching Christ with untiring fidelity and zeal, and with a strength of devotion and love which led him to exclaim, in a recent discourse before his Synod, that he would gladly accept a commission from his divine Master to continue preaching till the day of judgment! May a portion of his spirit rest on his Hindu namesake! Doubtless the church also prayed for this lad, and the Lord heard and answered. Let not such societies lose their confidence or waver in their support of schools and beneficiaries in heathen lands. The funds they contribute and the prayers they offer for such schools and heathen youth, have been owned of God. These schools have shared in special blessings and yielded precious fruit to the praise of his glory and grace. Truly thankful shall we be if the missionary ship, or any other object which can be presented for the gifts of the young, ever furnishes a tithe of the blessed results which have already accrued from mission schools. Young "Ashbel Parmelee" is now a preacher of the Gospel to his countrymen.

Will the reader recall the history of this seminary? Bear in mind that it was sustained ten years without one convert, and at two or three times the annual expense it was incurring when abolished; and that the tone of religious interest and feeling was constantly and rapidly increasing. In 1849 we find notices of this seminary in the *Missionary Herald*, as follows: "The seminary for boys in Ahmednuggur contains fifty-four pupils, and is under the care of Mr. Wilder. . . . It is in a very interesting state at the present time. Five of the pupils have expressed much solicitude to Mr. W. respecting their spiritual condition; and three have professed to believe in the Lord Jesus Christ, one of them having privately broken caste."

In December, 1849, the editor of the *Herald* thus introduces a letter describing the increasing interest in this seminary.

"The following extract from a letter of Mr. Wilder will be read with interest. It will awaken gratitude, and should call forth fervent prayer."

The letter is as follows:

"Just at present we have much to encourage us from the increasing religious interest in the seminary. A little band of five or six Christian youth, most of them connected with the seminary, have long been accustomed to meet me in my study one evening in a week, to pray for the youth connected with our schools. These meetings have gradually increased in interest, and the earnest prayers of some show true anxiety for the salvation of souls; and though we rejoice with trembling, yet we have the joy of feeling that some mercy-drops are descending.

"Some weeks ago, one young man in the seminary came, voluntarily, to converse about his soul. He repeated his visits, evincing a most gratifying earnestness, and soon there came another and another, and the number has now increased to *five.* Three of them profess true repentance and faith in Christ, and ask to be received into the Church. One has privately broken caste, and thus given proof of his firm purpose to renounce heathenism.

"The state of feeling in the seminary is so marked as to be quite observable to all who are praying for this object. One of our native preachers yesterday remarked that he thought this must be what we meant by a revival. Had we a different state of society we might hope, with the blessing of God, soon to see the whole school share in it, manifesting a deep and general interest for the salvation of their souls. As it is, we feel the most trembling solicitude. Of the five who come to me so frequently, no two are aware of each other's feelings. They come singly, and late at night, each supposing himself alone in his anxiety about his soul. Christians in America might suppose this to result from improper fear, and want of courage to confess Christ before men. But they will think differently when they know that the mere suspicion of these young men's state of feeling would lead their parents to remove them forcibly from our school and influence, and do all in their power to prevent them from ever professing Christ. It is this fact which dictates caution. Were the feelings and purposes of these youth known beyond the gates of our compounds, a sad excitement would result. The whole city would be in an uproar. The consequences would be fatal to our hopes in regard to others, if not, indeed, in regard to those already anxious; and many interesting youth would be removed forever from the reach of our influence. This state of things, rightly viewed, will give you a correct impression of the painful caution and extreme anxiety, to which we are constantly subjected in all our direct labors for the salvation of souls. (It should be understood that these remarks refer to the conversion of those of good caste. When Mahars are converted, there is no excitement. Few notice or care about it.) We have now quite a number of promising and well-educated youth in our seminary, whose consciences are enlightened and convinced of the truth, and who seem balancing the momentous question, hesitating whether they will yield to conscience, and the claims of God's word, or go back to the darkness of idolatry, or choose the third alternative and become absolute infidels. This third class is daily increasing in India, and we must expect it as an unavoidable result of an increase of knowledge, unsanctified and unaccompanied by that truth which alone can make wise unto salvation. Could we speak to your circles of praying Christians, we would say: Pray, pray earnestly that the Spirit of God may come and consecrate this talent, and save these precious souls. We have great hope that there is mercy in store for us, and that the faithful labors of so many years in this seminary are not to be without precious fruit."

And again at a later date:

"I wrote you in July, giving some little account of the religious interest in the seminary. The correctness of what I then stated, in regard to the extreme anxiety we are compelled to feel, about all good-caste youth who begin to manifest concern for their souls, has since been painfully verified. During our recent meeting, it was thought advisable to baptize one of the young men to whom I then alluded. His case is mentioned in the minutes of our meeting. He is a Koonbe of respectable talents, and we hope that God will make him greatly useful to his countrymen. His father is connected with the army, and all his friends, just now, are several hundred miles distant. On this account, we had reason to expect less excitement at his baptism, and besides, he was received into the Church in the middle of a vacation in the seminary From both circumstances combined, we hoped the event might pass without causing so much alarm as usual, to the seminary scholars. But such events do not take place without being known, and exciting commotion, among these hosts of idolaters. The young men themselves are not alarmed; but their parents are, and wish to remove them, at once and entirely, from our influence. The scholars are unwilling to leave us, and resort to entreaty, and sometimes deceive their parents, and continue to come under false pretenses. In the present case all have returned with the exception of three; but the only condition of their doing so, is that they be allowed to come as day-scholars. Not one remains in the compound. The parents of some are sadly alarmed; but we are much gratified to see the scholars appreciate their privileges and anxious to improve them. The religious interest among them increased steadily to the close of the term; and though they are now more reserved and cautious, yet I have good evidence that four or five still retain their convictions, and I trust they will, ere long, gain courage to give up all for Christ."

And well does the editor of the *Herald* add:

"Certainly prayer should be offered by Christians, not only for these young men, but for the missionary, who, at a time so critical, is their instructor."

Now, in view of the precious converts gathered in during the few last years of this seminary, and this increasing interest in it, was there not abundant reason to regard and cherish this institution with increasing favor? Commenced, as it was, at the express desire of the Secretary and Prudential Committee, though with the warm approval and coöperation of the missionaries, and commended through all its years of barrenness, how could it be otherwise than that all hearts should rejoice in the rich clusters of fruit it began to bear, and that they should foster it with increasing care?

Change of Policy, disparaging the Schools.

Strange to say, just at this juncture, when special blessings were resting on this seminary, a change of policy was developed in Boston, and a resolution taken to break up this promising school—to put out this "*eye of our mission.*" In 1845, when this seminary had been in operation nine or ten years at heavy expense and without a single convert, we find the Annual Report of the Board putting on record the following resolution:

"In regard to the mission at Ahmednuggur, your committee particularly notice the prosperous state of *the schools*, and the general interests of religion."

Of this very seminary the report says: "*It seems especially to call for commendation.*"

A similar resolution was recorded in the report of 1849, and the blessing of heaven was resting upon it and gathering its interesting and promising youth into the fold of Christ. In view of these facts, who can repress both grief and surprise at the sudden change of sentiment in regard to this seminary? In the Annual Report of 1851, we find the following:

"In this mission the boarding-schools, *of which the seminary at Ahmednuggur is one*, have not answered so valuable a purpose as to warrant a continued appropriation for their support"!

This change was sudden and suddenly enforced.

Dr. Anderson's Letter of May 10th, 1851.

In July, 1851, we received a letter from Dr. Anderson interdicting these schools, and removing Mr. Burgess at once, and Mr. Wilder after some delay, from Ahmednuggur, each to commence a new mission. In regard to the schools, the instructions were peremptory, as follows:

"1. The Prudential Committee have unanimously come to the conclusion, that they ought not to make appropriations, after the present year, for the support and continuance of the *seminary at Ahmednuggur.*

"2. As the committee see no proper use for *boarding-schools* at any of the stations, they will discontinue appropriations for such, after the present year.

"3. The Committee deem it their duty no longer to make appropriations for day-schools *taught by heathen masters*," etc.

It will be seen at a glance that this change was sudden and sweeping.

Action of the Mission.

How was it regarded by the missionaries? Did they show any disposition to disregard instructions? Far otherwise. Much as these instructions conflicted with their convictions and all their previous practice, and disastrous as they foresaw the results would be, they took prompt action in compliance with these instructions as follows:

"*Resolved*, That the allowance for food and clothing to scholars in the different boarding-schools be discontinued from the close of the present month.

"*Resolved*, That all free-schools taught by heathen teachers be discontinued from the close of the present month."

In view of this prompt action by the missionaries, and their readiness to obey instructions against their own convictions, may we not properly ask, what necessity for Deputations? Might not the unfortunate high-school in the Bombay mission have been interdicted in the same way in 1854, without involving so much expense of time and money in sending a Deputation for this purpose?

This summary action cut off the schools at a blow. It was modified a little, however, by subsequent action. The girls' schools under the care of Miss Farrar, though taught by *heathen teachers*, were made special exceptions. I knew that if the school at Newase should be disbanded it would cut off the connection of the native preacher with the people to a great extent, and render his longer residence there almost useless. I therefore begged my brethren to spare that school until I could represent the case and intercede for it with the Secretary and Committee in Boston. The brethren granted my request, and that school was spared and prospered till the Deputation suppressed it 1854.

Brother Hazen, too, begged the same favor for two or three of his schools taught by *heathen teachers* at Seroor, and his request was granted.

I made no effort to save the boarding character of the seminary, having gradually reduced that element till I felt prepared to try to retain the pupils by the inducement of *English* only. The great attraction to pupils of the higher castes had always been the privilege of learning English. And now, as our free-schools with heathen teachers were abandoned, this element of our seminary was our only effective link connecting us with the high castes. I therefore felt extremely anxious to retain this link unbroken, and as effective as possible.

Reduced Expense of the Seminary.

It may interest some minds to note the gradual and great reduction in the expense of this seminary its last six years. For its first ten years, its annual expense had been from Rs. 2000 to Rs. 3000. From 1842 to 1846, its annual expense, (including the primary department called the "Christian school,") as taken from the records of the mission treasurer, is as follows:

	1842.	1843.	1844.	1845.	1846.
	Rs.	Rs.	Rs.	Rs.	Rs.
Total expense,..........	2998	1925	2570	2749	1924

From 1846 to 1851, the period of my connection with it, the reduction of expense appears from the following items taken, as the above, from the records of the mission treasurer:

	1846.	1847.	1848.	1849.	1850.	1851.
Total expense,................	Rs. 1924	1311	1292	1349	1142	844
Number of pupils,................	49	80	80	82	63	83
Expense for board of pupils and incidentals,................	Rs. 1528	925	830	867	.687	389

The last row of figures shows what proportion of the entire expense went for the board of the pupils and the incidentals of the school, and how rapidly its boarding element was disappearing. Its boarding expense diminished more rapidly than its total expense, because in its first years native helpers were often employed in it as teachers, their salary being charged under the item of native helpers; but in the later years of the school, those helpers being removed to other duties, new teachers were employed, and their salaries charged to the seminary. With the eye upon the last row of figures, which indicate the boarding and incidental expense of the school, is it not manifest that a year or two more would have entirely removed its boarding character? There was much reason to hope, too, that by this *gradual* reduction the institution would lose nothing in the number and character of its pupils and still secure us valuable connection and influence with the young men of the higher castes.

The sudden suppression of its boarding character, gave an unhappy shock to the school, but anxious to save it if possible, I entreated my brethren to allow me to continue one lesson a day in English, and see if, by this alone, I could not retain these interesting youth under our Christian teaching. They granted my request for three or four months, till I should have time to urge my plea and hear again from Boston.

The result exceeded my most sanguine expectations. Instead of falling off, there was an actual increase, and the year closed with 83 pupils.

Reporting the seminary at this juncture, the *Missionary Herald* says:

"The seminary has from the first embraced many pupils from the higher castes. It was because of the difficulty of bringing such persons under the influence of the mission, that it was originally made a boarding-school. And this difficulty has been felt to such an extent, that heretofore a change has not been thought practicable. And even now we fully expected that many of the pupils would leave. But the school had in a measure become prepared for the change by a gradual diminution, for four or five years past, both of the allowance for board and of the number who received it; so that to our surprise more scholars have entered since the change than have left on account of it.

"The religious interest in the seminary has been such . . . as to encourage the hope that the convictions of several young men will prove deep and genuine, and ultimately result in a public profession of their faith in Christ. One of them indeed has made such a profession since the close of the year," and another in November.

Will it not be supposed that such pleasing results would have secured the perpetuity of this school? that the home officers seeing it able to go on and prosper without its boarding character, would rejoice in its success and withdraw their interdict? Oh! what a vantage-ground for good was here sacrificed. Anxiously we waited their permission to continue the school on this new foundation, but it came not, and this useful and favored seminary ceased to exist.

Unhappy Results of breaking up the Schools.

It will be readily inferred that this sudden change of policy must have shaken the mission severely. The intimations of this change, in the *Missionary Herald*, and of its results, are extremely laconic:

"Important changes have been made in the educational system at Ahmednuggur. All the boarding-schools . . . . were discontinued in September, together with such of the boys' free schools, nine in number, as were under the care of heathen teachers.

"The year has necessarily been much broken. . . . There is hardly a beginning made yet in reconstructing the schools."

The manuscript report of the mission brings to view the unhappy results of disbanding the free schools as follows:

"The disbanding our *nine boys' free schools* was a measure which we could not adopt without some concern. It proved, as we expected, an occasion of exultation on the part of opposers. These understand not the silent operations of the Spirit of God, and judge of our influence and the progress of our work only from our visible operations. No wonder that the disbanding of so large a number of schools furnished them occasion for a temporary triumph. The ready inference to their minds was, that our resources were failing, and many exultingly predicted that we should soon leave the country."

This impression was injurious to our work, and might easily have been avoided. It will readily be seen that if these schools were to be abandoned, it should have been done *gradually*, and the mission spared the shock of such a sudden and sweeping change.

The year before these schools were interdicted, one of the missionaries, while on a preaching-tour, wrote to Dr. Anderson, Aug. 8, 1850, as follows:

"The average expense of each school is about Rs. 6 per month. As the subject of schools is latterly receiving considerable attention from you, allow me to express my honest convictions of the wisdom of this expenditure, and the utility of these agencies. . . . Our common-school system is of long standing, and in my opinion does great credit to its originators, the former missionaries. It graduates the pay of the teacher according to the number and progress of his pupils, and consequently, the more strictly the rules are applied to a certain limit, the less expensive, and at the same time, the more efficient becomes the school. The schools for Christian children are an exception to this rule, the number of scholars being small and the pay of the teacher being fixed. Of all these schools I may say, every time I visit them, I am strongly impressed with a conviction of their importance. Their entire expense is about Rs. 80 per month, say Rs. 1000 a year. The annual expense of our station is some Rs. 18,000 or Rs. 20,000. You can easily compare the different kinds of labor, and judge whether too much goes to this department. *Preaching* is urged as the great work, and rightly too. But I must say I tour and preach with very different apparent success and pleasure, too, in this region where we are known by our schools. *I can not avoid feeling that in no way can we so speedily communicate a correct knowledge of the Christian religion to the masses of any particular district as by means of schools—in no other way can we do it so economically.*

"The *extra* expense of a missionary on tour, *alone*, varies from two to three rupees per day. [With his family, it is generally more.] It is safe to say the extra expense of two days on tour will support a common school a whole month. In two days a tourist may declare his message, perhaps in four villages—be partially understood, and hope and pray for a blessing on the seed sown by the wayside—on soil rocky and barren, or all rank with thorns and thistles—no previous preparation, no after cultivation. With God all things are possible, but it does not often *prove* possible to realize any manifest fruit from such labor.

"But the school—does fruit appear here? To me there does. Truth is fixed in the child's mind. The Lord's prayer, ten commandments and catechisms, become as familiar as the language of the nursery. They *must* be remembered. They *will* be remembered, in most cases for life. And to prevent their having an influence on the mind and character of the child, is to reverse the order of nature. They *do* have an influence. The children in all our schools are generally convinced of the absolute folly of idolatry and heathen superstitions. Some of them manifest this conviction by direct acts of disrespect—throwing stones, and showing other abuse to the idols. Now can any intelligent person avoid seeing and feeling that among the children of these schools there is a foundation laid for the most hopeful results in coming years? that such a process of education will of itself eventually undermine Hinduism?

"But must we wait for future generations to witness saving results from these schools? Not so. Have not all these children parents? and is not much of this truth communicated to them by the children? and in just the way to be received with the least prejudice? And not only the parents, but all the people of the village, many from the neighboring villages, and the traveller from a distance, come in contact with these children and schools, and thus with the truth. In some instances parents are enraged by the truth, and then the school must stop; but if they tolerate it, that moment truth gains a victory."

With such experience and convictions, it will readily be imagined that this great and sudden change of policy, involving the exclusion of English from the seminary, and its consequent extinction, as well as the suppression of our nine high-caste free schools, could not go into effect without causing much pain and sorrow to those of the missionaries most deeply interested in them. Some brief expression of their views in this connection, is necessary to a proper understanding of the case.

Letter from the Mission Secretary to Dr. Anderson.

The pastor of the native church being also secretary of the mission, forwarding the minutes of their meeting, at which action was takén abolishing the schools, according to instructions, wrote to Dr. A. as follows:

"In forwarding the minutes of our annual meeting, it seems to be a fitting occasion for the frank expression of individual views. The action of the mission in regard to schools has disbanded them, [as you directed.] You will not wonder that those of us who have been most deeply interested and engaged in these schools, see them disbanded with reluctance and some misgivings. I dare say you will more pity than blame us in this matter."

Pleading for the seminary, he writes:

"I feel constrained to give my opinion, and I think I can do so disinterestedly, from the fact that I must soon leave it and all my labors in this mission, [and go to Kolapoor.] Our good-caste free schools being disbanded, the seminary is now the only connecting link between us and the good-caste people. Exclude English and the higher Mahratta studies, and [by the certain withdrawal of our good-caste pupils] our acquaintance, intercourse, and influence with the intelligent part of the community, will *almost*, if not *entirely* cease. This would be a two-fold evil. While it would destroy our influence with those above, it would weaken it with those below. Such is human nature the world over. Our labors with the higher castes *do* serve to give us more favor with the lower castes. They also give us desirable facilities for elevating the lower castes. In our seminary, all castes, the highest and lowest, are brought together on the same seats, and in the same classes, without the slightest distinction—a state of things never hitherto tolerated in government schools. To understand the full value of this practice, you need to come in contact, year after year, with this abominable system of caste. The good influence of our seminary in this one particular will, I fear, never be fully appreciated in America. The gradual breaking down of caste prejudice, and the increasing conviction of truth in the minds of these young men, is something which can not be definitely estimated. We want a report of so many actual conversions, and then we can estimate progress. May the Lord grant us such evidence of progress. We will labor and pray for it in confident hope, and at the same time try not to undervalue the smaller tokens of his love."

Referring to the large number of converts of most hopeful promise, already gathered in from the pupils of the seminary, in the last five years, he next speaks of the inquirers:

"There has been a hopeful state of feeling in the seminary during much of the past year. For the last five months the twelve living on mission premises have been accustomed to meet with me or their Christian teacher for prayer and instruction, every evening in the week, when not engaged in public exercises. Nursoo, Narayan, Ramchunder, Vithoo, Hussana, and some others of the most advanced young men, are free to confess their honest convictions of the truth. Dada Meer and Dhondoo Sonar are asking for admission to the Church. Now *can* it be wise to thrust these young men entirely beyond our influence? We do so, of course, if we exclude English and the higher Mahratta studies.

"I shall be the last man to lack interest in efforts among the Mahars and 'village congregations.' . . . But I beg you will not imagine the two modes of labor at all conflict with each other. Our educational efforts for the higher castes serve the better to commend us to the lower castes, and give us facilities for elevating the latter as above stated. My earnest feeling, therefore, is, do not shut us up *exclusively* to the Mahars. Let us have at least one school in which we may hold out the inducement to good-caste young men of a thorough education in the higher vernacular studies, and *one third* of their lessons in English. Such a school in reality will involve little or no expense. The mission will always, I hope, have some Christian young men, like Rama and Vyenkutrao, who had better be engaged in the teaching and care of such a school than not. They will do very nearly, perhaps absolutely, as much good by preaching in vacation and out of school-hours, as if they had no school duties; whereas these constant, regular duties, furnish the most desirable kind of discipline in fitting them to become native preachers. Let us, then, by all means, have a school of this character—a good school, in which one third of the lessons may be in English, and the higher Mahratta studies shall be faithfully taught—and let us bring all these intelligent children and youth into it that we can, and then labor to convince them of the truth, and pray for the Spirit of God to convert them. The mission has put the school upon this basis for the present, and I trust it will meet your cordial approval as a permanent arrangement."

The disappointment of this hope, and the breaking up of the seminary at the close of 1851, have been already mentioned. Referring to the unsettled state of things around him, the mission secretary continues:

"The disbanding of the schools has produced some sensation. Opposers exult, thinking our resources are failing, and that our influence will consequently diminish. Some inquirers have gone back, and we have reason to fear will walk no more with us. . . . One result of the new state of things, which gives me much anxiety, is disaffection on the part of our native helpers."

The writer being in charge of the seminary, and still clinging to the hope that the officers in Boston would permit him to continue teaching English, had suffered the year to close without informing the students that the school was interdicted; and then he allowed a month's vacation, that he might have ample time to hear from Boston before the next term should commence. But when the vacation closed, and no reprieve came, he found it necessary to discontinue English, and witness the unhappy results he had so earnestly sought to prevent. Writing to the Secretary of the Board soon after this event, he says:

"It has cost me a severe struggle, and I have been unable to witness the result without much pain. About half our good-caste pupils have left us, and others are ready to follow them. The direction to discontinue teaching English I sent in to the head teacher from the villages while on a preaching-tour. Since coming in myself, I have been besieged by the pupils entreating me to allow them to resume their *one—only one* lesson a day in English. I must confess this interdict of English in the present state of our mission, seems to me most unwise. As I look upon these young men of high caste, on whom the mission has already expended thousands of rupees, (between two and three thousand rupees have actually been expended for board, etc., on these same young men,) with an amount of painstaking and strength-consuming labor which can not be estimated, and now see them leaving and scattering in every direction—many of them in such a state of mind that we had begun to regard them as near the kingdom, but now going to government schools, under Roman and heathen influences, at all events, thrust away from *our* influence, and that most likely forever; I confess I can not avoid feeling deeply and painfully. They had formed a personal attachment for us, and the mere indulgence of one lesson a day in English would retain them under our influence, attending all our religious services, and listening to Christian instruction an hour daily. But we turn them away! To be sure I can comfort myself with the *fact* that the responsibility of this act rests *entirely* with others, but this does not make amends for the lasting injury to this mission and the cause of Christ here. But the Lord is able to bring good out of evil and in him will we trust."

This exclusion of English virtually broke up the seminary at once, though a few Christian and low-caste boys remained. Not only did the good-caste young men leave, but several of our most promising converts left also, being influenced by a strong desire and purpose to obtain a good education. Rama Bhore, Vyenkutrao, Tukeram, Suddoo, and several others sought admission to the institution of the Scotch Free Church Mission in Bombay. A feeling of disaffection extensively pervaded the church and native Christian community at Ahmednuggur, and several children of our native helpers left and followed our converts and inquirers to Bombay. Three of these were children of Hurripunt, the first Brahman convert of the mission. With much anxious effort Mr. and Mrs. Hume diverted these into the girls' boarding-school of our Bombay mission, where under the faithful teaching of Mrs. Hume, two of them were hopefully converted.

In view of these results of disbanding the Ahmednuggur Seminary, few will wonder at the feelings expressed in a letter to the Secretary of the Board, under date of April 5, 1852, as follows:

"It is, perhaps, too late to urge any further plea in behalf of this seminary; but as I look back upon its history I can not prevent the question often arising in my mind, whence the special favor to this school for more than ten years, when its annual expense was from Rs. 2000 to Rs. 3000, and not a solitary conversion among its pupils, and the sudden and total reversion of feeling in regard to it since the expense has become some two thirds less, and the blessing of Heaven has begun to rest so largely upon it?"

I submit this question to the officers of the Board and the candid reader.

The unhappy results of disbanding our schools at Ahmednuggur led our brethren in Bombay to feel more than ever before the necessity of a high-school there. They saw our converts—the hope of the mission for native helpers in time to come—leaving us and going to other missions and institutions to prosecute their education. They knew they would be likely to remain in the connection where they received their education, or be diverted to secular pursuits, and perhaps fall away entirely. It was a time of intense feeling and painful trial to our brethren in Bombay, and they resolved to do what they could to stay the tide of evil. Hence those spirit-stirring appeals in Chapter IV., entreating the officers of the Board to authorize a High-School in Bombay. And here we arrive at the fact that the prohibition of English in the Ahmednuggur Seminary in 1851, was the exciting cause of the Deputation, with all its expenditure of time, and money, and feeling, in 1854–6.

I have thus far endeavored faithfully to exhibit the leading facts connected with the schools of the Ahmednuggur mission. If I have succeeded, comment is unnecessary. I may be frank enough to express my honest conviction that this authoritative suppression of our schools was a manifest departure from the broad and liberal principles of the founders and friends of the Board, and has proved unhappy and injurious to the best interests of the mission. But having said this much, let us throw a mantle of charity over the actors in this scene. Serious error was committed, but it was doubtless an error of the judgment and not of the heart. May the Lord so overrule events that the evils resulting may be soon modified, and valuable experience be gained for the future prosecution of our blessed work.

A gradual return to some of the former practices of the mission commenced long ago. No *boarding* or *English* schools are *reported*, but schools exist into which promising children of both sexes are received, *supported, and educated at the expense of the mission, and a few of the most promising scholars are instructed in English.* To be sure, some will doubt whether it is wise for a missionary to spend time and strength in teaching English to two or three Christian boys *alone*, when he might at the same time teach them and twenty or thirty young Brahmans with them, thus bringing the most intelligent Hindu youth under his Christian influence. But the fact that teaching English has been resumed at all in this mission, gives encouragement to hope that both English and general education will ultimately regain their proper place and importance there.

The shock to our mission from this sudden breaking up of the schools and sending back so many pupils to heathenism, can hardly be appreciated at this distance. The year 1851 commenced with about one thousand youth under our Christian teaching. It closed with only a few dozens. The report of the Board for 1852 says, "The mission have but one school for boys in Ahmednuggur," and their three Mahar schools in the villages contained in all only "sixty scholars." One school with a heathen teacher, that at Newase, was still tolerated, and the report admits: "*It is the object of chief interest to the Christian in that dark hold of heathenism.*" "*To this Ramkrishnapunt has the opportunity of imparting a large amount of Christian instruction.*"

Oh! why should we disband such schools and destroy such precious opportunities?

The testimony of friendly heathen to the value of these schools is worthy of record. The report of the Seroor station for 1852, says:

"In some places the people are earnest in asking a teacher to come and reside among them that they may learn the truth more perfectly. They say to us: 'You come here and talk to us once or twice a year, but before we see you again, we have forgotten all that you told us.'"

After our schools were broken up in Ahmednuggur and the new policy introduced, I was often told by frank and friendly natives: "You will never gain converts so. You must establish schools as Mr. Ballantine used to, and then the children and parents too will come into your religion."

It is well to learn even from our enemies.

First Good Caste School with a Christian Teacher.

So far as I am able to learn from a very careful examination of all the records of this mission, no common school was taught by a *Christian* teacher till 1848. The case then reported was that of a school for *Mahar* boys taught by a convert originally of the Mahar caste. Even this case elicited much joy, as an indication of very marked progress. The first school of *good-caste* boys with a *Christian* teacher, ever reported in this mission, so far as I can ascertain, was in 1853. This year the missionaries say:

"We have one boys' school in this city, taught by Dajeeba, a Brahman convert, in which heathen children are collected and instructed in secular knowledge and in the principles of the word of God. This school has been successful beyond our expectations, and had we teachers for this work, we should be able to collect other schools on the same plan."

But what was the "plan" of this school? When I first read the above paragraph in the *Missionary Herald* I thought, surely here is evidence of progress. I inferred that the quarter of a century during which this mission had employed so many heathen teachers, had witnessed such a giving way of heathen prejudices, that now at length good-caste youth could be induced to attend schools in Ahmednuggur taught by Christian teachers. And when I went there to meet the Deputation, at the close of 1854, I paid a visit to this school as something which was to furnish the most pleasing evidence of progress. But judge of my disappointment when I found, under this Christian teacher Dajeeba, the *heathen* teacher Mahadoo! This Mahadoo had been employed as a heathen teacher years before, but had been dismissed from service. He was now employed again in this school, to collect and teach the pupils, but was called a "monitor." We had often had Christian superintendents to look after our heathen teachers before. What real advance was there here? It is sufficient to say the "plan" did not please the Deputation; the heathen "monitor" was dismissed, and the school ceased to exist. So that the experiment of gathering a good-caste school with a Christian teacher, remains to be tried even in Ahmednuggur. When was dear Br. Ballantine right? When he wrote, unbiased, "*If Christian teachers should be employed good-caste pupils would not attend their schools*," and "*It is the only way they can obtain an audience*," (p. 101;) or when, under the influence of the Deputation, he ignored those pleadings, and wrote: "It will not probably be found necessary to make use of schools in order to collect a congregation"?

During these years of agitation very few converts were gathered into the Church. In 1851 there were eighteen converts; in 1852, only five; in 1853, nine.

After such a breaking up of the most effective agencies of the mission, what wonder that we find in the report of 1853:

> "In Ahmednuggur itself it has been found difficult the past year to gain much access to the heathen. The congregation, on the Sabbath, with the exception of a few in the employment of the mission, who attend because they are required to, is chiefly made up of those who have already taken a stand in favor of Christianity. . . It is just now discouraging to see that so few of the heathen around us are reached by any of the operations now in progress here."

No doubt this state of things, resulting from the suppression of so many of their schools, had its influence in leading the missionaries so warmly to second, at this date, those earnest appeals for a high-school in Bombay.

In the report of 1854 we read: "The female schools of Miss Farrar, taught by heathen teachers, have been abandoned." By interdicting these and the other good-caste schools the Deputation completed the work commenced in 1851, and almost entirely severed our connection with the higher castes. And yet, of the thirteen converts of this same year, 1854, *nine* were *pupils*, and attested God's special blessing on the schools. During these years of agitation and change the Ahmednuggur mission did not publish its usual annual reports in India. It commenced again in 1855, and apologizing for its long silence, it mentions as a reason "the gradual change of missionary policy which had been going on for three or four years past." Why this "change of policy" should have prevented a report, does not appear. In defining this "change of policy," the report says:

"1. In former years boarding-schools for boys and girls were sustained at great expense, in the hope that many of those thus educated would become converts, and be fitted for the work of extending the knowledge of the truth among their countrymen. These boarding-schools were commenced under instructions from home, and the great schools of the American mission in Ceylon were held up to us as models after which to copy. Our Secretaries, however, several years since, began to change their policy in this respect, and in 1851 the abandonment of the old system was commenced in this mission, and completed in 1854 by the coming of the Deputation."

In regard to this extract it is worthy of remark:

1. That the missionaries do not state whether the hopes which led to the establishment of these schools were realized or not. Their sudden and entire abandonment would lead to the inference that those hopes had been disappointed, whereas the whole history of the mission shows conclusively that the boarding-schools were our most effective agency for bringing the low castes to instruction and conversion, and

that in securing converts from the higher castes, they were second only to the schools with heathen teachers.

2. It is also worthy of notice that the missionaries throw the responsibility both of establishing and suppressing these schools entirely upon the officers in Boston. "They were commenced under instructions from home." "Our Secretaries began to change their policy."

All who have attentively perused the history of the mission will agree that a very great change of policy had been effected. And yet the Senior Secretary maintains that his views are unchanged from what they were eighteen years previous. [See report of Deputation to special meeting at Albany, p. 9.] Are the missionaries in error here, or did Dr. Anderson effect this great and radical change in the policy of our missions without any corresponding change of views on his own part?

Again, we see this "change of policy" dates as far back as 1851, and what must be the bearing of this fact on the statement which has been repeatedly made, that the Deputation had no fixed views and theory before they left America? Is it not evident that they "began to change their policy in 1851," as the Ahmednuggur mission affirms, and that this change was only "completed in 1854 by the coming of the Deputation"? Is it not evident that the experience, judgment, and convictions of every American missionary then in Western India was opposed to this "change of policy," when, in 1853 and 1854 they all united in those earnest appeals for a High-school in Bombay? And was it not expressly to resist and extinguish these deep and united convictions of the whole body of their missionaries that the Deputation went to India?

And how does this action accord with the statement that "the various missions of the Board are *organized and self-governing bodies*"? On this point the Senior Secretary affirms:

"The *missions are all organized bodies*, and they are so for the purposes of *self-government;* and the administration of their internal affairs, just as far as possible, is intrusted to them. Each mission, when of proper size, is left to determine the stations of its members, to manage its *schools*, etc., and virtually to dispose of all the funds committed to it by the Prudential Committee."

And was not the whole body of missionaries in Western India sufficiently large to be a self-governing body, and manage their *schools?* Were they not entirely unanimous in their opinions of the necessity of a high-school in Bombay?

Another change mentioned in this report of 1855 is:

"2. We formerly had a large number of schools for boys and girls, taught by *heathen teachers*. We now have none."

This change would authorize the inference that these schools had proved unwise, and yet in the same report we find the frank admission that the heathen teachers had been converted "*and these form now our most efficient laborers. Our native pastors were both originally heathen school-teachers, and in this way were brought under the influence of truth, and converted.*"

This frank admission is worthy of notice. The history of the mission is an invincible argument in favor of such schools.

Ordination of Native Pastors.

The ordination of Hurripunt and Ramkrishnapunt as native pastors had been deferred some months, that the Deputation might be present. It occurred during their visit, and was an occasion of much interest. "It was a day never to be forgotten, especially by those who could remember the time when these two pastors were idolaters like their countrymen, and when, after many struggles and much opposition, they first came forward and professed their faith in Christ."

"In the beginning of 1839 only one of the present members of these two churches was a Christian. All the rest were enveloped in the darkness of heathenism. At that time the whole number of church-members in this mission was only eleven, and these were mostly inmates of the poor-house. What a change! Surely this is the work of God." And may we not add, just so surely are those schools, in which these native pastors were first employed as heathen teachers, and thus converted, approved of God, and bear the seal of his own favor and blessing?

Connection with Higher Castes Broken.

The breaking up of our schools broke the effective link between the mission and the higher castes. The former pupils of these schools had become warmly attached to us, and I have large files of letters received from them since they left us, showing their appreciation of our kindness, and their honest conviction of the truth; and several of them have professed their faith in Christ since the schools were abandoned. The influence of the schools has thus been felt for good even since they were broken up.

In 1856 four young men of good caste came out and received baptism in Ahmednuggur. Their cases were reported at length. Years before they had been pupils in our mission schools, and there learned the Gospel. Two of them had been in our mission seminary for years before it was suppressed. One of them, Sawalya, was long a boarding scholar, and I then regarded him as thoroughly convinced of the truth, and he seemed on the point of professing Christ before the world. Another, Cassim, was a brother of Daood, who was baptized in 1847. Cassim was then in the seminary too, and his friends removed him lest he also should become a Christian. The two other converts were pupils for years in our schools taught by heathen teachers. At the time of their baptism they were students in the government school, and the immediate agency in bringing them to an open profession of Christ seems to have been the earnest and eloquent appeals of Dr. Duff, followed by those of Nilkunt Shastri, a converted Brahman, though the origin of their convictions and the foundation of their Christian faith is clearly traceable to our mission schools.

Since the baptism of these young men in 1856, I have

heard of no convert from the higher castes in that mission, except two or three children of Christian parents. The agencies of the mission and their results seem to have become restricted almost entirely to the lowest castes.

Why were the Schools abandoned?

I am often asked the reason for the sudden abandonment of our schools. Why this sudden and sweeping change of policy? I can give no satisfactory answer. The Secretary used to say to us in India: "The apostles had no schools, why should you have?" Some of our brethren replied: "The apostles had the gift of miracles; we have not." One brother, an amiable one, too, looked up with much simplicity, and said: "The apostles had no secretary to superintend their labors, why should we have?"

The *fact* of a change of policy is unmistakable. For its true cause we must continue to refer to the Deputation. In the *Missionary Herald* of 1851, p. 8, we read: "The Mahar caste still affords peculiar inducements for all description of missionary labor, and is one of the proofs that it is better to direct our principal efforts toward the people of the lower castes, rather than the higher."

Is this the rock which caused the shipwreck? Is it possible that the Secretary did not know that our boarding-schools were our most effective agency in securing connection and influence with the Mahars even, and that while they constitute less than a twelfth of the people, their influence does not extend upward; that if we would aim at the conversion of India we must have agencies that will affect the middle and higher castes?

The same progress, nay, even greater progress, might have been secured among the Mahars, and at the same time our labors been continued for the higher castes. Had they been continued, and the blessing of God rested upon them as formerly, the ratio of good-caste converts would have increased till the upper strata of Hindu society would have been affected as thoroughly as the lower. And the importance of infusing the leaven of the Gospel into these upper strata can hardly be over-estimated, whether we consider their position and influence or their comparative number. The two or three hundred Mahar converts gathered into the Church before our schools were abandoned had brought around the mission a large number of their friends and acquaintances, many of whom have given up much of their superstition and idolatry, and constitute a nominal Christian community. The progress already made among these Mahars secured us a hold upon them which we hope will be permanent. A good number of converts are gathered into the churches from them every year. For this we will rejoice and thank God, while we can not cease to regret that the schools, so greatly blessed of God for winning and saving those of the higher castes, have been so unwisely abandoned.

I have expended much labor in efforts to prepare a Tabular View of the schools of this mission, but in vain. The statistics are imperfect, and for more than half the years of its existence, none are given in its reports. I find no account of native *Christian* teachers till the mission had been prosecuted more than ten years, and then only two or three converts taught a part of the time, and in the *boarding*-schools. The first Christian teacher in a common school was a Mahar convert in 1848, and a school of good-caste children has never been sustained, without a heathen teacher, so far as I know, even in this old mission.

Imperfect as the statistics of the schools are, they are sufficient to establish the fact that from 1832 to 1852—20 *consecutive years—this mission constantly employed an average of 15 heathen teachers.* Now, if the good brethren who adopted and sustained these schools pronounce them "a failure," what is their apology for supporting them so long? And if the officers of the Board are alone responsible for these schools, and have just discovered that they are a failure, then may we not with propriety ask, how came they to be more than forty years making this discovery? And if it took forty years to discover this error, then what security has the Church that there is not an error of equal or greater magnitude still existing? If the funds of the churches have been misapplied for forty years past, then what security that they will not be for forty years to come?

But such questions are suggested with much deference, while we cease not devoutly to thank God for the precious tokens of his favor and blessing upon these schools in all the past history of the missions.

The history of the schools in this mission must here close for the present. It is sufficiently manifest that they proved its most effective agency for bringing the heathen to a knowledge of Christian truth. The "change of policy" in 1851 presents cause for sincere regret, and results in the necessity of changing again. A gradual return to the former policy of the mission has already commenced. Promising children and youth are received into schools and *supported by the mission*, and a few are instructed in English. The desirableness and necessity of a good English seminary is still imperative. If such a school can be revived, and bring the intelligent good-caste young men of the city under daily Christian instruction, it will be a bright day for the mission, and one full of hope for the salvation of those precious youth. The memories of my delightful years of labor in this mission make all its interests dear to my heart. God bless and prosper it forever.

Tabular View of the Laborers in the Ahmednuggur Mission,

From the origin of the Station to the close of 1856, (prepared from the MS. records of the Mission.)

	Joined Mission.	Left Mission.	Length of Service. Yrs.	Mths.	Days.
Rev. Allen Graves,	Dec. 20, 1831.	To Am. and Bombay, July, 1832.	0	6	10
Rev. Hollis Read,	"	" Nov. 1834.	2	10	10
Rev. William Hervey,	"	Died, May 13, 1832.	0	4	23
Rev. G. W. Boggs,	Dec. 29, 1832.	To Am., Oct. 2, 1838.	5	9	3
Rev. D. O. Allen,	Jan. 1834.	To Bombay, Nov. 18, 1836.	1	10	18
Rev. Henry Ballantine,*	Oct. 20, 1836.	....	16	0	20
Rev. Eben Burgess,†	Oct. 21, 1839.	To Satara, Nov. 21, 1851.	10	0	0
Rev. Ozro French,	Oct. 24, 1839.	To Am., Jan. 1849.	9	2	6

* Absent in America 3 years and 20 days. † Absent in America about 2 years.

	Joined Mission.	Left Mission.	Length of Service. Yrs.	Mths.	Dys.
Rev. S. B. Munger,*	Feb. 1837.	To Satara, Feb. 1855.	11	6	0
Rev. R. G. Wilder,	Oct. 27, 1846.	To Kolapoor, Nov. 17, 1852.	6	0	20
Rev. S. B. Fairbank,	"	To Bombay, Nov. 1849.	8	0	0
Rev. Allen Hazen,	March 30, 1847.	To " Jan. 1855.	7	9	0
Rev. Lemuel Bissell,	Aug. 27, 1851.	....	5	8	3
Rev. W. Barker,	Jan. 9, 1854.	....	2	10	21
14.			83	1	14

Assistant Missionary.

Mr. Amos Abbott,	Oct. 1834.	To Am., Dec. 1846.	12	2	0

Female Assistant Missionaries.

Mrs. Mary Graves,	Dec. 20, 1831.	To Bombay, July 1832.	0	6	10
Mrs. Caroline Read,	"	To Am., Nov. 1834.	2	10	10
Mrs. G. W. Boggs,	Dec. 29, 1832.	" Oct. 2, 1838.	5	9	8
Mrs. A. Abbott,	Oct. 1834.	" Dec. 1846.	12	2	0
Mrs. E. Ballantine,†	Oct. 20, 1836.	....	16	0	20
Mrs. M. Burgess,	Oct. 21, 1839.	Died, June 24, 1842.	2	8	3
Mrs. A. Burgess,	March 30, 1847.	To Satara, Nov. 21, 1851.	4	7	21
Mrs. J. French,	Oct. 24, 1839.	To Am., Jan. 1849.	9	2	6
Miss C. Farrar,	Oct. 19, 1839.	....	16	1	11
Mrs. Mary Munger,	Dec. 1854.	To Satara, Feb. 1855.	0	2	0
Mrs. E. J. Wilder,	Oct. 27, 1846.	To Kolapoor, Nov. 17, 1852.	6	0	20
Mrs. Abby Fairbank,	"	To Bombay, Nov. 1849.	8	0	0
Mrs. M. Hazen,	March 30, 1847.	" Jan. 1855.	7	9	0
Mrs. Bissell,	Aug. 27, 1851.	....	5	8	3
Mrs. Barker,	Jan. 9, 1854.	....	2	10	21
15.			95	1	8

From the foregoing table it appears that of the 14 missionaries,

	Died in Serv.	Ret. to Amer.	Transferred.	Remained in 1856.
	1	3	7	3
Of the 15 fem. assist. miss.	1	4	6	4

The assistant missionary had also returned to America.

	Yrs.	Mths.	Dys.		Yrs.	Mths.	Dys.
The average period of service of the missionaries,	83	1	14				
		14		=	5	11	7
Ditto of female assist. "	95	1	18				
		15		=	6	4	8

* Absent in America twice, about 6¼ years. † Absent in America, 3 years and 20 days.

Compare this table with that of the Bombay mission, p. 155, and it is easy to ascertain the *whole length of service* of any one missionary or assistant missionary. For instance:

	Yrs.	Mths.	Dys.
Rev. Allen Graves was in the Bombay mission, ...	21	3	16
in Ahmednuggur, (see Table,)	0	6	10
This shows his whole period of service to be, ...	21	9	26

And so of all, though in case of two or three, the tables for Satara and Kolapoor missions also will need to be consulted.

CHAPTER VI.

SCHOOLS OF THE SATARA AND KOLAPOOR MISSIONS.

SATARA.

THE origin of this mission dates from December 2, 1851, though it had been a station of the Bombay mission from June 1, 1849, and it had been repeatedly occupied before, for short periods, by Mr. and Mrs. Graves.

"The position of the place is singularly beautiful. It stands about a mile from the bank of the Vena, where that stream emerges from its narrow mountain valley, into the more open vale of the Krishna, with which it forms a junction below the city. Round the borders of the two rivers rises an amphitheatre of hills, some of considerable elevation. . . The city of Satara contains a population of 32,000."

Schools secure Ready Access to the People.

Three weeks after commencing the station, Mr. Wood reports: "I have opened a vernacular school for boys in the bazaar." He soon adds: "The school continues in successful operation. One hundred or more are in regular attendance, and as many as that meet in Sabbath-school every Sabbath morning. I have lately taken another school of boys of 100 or more, under my care." Thus here, as in the other missions, the schools proved the most ready and effective means of access and influence with the people.

In 1851, we find in the *Herald*, "The new station at Satara promises to be one of much importance." But it suffered a severe loss, August 27, in the death of dear Mrs. Wood, whose zealous and useful labors for the girls and women were thus early terminated.

Mr. and Mrs. Burgess, from Ahmednuggur, joined this station, December 2, and from that date it became a separate mission.

Mahabuleshwur, formerly a station of the Bombay mission, was now transferred to Satara.

In 1852, a third school for boys and two for girls, were in operation, and we find "the teachers were heathen Brahmans." "Mrs. Graves has still an interesting school of about 25 pupils, five or six of whom give evidence of being Christians." "The schools both for boys and girls are quite promising."

One convert, Krishnarao, was this year baptized and received into the Church. The Report of the Board speaks of him as "a young man of the Brahman caste, of pretty good English education. As he had an extensive circle of friends and acquaintances, the influence of his profession of Christianity was extensively felt, and he gave promise of being a very useful helper in the mission. But in May last the desire of a higher education led him to join the school of the Scotch Free Church mission at Bombay.

The baptism of Krishnarao was the signal of alarm to the high-caste pupils in the schools, and many of them left, but after a few weeks most of them came back again.

In 1853, the death of dear Mrs. Burgess brought another heavy affliction upon this mission and weakened its working force. Her life was useful and her death happy.

Religious Interest in the Schools.

Of the success of their labors the missionaries write:

"Four or five of the pupils, together with the teacher, give evidence of being much interested in the truth of Christianity." "Mrs. Graves has continued her school at M., a part of the year, as her health would permit. The number of her pupils is from 20 to 25. This school attracts considerable attention from English residents who resort to the Hills during the hot season; and liberal subscriptions are made by them for its support."

Mr. Wood, having spent a Sabbath at Mahabuleshwur, and being delighted to see some 30 girls present at his religious services, writes: "They were from Mrs. Graves' school, having received instruction at her hands for years. . . . Mrs. Graves thinks that some of them give evidence of being born again."

Of his schools in Satara, Mr. Wood writes: "Three of the larger boys in one of our schools, came to Mr. Burgess a few days ago, desiring him to converse and pray with them. They said they were convinced of the truth and claims of Christianity, and that they believed in Christ, as their only Saviour and Redeemer. Having been in the school from the first, they have obtained a pretty good knowledge of Christian truth."

A few months later, Mr. W. writes again: "Many of the older boys appear to be fully convinced of the folly and sinfulness of idolatry; and we are not without evidence that the truth is finding its way to their hearts." Speaking of a precious interview with some of them, he says: "They avowed their belief in Christ, and desired to be baptized and confess him before the world. We do not think they are prepared for such a step, but we hope they will be hereafter. We have evidence, moreover, that *we preach to the parents of the children, and to others through these schools.* The books are read at home; and some of the boys are known to engage in discussions, setting forth the folly and sinfulness of idolatry."

The Schools Disbanded.

1854.—These interesting schools continued to prosper till near the close of 1854, when they were all disbanded by order of the Deputation. The Report of the Board says: "It has been thought best to give less attention to education, and more to the direct preaching of the Gospel, and the schools were all closed at the end of the year."

Soon after this event we do not wonder that the missionary at Satara speaks of "finding no regular congregation." He felt the want of one much, and as he was one of the brethren who had yielded their views to the Deputation, and joined in abolishing the schools, it is to be presumed that he exerted himself faithfully to secure an audience without schools; and some minds will be interested in knowing to what appliance, in this emergency, he resorted. It was simply this. He carried with him to his chapel, a bag of copper coin, and after sermon distributed it to his hearers. This drew an audience of forty or fifty paupers, instead of the intelligent and interesting audience of good-caste young men which had before been gathered, both on Sabbath and week-days, by means of the schools.

I need not express my regret at the loss of those valuable schools. Had their number been increased and a good English school been established, the prospects of the mission would have been full of hope. Precious youth there might have been won to Christ. But since those schools were abandoned, what young men have come to the missionaries to tell their convictions and ask for prayers?

I have repeatedly visited Satara, and have had the pleasure of preaching Christ in her streets, her temple-courts, and the mission chapel. If there was any thing hopeful and animating in the mission, it was the bright intelligent faces and fixed attention of those Hindu youth in the Sabbath audience, gathered in from the schools. If there was any promise of future success, it centered mainly in those schools. Their suppression with a view "to give less attention to education and more to the direct preaching of the Gospel," resulted in banishing those interesting children and youth from the Sabbath audience, and reducing it to a band of paupers and a few servants and dependents of the mission. In saying this, I speak only of what I have seen. I have ridden to the chapel with the good brother (M.) and his bag of money, and seen him distribute it after sermon. I witnessed the result of disbanding those schools, with much sorrow, and look forward in hope to their future revival as the most effectual means of securing the success of the mission.

In 1856, the Report of the Board says of this mission: "Two persons of the Mahar caste have been received into Christian fellowship. The present number of communicants is supposed to be six. None of them, however, can be considered as strictly belonging to the people of Satara. 'No inroad in the way of conversions,' Mr. Munger says, 'has yet been made upon the ranks of the Prince of darkness, in this benighted city.'" These two Mahar converts had been educated in mission schools, and baptized in infancy. The other converts in this mission had been transferred from Ahmednuggur.

The following significant statement in the *Missionary Herald* of 1859, is from the pen of the same brother who, without his schools, felt driven to collect a Sabbath audience with the use of money. He writes: "My audiences are less numerous, and fewer of the educated part of the people attend. The consequence is, that there is less discussion and less opportunity of the kind which discussion furnishes, to bring distinctly into view facts which stand opposed to the objections in the minds of the people. . . . . The conviction has gained strength by all our experience in Satara and in India, that the devil cometh and taketh away the word out of their hearts, lest they should believe, and be saved. . . We have need of patience, much patience. The truth does not readily find a way into these Hindu minds."

Such, doubtless, is the conviction of every missionary of much experience in India; and hence the imperative necessity of schools to gather and *hold* the people under stated Christian instruction till the focus of God's truth can be brought to bear on their minds and hearts.

Tabular View of the Schools in the Satara Mission.

Year.	Boys. Schools.	Pupils.	Girls. Schools.	Pupils.
1849,	1	100	..	..
1850,	1	100	..	..
1851,	2	200	3	60
1852,	3	220	3	65
1853,	2	120	2	55
1854,	2	120	3	75
1855,	Abandoned			
1856,	"			

No Christian teachers were employed in these schools.

Tabular View of Missionaries at Satara from the Origin of the Station June 1st, 1849, to the close of 1856.

Missionaries.

	Joined the Mission.		Length of Service. Yrs.	Mths.	Dys.
Rev. William Wood,*	June 1, 1849.	Returned to Amer., Nov. 1854.	5	5	0
Rev. E. Burgess,	Dec. 2, 1851.	" Nov. 5, 1853.	1	11	3
Rev. S. B. Munger,	Feb. 1855.		1	11	0
3			9	3	3

Female Assistant Missionaries.

	Joined the Mission.		Length of Service. Yrs.	Mths.	Dys.
Mrs. Lucy Wood,	June 1, 1849.	Died Aug. 27, 1851.	2	2	26
Mrs. Abigail Burgess,	Dec. 2, 1851.	Died April 26, 1853.	1	4	24
Mrs. Mary Munger,	Feb. 1855.	Died June 3, 1856.	1	4	0
Mrs. Mary Graves,	Dec. 2, 1851.	†	5	0	29
4			10	0	19
Average years of service by each missionary,			3	1	1
" female assistant,			2	6	4

* Rev. Mr. Wood returned to Satara early in 1857, and resumed his labors.

† Blanks in this column show that the person remained in the missions after the close of 1856—the limit of these statistics.

KOLAPOOR MISSION.

Kolapoor is an "independent native kingdom," beyond the limits of British rule. It has a population of 550,000, among whom no mission had existed previous to 1852. "Rarely, indeed, had missionaries entered the kingdom on their hurried tours, and the great mass of the people was entirely unacquainted with the Gospel."

It was my privilege to commence this mission December 4, 1852. At no wish of my own, the Prudential Committee of the A.B.C.F.M. detached me from my pleasant and engrossing duties at Ahmednuggur, and sent me to lay the foundations of a *new* mission in this dark region of unbroken Hinduism. I found it a difficult enterprise, involving severe labor and some special exposure and hardship.

Kolapoor, the capital of the kingdom, has a population of 44,000 inhabitants, and a high reputation for sanctity. There is a tradition among the people that the gods once assembled in grave council to decide which was the holiest place of all the earth—that the claims of Kolapoor and Benares were found to outweigh all others, and that on putting these two cities in the opposite scales of the balance, Kolapoor exceeded Benares in holiness by just one grain! "It could not be expected that a missionary would be welcomed among such a people. On our first arrival they sent a petition to their king, praying him to banish us from his kingdom, and for some weeks all the respectable inhabitants kept themselves entirely aloof from us."

As seen from a distance the city is "beautiful for situation." The most commanding object, next to the king's palace, (see frontispiece,) is the white dome and towering spire of the temple of Ambabae. But this is only one among two hundred and fifty-two temples in this stronghold of heathenism. The city is full of them, and like Athens of old, "is wholly given to idolatry."

Opposition overcome by Schools.

Earnest and persevering efforts were made to obtain regular and stated audiences in this mission without schools, but in vain. Indeed, the first attempts to establish schools encountered resolute opposition. The Brahmans of Nassik and other places hastened to apprize their caste-mates at Kolapoor of the many evils *they* had suffered from the schools of the missionaries, and warned them to be on their guard against us. It was some months before we succeeded in commencing a school, and then began with only two little boys. Both they and their parents consented to their coming with much hesitation, fearing the priests would execute their threats, and put them all out of caste. It was painfully amusing at first to observe the timid, anxious looks of parents and friends as they came near enough to peer in at the door of the school-room, to see what we were doing to those two little boys. But observing our kind manner, and finding that neither they nor the boys received any harm, they gained courage, their prejudices and fears rapidly gave way, other pupils came, and our first year closed with two hundred and five boys and twenty little girls under our Christian teaching.

Those who would rightly estimate the value of these schools, should know that a short time before we commenced the mission there was not a respectable girl or woman in the whole kingdom who knew how to read, and only four hundred boys receiving any education, even in their indigenous schools. They should know, too, not only that the prime elements of Christian truth were a part of the daily lessons of these children and youth, but that the pupils formed a nucleus around which gathered parents and neighbors, thus furnishing an interested and delightful audience for my preaching services.

The attempt of Mrs. Wilder to bring the little girls and their mothers under her influence and teaching was attended with peculiar difficulties; but persevering efforts triumphed over them. The hundred and twenty girls brought under her teaching in a few years marked progress which gladdened our hearts, and not only ours, but the hearts of all who knew the facts and felt any sympathy in our work. These schools were of special value in conciliating the favor of the higher castes, and changing public sentiment towards us. In the course of two years, the very men who signed the petition praying for our banishment, were frequently coming to our house, schools, and preaching-places, and seeking opportunities for acquaintance and conversation; and when I wanted land, the king, of his own accord, proposed to give me all I desired. Speaking of this friendly disposition of the native Government, the Political Superintendent, Colonel Malcolm, wrote: "The Durbar would cheerfully give you twice as much ground as you ask for."

LETTER FROM MRS. WILDER.*

The City of Kolapoor.

(See Frontispiece.)

"To the Readers of the Dayspring:

"I have long had in mind to tell you something about Kolapoor, which is one of the most interesting cities of the Southern Marathi country. It has 44,000 inhabitants, and occupies a circumference of four and a half miles, on the southern bank of the river Punchagunga. The Hindus regard it as a very sacred city. In their books it is spoken of as the 'Benares of the South,' because it has so many sacred shrines. It contains more than two hundred temples. At a little distance, as I now see them from my window, their white domes and minarets, among the tall old trees, make a fine appearance. But could you come and walk with me through the winding streets of this city, you would see much to make your hearts sad.

"Temples and Sacrifices.

"Crossing the river, we see people descending the banks, thinking to wash away their sins in the sacred stream. Passing on, you hear the sound of drums and tomtoms, and soon meet a crowd going with their offerings to some heathen temple. Among them are priests with hideous faces covered with ashes.

* *Dayspring*, June, 1857.

At the turns of the most pleasant streets, and under the shade of the tallest trees, you see temples where men, women, and children meet to worship some senseless little idol. Crossing a broad street, skirted with trees on each side, we soon reach the great temble Ambabae, which is the largest and most frequented temple in this part of India. It is very costly and beautiful; the cut and carved work being most tastefully executed. We are not permitted to enter it, but standing at the door, we can see the deluded people falling upon their faces before the idol. This temple is visited by people from distant parts of India, who make large contributions to it. In former years its annual revenues amounted to 30,000 dollars.

"You know, dear children, the Hindus do not spare expense or trouble in doing honor to their false gods. See that little ill-shaped image! Would you think it possible that any one can be so foolish as to call it a god and worship it? Yet every year it is borne through the city on a triumphal car, and followed by immense crowds of people. A few days ago it was place in a palanquin and carried in procession past our house to the temples of Temblaee, where upwards of 15,000 people met to worship it. Foremost was the king and his retinue, on elephants, camels, and fine horses, moving on in slow procession to worship that senseless little idol. On these occasions, a young buffalo is slain and offered in sacrifice to the goddess. Thus, you see, they worship these idol gods instead of the dear Saviour who died for them. These sights make our hearts sad, and we know that God is grieved as he looks down from heaven upon them. But he loves the people still, and commands us to make known to them Christ and the true way to be saved.

"The Mission School.

"You will be glad to come with me to a brighter scene. What pretty building is this on the main street, with little trees rising in front of it? Rejoice with me, dear children, that in this dark, heathen city, there is *one* bright spot, one *sacred* temple, appropriated to the service of the *true* God. Ascending a few steps, we enter a large and pleasant room. It is well filled. Among those present are some two hundred boys; and at one side, ranged along near the pulpit, are fifty or sixty little girls, and a small group of women. On the other side, and in front, are many older people. The children rise and sing a hymn, and remain standing while the missionary asks them many questions from the Bible and catechism. You can not understand their language, but you will be pleased with their happy looks and tone, as they answer the questions so fluently. Their lessons are the same that you are accustomed to recite in your own loved Sabbath-schools in America. Some of them have learned two or three catechisms, and a great deal of Bible truth. Will you not pray that it may affect their hearts, and that they may be prepared to meet you in heaven? It is pleasant to see how attentively they listen as the missionary entreats them no longer to worship their idols, but to believe on Christ as the only one able to take away their sins. Their interested countenances show that they understand his words. Sometimes the men give an audible assent to the truth of what he says. Two of our school teachers, of the Brahman caste, seem quite convinced of the truth, and resolved to give up all for Christ. We hope they will soon be baptized.

"**Ladies of the Palace.**

"When we came to Kolapoor, a few years ago, it was found difficult to persuade parents to send their children, especially their girls, to our schools. They even tried to prevent our having a mission here. But these schools have secured us much favor with the people. The king's sister, hearing of the progress of our scholars, sent her two little adopted daughters, and also a nephew of the king, to attend our schools. She one day sent to one of our schoolmasters to borrow a Testament to read. Not long after I paid her a visit, and gave her a Testament. She seemed quite taken with the story of the 'prodigal son,' (Luke 15th,) which I read to her, and expressed her surprise at the great love and compassion of the father, in receiving and forgiving so wicked a son. I have recently been to the palace several times to see her and the queen. They always receive me very kindly. I was pleased to see that some of our Christian books had found their way into the palace, and were in the hands of several of the children there. Among the ladies of the palace, the king's sister is the most intelligent, and has quite a noble bearing. She is a lineal descendant of the great Shivajee who founded the Marathi empire. Her great-grandmother was a most cruel woman.

"Human Sacrifices.

"In front of our house, a few miles distant, is a hill-fort which used to be the stronghold of native princes, and where this cruel old queen used to offer human sacrifices to please the goddess Karle. When I was there, a short time ago, the very spot was pointed out to me where the poor victims used to be sacrificed. It is within a pretty inclosure on the summit of the hill, under the dense foliage of beautiful trees that surround several old buildings, where kings used to keep their treasures. It was her custom to send men down in the night to search for victims, and the poor villagers were kept in constant terror. When we think of her cruel character, and now see this young princess reading the New Testament, and sending her children to the mission schools, have we not reason to thank God, and hope that a still greater change and choicer blessings are in store for this idolatrous city?

"Your affectionate friend,

"E. J. W."

Christian Teaching in the Schools.

The schools of this mission were all *vernacular free* schools. We taught no English in any of them. Their character may be inferred by the following extract from the report of the mission:

"All past experience combines to make us retain a high estimate of these schools. As a connecting link with the people, a means of securing kind feeling and friendly relations, of communicating most understandingly and effectively the largest amount of Christian truth both to the pupils and their parents, as also of securing large and intelligent audiences for preaching services, such as can be obtained here in no other way, these schools still seem to us, not only extremely desirable, but quite indispensable in a new mission.

"While a thorough course of secular studies is prosecuted in these schools, our primary and controlling object is to communicate a full and correct knowledge of the Christian Scriptures. This object we are happy to know, is secured to a very good extent. The Scripture lessons being made most prominent in the frequent visits and examinations by the missionary, the teachers and pupils soon come to regard them as the most important, and a failure is less frequent in these than in any other lessons.

"Thus a large amount of knowledge and an intelligent understanding of Scripture truth is secured; and as 'God's word shall not return unto him void,' so surely shall not this divine seed, sown in youthful minds, fail of a permanent influence on their future lives and characters."

Converts and Inquirers.

As soon as our schools had won upon the feelings of the people so far as to bring them under Christian instruction, it was easy to mark the influence of truth on their minds. Within the first twelve months five serious inquirers avowed their convictions and asked for baptism.

Govind Apa Chowhan.

The first of these inquirers was Govind Apa Chowhan. The first time I ever saw him was in one of my schools, then recently established. He had heard of this school, then exciting interest and conversation among the thousands of Kolapoor and the surrounding villages, and though too old to take the place of a regular pupil, being a man of some forty years, yet day after day and week after week, whenever I visited the school, I found him there, eager for knowledge. He purchased books of science and portions of Scripture, and studied them diligently. His convictions deepened, and he was subsequently baptized and received to church fellowship. The mission report gives the following account of him:

"Govind was born of respectable parentage, being a distant relative of the king. Several of his relatives still rank among the nobility, and hold their enams, or landed estates, in virtue of their rank and past services to the government. Govind's branch of the family became impoverished by a train of reverses, and in his youth and early manhood he obtained a meagre support by teaching school, but was glad to change this profession for that of a sugar-merchant.

"At one time he became connected with a band of evil-doers, whose occupation was to obtain money on false pretenses. Their common practice was to represent that they had discovered buried treasures, but wanted money to perform certain idolatrous rites to prevent evil spirits from removing it, while they should dig for it. They would thus take advantage of the superstition and covetousness of some wealthy Hindu, promising to give him a portion of the treasure; and having obtained from him a few hundred rupees for the expense of the proposed rites, they would disappear with the money. When Govind became acquainted with Christian truth, his conscience rebuked him for this as for all evil practices, and he resolved to abandon them and his wicked companions, and commence a new course of life. He was resolute in his purpose, and made restitution so far as he could, to those whom he had helped to defraud. But his associates, either in revenge because he left them, or fearing he would inform against them, hastened to accuse him to government, and got him apprehended and condemned to a year's imprisonment and a heavy fine. The case having come before an English officer, Capt. Hervey, it appeared so evident that Govind had forsaken his wrong-doings before his apprehension, and that the charges had been preferred in malice by his old associates because he had reformed and left them from the promptings of his own conscience, that the magistrate remitted his fine and imprisonment, and took him into favor. Govind's examination before government elicited the facts mentioned, as also his satisfactory knowledge of Christian truth. Two questions and his replies, taken from the records of government, are as follows:

"'*Question.*—You have said that you began to think of making restitution to those you had wronged; what led you to this?

"'*Answer.*—I had been reading portions of the English Scriptures given to me at Kolapoor by the Rev. Mr. Wilder, the American missionary, who had also given me a great deal of good advice; and I perceived that such ought now to be my conduct, and that I should leave off all such bad courses as

I had been addicted to. I had resolved to enter into the Christian faith by being baptized, and I had quite forsaken my evil ways.

"'*Question.* — What do you understand by the Christian faith?

"'*Answer.*—In the Hindu faith no one had ever offered any atonement for the sins of the world; in the Christian faith I felt that there had been a Saviour; I felt that I had been a great sinner, and that there was no hope left me of pardon except through that Saviour, Christ. Such was and is my faith. Neither had Ramkrishna, Brahma, Vishnoo, Siva, Maroote, nor any one in the Hindu faith, not even the Mussulman's prophet, nor any one in any creed whatever, taken upon themselves and given up their lives for the transgressions of mankind; and it was from the Christian religion alone that I came to feel I was a great sinner, which I did not perceive according to any other religion. I had not either in my heart, acknowledged any fear of God (Permeshwur) hitherto. I did so now by the Christian religion. I felt that God was near me and saw every thing I did. I felt convinced for this, and therefore I began to repent.'

"The date of the instruction and feelings here described was in the spring of 1853. After further instruction and the evidence of his sincerity for four years, he was baptized and admitted to church fellowship, witnessing a good confession. The influence of this convert was being felt for good, and two or three of his relatives were asking for baptism, when we were obliged to leave the mission. To leave him thus, with no missionary to direct his efforts, or to watch over him and encourage the development of his Christian character, and to foster the convictions in the minds of others — this rendered the necessity of leaving the mission one of the severest trials of our lives. Our thoughts often go back to him and others, and the interests of the mission, with intense anxiety. A recent letter from Rev. Mr. Wood, of Satara, reports a visit from Govind to that mission, seventy miles from Kolapoor, and says: 'He appeared very well. He went to Mr. M.'s meeting on Friday evening, and spoke for half an hour to a large audience.'

"He soon returned to Kolapoor, with no missionary to watch over and encourage him. May the Lord keep him and make him a bright light in that dark place!"

The number of inquirers increased, and the whole number baptized, at Kolapoor, or after removing to other stations, was *five*. All of them were for months or years under our daily teaching, either in our city schools or at our house. Several of our teachers became thoroughly convinced of the truth, and were free to admit their convictions; and some of them often came to read the Bible and pray with me alone, and seemed almost ready to profess their faith in Christ.

The Schools abandoned by the Deputation.

And here I have to record, with sorrow, the abandonment of these interesting schools which had cost us so much effort, and which gave us so valuable a connection with the people and such bright promise for the future. The report of the mission for 1855, after speaking of the influence of the schools, says:

"Such being our estimate of these schools, the necessity of abandoning them has proved a severe trial. Our late Deputation pronounced sentence against them. In respectfully yielding to their authority these schools have been suspended. They have been more prosperous the past year than formerly, owing to the diminishing fears and prejudices of the people, and at the date of their suspension they embraced some five hundred boys and young men and about one hundred girls, of whom some four hundred of the former and fifty of the latter were in regular daily attendance.

"Notwithstanding our very great deference to the wisdom of our Deputation, we have been unable to close these schools without feelings of sincere grief and sorrow. We can not avoid being conscious of the fact that their suspension is proving a cause of triumph to every opposer of the Gospel in Kolapoor; while our deepest convictions from all past experience, assure us that the loss of these schools involves the sacrifice of our most effective agency for prosecuting our missionary labors. We may still be able to come in contact with *individuals*—one here and another there. But this we could do before and with how vastly greater advantage and effect when daily and weekly instructing *hundreds* in the precious truths of the Gospel!

"If our Deputation could exchange places and labors with us for a twelve-month, we can not for a moment doubt that they would advocate these schools with all the persistency and authority with which they now oppose them; and in case of their suppression, would not only grieve for their loss, but spare no pains or efforts to win again the confidence of the parents, and recover this most economical and effective agency for making known Christ to these perishing idolaters.

"We still cling to the hope that our Deputation and Home Committee will yet reverse their action and allow these schools to be reöpened, but for the present they are all suspended.

"Our friends in this country have manifested a very kind interest in these schools from the first, and it may gratify them to know that their generous contributions have wholly supported them. *Not a farthing of their expense has come from the home funds of the Board since their origin.*"

The Schools re-authorized by the Prudential Committee.

No one understanding the history and value of these schools can wonder at the earnest appeal which was sent to the Prudential Committee at that date, in their behalf. (See p. 144.) That appeal reached America about the date of the special meeting at Albany, March 4, 1856, and received a kind hearing from the Prudential Committee. Permission to resume our schools was promptly sent, and reached us in June. In the report of the mission for 1856, this event is thus noticed:

"At the close of last year it was with much regret that we reported our schools disbanded in deference to the wishes and authority of our late Deputation. . . They had adopted views adverse to the employment of heathen teachers. . . . But our best endeavors to obtain Christian teachers for Kolapoor had been in vain. We had no alternative. We must employ heathen teachers or none at all. And what made the case more emergent, experience had shown us that by means of these schools we could obtain regular and stated audiences for our preaching services, and much most desirable intercourse with the people; while without them our intercourse with the people was extremely limited, and we could obtain no regular audiences whatever. In view of these facts few will wonder that we very much regretted the loss of our schools. But our Deputation did not find time to visit Kolapoor, and hence gained no personal knowledge of the peculiar difficulties involved in the origin of a mission in this part of India. Our best arguments, while with them at Ahmednuggur, failed to change their views; and our request to be allowed to continue our schools on our private responsibility—drawing no support for them from the home funds of the Board, and not even reporting them to the Board as a regular part of our mission operations—failed of securing their assent. Their official letter to this mission, after leaving the Bombay presidency, contains the following specific instructions: 'The appropriations for boys' schools will be discontinued next year, unless the committee hear from you, that you have schools not under heathen masters, which the Board can properly sustain.'*

"Our schools were accordingly disbanded, all our efforts to obtain Christian teachers having proved unavailing. These facts having become a part of the history of our mission, it seems proper to place them on record.

"At the same time it is with devout gratitude we record also, that our Home Committee and Deputation kindly reconsidered their action, and in June we received a renewal of their sanction for these schools. They were reëstablished without loss of time—the same teachers being employed as far as possible, and the same pupils gathered into them so far as they could be found and persuaded to return. The schools have not yet regained their former character and numbers, but are gradually improving. Among the pupils of these schools, up to the time they were disbanded, were the nephew of the king and three or four other children from the palace. This introduced our Christian books there. Our schools, from the first,

* This interdict covered not only the home funds of the Society, but also local contributions received in India.

have had a very manifest influence in awakening more interest on the subject of education, and in winning the favorable regards of the people.

"The Kolapoor mission is still in its infancy, and must be content to rely for growth and progress, on the same agencies which the Lord has so eminently blest in all our older missions.

"Two of our Brahman teachers have manifested increasing interest in the truth for some months past, coming often for private instruction and freely stating their convictions; and we hope and pray that they may soon have grace and courage to profess Christ before the world. Several other inquirers also encourage our hopes that a good work is begun in their hearts."

In the printed report of 1857 we read of these schools:

"They continued to prove one of our most valuable agencies, till we were obliged to suspend them, with all the operations of the mission, when we left India. To these schools, more than to all else, do we owe our preaching audiences, and the wonderful changes in the feelings of the people from open hostility to kindly civilities and friendly intercourse. These schools have introduced our Christian tracts and books into the king's palace, and into thousands of the best families of Kolapoor. One of these schools arrested the attention of our first inquirer, and drew him to us for instruction which, with the blessing of God, resulted in his becoming the first convert baptized in the kingdom. To these schools may be traced the influence which brought around us, on leaving Kolapoor, crowds of Hindus to utter their parting salutations, and express their desires and hopes, some of them with tearful interest, that we might soon return."

Outbreak of the Sepoy Mutiny.

We left India the day after the sudden outbreak of the terrible mutiny of 1857. But our leaving had no connection with that event. It was not even known to us at the time we sailed. Under the severe labor and exposure involved in laying the foundations of this new mission, my health entirely failed, and I had remained at my post a whole year against the advice of my brethren and medical attendants, still hoping my system would rally; but in vain. We came to America with the cordial approval of the executive officers of the Board. The necessity of coming involved a severe trial. We had just completed a mission-house near the city, and the increasing interest of the people, the hopeful conversion of some, and a large band of earnest inquirers, all the circumstances of the mission, in fine, combined to make us regret the necessity of leaving as we did. From a note addressed to one of the officers of the Board, as we were embarking at Bombay, the following extract indicates something of our feelings:

"This is a very, *very* sad day to us. Our brethren and the doctors combined, have persuaded us to turn our backs on the mission and work where we have experienced so much joy and sorrow, hope and disappointment; and we feel as though detached from all that was most dear to us on earth. Many times during our hasty preparations and journey thus far, have we almost resolved to turn back to our people and work at Kolapoor. Had I anticipated the severity of the struggle in my own feelings, I should have much preferred to remain at all hazards, doing what I could at my post of duty, and going thence when the Master should call. But friends say he is calling us now, to do what we can to save and restore health for longer labor in future. It *may* be so, and we will hope yet to become resigned, though at present it is by far the hardest trial of our lives."

The printed report of 1857 adds:

"These strong feelings of reluctance to leave our mission, doubtless indicated a spirit not properly resigned to the orderings of God's providence, and they were signally rebuked by subsequent events. The voyage was blest to the moderate improvement of health, and we reached our native land in safety, but to hear of the fearful atrocities of the Sepoy mutiny which had commenced the day before we sailed, though we knew it not then; and still more startling was the fact that the most violent outbreak in Western India occurred at Kolapoor after we left there, involving the murder of our nearest European neighbors, and leaving us no reason to hope our lives would have been spared, had not the Lord removed us as he did. We would record this special providence to his praise, and with thankful hearts for the hope we now cherish of being able ere long to return to our deserted mission."

The terrific scenes of the mutiny were mostly confined to the central regions of Northern India. But the tide of disaffection swept over Western India, and conspiracies were plotted at every military station, and held in check only by the unceasing vigilance of the British officers. Even this did not avail at Kolapoor, where a violent outbreak occurred only a few weeks after we left. It was shrewdly planned with a view to cut off all the officers and families connected with the regiment. The mutineers issued from their barracks about eleven o'clock at night, the darkness intense and the rain pouring in torrents. Most of the officers were in their public mess-room, and the ladies had an evening visit at the house of the commanding officer, Major Rolland, near by.

A friendly native saw the mutineers as they came out of their quarters armed, and perceiving their bloody purpose, he ran to the mess, and his old mother to the ladies, and gave the alarm. All ran in haste to the Residency, half a mile distant in the opposite direction. The great darkness was in their favor. The mutineers surrounded the buildings and began to fire in at the doors and windows before they knew their victims had escaped. In their rage they cut to pieces the poor native woman who informed the ladies; and plundering and burning the houses, they at the same time extended themselves across the camp in such a manner as to cut off the escape to the Residency of any Europeans who might be in their houses. Three unfortunate young officers had remained at home, and fell victims. The mutineers then hastened to the city, passing my house, but strangely leaving it untouched. With many of them I was personally acquainted, they often having visited me for conversation and Christian tracts. I would gladly hope their friendly regards would have led them to spare us had we been there; but the twelve martyred missionaries, who perished with their families in the horrors of this mutiny, forbid the hope. They knew we had left a few weeks before, and that the house contained no plunder that would be of service to them.

They hastened to the city and sought to gain access to the forces of the king, and induce them also to join in the rebellion. But a formidable wall makes the city a strong military fortress, and no access was possible without bribing the gate-keepers. In this they failed, and remained outside the walls.

The little party of European officers and ladies in the Residency was still agitated with the most painful apprehensions lest the other regiment near them should rise and join the rebels, in which case not a soul of them could escape. But some of the more courageous officers ventured to hold a parley with this regiment, and finding them faithful, those officers put themselves at their head, and marching down upon the mutineers, still in the suburbs of the city, they poured in upon them a sudden and effective fire which destroyed most of them on the spot. That morning's sun revealed not only the devastations of the mutineers, but the sudden and terrible vengeance that overtook them. Their few flying fugitives were pursued and brought to punishment, and probably not one of the Kolapoor rebels now lives to tell the tale of that fearful night. We can never recall the events of that terrible mutiny, and the beloved friends who perished in it, without remembering with gratitude the special providence which removed us from its perils.

The Mission abandoned.

Being alone at Kolapoor, our return to America suspended all the operations of the mission. But they were *only suspended*, and we fondly clung to the hope that we should be able to return and resume our labors. The sea-voyage did much for my broken health, and it continued to rally in the bracing air of my native land. After some twelve or fourteen months, I mentioned, in an incidental letter to the Secretary, my improving health, and expressed a hope that we should soon be able to return to our mission. A reply of Oct. 6, 1858, says:

"The Prudential Committee [yesterday] voted to discontinue the Kolapoor Mission"!

Let those who would judge of our grief at this event, go and toil in such a dark field as Kolapoor, struggling with opposition and difficulties with a strength of purpose and interest that winds the heart-strings around the converts, inquirers, schools, and all the interests of the mission, so closely that they can not be severed without leaving them mangled, bleeding, and palpitating from the effect of such violence.

This abandonment of the mission was just after our annual meeting, and there was no chance for an appeal to the Board for nearly a year. Why is it that such business is never brought before the whole Board before the Prudential Committee have taken action? Why did the Deputation start for India with such absolute powers, to speak and act for the Board, just *before* the meeting of the Board, and without seeking advice and authority from its proper source?

Appeal from the Prudential Committee to the Board.

At the next annual meeting of the Board held in Philadelphia, Oct. 4, 1859, an appeal was presented in behalf of this mission. My first request for a hearing, was declined, but at a subsequent stage of the meeting when no *business* was ready and missionaries were called out to fill up the time, a gentleman in the audience, a stranger to myself, arose, and with dignified firmness, asked: "If missionaries are to be heard, why not hear Mr. W., who requested a hearing this morning?" The inquiry was opportune, and secured a kind hearing for the following

Appeal.

"MR. PRESIDENT, FATHERS AND BRETHREN:

"It has been announced to you that one of your missions in Western India has been abandoned. In the official announcement of this action to myself, the reason assigned was in the following words: 'It is thought that the funds placed at the disposal of the Board can be expended in India to better advantage, than in a merely protected state, where the toleration and protection for the missionary and his converts are but partial, as is the fact in Kolapoor.'

"In closing my reply to the Prudential Committee on this subject, I remarked: 'I believe there is proper provision for an appeal from such action of the Committee to the whole Board. In proper time and manner I shall wish to avail myself of this right of appeal in the present case. If you think of any suggestions that may be of service to me in preparing and presenting such an appeal, please send them to me at your earliest convenience.' The Committee have not favored me with any such suggestions, but supposing the proper time has come, I desire respectfully to appeal from this action of the Committee, to the judgment of your larger body. In doing so, I beg to submit that the reason assigned for abandoning this mission, (namely, that Kolapoor is 'a merely a protected state,') though a proper consideration to be weighed at the *inception* of the mission, is no valid reason for abandoning it after some five years of successful labor. Perhaps I should say just here, that the origin of the mission is traceable to no wish of mine, but rests entirely with the Committee. Waiving all allusion, however, to past action, I beg to submit the following reasons why the Kolapoor mission should be at once resumed and vigorously carried on by the American Board:

"1. *It is a large and interesting field of labor.*—Just under the window of my '*home*' in India, is the city of Kolapoor, with a population of 44,000 idolaters. So frequent and flourishing are the villages around it, that within twenty miles of my door is a population of 120,000. And beyond on every side, is a wide region of unbroken Hinduism, embracing three or four millions.

"2. *It is a needy field.*—Darkness reigns there such as may be felt. Human victims have been offered to their cruel gods within the memory of many still living. . . . A few years ago, British officers canvassed the whole kingdom, and found only 400 boys, and no girls, receiving any education. They need the Gospel, and this alone can elevate and save them.

"3. *It is an unoccupied field.*—No other missionary society is laboring in that whole region. I am the only missionary who was ever sent to live and labor in it. My nearest missionary neighbor is at Satara, seventy miles distant.

"4. *It is a promising field.*—It is true that at first the people showed great prejudice and determined opposition. They sent to their king a numerously signed petition praying him to banish us from his kingdom. And when they found we were not banished, they adopted a rigid system of non-intercourse. Our best efforts to gain a hearing from the people were quite in vain. But when at length we succeeded in gathering some of their children into schools, their prejudices and opposition rapidly disappeared. The very men who petitioned our banishment came in numbers to converse and listen, and with the nucleus of the schools we were always able to secure an audience of eighty to two hundred hearers.

"More than a dozen became enlightened, and admitted their convictions of the truth. Of these, five were baptized and admitted to church fellowship.

"Not less than 500 youth became well instructed in the fundamental doctrines of our Christian faith, and an amount of Christian knowledge was widely disseminated among the people, at thought of which our hearts always swell with gratitude and hope. We left some fifty girls able to read the Bible, recite catechisms, and repeat and sing Christian hymns, where before not a respectable girl or woman in the whole kingdom knew her letters. Here was progress which gladdened our hearts, and we know of no mission of this Board in India upon which the Lord has bestowed a larger blessing, in proportion to the amount of labor, in its first years.

"5. *It has a good climate.*—Situated a little east of the mountains, it is free from the very heavy rains of Bombay and the coast, while its proximity to the ocean secures a sea-breeze to modify the intense heat of the hot season, and thus the climate is a little more favorable than that of any other station occupied by our Board in Western India.

"6. *The native government is friendly.*—The king did not

banish us at the request of his subjects. Myself and wife have always been cordially welcomed at the palace.

"After our schools convinced the people that we desired to do them good, four or five children and youth from the palace attended them *till they were suppressed by your late Deputation.*

"At the outbreak of the late terrible mutiny, when the houses of some of the British officers were plundered and burned, our mission-buildings remained unharmed. We never lacked protection for ourselves or our converts. When your Committee authorized us to build a mission-house, the king offered us all the ground we desired. The day we were obliged, in broken health, to leave Kolapoor for America, he sent his court officers to express his regrets and a kind farewell, and some hundred natives gathered around our house, remaining from early morning till four o'clock P.M., and then accompanied us some distance from the city, repeating their kind wishes and hopes for our return, mingled with their touching farewells.

"7. *A good foundation has been laid.*—The special difficulties involved at first, in the prejudices and opposition of the people, have been outlived. A dwelling-house, chapel, and school-house have been built. A beginning has been made full of promise.

"Col. R. Phayre, Quarter-Master-General of the Bombay Army, a man in character and piety quite of the Havelock stamp, sending a monthly subscription for our schools, wrote as follows: 'I wish particularly to support your work, which I look upon as second in importance to none that I have seen.' 'I must say that I have nowhere seen a more satisfactory state of matters than I witnessed that Sunday in Kolapoor.' 'When I visited your mission-house, and saw the practical working of your own and Mrs. Wilder's faith and love, I could not help offering heartfelt thanksgiving to God, who had implanted so promising and flourishing a nursery in the very heart of one of the most bigoted and perhaps hostile cities in the Southern Mahratta country.'

"Similar statements have been sent to me by some twenty or thirty devoted chaplains, missionaries, and Christian laymen in India.

"*The Oriental Christian Spectator*, an able periodical published at Bombay, making a kind note of our departure from

India, after speaking of our life and labors several years at Ahmednuggur, adds: 'Of the Kolapoór mission, in the same province, Mr. Wilder has been the father and founder, laying by wise educational and other evangelistic measures, a good foundation for the time to come, and on which, we trust, he will in after-years be spared to build.'

"Here, then, is your *Kolapoor mission—A large field—A needy field—An unoccupied field—A promising field— With a good climate—A friendly native government, and 'a good foundation for the time to come,' already laid.*

"Your Committee entered upon this field of their own free will and accord. Are there not strong reasons for holding on and prosecuting the mission with vigor? I need not speak of the pernicious influence upon the minds of the Hindus, of fickle and hesitating efforts, of beginning to build and not being able to finish. I need not remind you of the scriptural estimate of those who put their hand to the plow and look back; but I do urge that Kolapoor is a noble field for missionary effort. It is embraced in the title-deed of Christ and his great commission to the Church. The idolaters there *need* the Gospel, and must have it, or perish forever. You have voluntarily entered the field. Are there not weighty reasons why you should prosecute your mission there with increasing energy?

"In urging this Appeal, I present only such arguments as remain valid whether I live or die. I say nothing of our own personal attachment—of the closeness with which our heart-strings have become entwined around the dear children and youth, and all the interests of that forsaken mission. Our years of toil, discouragement and suffering, while continuing to hope against hope till we outlived the peculiar prejudices of the people, have only bound our hearts more closely to them and the work to which we have devoted our lives. But the arguments here urged will remain valid in any possible event.

"With becoming deference to your honorable body, this appeal is respectfully submitted; and I sincerely hope the Lord may incline your hearts to pass a resolve at once, unanimously resuming the Kolapoor mission.

"But, if not—if you disregard this appeal—when the memory of our forsaken mission comes over our souls with sorrow, we shall at least have this consolation, that *we have done for it what we could.* R. G. WILDER."

Could a vote have been taken when this appeal was listened to so kindly, would not the mission have been instantly resumed, as unanimously as the assembly at the late Jubilee Meeting declared for $400,000 the present year?

This appeal was referred to the Committee on the Mahratta missions, who reported:

"The Prudential Committee have judged it best not to reoccupy the field, (Kolapoor,) for the reason that four independent centres of operation in Western India, are found to be too many for the amount of funds that can be devoted to that part of the heathen world. The cause here assigned is one of those financial trials overtaking the Committee, in the pressure of the times and the exigencies of the Board in regard to funds. . . .

"Your Committee heard with great interest the appeal of the worthy missionary, (presented with so much ability, zeal, and earnestness,) whom ill-health forced from this important field; and they would urge, in view of all the facts of the case, that amid other and even more important fields in Western India, the one in question should be kept in sight by the Prudential Committee, and be reöccupied when the funds of the Board and men at its command, shall justify such action."—*Ann. Report for* 1859, *p.* 18, *and Missionary Herald, p.* 333.

This report referred the case entirely to the pleasure of the Prudential Committee, who had before abandoned the mission. Does not this result fully verify the recent statement of one of our leading editors of the religious press, that, "If the Prudential Committee err in judgment in a case like Mr. W.'s, it is hardly practicable, as such cases are managed, for the Board to correct the error"? The Prudential Committee did not reconsider their action, and the mission remains abandoned.

Re-establishment of the Mission.

But "there is hope of a tree, if it be cut down, that it will sprout again." There is deep and abiding interest in this forsaken mission. Many praying men and women are unable to understand why it should be abandoned. In the midst of a dense population of heathen, seventy miles from any other mission, with millions of perishing idolaters around it—why, *oh! why* should it be abandoned? Why should the strength of a mission family for some five years, and $10,000 in money expended in laying its foundation, be thus sacrificed? Is it not a good locality? All testimony confirms the statements of the foregoing Appeal. Dr. Anderson himself writes:

"*Kolapoor is a better place*," *and* "*I could not but hope it would take the place of Aurungabad in our plan of enlargement.*" "*You have* [at Kolapoor] *one of the most eligible posts in the Deccan.* In my own mind its aspects stand related to the very delightful ones of Satara, *one of the finest missionary localities I have seen in India.*"

The friends of missions are not satisfied that this interesting field should be thus given up. And how *can* they be? The plea that it is in "a merely protected state," does not satisfy, for this should have been considered before so much toil and money had been expended. Besides, the Government is to all intents and purposes British, the king having little power, being decidedly friendly to the mission, and allowing no hindrance whatever to our labors.

The plea based on a *want of funds* is not satisfactory, for $2000 a year—less than the salary of our treasurer—for the whole expense of the mission, is too small a sum for which to abandon *such* a field. Besides, the Prudential Committee immediately commenced another station at Sholapoor, more remote from any occupied station than Kolapoor, and where foundations must be again laid at heavy expense!

Ecclesiastical Action.

Many of the best friends of the Board have felt troubled and grieved by the abandonment of this mission. Two large ecclesiastical bodies, whose members have ever been among its warmest friends and zealous supporters, have felt constrained to put on record the following resolutions:

Action of the Champlain Presbytery.

" *Whereas*, from long and intimate acquaintance of some of us with the Rev. R. G. Wilder, and in view of his present circumstances and his earnest desire to return to his missionary field, we feel it to be a matter of justice to him and to the cause of our Lord Jesus Christ to express our sympathies and sentiments; therefore,

" 1. *Resolved*, That we have implicit confidence in the Christian and ministerial character of brother Wilder, his strict integrity and exemplary fidelity while in the service of the A.B.C.F.M., [15 years,] as well as in his assiduous efforts to excite and increase in our home churches the true spirit of Christian missions.

" 2. *Resolved*, That we consider him possessed of rare qualifications for the missionary enterprise, and regret that impaired health obliged him to leave the foreign field, where he had labored with great success, and to which he was ardently attached.

" 3. *Resolved*, That as brother Wilder's health is now so far restored that he deems it safe, and is earnestly desirous to return to Kolapoor, and being already familiar with the Mahratta language, we consider it very desirable that the way be opened to secure this important object.

" 4. *Resolved*, That we will cheerfully assist him ourselves, and we cordially commend him to all whose hearts the Lord may incline to aid him with their prayers and contributions.

" STEPHEN H. WILLIAMS, Stated Clerk.

"*Chateaugay*, *June* 20, 1860."

Action of the St. Lawrence Consociation.

"*Resolved*, That having listened to the statements of Rev. R. G. Wilder, returned missionary from Kolapoor, India, we commend him to the sympathies, prayers and contributions of the Churches of Consociation, and to all who love our Lord Jesus Christ, in the hope that he may be encouraged and sustained in his noble determination to return and resume his labors among the perishing Hindus of Kolapoor.

"Attest, P. MONTAGUE, Register.

"*Madrid*, *June* 27, 1860."

If this action were for my sake alone, it should have no place here. Will the reader kindly dismiss its *personal* bearings, and consider it only for its relation to the interests of our dear mission? For this it has a permanent value, and deserves a record in this connection. With this kind and effective encouragement, and the ready favor of many other dear friends, whose sympathy and interest will never be forgotten, a few months' effort has resulted in gathering resources sufficient to authorize the attempt to reëstablish the mission. We go back with joy, trusting that the prayers and aid of friends, and the promised grace and presence of *Him who gave our commission*, will sustain us in that dark field. In view of the hindrances that have obstructed our return for a time, let no friend ask, Why do you not remain in your native land? Dear native land! precious "high places of Zion!" beloved friends of our early years! Do we not *love* them? God knows.

> "Yes, my native land, I love thee;
> All thy scenes, I love them well."

But did not the Son of God love the presence-chamber and glory of the Father? And, in suffering for us, did he not "leave us an example, that we should follow his steps"? And has he not said, "Go ye into all the world and preach the Gospel to every creature"? Is the Gospel heaven's choicest gift to man, and shall the millions around Kolapoor be left to perish without it? Where, oh! where can we do more for Christ and the salvation of precious souls, than in that dark kingdom? With 44,000 idolaters under my window, 120,000 within a few miles of my door, and millions around me a little more distant, with no other missionary to care for their souls—where, oh! where on the globe can I find a more needy or noble field for Christian effort?

Testimony of European Friends.

This sketch of the Kolapoor mission must here close for the present. But of the many statements of European friends, elicited by the suppression of its schools and its temporary abandonment, it is proper that a few brief extracts should find a record in this connection—the more so as they have a direct bearing on the great interests of our missionary work; and it is well for the friends of this cause in Christian lands to know the honest convictions of intelligent laborers and patrons in the field.

Of the able and efficient missionaries of the FREE CHURCH OF SCOTLAND, the Rev. Messrs. James and Kinnaird Mitchell write, (the former with some forty years' experience:) "My dear Mr. W., the Lord had signally blessed your well-conceived plans for collecting parents to public worship, along with the pupils of your schools. Such a fact is much to the point, for showing the connection between preaching to adults and educational institutions. It ought surely to be taken into account." "We have no hesitation in employing properly qualified heathen men to conduct the literary branches of our seminaries, rather than be without them. We would have just so many of these schools as we could properly superintend. *In India these schools present one of the best possible agencies for inculcating the truth as it is in Jesus.*"

After testifying to the value of the different schools, and especially of English schools, they say: "It is our undoubted experience that most, if not all, the useful converts, have been converted through these institutions. Every Indian mission ought to have them from the first, and they should be continued in full energy as long as it exists. They should never be extinguished, as we are sorry to hear has been the case at some of the stations of the A.B.C.F.M. *It is a narrow and mistaken policy to discontinue the schools.*"

The Rev. A. White, missionary of the same church, writes: "Every way of gaining hearers for the Gospel, especially such a good way as instructing those who are in brutish ignorance, and quickening the torpid mind into activity by a sound education, must be faithfully followed. I trust that ere long your schools will be all restored."

The Rev. Stephen Hislop writes: "I believe the Hindus, fortified as they are by the buttresses of an ancient superstition, trammelled by the fetters of a tyrannous caste, perverted by the sophisms of a false philosophy, and corrupted by the impurities of a degrading mythology, are in a worse position for giving an intelligent consideration to the statements of God's word, than any other nation at the present time." Resting an argument for schools upon this basis, Mr. H. adds: "The Gospel is made known by missionaries in the schools as well as in the streets, only there are advantages for making it known with effect in the former locality, which can not be secured in the latter." After describing long-continued and faithful labors in oral preaching, Mr. H. says: "Not one soul was awakened, so far as man could judge, by the preaching of the word in the city and villages." "I can not fancy any thing more paralyzing to the hands of a missionary, than to be debarred from using that mode of work for which he is best qualified, or which, at all events, he conscientiously believes to be the one most suited to his field of labor."

The Rev. J. M. Mitchell, D.D., writes: "Were the Deputation offering their cherished plan of missionary operations for the imitation of all missions in India, I should strongly protest against a scheme so exclusive. For a mission planted in a large city to leave out education—to leave out even *English* education—is, I think, in the present condition of India, *the same as cutting off a right hand.* Towns of the size of Ahmednuggur and Kolapoor can not be efficiently acted on, without education coming in as a part of mission work. In a new station like Kolapoor, the prohibition of schools seems a very serious evil, and I heartily sympathize with Mr. Wilder in his deep regret on this subject."

The Rev. John Wilson, D.D., of thirty years' experience, attests the necessity of schools "on a very large scale, to bring the Hindu mind to any thing like a resemblance to that of the generality of unconverted persons in Britain and America." "The effect of mission schools in the west of India," he adds, "has certainly not been that of diminishing either the amount or efficacy of any other method of promulgating divine truth, but the contrary. For every form in which they exist in the mission to which I belong, they have received the divine blessing in actual conversions. Even those of them which have been taught by heathen teachers, in the want of Christian teachers able to secure a due attendance at them, have been thus acknowledged of the Lord." "I am not aware of a *single European* missionary who approves of the policy which they [the American Deputation] are understood to have recommended in reference to education, either through the vernacular or the English language."

Rev. James Aitken of more than twenty years' experience, says: "Is there no advantage in getting the poor children of darkness before their corruptions have been thoroughly developed, and their minds preöccupied and prejudiced?" "I can not without deep interest, advert to the fact that, so far as my own observation and experience go, all the really satisfactory converts I have ever known any thing of in India, have been the fruit, either of educational seminaries, or of a process of laborious and protracted tuition, equal to that which is practised in these seminaries."

Of our worthy brethren of the IRISH PRESBYTERIAN CHURCH, Rev. Dr. Glasgow very fitly remarks: "Our great commission is to 'teach all nations,' and by what logic the teaching of the young and of science is to be excluded, I do not know." "I can testify from long experience that the conducting of schools does not decrease but increase the actual amount of direct preaching of the Gospel, by furnishing occasions of time, place, and audience."

Rev. James McKee of the same mission, writes: "I confess I sympathize with you, and have done all along, in deploring several of the changes effected by your late Deputation. Necessity as well as wisdom must soon compel you to reëstablish your schools." "I am, I confess, amazed, that men such as those deputed by your Board, could so ignore the opinions and practices, not only of their own missionaries in India, but of the missionaries of every other body of which I know any thing. By their decision regarding schools, they have virtually pronounced regarding most of the missionaries in India that they are unfit for their office." "I am constrained to believe that the closing of the schools belonging to the American missions in this Presidency, was a rash and unwise proceeding, and that the sooner this resolution is rescinded and these schools reöpened, the better."

I have before me very full statements from our excellent brethren of the LONDON MISSIONARY SOCIETY, stationed at Belgaum, Bellary, Bangalore, and other places. Their testimony is unanimous and earnest in favor of schools, and that too after missionary experience, in some individual cases, of twenty, thirty, and even forty years. I would gladly place their valuable statements on record in detail, but can find room for only a few brief extracts. After developing their educational views and plans at length, their Corresponding Secretary, Rev. J. Sewall, adds : "In order to carry out these educational labors, it is considered :

"That *boarding-schools* for boys and girls should be established, and vigorously and prayerfully conducted at each of our stations. . . .

"That a *superior English* and vernacular day-school should be established at each principal station — as this appears to be almost the only method of reaching that important class of society, the children of the middle and upper ranks of the people.

"That we regard it equally essential that purely *vernacular* schools be established for the benefit of the masses of the people," etc.

The views and practice of the able and successful missionaries of the CHURCH OF ENGLAND, are so well known to be decidedly in favor of schools as one of their most effective agencies, that I need not quote them here. I have them in their reports, and in the letters of individual missionaries and chaplains, and would gladly place them on record, especially the statements of esteemed friends, as the Rev. C. Laing and the Rev. H. H. Brereton, who have expressed their very high estimate of our schools and personal labors, in terms of special kindness.

And it should be known that the Christian laity in India

appreciate the effective agency of our schools, no less readily than the missionaries themselves. The cheerful liberality with which they give to support these schools, has already been mentioned. Some statements of Col. R. Phayre, Quarter-Master General of the Bombay army, were quoted in the appeal for the Kolapoor mission. In the same connection, speaking of our schools and Sabbath services, he says: "There I witnessed the *children* receiving instruction in the way of salvation, and the *fathers* naturally interested in the progress of their offspring, attending to *hear*. Now we know that faith cometh by *hearing*, and there can be no more auspicious moment for a man to hear to the saving of his soul, than when his heart is softened toward the preacher by gratitude for kindness to his child. I have now been about twenty years in India, and have long felt that teaching and preaching must aid each other." "Oh! what a pity to give up such agencies. What *can* you do without them in such a place as Kolapoor? Those good men [the Deputation] have not *faith* enough. Why can they not trust God, and the experience and conviction of their brethren who have already toiled in this work so many years?" This large-hearted Christian always gave us $30 a year for our schools in Kolapoor, and when they were suppressed by the Deputation, he kindly offered to increase his subscription, if that would avail, and even give $100 or $200 at once to start them again.

F. L. Yonge, Esq., another contributor, and one who observed the working and influence of our schools for years, writes: "I think it a thousand pities that your schools should be given up."

Edwin Checkley, Esq., inclosing Rs. 50 for our schools at Kolapoor, writes: "I can not express how very greatly I sympathize in your feelings regarding the very great mistake made by your Deputation in closing your schools."

Similar letters of sympathy came to us from many European friends scattered over Western India, most of them entirely unsolicited, the facts in the case being known because our previous agencies were known, and all changes by the

Deputation were manifest to all around us. Each mission in India is a city set on a hill, and can not be hid. The doings of the Deputation became known to the public press, and hence when permission came from the Prudential Committee to resume our schools at Kolapoor, the *Bombay Guardian* of July 5, 1856, in a leading editorial says: "We rejoice to learn that the Prudential Committee of the A.B.C.F.M., have restored to the Rev. R. G. Wilder, missionary at Kolapoor, the liberty of having schools, which was taken away from him on occasion of the visit of the Deputation to this country. This gives us pleasure quite independent of any opinion we may entertain as to the value of schools to a mission. We think that a missionary, about whose fitness to be a missionary there can be no question, should be allowed to adopt such modes of labor as he conscientiously, and after due experience, believes to be the best for him in his circumstances. It is certain that if he be hindered from laboring in the way that he regards as the most suitable, if there be no margin left for his own convictions, and the teachings of his own experience, he will occupy a position unbecoming a missionary of the Lord Jesus Christ. If the aim be to degrade the calling of the missionary, and reduce him to the standing of a mere agent of a missionary Board, then let him be subjected to a code of rules and regulations; let him be told, not merely what he is to do, but in what mode he is to do it.

"But the true idea of a missionary is, that he is one whom the Head of the Church hath called, qualified, and sent forth; and so long as he is viewed as a missionary, his convictions of duty must be respected." As to the best agencies: "Who is fittest to decide? He that is acquainted with his field by personal labors performed in it for years, acquainted with the character and customs of those among whom his lot is cast, informed by experience of the particular difficulties he has to encounter, he or the Secretary of the Society, who may indeed, pay a flying visit to the foreign field on Deputation, but whose years are spent in a land of churches and Bibles?"

"What made the prohibition laid on Mr. Wilder the more surprising was, that he asked no allowance from the funds of the Board for his schools, but was prepared to carry them on by the aid of Christians in this country, who approve of this mode of evangelistic labor."

J. T. Molesworth Esq., author of our invaluable dictionaries of the Mahratta language, a profound scholar and eminent Christian, expressing his grief for the loss of these schools, writes: "I am distressed beyond measure that good men should have been left to make such mistakes." And again: "I had the pleasure of seeing in the last *Bombay Guardian*, that *permission has been granted*, (alas! that man should be found audacious enough to refuse permission,) for the restoration of your Kolapoor vernacular schools." "To restore things not merely abandoned but abjured, is difficult; but you will do your best, and He *to whom power belongeth*, (Ps. 62 : 11,) will prosper you. I have much pleasure in sending you Rs. 100 to help you at the outset."

The Oriental Christian Spectator, an able periodical published at Bombay, says, June, 1857: "Mr. Wilder has proved a most faithful and able missionary while in the midst of us. He was for several years stationed at Ahmednuggur in the Deccan. Of the *Kolapoor Mission*, the latest report of which we insert in this number of our periodical, he has been the father and founder, laying, by wise educational and other evangelistic measures, a good foundation for the time to come, and on which we trust, *he will in after-years be spared to build.*"

"AND THIS WILL WE DO, IF GOD PERMIT." (Heb. 6 : 3.)

CHAPTER VII.

CHARACTER AND RESULTS OF MISSION SCHOOLS IN OUR CEYLON MISSION.

CEYLON, the ancient Taprobane, is an island at the southern extremity of India, some 300 miles long by 170 wide. Its population in 1831 was 950,917, of whom 20,656 were slaves. The Cingalese are most numerous, especially in the interior and southern portions of the island, while in the northern and eastern portions the Tamil race prevails.

The natural resources of the island are abundant, and it furnished a very extensive commerce to the nations of Western Asia as early as the sixth century. It was lost sight of during the dark ages, but the Portuguese discovered it in 1505, and for a century gradually increased their possessions upon it, and were then supplanted, in the first half of the seventeenth century, by the Dutch. The first aggression of the English on this island dates from 1782, and in fourteen years they entirely supplanted the Dutch. In 1803 they came in conflict with the native government, and as early as 1815 gained possession of the whole island.

During the successive reigns of the Portuguese and the Dutch, the Roman and Protestant religions had been introduced and propagated by the influence and power of the state, but the British treaty provided that the old religious rites and superstitions of the natives should be inviolably protected and maintained by the government, and hence Christianity, both Roman and Protestant, soon became almost extinct.

Feb. 24th, 1813, there embarked a lone stranger from the Isle of France, and directed his course to Ceylon. He was a man of affliction. His earthly hopes had been dashed, and he had drained the cup of sorrow to its dregs. But on his thoughtful countenance there was stamped a purpose in unison with that of Him who came from heaven to earth to die for man, and in his eye there shone the light and glow of a holy enthusiasm. He was a voluntary exile from this, his native land, and the Governor-General of India had made him a forced exile from the territory of the Hon. East-India Company. That cruel order of the Governor, which drove him from Calcutta, by the discomforts of a hasty and untimely voyage, consigned his beloved wife and child to their martyr-graves; and now, having deposited their precious dust with many tears on that lone isle of the ocean, Samuel Newell turned back to seek his companions in toil and persecution, and soon landed at Colombo. He did not find his associates in Ceylon. Hall and Nott were at Bombay, prosecuting that noble struggle which, with God's blessing, ended in breaking up the exclusive policy of the East-India Company, and letting in the light of God's truth upon the degraded millions of India.

Newell remained, teaching and preaching Christ, some ten months at Colombo, and then joined his brethren at Bombay. But this event was the starting-point of the Ceylon mission of the A.B.C.F.M. The representations of Newell to the American Board availed, and Messrs. Warren, Richards, Meigs, and Poor were sent out to establish a mission in Ceylon. They reached the island March 22, 1816, and established themselves in the district of Jaffna early the following October. This district, some 40 miles long, by 15 broad, consists of a cluster of islands at the northern extremity of Ceylon, with a population of 147,671, mostly of the Tamil race. Sharing the favor of the British government under the influence of Governor Brownrigg, the commencement of their mission was auspicious.

Chief Interest centres in the Schools.

Among the earliest notices of their labors we read of "ten or twelve boys" who became pupils, "and began to learn the English alphabet." "Early in December teachers were engaged to open schools under the superintendence of the missionaries." In 1817 the progress and brightening hopes of the mission are found to centre in their schools. "In October the weekly meeting with the school-masters and others, for prayer and personal conversation on religion, was commenced," and a *boarding-school* opened, "with ten or twelve of their most promising boys."

The first notice of a hopeful conversion is recorded of one of these pupils. "He appeared deeply interested in divine truth, and in a short time declared his belief in Christianity, and his desire to embrace it publicly, at any sacrifice."

The missionaries became so deeply impressed with the value of these schools that the progress and enlargement of the mission is uniformly marked by their increase.

In 1818 Mr. Poor had eight free schools under his care, with four hundred pupils, and a boarding-school of twenty-four. "Mr. Meigs had five schools, and was about to open two more." Their Sabbath audiences were composed of the pupils, with such of their parents and friends as the presence of the children induced to come.

In 1819, though the mission was weakened by the failure of health, "still, the schools were carried on and enlarged. There were fifteen free schools, with seven hundred scholars." "There was also a boarding-school at each station," with "forty-eight boys and girls." The "good influence" of these schools "was manifest, and the mission entreated for funds for the extension of the system."

First Revival in the Schools.

This year witnessed the first revival in that favored mission, and it seems to have been confined entirely to the schools. Its first converts were Gabriel Tissera and Nicholas Permander, two *heathen teachers*, who had been taken into service at the commencement of the mission. ' There were some who gave evidence of piety at each of the stations, and several of the boys in the schools were subjects of special seriousness." The mission was reïnforced at the close of this year by Messrs. Winslow, Spaulding, Woodward, and Scudder.

In 1820 "pecuniary embarrassments crippled the mission," and the British government interdicted any further reïnforcements. Still, "the number of boarding scholars was enlarged, and several new free schools were opened," and "the convicting and sanctifying influences of the Holy Spirit were manifestly present."

In 1821 "the want of funds was severely felt, and several of the free schools were discontinued for a time." But the record of the year gives four boarding-schools, with 72 boys and 15 girls, and twenty-four free schools with 1117 boys and 36 girls. The strong prejudice and opposition of the heathen had broken up one of the girls' schools, and the missionaries say: "It was doing much, therefore, to have 51 girls in school."

Second Revival.

This year the mission enjoyed its second precious revival. "On the 22d of April, two boys from the boarding-school at Tillipally were received as members of the Church." "On the last evening in June four girls came to Mr. Poor, in distress on account of their sinfulness, and anxious to know what they must do to be saved." Scarcely had they left when Nicholas came to ask how he should converse with those who were anxious about their souls. Among the pupils the seriousness increased, and at an inquiry-meeting soon after, twenty or thirty were present, and several expressed hopes in Christ. "On the evening of the 23d, (July,) seven girls came, with earnest inquiries after the way of salvation. Early in August four were added to the Church;" and in December a servant and two boarding-girls were received into the Church. Three of the first converts, who had been brought under saving influences by being employed as teachers, were licensed to preach the Gospel.

In 1822 the special utility of the schools appears in the active efforts of the pupils, both boys and girls, to make known the truth to their parents and neighbors. The same appears in the first Christian marriage. This took place between two pupils, Daniel Smead and Miranda Safford, and the parties being of different castes, (the Vellale and Chanda,) it furnished a severe test of the influence of the schools, and of their value in the estimation of the natives. "The heathen thought that the new religion was indeed fitted to turn the world upside down," but "the immediate effect on the cause of female education was decidedly favorable."

Origin of the Batticotta and Oodooville Seminaries.

In 1823 the progress of the mission is still marked by "an increase of the number of schools and pupils." The missionaries became so deeply impressed with the value of educational agencies that they resolved to establish a "mission college." "The immediate objects proposed were:

"1. To impart a thorough knowledge of the English languagn, as the only way to unlock the treasures which that language contains.

"2. The cultivation of Tamil literature, which is necessary in order to oppose idolatry successfully, and in order to raise up a reading population.

"3. The study of Sanscrit by a select few, from among those who may be designed for native preachers.

"4. To teach Hebrew, and in some cases, Latin and Greek, to those native preachers who may be employed as translators of the Scriptures.

"5. To teach, as far as the circumstances of the country require, the sciences usually studied in the Colleges of Europe and America."

This "seminary was put into operation as a central school, at Batticotta, under the care of Mr. Poor, on the 22d of July. It was opened with twenty-six scholars, selected from the boarding-schools." This number soon increased to forty-seven.

"A central school for girls was opened at Oodooville, under the care of Mrs. Winslow." It commenced with twenty-two girls, and soon had twenty-nine.

Thus each year and each revival increased the convictions of the missionaries as to the value of these schools, and therefore they enlarged and improved them.

Third Revival in the Schools.

1824.—This year a third and more powerful revival in these schools attests the marked approval and special blessing of God upon them. We find they had fifty free schools, with some two thousand pupils, and two hundred boarding scholars.

The revival commenced in the boarding-school at Tillipally, on the 18th of January. Mr. Woodward first noticed that some of the boys were much affected during the morning service. He appointed other meetings, and the next day sent for Mr. Winslow. He came, "and found seven or eight of the boys manifesting much anxious concern for their spiritual welfare, and others more or less serious. Most of them belonged to the *boarding-school.*" "The Spirit of God seemed evidently present."

"The disposition to serious and anxious inquiry continued to increase till all the members of the school, (about forty in number,) the domestics of the family, and two or three *heathen* schoolmasters were among the inquirers. The result was, that most of the older boys, and two girls, gave pleasing evidence of a change of character."

The very next Sabbath a like blessing came down upon the girls' boarding-school at Oodooville. While Mr. Winslow was addressing them, "some were much affected, and tears began to flow from those unused to weep."

Other meetings followed; deep convictions took hold upon the hearts of the pupils, "and the Lord graciously caused the work to proceed, until no one in the school remained wholly unaffected."

The next development of the revival was in the monthly prayer-meeting at Batticotta, Feb. 2d. "We had scarcely assembled in the afternoon and sung a hymn, when the Holy Spirit seemed to fill all the place where we were together. The brother who was leading in prayer was so much overwhelmed with a sense of the Divine presence, that he could scarcely proceed. The same influence was felt by all, and the afternoon was spent in prayer, interrupted only by a few passages read from the Scriptures, and by singing and weeping."

"The next Sabbath," a precious season was enjoyed at Manepy. "When, in the afternoon, the children and youth of the boarding-schools of that and the other stations came together, an affecting scene was exhibited. Many were in tears. More than thirty expressed a desire to forsake all for Christ. The Lord carried on the work, till, in a school consisting of about forty-five boys, many of whom were young, nearly half *professed* themselves to be the Lord's."

A still more special blessing was enjoyed at Panditeripo, commencing February 12th. "After the boys had gone to their room, and were about to lie down to sleep, Whelpley, (a native member of the church,) was induced to exhort them most earnestly to flee from the wrath to come. They were roused and could not sleep. By little companies they went out into the garden to pray, and the voice of supplication was soon heard in every quarter. It waxed louder and louder, each one, or each company, praying and weeping as though all were alone. More than thirty were thus engaged in a small garden. The cry was, 'What shall I do to be saved?' and 'Lord, send thy spirit.'" "The next day they seemed to be earnestly seeking for the salvation of their souls. More than twenty, at that place, indulged the hope that they had obtained the forgiveness of their sins."

In the farther progress of the work in the seminary at Batticotta, it is stated that "about *ten* of the youths expressed a determination to forsake all for Christ, and scarcely one in the school was altogether unmoved." "Of the subjects of this revival, . . in all sixty-nine, were thought, in March, to give some evidence of a change of heart. The special interest continued through the summer. At times, nearly all the members of the boarding-schools, and many others, avowed more or less anxiety for the salvation of their souls; but it was almost wholly confined to those whose long acquaintance with the mission, *either as pupils, as teachers, or servants* in their employment, or as neighbors, had given them some knowledge of Christian truth."

Fourth Revival in the Schools.

In October of this year, the mission enjoyed another gracious visitation of the Holy Spirit upon the youth gathered in their schools. Mr. Winslow writes: "The year closed, as it began, with a revival. The last two months have been a time of silent, but we trust, effectual operation of the Holy Spirit on many hearts." After mentioning some special cases of conversion among the *pupils*, he adds: "Many of the [*heathen*] school-masters also, at the different stations, are more or less serious, and eight or ten may be said to appear well. Of the lads in the central school, and the children in the boarding-schools, several have of late hopefully passed from death unto life."

What more positive testimony is possible to the value of these schools than is furnished in the history of these revivals? Is it possible for God to give the seal of his approval and blessing to such schools more unequivocally than he has here done? Who can wonder that the missionaries came to value these schools as the right arm of their strength? Who can wonder that the old missionaries, who knew their history, and had witnessed these showers of God's grace and mercy upon them, clung to them till they were suppressed by the Deputation, and then mourned over their ruins with many tears, and bitter and touching lamentations?

The year 1825 "opened joyfully." "59 free schools contained 2414 boys and 255 girls, taught by 58 masters; and in the boarding-schools were 126 boys and 31 girls, making in all, 2824 pupils from among the heathen. Several of the teachers had become pious, [all were *heathen teachers* at first, and most were still *heathen,*] and with the more advanced scholars, assisted greatly in the missionary work. The central school at Batticotta, which was intended as the germ of a college, was highly useful, and received the decided approbation of statesmen and divines in different parts of India; insomuch that about $1800 was subscribed for it in Calcutta, and considerable sums at Madras and in Ceylon."

The fruits of the precious revivals in the schools during 1824, were gathered into the Church in larger numbers this year. On the 20th of January, *forty-one* were received into the Church, in the presence of some twelve hundred to fifteen hundred people. Of these forty-one converts the missionaries say: "*Thirty-six belonged* to our charity boarding-schools, and five were from among the people." "Eight more were admitted to the Church" on the 21st of July.

The second revival of 1824 continued with much special interest through 1825, and is spoken of by the missionaries as the *fourth* revival in their schools. Near the close of this year, December 20, Dr. Scudder writes: "There was scarce a careless boy in the school at Batticotta. Dwight and Niles, two members of that school, came to Tillipally, and exhorted and prayed with the pupils there, and a few days afterwards eighteen of the boys were found to be seriously attentive to religion."

In 1826, we find both the missionaries and the officers of the Board regretting that the British government would allow no more American missionaries to settle in Ceylon, and no college unless under British instructors. "This decision, however, did not defeat the main object of the undertaking. It was still possible to sustain a school of a very high order, which should give an education nearly or quite equal to a collegiate course. Encouraged by liberal subcriptions in India, and by favorable opinions both there and in America, the brethren erected buildings "and persevered in their general purpose. The Batticotta Seminary, as it was called, had fifty-three students, of whom twenty-two were members of the church, "and its influence was highly gratifying." Eighteen more students were received into the seminary from the preparatory schools, and the value of the schools and their influence in conciliating the good will of the people, are attested by the fact that there were two or three times as many candidates for vacancies, as the missionaries could receive.

1827 "was a year of quiet and silent progress." "There were 93 free schools, containing 3378 boys and 942 girls." The seminary had 67 students, of whom 24 were church members, and the whole number of pupils under instruction was 4500.

In 1828 "from want of funds it was found necessary to give up a few of the free schools, several of which were transferred to the" Church Missionary Society. A class of 15 left the seminary, having completed their course of study, and a class of 29 entered the preparatory school, selected from not less than 200 applicants, whose claims were clamorously urged by their relatives and friends. What a change since the time when it was difficult to procure a single pupil!

In 1829 "the system of schools was steadily accomplishing its work, laying broad and deep the foundations of future success. The whole number under instruction was 3436. Their improved system of education was attracting the attention of all orders of men. The seminary, especially, was made to bear powerfully on the question whether the Brahmanical religion is true." This it did by teaching the facts of true science, geography, astronomy, etc. A celebrated Hindu astronomer, Vesuvenather, calculated an eclipse of the moon by his Hindu tables. He differed from the calculation of the missionaries fifteen minutes in the time of its commencement, two eighths of the moon's disk in extent, and twenty-four minutes in its duration. The minds of the natives were excited, and many predicted a great triumph for Hinduism. The eclipse came, and verified the calculation of the missionaries—a heavy blow to the claims of the Brahmans, and an equal triumph in favor of the missionaries.

Fifth Revival in the Schools.

In 1830 (October) commenced the *fifth revival* in the mission schools, and it "increased in power and interest to the end of the year. Nearly all the students in the mission seminary were more or less awakened; evident tokens of the Divine presence were seen in the boarding-schools at all the stations, and many of the [*heathen*] teachers and superintendents of free schools received deep religious impressions."

1831.—The revival in the schools continued into this year, and 63 were received into the Church as the fruits of it. The 170 native members were now divided into five churches—one at each station. Of the 93 teachers of free schools, some 30 had become members of the Church, and two of the early converts were licensed to preach. If any doubt the propriety of employing "*heathen teachers*" let them mark the result in this mission.

1832 was a "*good year.*" The schools prospered; 27 persons were received to church fellowship, and the Governor gave leave for additional missionaries from America.

In 1833 the permission of the British Government was gladly welcomed by the Board, and a reïnforcement of five missionaries, Messrs. Todd, Hutchings, Hoisington, Apthorp, and Ward, with their wives, were sent to Ceylon.

Sixth Revival in the Schools.

In 1834 two new stations were established. "The whole number of children and youth under instruction, including 124 in the seminary, was 5367." "But the great event of the year was the commencement of another revival" in the mission schools. It commenced at Batticotta, and "soon spread to all the stations."

1835.—The chief power and results of this revival were developed this year. "Every member of the seminary appeared to be deeply impressed with the truth and importance of vital piety, and a considerable number appeared to become truly penitent." In March, fifteen students of the seminary and two others were received to the church, and there were some twelve other candidates. The work soon spread to the girls' boarding-school at Oodooville, and proved "remarkably rapid and powerful, indicating that its subjects had very clear views of their duty, before they were thus awakened to perform it." "Eleven girls of the boarding-school, and two others, were received into the Church in March," and there were more candidates.

At Tillipally, "in a short time 20 gave evidence of a change of heart, and 13 were added to the church." "The whole number added to the church in March was 51, of whom 48 were received at one meeting at Batticotta. The admissions during the year were 76."

Seventh Revival in the Schools.

A *seventh* revival commenced in the Batticotta Seminary, in November of this year, in which "eighty-five professed their resolution to follow Christ." At the same time a precious blessing came down upon the Oodooville school, and several of the girls were converted.

The special value of these schools appears very distinctly in these successive revivals. In no other conceivable way could such masses of heathen minds have been brought under stated teaching in the very focus of Christian truth, and impregnated with it, so as to have become prepared for the descent of the Spirit and his gracious operations in their rapid conviction and conversion. So long as human agencies are owned and blessed of God, we can not fail to approve the wisdom which devised and sustained these mission schools. The seal of God's own blessing is upon them.

Eighth Revival in the Schools.

In 1836, another precious revival marks the favor and blessing of God upon the schools of this mission. It commenced in the girls' boarding-school at Oodoovillo. With no previous indications of the Spirit's presence, the missionary was aroused from his sleep at night by the voice of some one in distress, and on going to the verandah, found it to be "the voice of prayer and weeping." In a few moments one of the girls came, saying: "We want some one to come and talk and pray with us." The voice of weeping, prayer, and singing did not cease till one or two o'clock in the morning, and some had little or no sleep during the night. Special meetings continued for days, and at the close of one of them, "when the last girl prayed it seemed that it was not her prayer, but the prayer of the Holy Spirit, as if some other person was speaking." The missionary writes: "More deep feeling and fervent wrestling prayer, I never witnessed. The last thing I heard at night, and the first in the morning, was the voice of prayer and praise."

One of the pupils speaking of the revival and of that particular prayer, writes: "Her prayer was as when a miserable beggar pleads with a rich man, or as when a child entreats favor of a parent, or as when a person agonizes for a friend who is about to be hung. When she had closed her prayer, some of us were exceedingly agitated and were unable to speak, for we saw all our sins and defects. Then some of us had a thought, namely, that we could not expect peace of mind until we had called some of the older girls who did not seek Jesus Christ with all their hearts, and seriously talked with them. We, however, concluded that we must first acknowledge our own faults and ask forgiveness of God, and then call the girls and speak with them. After we had done according to this our determination, we called up those who were asleep, and conversed with them. At that time they were aroused to anxiety about their souls. For this we praise the Lord. From that day to this they lift up their voice in prayer to God day and night. We do not believe there is one girl in the school who does not thus pray."

This revival extended to the other schools, and of the thirty-nine received to the Church this year, most were from the Batticotta Seminary.

Value of the Schools.

We do not wonder that these frequent revivals deeply impressed the minds of the missionaries with the value of these schools. These gracious harvests were manifestly the result of seed sown in soil well prepared. The minds of these pupils had been long under Christian teaching and impregnated with Christian truth; hence when the rain of heaven came, the seed of the word sprang up unto life eternal. What right have we to expect such harvests where the soil is not thus cultivated?

Of the girls' boarding-school at Oodooville, the missionaries recorded their estimate this year as follows:

"God has in a singular manner blessed this school from its commencement. *Not one* who has completed a full course in the school has left without giving evidence of decided piety, a fact which should call forth expressions of gratitude from all the friends of missions. The whole number of those who have completed a regular course of study is thirty; all of whom are married to pious young men, most of whom are in mission service. Of the seventy-five who remain, thirty or more give decided evidence of piety. Of those who have left the school it should be remarked that *not one* has disgraced her profession. In several instances where their husbands have fallen into sin, . . they have been the means in the hands of God of leading them back to the fold.

"This institution is viewed with interest, not only when in contrast with the surrounding population, but in view of the bearings it may have on future generations. Having enjoyed the advantages of a Christian education, and having been brought to taste the love of Jesus, they can but feel a deep interest in the welfare of their offspring, as well as their relations and neighbors in general. A desire for the salvation of their heathen parents often leads them to the throne of grace, and often makes them sad."

The Sad Girl.

Of the anxiety of these educated and converted children for the salvation of their parents, take the following instance, which occurred in this same revival:

One of the girls was asked how she felt. Her reply was that she was "sad." "Why? have you any difficulty with the girls? do they not behave well?" "Yes, they behave well." "Then have you not joy on their account?" "Yes." "Why then are you sad?" "My parents," she replied, and tears choked her utterance. "She loved Jesus, but her parents were idolaters. Such persons need the prayers and sympathies of the friends of the blessed Jesus in our favored land."

Speaking of their *heathen teachers* the missionaries say: "Our school-masters are generally men of respectability, and of good caste; the majority of them are *heathen;* a large number, however, have become hopefully pious."

This year (1836) closed with 155 free schools, containing 6272 pupils, of whom 994 were girls.

The whole number of pupils educated in the free schools of the mission from its commencement, (20 years,) was estimated at 15,500. In the Batticotta Seminary were 166 students. A class of 46 being admitted, were selected from 130 candidates, of whom "at least 50 rejected applicants were as well fitted as the class admitted the year before; showing that the desire for admission was raising the standard of education."

Of the graduates of the seminary "57 were in the employment of the American missions, ten were employed by other missions, and twenty-two were in the service of government."

The whole number which had graduated up to this time, or left without completing the full course, was 147.

"To show the Christian influence of the seminary on lads and youth who when they entered were nearly all heathen, it may be mentioned that of those who have left (147) 81 had made a public profession of their faith in Christ, and been received to the Church before leaving. Most of them have continued to conduct themselves in a manner consistent with their profession."

Which of our American colleges has shared a larger blessing than this? Of which of them can we find a larger proportion of graduates turning away from secular pursuits and entering upon the special service of Christ? Ought not *such* institutions on heathen ground to be generously supported, and become embalmed in the affection, sympathy, and prayers of the people of God?

Ninth Revival in the Schools.

1837.—The previous year had closed with marked religious interest in the schools. Of a day of fasting and prayer the missionary writes: "It has been an uncommonly interesting season in the seminary. There are indications that the Lord is with us indeed. May his presence be gloriously manifest."

Of the monthly prayer-meeting he says: "I was still more encouraged, and could not but feel that the Lord was at hand." "There are several who declare themselves ready to live for God and Christ. Some we have good reason to believe are converted. To God be all the glory." "We do not doubt but that the judgment-day will disclose much fruit to the praise of God's abounding grace."

But the special revival of this year occurred in May and June, and as heretofore, its special fruits appeared in the schools. In the Batticotta seminary were "twelve or fifteen" hopeful conversions, and "at Oodooville, sixteen were afterwards admitted to the Church, as the fruits of this gracious visitation." The whole number received during the year was 46.

Notice of Magee, a converted Pupil.

This brief notice of one of the converts, was prepared by a school-mate in the seminary, and its correctness attested by the missionaries. It is given here, not for any thing remarkable in itself, but to illustrate the readiness with which the minds of the pupils came under the influence of Christian truth, and their fidelity in making it known to their parents and friends.

"Before Magee entered the seminary he was an opposer of Christ and his religion. He entered the seminary in October, 1835. His mind was soon changed, so that during his first vacation, he talked with his parents, and told them: 'The gods whom we have worshipped to this time are false, and it is dangerous to believe in them.' He spake many words against the religion of his parents. 'If you,' he added, 'continue in this state, you can not get to heaven, but must go to hell.' To prove this he read a portion of Scripture, and then entreated them, saying: 'Believe Christ; follow him. If you do so, you may enjoy heaven.' His parents replied: 'Son, it is not lawful for you to revile our gods, whom, till this time, we have worshipped and believe.' Magee declared his purpose to believe in Christ, and to join the Christian Church. At this time his father was displeased and forbid him doing it for the present, saying: 'If you leave the worship of Siva, and embrace this new religion, our relations will forsake us, and the people will mock us. If you wish to become a Christian, you may do it after you have left the seminary and become older. You are a little boy, you need not join the Church now,' etc. With these things in mind, Magee returned to the seminary, having no further argument with his father. He soon after joined the Church, of which he informed his father by a letter. The father read the letter, and reported the same to his mother. The next vacation Magee feared to go home, and took refuge with a school-master near by. The master took him to his father's house. His parents would not at first speak to him, and exhibited strong marks of displeasure. Soon the boy's uncle came in with a stick in his hand. The boy seeing this fled to the school-master, who still remained there. The school-master seized the stick and prevented the beating of the boy. Magee spoke to them so mildly as to assuage their anger. His parents then told him that henceforth he should live with the missionaries, and should never see their faces. According to their word, he never returned to them, but before another vacation went to dwell with Jesus Christ, whom the missionaries preach."

Conversion of a Girl in a Free School.

This account was written by herself at the request of one of the missionaries, "and may show," he remarks, "the influence of our native free schools."

"I have four sisters and one beloved brother. My father gave my two older sisters their dowry, and married them to heathens. Both they and we then worshipped devils, and were on the way to hell. At that time a teacher of the Christian religion (missionary) came and asked my father to send his children to school. Though he told the missionary that he would send them, still, as soon as he was gone he said to us: 'Well, after I am dead, let it go as it may, but while I am alive you shall not go beyond the gate.' As I was desirous of learning, I used to beg my grandmother to go with me to the school. She promised, but deceived me. After that, the cholera came, and both my father and mother died in one day. As we four children were small, we could not live alone, so we went to our grandfather. Our grandparents loved us more than their own children, and instead of neglecting us, sold their own property to support us. After that, God was our father and mother, and caused my younger sister and brother to be taught in the mission schools. Though I was very desirous of learning, still they would not let me go, on account of my age. I learned my alphabet, however, of my sisters, at night, in leisure moments.

"After that, by the grace of God, I went to a school, learned as fast as I could, and became even the monitor to those who had been in the school before me, and in about six months I could read readily. After that, I read Matthew, Mark, Luke, John, and the Acts of the Apostles, and was much struck with the miracles and wonders which Jesus Christ had done. In consequence of the joy of mind which was given me, I meditated on that I had read, and committed to memory by day and by night, while in the house and by the way, committing in one month three or four hundred verses.

"About that time all the people began to speak about the wonderful fact, that a man had cut off his tongue at Skanda Swamy's temple, and still lived. They praised their god, and said, 'The God of the missionaries is defeated, and our god has conquered;' and all ran to see the wonder, and spoke of it to me. I was then in great distress, and cried out: 'Alas! what shall I do? which God shall I worship? I have put my feet into two boats,' (meaning one foot in each, and would of course fall into the sea between them.)

"When I heard the missionary preach about the man who had cut off his tongue, I prayed, and said: 'O God! my Creator, I am a poor ignorant girl; have mercy on me and save me.' In this way I obtained relief.

"Mr. Woodward urged me to commence a school, though I should get only five children. I commenced accordingly, and collected about forty children. Not only this, I had a meeting once a week, and exhorted the women. After a short time, I joined the Church, according to the command of our Lord Jesus Christ. Now, not only I, but, including myself, four, two sisters and my brother, belong to the Church.

"After that, in consequence of the death of our teacher who did so much for us, I was in great distress, and said: 'Now who knows our poverty and will have compassion on us? Our father and mother are dead. Our property is spent, our relations cast us off, and our minister, who was our benefactor, is also dead!' Thus for six months I sorrowed and was like the stock of a tree, lying near the bank of a river, tossed by its waters. . . .

"In the mean time I wondered at the way in which I had been saved. As I had no guardians, I committed myself to the missionaries, and through their help I am safe. Were it not for this, I should have been lost like my companions.

If my father and mother had lived, they would not have let me go to school. Though I had studied, still if I had had property, then that would have hindered me from teaching a school. It is very astonishing that God has delivered me from all these hindrances. Moreover, it is hard for a rich man to enter into the kingdom of God. Therefore I greatly rejoice, because it is better for us to be poor, and serve Jesus Christ, and be saved through him, than to be with our father and mother, or to be rich as my elder sisters are."

To this account the missionary adds: "She is now married to a Christian husband, and has one child named Daniel. On the day when the child was baptized, I said to her: 'Why do you call its name Daniel? Are you going to throw it into the den of lions?' She replied: 'Yes, if that is the Lord's will.'" "She still continues to keep her school."

Of the girls who had been educated in the schools up to this date, the missionaries say: "They already exert a good influence, and are mothers of more than 40 children, whom they train up in the fear of God, and in the knowledge of Jesus Christ. Several of these children are in our boarding-schools, and two are members of our church."

With such evidence of the value of these schools, in the rich blessing of God upon them, we do not wonder that the mission enlarged them to the extent of their means. In July of this year, the schools were at the climax of their prosperity. Their "187 free schools contained 6996 pupils." The seminary had 151 students, and the girls' boarding-school 98.

But the funds of the Board failed, and painful retrenchment was unavoidable. With much grief the missionaries suspended all but 16 of their free schools, dismissed some of the pupils in the girls' boarding-school and the seminary, admitted no new class, and made other "painful retrenchments."

"The heathen triumphed. They said the mission was going down. Native church-members were discouraged, and resisted ridicule, threats and temptation, less firmly."

Lamentations of the Mission for the Reduction in their Schools.

The year 1838 opened in gloom. The mission seemed clothed in sackcloth. The circular from the officers of the Board had reached them, requiring prompt and severe retrenchment. It was painful work, but there was no alternative. Funds failed, and the expenses of the mission must be reduced, or the Board become bankrupt. The missionaries entered upon this work of retrenchment with sad hearts. They sent away 45 students from the Batticotta Seminary, limiting its number to 100, and receiving no new class for two years. From the Oodooville school they sent away 8 girls, though with evident misgivings. In their letter to the Secretaries, they say: "We could not cut very deeply into that institution, without striking a destructive blow at the cause of female education and female piety in the land, and thus marring our highest hopes." They also turned away some of their native helpers, reduced their printing operations, and stopped the erection of buildings.

But the reduction which grieved them most severely, was in their schools. They were obliged to abandon all but 16 of their free schools, and thus to turn back more than 5000 pupils into ignorance and heathenism. We do not wonder they wrote: "We have cut off the arms and limbs of our system, close to the trunk! If we must cut to the amount of £100 more, it must be '*next the heart!*'"

In reply to the circular requiring these reductions, the mission sent a general letter, filled with touching lamentations. The bitter grief of the missionaries at this emergency, shows their estimate of these schools more eloquently and impressively than their positive testimony in the strongest language could have done. "Looking at the results as a whole," they write, "we see evils too great for human computation. In the work of changing the religion of a whole people like this, which involves an entire change of education, manners, and customs, and modes of thought and feeling, nothing is more important than a fixed impression on the minds of the community, of the permanence of those causes which are to bring about the change.

"After many years of toil, our labors were resulting in a strong impression throughout the land, that the Christian religion would certainly prevail. And this impression, to a very great extent, was based on the conviction that the missionaries would never give over; that their means of influencing the community, and especially the rising generation, would never fail. And this impression was fast preparing the way for breaking over those bonds of caste, and clanship, and family, which, with a strength that can not be appreciated in America, bind the people to the religion of the land. The prophecies that the missionaries would by and by give up in discouragement, had been proved vain. Every year their cords were seen to be lengthening, and their stakes strengthening. But the blow which has been struck has weakened, every where, the strength of this impression. It has staggered the weak in faith in our churches, and taken away their confidence in the presence of opposers; it has quieted uneasy consciences among the people; it has caused the whole community to feel that what has been, may be only the precursor of greater reductions to come. This impression we meet with constantly. We feel its influence in almost every department of effort. In many cases it takes away the edge of our words. It often closes the mouths of our helpers. It is an evil which can not be written so as to be appreciated abroad, but it is an evil, disastrous, not only to the progress of our cause generally, but also to the increase of true piety in the land. This, time and steady toil only, can remove.

"The breaking up of our schools has been a grievous blow. On account of the pressure which we then began heavily to feel, we were driven to a temporary suspension of our schools in July last. We then made our retrenchment in that department, because there was no other department of our labors which could so easily be resumed, after a temporary suspension. But it was with aching hearts that we turned 5000 children out into the wilderness of heathenism, to be exposed to the roaring lion, even for the short period of three or four months. It was painful to miss them at the house of God on the Sabbath, and on Tuesdays, when they were accustomed to come together to study and hear the word of God. So deeply did we come to feel the evils of this suspension, that when we came together at our annual meeting, it was a general feeling that, at almost any sacrifice, we must resume the schools to an important extent. *But we could not.* We have left the children to wander. They hear not the word of God; they come not to his house; they study not the way of life; their education is strictly heathen; their minds are being filled with prejudice; they are trained only in sin.

"By the breaking up of the schools, the Sabbath congregation is almost broken up at a number of our stations. The children and masters formed the nucleus of the congregation. By the breaking up of our schools, one of the rods of our power is broken. No man who has not tried it can tell how difficult it is to bring the simplest truths of the Gospel into contact with the mind of an adult, trained from his earliest years in Hinduism. The rising generation, by a course of instruction, to a very important extent liberal, were getting Christian ideas in connection with language, and were being shut out from those heathenish associations with every important word, which prevent the adult from feeling the force of the preached truth. But we have no heart to dwell upon this point. Our children are no longer ours. They are almost certainly shut out from the way and the hope of heaven.

"The results to the seminary, and the important Christian interests which cluster around that institution, are very painful. For want of funds, we took no class at the regular time in October last. And our funds will not authorize the reception of a class the coming October. By this, the whole arrangement of the institution is necessarily thrown into disorder, and it will take years to bring it to the previous state of regularity. There will now, necessarily, be a chasm of two or three years between the present fourth class and that which will succeed it. A year ago, in a printed card, we told the whole community that we should take a class of

40 the then coming October, according to the terms of admission therein stated. In October we were compelled to say: 'For want of money, we can not fulfill our promise, but we shall be able to do it the year following.' But we can not do it, and a failure to do it will add new strength to the impression that the missionary efforts and means are declining, and may by and by cease. But this is not all. At the commencement of our annual meeting, we carefully ran over the list of students, with a view of selecting all who were so deficient in promise, either on account of scholarship, conduct or ability, that they might be dismissed without serious injury to the institution, or the general cause. Feeling our pressure, we numbered in that class some whom we would willingly have retained. We marked the names of 14. To these we have been compelled to add 30 more, making in all 44." "Among these are some lads of fine promise as to scholarship, and from the most influential families in the land. If they had continued with us, doubtless many of them would, by the grace of God, have been truly converted, and thus been prepared to build up the Redeemer's kingdom in the land. But they are now thrown back, with minds soured by disappointment, to grow up its strongest opposers. We could have wished the Christians in America could have turned aside for a day from buying and selling, and getting gain, to see these 44 boys, as they left the seminary, to go back to their heathen homes!

"But the loss of these is not the only loss. Through the strong desire waking up in the land for a knowledge of English, the seminary was fast coming to have the virtual control of the whole education of the district. By requiring a knowledge of our Christian books as the terms of admission, we were securing the careful study of these, even by many not connected with mission schools. But our inability to take new classes for two successive years, together with the excision of so large a number already, has, to a great extent, cut off the hope of future admission. The consequence is, that scholars are leaving our English day-schools at the stations, some of which will probably be broken up.

These schools, bringing boys daily under the eye and Christian instruction of the missionaries, are in a peculiar degree the nurseries of the Church.

"We might go into the detail of many other painful particulars; but we will not. They have come upon us suddenly, and we must bear them. We can not write them so that they will be felt in America. If we could have foreseen the coming blow, though grievous, it would not have been so destructive. It has come like a thunder-bolt, and compelled us, with but little time for deliberation, to break up or render inefficient, plans and operations, whose success, under God, depended mainly on their permanence." . .

"In these circumstances, the reduction which the Committee have been compelled to make, is well-nigh destruction to your mission in Jaffna. We make no complaint. We see not how the Committee could have done otherwise. But, as the messengers of the churches, we ask the privilege of saying to the friends of missions in America: 'If you would not waste your money in the missionary work—if you would not waste the labors and the lives of your missionaries in fruitless toil—if you would not do only to undo again, *you must give a steady and unchanging support to your established missions.* Better not establish a new mission for years, than throw one already established into a state of bankruptcy.'

"We know the state of universal pecuniary distress which has visited our land. It is indeed unparalleled. We learn, too, with gratitude to God, that, even in that year of distress, the receipts of the Board exceeded those of former years. But, brethren, when, in your stead, we went down into the deep cavern, you told us that, come storm or come sunshine, you would never release your hold. And now, when after much toil, we have gathered around us many of those whom we were sent down to rescue, will you forsake us? We plead not for ourselves. On that score we have no anxiety. We plead for this dying people; that having begun to lead them in the way to heaven, you would not, for any worldly consideration, leave them to turn back to hell."

What praying man or woman can read over these tearful lamentations and touching appeals without deep and strong sympathy? Did not the failure of funds and the consequent abandonment of these schools involve a terrible calamity, over which those devoted missionaries did right to mourn? And how can a man, who has been observant of the operations of the American Board for the last twenty-two years, avoid the inquiry, What greater calamity was the breaking up of such schools in 1837–8 than in 1854–5? What greater calamity in their being broken up for the *want of funds* than by the *dictum of a Deputation*, "clothed with full power and authority"? The schools which were broken up in the two cases were precisely alike in character and results. Was it not as sad to send Hindu children away from mission schools, an offering to the Hindu Moloch, in 1854, as it was in 1837? Was it not as sad to see them sent away by the mere caprice of erring man, as by the stern necessity involved in the failure of funds?

Does any one fancy the circumstances of the case had changed? Impossible. The Batticotta Seminary of 1837 was also the Batticotta Seminary of 1855. The failure of funds in 1837 sent away only forty-five of its students. The action of the Deputation in 1855 extinguished the institution entirely. The Bombay high-school was like it in character, and this, too, was suppressed by the Deputation. Does any one fancy that want of funds led the Deputation to suppress these schools in 1854–5? Then why did they suppress schools which had never cost the home funds of the Board a farthing? Why did they "turn out into the great and terrible wilderness of the heathen world" five hundred children and youth under daily Christian instruction, and that too when we plead for them with tears, and pledged ourselves that if they would only allow the continuance of the schools, they should never be any expense to the Board?

Ah! why is it, that the unavoidable abandonment of these schools in 1837, for want of funds, filled the periodicals of the Board with bitter lamentations, while their needless suppression in 1855 is passed over in silence, or gloried in as a shrewd stroke of policy?

And there were lamentations, too, in 1855, as tearful and touching as any in 1837. They may not find a place in the records of the American Board, but if the history of missions records them not, she will be unfaithful to her trust. More touching lamentations never found utterance than some which were wrung from the hearts of long-tried and faithful missionaries—hearts torn and crushed by the magnitude of the evil which had come upon them.

Father Spaulding's Lament.

In view of the desolations caused in the Jaffna mission, in 1855, the touching lamentation of this dear devoted missionary shall stand here as the representative of many; uttered hesitatingly, tremblingly, in most cases, as if under some painful apprehensions, and yet uttered with a force and meaning that could not be repressed.

Father Spaulding is the oldest American missionary in Ceylon. Through some forty years of faithful labor there he has gathered up rich stores of personal experience and observation; he had found the schools to be the right arm of his usefulness and power in the mission, and he could not see them suppressed, even by his best friends, without grief. Amidst the wreck and ruins of his schools and life-long labors, with a broken, stricken, *grieving* heart he gives utterance to his sorrow in patriarchal simplicity: "'*Joseph is not and Simeon is not.*' *Our village-schools are ragged schools. Our health is pining — our strength weakened — our church in sackcloth—and the crown is fallen from our heads to the dust, and woe is me, for we are undone—is my wailing even in the night-watches.*" "*We are very small and oppressed. We have lost much in native assistants,* (*now the glory of other missions;*) *much in our village-schools; much in unity and liberality of counsel and effort; and much of the confidence of the people. Who will be responsible in the day of judgment?*"

The question is urged here, not in bitterness but in kindness, not in anger but in sorrow, and yet in all its solemn gravity, ought not this suppression of the schools in 1855, by a Deputation sent out at an expense of some $10,000, to stir as deep and lasting regret in the hearts of all who love the cause, as did their abandonment in 1837 for want of funds? "Who will be responsible in the day of judgment?"

Grief of the Board for the Loss of the Schools.

In 1837–8, in view of the terrible disaster involved in abandoning the schools, and of the lamentations of the missionaries, the officers and patrons of the Board seemed almost to vie with each other in the depth and extent of their grief, and their efforts to retrieve the loss. The editor of the *Missionary Herald* introduced the letter and enforced the appeals of the mission in impressive and touching terms. He says: "Let every Christian reader of this letter imagine himself as nearly as he can, in the place of his missionary brethren and sisters in Ceylon, and sympathize with them in their disappointment and grief, while stripped of almost all their facilities for extended usefulness, and left to mourn over apparently lost labor; let him see the schools disbanded and the youths turned away from the seminaries, and follow them all to the haunts of heathenism and temptation; let him hear the triumph and scoffs of the heathen, renewing their confidence in the strength and permanency of their idolatrous system, which had begun to fail them; let him think how the native assistants and church members are disheartened and their faith shaken, subjected as they are to new assaults and temptations; and say whether the poverty of the Christian community at home is such as to justify the patrons of the Board in permitting this mission any longer to remain in this prostrate and paralyzed condition." "Let each one of the patrons of the Board regard this appeal as addressed to himself, and let him in his own mind make out such a reply to it, in his own defense, as he would be willing to meet the afflicted brethren with, could he see them face to face; such a reply as he would be willing to make before the throne of Christ to the deceased brother who penned it." At the annual meeting of this year, 1838, one of the secretaries read a paper from which take the following extracts: "The effects of the curtailment were first felt in the free schools and seminaries connected with the missions; and they were disastrous and painful nearly in proportion to the extent and success with which these had before been conducted. In Ceylon five thousand pupils were dismissed from the free schools at once, leaving only sixteen schools remaining. 'The breaking up of our schools,' say the missionaries, 'has been a most grievous blow. It was with aching hearts that we turned five thousand children out into the wilderness of heathenism.'"

Five Thousand Pupils sent back to Heathenism.

"After my usual lessons," says one of the older missionaries, "with the readers in the schools yesterday, I gave each a portion of the Bible as a present. I told them the reason—exhorted them to read it, not to enter into temptation, and to keep the Sabbath holy—prayed with them, commending them to the Friend of little children, and then sent them away—from me, from the Bible class, from the Sabbath-school, from the house of prayer, to feed on the mountains of heathenism, with the idols under the green trees—a prey to the roaring lion, to evil demons, and to a people more ignorant than they, even to their blind, deluded, and deluding guides; and when I looked after them, as they went out, my heart failed me. Oh! what an offering to Swamy!—*five thousand children!*"

"But the bearing of this curtailment on the system of education in this mission, did not end with the free schools. Eight girls were cut off from the female boarding-school—a school which the mission regard as vitally connected with female education and female piety in the land. The seminary for educating native preachers, and other helpers, could not escape. No new class could be taken at the usual time for admitting one, in the autumn of 1837. Still less could the missionaries open the door for one the present autumn. Thus the hopes of about one hundred candidates were disappointed, and their progress in obtaining an education, which should bring them under Christian influences, and ultimately qualify them for usefulness to their countrymen and the Church, probably arrested forever. There was a more painful step still, which the mission could not be spared. Forty-four must be cut off from those already in the seminary, who had enjoyed their instructions, and on whom their hopes were set as future coädjutors in their work."

"This retrograde movement has, in some instances, exerted a most unhappy influence upon a whole heathen community. In Ceylon, no sooner was it known that the resources of the mission had failed, and the schools were dismissed, than a general exultation and triumph prevailed." "Native teachers are turned out of employment, and are exposed to a life of idleness and temptation. Instead of being coädjutors to the missionaries in doing good to their own countrymen, they are in danger of being ruined themselves, and becoming the means of ruining others.

"The native church members are disheartened and perplexed. With the little knowledge and enlargement of mind, which they can be supposed to possess, it is not strange that it seems to them now as if that cause to which they had attached themselves, and which they supposed was to rise steadily as the sun, and universally prevail, was now about to set in confusion. This fills them with doubt and dismay.

"Nor does the character of the missionaries, and through them the character of Christianity itself, escape reproach. They have disappointed expectations, and, as the heathen regard it, broken the pledges which they had previously given. In Ceylon, the missionaries were regarded as pledged to carry the pupils already received through their respective branches of instruction, and to receive additional classes to the seminaries from year to year. When they turned away five thousand pupils from the free schools, and forty-four from the seminary, and refused to receive classes for two successive years, they were charged with breaking their promises.

"The Committee repeat what they said on introducing this subject, that what we now see are only the beginnings of the consequences which are growing out of this curtailment. The results which are to be developed in the future life and in the eternal existence of the multitudes affected by it, none can foretell but He who sees the end from the beginning. Of how many was probably the character and the everlasting destiny fixed that day, when the Ceylon mission, compelled by the scantiness of our contributions, decided to turn five thousand pupils from their schools? Who is willing to look at the consequences of this curtailment to that student of the seminary, turned away with his pride wounded and his mind soured, to become a hardened idolater, or a leader in infidelity; or to that convinced but unconverted school-master; or to that weak church-member; or to those girls shut out from the boarding-school, and turned over again to heathen parents and friends, without restraint, to be trained for idol-worship, or scenes of pollution and infamy; or to those Brahmans and learned men, whose faith in their Shasters began to waver, but who now are convinced again that Siva is mightier than Jehovah; or to those whole nations of heathen to whom we have been virtually shutting up the way of life, and as it were clearing out the impediments from their broad way to perdition, which the missionaries had been throwing in to obstruct their progress?"

These regrets and lamentations of the missionaries, officers, and patrons of the Board, for the reduction of their schools in 1837, found fitting expression in the following resolution, which was adopted by the whole Board:

"*Resolved*, That this Board deeply sympathize with its missionaries under the grief and disappointment they have suffered, in consequence of the curtailment of their means of usefulness, and would assure them of our prayers and efforts that they may be speedily furnished with the aid necessary for executing their former plans, and extending their operations."

Now these vivid representations of the sad results of the curtailment in 1837, and this resolution of the Board to retrieve the loss as speedily as possible, are surely fitting. But why more fitting in 1837 than in 1855? Was it any less disastrous to turn away heathen teachers and pupils in 1855 than in 1837? Were these schools any more needed in Ceylon, in 1837, after twenty years' progress, than in *new* missions in 1855? Was it not as sad for native converts and inquirers to be thrust away from the mission at Ahmednuggur in 1851, by the summary suppression of the seminary there, as by the curtailment in Ceylon in 1837? Does it really change the character of the results because in the one case the schools were disbanded for the want of funds, and the calamity elicited a burst of regret, sympathy, and lamentation from missionaries, officers, patrons, and the whole Board, while in the other the schools were suppressed by the Deputation, and only a few of the old and long-tried missionaries ventured to give utterance to their grief?

Here are two correlative pages in the history of missions, the lessons of which the churches can not afford to lose. The Officers of the American Board, by their changing policy, have developed conflicting acts and series of facts and results which are painfully instructive. If they can reconcile their regrets and lamentations for the loss of their schools in 1838, with their voluntary suppression of the same schools in 1855, they certainly owe it to the Church and the world to do so.

Efforts to Retrieve the Loss.

1839.—The shades of light and darkness alternate, and sometimes intermingle, in the picture of this year. The general summary at its commencement speaks in tones of grief of the sad reverse which had fallen upon the mission. "It was never making more rapid progress in its work, never exerting a happier or greater influence, never blessed with more cheering prospects, than when, as by a blast from the desert, the numerous children in its schools were driven away and dispersed among the heathen."

The convictions of the missionaries as to the vital importance of these schools are recorded in terms which can not be mistaken. "Aside from the training of teachers of Christianity," they say, "the seminary is doing much to introduce the Gospel into the country, by the tone it gives to religious education, and the encouragement it affords to Christian schools. The missionaries find no difficulty in making all their schools as thoroughly religious as they choose. And parents who wish to have their sons educated make no objections to the study of Christian lessons."

"Christianity, without an education suited to its nature and genius, will exist only in embryo. It will exert no living, self-propagating power. The mere repetition of Christian precepts is not enough to feed and furnish the mind. In regard to this people, their whole moral organization is defective, from never having enjoyed a single healthful influence in their early education. To give them an elevated piety there is needed, after conversion as well as before, the patient and persevering efforts of parental training, more necessary and difficult as they are met and resisted by the powerful influences of habit, confirmed by years of sin, and example that is almost universal. What we regard, then, of essential importance to the permanence and growth of Christianity in this land, is the formation of a community that shall be governed by enlightened Christian sentiments."

"You are aware that but little has been done the past eighteen months in the department of native free schools. Our direct influence upon the people has in consequence been very limited. The schools, as has been often remarked, are an important channel of communication with the parents and friends of the pupils. Without them we labor under great disadvantages in securing their presence and gaining their attention. We hope to be able to resume a sufficient number of the schools the present year to give efficiency to our system."

"We are as much as ever convinced of the adaptation of our general system of effort to the great object of turning this people from idolatry, and of converting them to God. We do not see how Christianity can be permanently established, in this or in any land, without the aid of a system of Christian education. We are not aware that it ever has been established without such aid. In this land, even preaching the Gospel almost necessarily partakes of the character of elementary teaching. Schools, under Christian influence, are the most economical means of giving to the mass of the community a great deal of instruction that is necessary to the understanding of the truths of the Gospel. We do not say they are a means necessary to conversion; but for the growth and permanence of Christian principles in a heathen community, we consider them, in connection with the preaching of the Gospel by the missionary, as of very essential advantage. We have sometimes thought the American Church did not appreciate the advantages she derives from the Christian education of her youth, and therefore does not admit, to the extent that we think she ought, the importance or the obligation of connecting a system of religious education with the efforts of her missionaries. But if every Christian school and every pious mother were withdrawn from America, what would be the result to the Church? And if the influence of a polluting and idolatrous system of religion were substituted, what would be her future prospects? We ask no more than that she would do unto others what she would that they should do unto her, if the circumstances were reversed."

These views and convictions of the missionaries were promptly and warmly seconded by the Board, as already shown, and the Committee sent a letter by "the shortest and most expeditious route," and relieved the mission from the restriction which had been imposed upon it.

"The mission kept a day of special thanksgiving when they heard that the churches had enabled the Committee to relieve them from their embarrassments." The Ceylon government generously contributed £200 a year for its schools, and though "so much ruin could not be repaired at once," and the schools were but partially resumed, still the state of the mission was greatly improved, and the year closed with "fifty-one free schools, containing 1824 scholars," and 260 boarding-scholars, of whom 86 were members of the Church.

Tenth Revival in the Schools.

Another "precious visitation," too, was enjoyed in the schools. It commenced near the close of the previous year, and ten persons were soon admitted into the Church, of whom "nine were members of the girls' boarding-school." But the more marked results of God's gracious presence were enjoyed in May. Special religious meetings had been held, and the minds and hearts of the pupils were found prepared for the silent operations of the Spirit, as on former similar occasions. "From that time a considerable number regularly attended a meeting of inquiry, held every Sabbath. This class of candidates for the church numbered about fifty during the last term. From them thirty-one were received to the communion of the Church, on the 19th inst., (May,) making the number of students now in the seminary, who are members of the Church, in regular standing, eighty-four, while of the sixty-six remaining students, about twenty were candidates for admission." Well do the missionaries say: "From this view we feel ourselves called upon to thank God and take courage."

In September of this year they write again: "The moral and religious state of the seminary is encouraging. At no time previously has there been so large a proportion of the students members of the Church. It has been a leading feature in the boarding-school system from its commencement, that a large proportion of the pupils come forward to profess their faith in Christ."

Thus the missionaries proved the truth of their own judgment and prediction when they wrote: "As the word of God shall not go forth in vain, we may confidently expect that, if any where, there will be true converts among those who are daily and for a long time brought into immediate contact with divine truth, and who are in a great measure removed from the adverse influences peculiar to this country."

Near the close of this year, reverting to the reduction of the schools, and the success of efforts to retrieve their loss, they say: "Most of the native free schools at the station, which were for many months suspended, have been reëstablished. Few, however, of the older pupils are now in attendance. The blight occasioned by the dearth of funds will long be felt at every station." And yet, "the readiness of the people to send their children to Christian schools, even their female children, furnishes pleasing evidence that there has been a leavening of the whole mass of the community."

Converting Influence of the Schools.

1840.—Among the notices of the schools this year we find the following in regard to the girls' boarding-school: "The whole number admitted to this school since the commencement is 167." It has been before stated that *all* who had left after a regular course of study, gave evidence of piety. And now it is stated that "of the 90 now in the school, 25 are members of the Church, 25 the children of church-members, and several others are the sisters of pious lads in the seminary at Batticotta. The influence of the pious girls on the morals of the school is most happy. Meetings among themselves, and with the other girls, for reading the Bible, exhortation, and prayer, are a delight."

"It is not uncommon that these children exert a very favorable influence on their parents and other friends, when they go home in their vacations, by reading portions of the Bible or tracts, by answering inquiries, and by urging the claims of Christianity."

"The bearings of this school on the future prospects of the mission are most interesting. The objections and prejudices against female education are shown to be without foundation, and the happy contrast between an educated and pious wife and an ignorant heathen one, is seen and acknowledged, not only by Christians, but by many heathens around us. Besides, it should never be forgotten, that, until the females are raised by education so as to hold their proper rank in society, and until their hearts are brought under the influence of Christianity, there is little hope that the people of India will rise from idolatry and sin to the dignity and happiness of a Christian people."

The Batticotta Seminary "continues to be, to a very great extent, our principal dependence in view of the future prosperity of Christianity in this part of the world. Successive classes rise gradually above the preceding in their attainments, and we are able to fix our terms of admission higher, and to subject candidates to a more rigid examination."

"There has been a class of professed inquirers varying from forty to sixty. Some of those, it is expected, will be received to church fellowship soon. We have reason to think that the church is rising, both as to her views of doctrine and duty, and to her approaching freedom from the 'yoke of bondage' of heathen superstitions and national prejudices."

"The whole number of church members connected with the seminary, including six teachers, is 105." 31 of the students were received in August of this year. The whole number received into the Church this year was 48, showing that the presence and influence of the Spirit was not less marked than in the year previous.

Of all the converts of the mission up to this date it is said: "In our printed list of church members there are 491 names. Of these 311 have been educated in our schools, or are now in a course of education. Many of the remaining 180 are or have been [*heathen*] *schoolmasters.*"

What more unequivocal testimony to the value of these schools is possible? *Nearly all the converts brought under Christian teaching and influence, and converted to God, by means of these schools!*

Success of the Schools in training Native Helpers.

In 1841, the mission found so much progress had been made in overcoming the prejudices and opposition of the people by means of their schools, that they could modify their regulations and require the students of the seminary to furnish their own clothes, and give security for the subsequent payment of their board—a decided step in advance, which greatly encouraged the missionaries. The religious interest in the seminary is indicated by the statement that: "There are from fifty to seventy-five who wish to be regarded as candidates for church membership. We hope some of them will prove themselves worthy."

"To show to what extent the seminary is accomplishing its *object of training native helpers* in the missionary work, the missionaries stated more than two years ago, that of those who had passed through its course of study, *sixty-seven*," exclusive of eight teachers in the seminary, one of whom was a preacher, "were in the employment of different missions in Ceylon and Southern India. Four of them were preachers, and others were preparing for that office.

In 1842 "a theological class of eight" is reported in the Batticotta Seminary. Of the schools it is said: "The school system is gradually recovering from the desolations of 1837. In the centre stands the *noble seminary*." Of the value of these schools in the estimation of the missionaries and of the Board at that date, what better proof is possible than the prompt vigilance and energy with which they were resumed, after the terrible disaster which disbanded them in 1837 had a little subsided? This year the seminary reports 207 pupils; and some 70 free schools, with the English and other boarding-schools, present the sum total of 3541 pupils under Christian instruction.

Direct testimony, too, continues to be placed on record in most unequivocal terms. The pages of the *Herald* abound with statements like the following:

"There are no such occasions for going 'from house to house,' and of holding intercourse with the people 'in season and out of season,' and no such occasions for going about doing good to soul and body, and certainly no such opportunities for holding friendly intercourse with adults, male and female, as those afforded by the establishment of a system of native free schools. *It furnishes, probably, the happiest combination of influences for doing good to soul and body that can possibly be devised by the missionary.* It is far more acceptable to the people of this country than would be the same amount of expenditure even for medical purposes."

Compare with this testimony the fact that though the report of last year gives 105 members of the seminary as communicants in the church, the whole membership of that church this year is reported to be only 131. And also the fact before mentioned, that of the first 491 admitted to the church, 311 owed their conversion to being pupils, and many of the remaining 180 were converted while employed as heathen school-teachers.

In 1843, the number of pupils had increased to more than 4000. Reviving influences had also come down upon the schools, and while reporting the admission to the church of fifteen girls from the boarding-school in March, the missionaries add: "We have reason to believe that a few more are under the teachings of the Holy Spirit. They are all—even the least of them—in the habit of prayer, which has been characteristic of the school from its commencement. When a girl is admitted to the school, this is the first lesson taught by her little associates, not by our request or interference, but as a thing of course."

Who can wonder that the missionaries say of these schools: "It seems impossible that in this way the families of the next generation should not be greatly modified and improved. In our efforts to bring girls under instruction, the influence of fathers who were educated in our native free schools in the early stages of the mission, is very serviceable. These fathers are comparatively free from prejudice against Christianity; and they have a vague impression that it is well for their children to become acquainted with it."

"Though Seed lie buried long in Dust."

If any fancy that the unconverted pupils of mission schools become the worst opposers, let them ponder the last statement. Let them consider, too, hundreds of cases like the following:

"When at Manepy, in 1827–8, I was pleased with the progress of a lad who was once a monitor in a village school. He had left the school and gone to his fields and gardens. I used to see him at work on the Sabbath, and always reproved him, but he used generally to return some saucy answer. One Sabbath afternoon I was riding to the place of meeting, and seeing him at work, I began to repeat the fourth commandment. In a moment he caught it out of my mouth, and looking significantly at my horse, said, '*Nor thy cattle!*' and then stopped. After preaching at Manepy, a few days ago, I proposed to meet those who professed to be inquirers, and was surprised to see this very monitor boy. . . . On inquiring the cause of his wishing to be a Christian, he told me that it was simply the truth which he had formerly learned in the school, adding: 'He who knows his Master's will and does it not, must be beaten with many stripes.' He quoted many passages from the Bible readily and appropriately, thus giving evidence that he still remembers what he then learned, and that the husbandman has encouragement to wait in hope."

Next to the band of living converts in our mission churches, no brighter prospect meets the eye or gladdens the heart, on heathen ground, than the thousands of youth who have been, or are being educated in mission schools.

1844.—The records of this year continue to abound in facts and testimony to the very great value of the schools. The missionaries say:

"The entire system of schools is itself a proclamation of 'peace on earth and good will toward men,' which the wayfaring man, though a fool, may understand. As a means of access to the adult population, moreover, schools are an almost indispensable auxiliary to the missionary."

The Native Church gathered from the Schools.

A brief history of the native church is crowded with facts and statements as follows:

"The native church in Jaffna, so far as human instrumentality is concerned, is the offspring of the school establishments in the district, more especially of the mission boarding-schools. This might be clearly shown by a chronological notice of admissions to the Church from the year 1819, when Gabriel Tissera and Nicholas Permander—the first teachers in our boarding-schools—were received, down to the present time."

"It should also be stated that those precious and repeated seasons of revival with which we have been favored, and which are the most prominent events in the history of our mission, were always closely connected with the boarding-schools.

"Hence, with a very few exceptions, the members of the Church have been gathered, not from the general mass, but from certain select classes of idolaters who have been brought under the influence of the mission from secular considerations," namely, the desire for education.

This sketch of the native church brings to view the fact that of 460 living communicants, 365—about four fifths—owed their Christian knowledge and conversion to the schools.

As a general result of all past experience, the missionaries write:

"We are now prepared to say in conclusion, that *in every village throughout our field*, which can be statedly reached by the missionary for the purpose of preaching the Gospel—whether it be weekly, monthly, or quarterly—*a Tamil free school for both sexes should be established and efficiently sustained.*

"It is for the Board and for the Christian public in America to determine to what extent men and money, faith and prayer, shall be made subservient to a vigorous prosecution of the work we have in hand. But let it not be forgotten that the special object of this communication is to reconcile the minds of all concerned to our making the Tamil free school system for both sexes, coëxtensive with stated village preaching.

"*In a word, the village school is a fulcrum, with the aid of which the combined powers of the missionary and of his native assistants may be made to bear advantageously upon the mighty masses to be moved; and, other things being equal, the result will be in proportion to the length and solidity of the lever applied.*"

1845.—The pupils in the schools this year show an increase of 1354, the whole number being 4080. Of some 120 teachers only 54 are reported as members of the church, showing that the larger proportion were still "*heathen teachers.*"

The report of the Board says: "The testimony of the three brethren from the Tamil missions as to the value of the school system, is united and strong. They say it has risen in their estimation, and never was in higher repute."

The testimony of the Home Committee is, that the Tamil missions "are conducted on principles long tried, and which appear to have the sanction of experience and of the great Head of the Church."

A refreshing season was enjoyed in the seminary this year; a meeting for inquiry was attended by some 50 students, of whom some 15 or 20 gave "some evidence of having been born of the Spirit."

1846.—The number of pupils slightly diminished this year, but the schools prospered, and "on the whole, the seminary has never been in a more healthful state than during the last year." A gracious influence was manifest in the schools, "Christians seem revived and encouraged, and a great majority of the students are very seriously impressed." Several students and pupils of the girls' boarding-school were received into the Church.

1847.—The annual report of this year finds nothing worthy of higher commendation than "the admirable system of schools and higher seminaries of learning, which forms so striking a feature in these [Tamil] missions."

The Old Heathen Teacher.

The reader will have observed that in the first years of this mission all its native teachers were heathen—that up to the present date the larger proportion of the teachers employed were heathen, though many of them had thus been brought under the influence of Christian truth and converted. It is well to mark the blessing of God which rested so largely upon these schools, and resulted in the conversion of so many of these teachers. Nathaniel is an instance of one of these teachers who long resisted the truth. He was employed for many years as a teacher of Tamil in the seminary. The following brief account of his conversion is from the pen of one of the missionaries.

"Through all his former labors with us, he was a consistent heathen, and was often designated as 'the devout heathen.' He now seems as decided and devout in the Christian way. Though he had received much instruction in the doctrines of Christ, and through the course of many years, yet he steadily pursued his mystic studies, and took one step after another in the prescribed course of Hindu religious life. A few months ago he was doubtless cherishing the sentiment that in his next birth he should be near the gods. After his dismission from our service, he had several classes of disciples whom he led on in the same alluring, delusive path. While thus engaged, he was brought very low by sickness, 'nigh unto death,' indeed, as he supposed. It was then, as he says, that 'God spake to his heart, reminded him of the Christian instruction which he had received, and made him feel his sins and his lost condition.' As soon as he was able to walk so far, he came to me and declared his purpose to be a Christian. Since that time he has given increasing evidence of having been 'born of the Spirit.' The day previous to his reception to the Church, I asked him if he intended to be baptized by his heathen name. 'Oh! no,' said he, 'I must have a new name. I wish to have all new.' He chose the name of *Nathaniel*, in view of John 1 : 47."

This man at once consecrated his children to Christ in baptism, and entered upon the Christian life with mature knowledge and full purpose of heart. In 1848, the whole number of pupils reported in this mission is 4640, and about half the teachers had become members of the Church.

The reports of the mission are crowded with direct testimony to the value of the schools. After giving a series of facts as the basis of his conclusion, Mr. Fletcher writes: "Thus you see that a thorough Christian education is one of the most powerful levers by which to overthrow the superstitions of India. The system of education here is full of hope to this people. A young man who has passed through our common schools and the seminary, although he may not be a professed Christian, and may mingle with the heathen, still can not be such a heathen as he otherwise might be. His mind has received such a shape, that it can never for one moment admit the truth of the system of idolatry. Thus he never will be a sincere worshipper at its shrines, nor a zealous, conscientious inculcator of its principles. There is also a growing conviction among all classes, that the missionaries are right; that they teach the truth, and are seeking the welfare of the people." Mr. Howland writes: "I must not neglect to mention what an interesting field for preaching the Gospel I have among the 700 children in my free schools." And after stating the influence of true secular knowledge on their minds, he adds: "They are made familiar, too, with the Bible and with the whole plan of salvation. From the first day they came into the school, they have heard these truths. Scripture lessons and Scripture reading form the great part of every day's instruction. I often resolve that I will spend more of my time in these schools, with the conviction that it is perhaps my most hopeful field for preaching the Gospel."

Some persons have advanced the idea that so much attention to mission schools by the missionary must detract from his time and strength for oral preaching. On this point doubtless the experience of every missionary would accord with that of Mr. Smith, who says: "The care of the schools is not, and never has been a hindrance to my going among the natives. . . . I regard these schools as a very important connecting link between us and the heathen. To cut them off, to any great extent, would greatly diminish our means of access to the people. *The fact is worthy of notice, that all who have come to this field with strong prejudices against schools, and strongly in favor of preaching as the only means to be used, have, as soon as they have really entered into the work, seen and felt that schools are a very important means of getting access to the people.*"

Thus, instead of the schools being any hindrance to oral preaching, experience amply shows that they furnish opportunities for stated oral preaching ten times as often and to twenty times as many hearers, as would be possible without them.

In 1849 the number of pupils was 3485, and the controlling influence of the schools in favor of Christianity was such that the Romanists and Hindus found it best to resort to the same agency in their efforts, but found it necessary to introduce the Bible into their schools to win popular favor. Fitly do the missionaries say: "Understanding these facts, no one can be at a loss as to the bearing of our seminary at the present time on the best interests of our cause, as well as on the general prosperity of the land." It was these schools which enabled them to say: "A broad foundation for future success has been laid in the dissemination of Gospel truth throughout the province."

The spontaneous testimony of the native converts refers the blessed change that had come over the province to these same schools. "It is the privileges of this seminary," they say, "that have raised us in point of civilization, education, and religion. . . . Since the establishment of this seminary and other schools, the people are greatly improved in their customs and manners; and deserve, we hope, in a few years to come, if not now already, to be ranked in a higher class."

After enumerating the many benefits derived from the schools, by way of education physical, intellectual, moral, and religious, they very fitly add: "In short, we could say with the blind man in the Gospel, 'that whereas we were born blind, now we see.'" Even the heathen join in this same testimony. An old unconverted moonshi, noting the wonderful change that had come over the people, exclaims: "I seem as one born blind and now just made to see. Every thing is so changed!"

We need not wonder, then, that the toiling, hoping missionary writes: "The good work is evidently making progress, slowly indeed, for God does all things without haste; and I can not but hope before another century the sun will rise upon Christian Jaffna, and that this little spot with its Puritan institutions, the village church and *school*, will send out influences to leaven India."

In 1850 the number of pupils in the schools was 4165. The seminaries continued to be the centres of religious interest and influence, and "an unusual degree of religious feeling" in the seminary this year, was "characterized by unusual quietness and depth of conviction. Mr. Howland remarked that he had not seen before in India, such deep conviction for sin. It appeared more like the operations of the Spirit as seen in America than like those he had heretofore seen here. Some interest is felt by nearly all the boys, and some 12 or 15 are hopeful subjects of renewing grace."

In the statistics of this year are recorded the fact that of 680, the whole number of converts received to church communion from the first, 300 were educated in the Batticotta Seminary, and 180 in the Oodooville boarding-school. Of all who had been educated in the Batticotta Seminary, fully three fourths had become church members, while, in the girls' boarding-school nearly all had become pious, and the numerous Christian families are spoken of as presenting the brightest hope of the mission for coming years.

The value of education continued to increase among the natives, and crowds of candidates pressed for admission—many more than could be received, even though the mission had changed its terms and required the full pay for board *in advance.*

In 1851 the whole number of pupils was some 4250. Of these more than 500 were students of English in 15 schools, 9 of which were generously supported by the government. The seminary continued to prosper. "It has afforded us a very valuable corps of native assistants, and sent abroad through the island, a large number who are well instructed in true science and the doctrines of Christianity." The female boarding-school "has exerted a wide and powerful influence in overcoming the prejudices of the community against female education."

Eleventh Revival in the Schools.

The mission was blessed with another precious revival this year, which commenced, as the previous revivals had done, in the boarding-schools. After describing the preliminary indications of the Spirit's presence in the schools, the missionary writes: "In the afternoon there was an unusual stillness in the seminary, except as it was broken by the voice of prayer. Almost every countenance had an expression of thoughtful tenderness and solemnity. At the close of the Bible exercise at four o'clock, instead of going out to distribute tracts among the people, as is usual, the church members and teachers met in the school-room, and were soon joined by most of the impenitent. Their voices were heard in fervent prayer until sunset. At our evening meeting, there was a stillness, such as exists only when the Spirit of God is present. At the close of the exercise many lingered in the school-room; and as soon as they were left alone, their voices were heard in prayer. It was after ten o'clock when I went to sleep, and they were still praying. I learned the next day that they continued until nearly midnight; and at half-past four I was awakened by the same sound." "They have held a morning prayer-meeting nearly all the term; but never before had I heard them pray so early or so fervently. It was not merely the form of prayer, but the earnest pleading of burdened hearts; and I could not but feel that the Lord was indeed among us, stirring them up to take hold of him, and plead his promises; and I felt that a cloud of mercy was hovering over us.

"Though they had gathered so early, the sun had risen long before they dispersed. . . . At our morning devotions we spent an hour together, and then went on with school duties. But the bell for twelve o'clock, which released them from study, had hardly done ringing, when the voice of prayer was heard in the school-room. At first only a few of the church-members were present; but as they continued in prayer, others came, until nearly all the members of the seminary were there. Many did not go to dinner. Some who entered the room thoughtlessly, and because they saw others going, were soon in tears; and church-members, who seemed lifeless and dead, spoke and prayed in a manner which the Spirit only could inspire. The Spirit seemed literally *poured out;* and all were moved, as by an unseen yet mighty influence. The bell rang at two o'clock to call them to their studies, but still they lingered more than half an hour; and then I sent and advised them to adjourn until evening. I never before witnessed such a simultaneous movement on so many minds, when there was no special apparent cause.

"Tuesday was spent as a day of social prayer; and it was truly a most solemn and interesting day. From four o'clock in the morning until nearly midnight, except during the public meetings, the voice of prayer might be heard from the class and prayer-rooms, and indeed from every place where one could be alone or unite with others in small circles. . . .

"Much prayer was offered on Saturday that the Sabbath might be a day of God's power, and so it was. The scenes of that day it is not easy to describe. The most careless seemed aroused; and on every countenance there was a solemnity which showed the inward workings of the spirit. The interests of the soul seemed the only topic of thought and conversation. Often did we wish that the patrons of these boys might be here to witness what we did, and share our joy. They would have felt a thousand times repaid for all they have done. To us that Sabbath was a day never to be forgotten. We had hoped, but hardly dared to expect, to see such scenes in this dark land; and we could hardly believe what our eyes saw, and our ears heard."

Shall we wonder that the hearts of the missionaries became strongly bound to institutions thus crowned the *eleventh* time with such a choice blessing from Heaven? Shall we wonder that the Committee upon this mission, at the annual meeting of the Board, placed on record that, "the two very important schools which have been long established on 'Ceylon's Isle,' have shared largely in the divine blessing;" "and results of a desirable and permanent character show the wisdom of the plans adopted by the excellent men who first went to that field"?

And is it possible that at this very time doubts were being entertained by our Secretaries about the wisdom of continuing these institutions, and that plans were being formed for their suppression, even against the judgment and convictions of those same "excellent men"? Let us not anticipate. A fact so sad needs no heralding, and results so disastrous as followed it should be spoken of only in sorrow.

In 1852 the schools were prosperous, and the testimony of the periodicals of the Board is: "The village schools are spoken of as 'still worth vastly more than they cost as simple instruments of preaching the word.'" "The influence of the Batticotta Seminary and of the female boarding-school is 'deepening and widening.'" The Annual Committee speak of "the continued and spreading influence of the seminary and boarding-school," and complimenting the "fidelity and wisdom" exhibited in the conduct of the mission, add: "It is also a signal token of good that young men educated in the mission schools, and fast becoming influential and valued members of society, are helping to create a public sentiment favorable to Christian institutions."

"Every year adds to the evidence that our plans and our course have been laid by Him who had far more foresight and forethought than we had."

A blessed "season of refreshing" was enjoyed in the

schools, to the results of which a brief allusion is thus made: "Several leading members of the Church have been greatly revived by this outpouring of the Spirit." "They seem to speak with other tongues and with a great increase of power."

"Three schoolmasters and two others who were formerly teachers, profess to have experienced a change of heart, and are very desirous of becoming members of the Church. Several of the larger girls in the school at the station give more or less evidence of having passed from death unto life." The pupils of the other schools were also "deeply impressed by the power of truth." Thus a precious work of grace was often enjoyed, such as can prevail only where the elements of Christian truth have become fixed in minds and hearts by a long course of stated and continuous instruction.

1853.—The report of this year shows some 4242 pupils in the schools, and says: "The missionaries are seeing more and more of the fruit of what has been done in the schools in former years." They have proved "emphatically the door of access to all classes of the people."

Of the former graduates of the seminary it is stated: "Those of whom we have hoped the least and feared the most have shown in some instances that the labor bestowed on them is not all lost, and we believe facts will show that as few fail of fulfilling the high object for which they are educated, as in Christian lands, and fewer than we should expect, when we consider 'the hole of the pit' whence they are taken."

This statement is amply supported by facts. Of the girls' boarding-school it is shown that out of 204 graduates 136 were church-members when they left, and 13 more became so. Of the 753 who had been admitted into the Batticotta Seminary, 365 had been received to church-fellowship, and 103 were still students. Of those who had graduated, 96 were in the service of the mission, "a fact which shows the usefulness of the school in the way of furnishing missionary helpers."

Very fitly does the Annual Committee on this mission say: "Several precious seasons of spiritual refreshing have been enjoyed, more especially in the mission seminaries and boarding-schools. A large proportion of the members of the churches, amounting at the time of the last returns to 385, have been educated in the mission schools, and belong to the more influential classes of society." How could it be otherwise than that the Committee, and officers, and patrons of the Board should appreciate the wisdom and fidelity of "the good men and women" who devised, and brought into use these successful agencies of the Ceylon mission?

Testimony of the Rev. Daniel Poor, D.D.

Among the faithful and devoted missionaries who labored some forty years in this mission, it is fitting that the testimony of such a man as Dr. Poor find a brief record here; all the more so as the convictions of his lifetime have, in some quarters, been misrepresented. He has left his testimony in utterances, which give no uncertain sound, as follows:

"I would now ask whether it is not notorious, that by means even of the worst conducted mission schools, the Gospel has been preached to adults to a two-fold greater extent than though the missionary had devoted his time exclusively to preaching without the aid of mission schools? My observations lead to the conclusion that he will do four times the amount of preaching to adults, by means of a large circle of schools, that he would were his exclusive business to preach without them. In this statement I give due weight, and only due weight, to the importance of addressing persons under circumstances favorable for securing the ear, to say nothing of the kindly and respectful feelings of the heart. The difficulty of getting a hearing from adults, after their curiosity has been gratified by hearing a foreigner attempt to address them in the native language, can never be conceived of but by those who have made the experiment. To preach in bazaars and in the highways to men with whom we have no acquaintance, and over whom we have no influence, but by whom we are regarded with deep-rooted aversion, or with dread, is like sowing seed upon a mighty and rapid stream. It is barely possible that some grains may be washed to the river-side and take root.

"Attendance, by adult heathens, for any length of time, at appointed places for hearing the Gospel preached, is a thing scarcely known in India. If a man wishes to attend, he must in some way become so allied to the missionary that he may have some ostensible reason for attending that will excuse him in the sight of his countrymen. It is still more difficult to have any profitable access to children not in mission schools, than to adults. They are indeed like wild asses' colts, entirely beyond our reach.

"It is, therefore, a question of immense difficulty, as well as of importance, to every one who would preach the Gospel to this people, What is the medium, or method, of access to them for the purpose of delivering the Gospel message?

"This question I have deeply pondered in my mind, from year to year, from the time of my first arrival in the country, and have adopted different methods at different periods. The course of preaching to adults which I review with the greatest complacency, is that of having preached in the villages, by previous appointment, in the school-bungalows connected with the mission.

"Our success in assembling the people on special occasions, and at protracted meetings, was in close connection with the influence of our school operations. With the exception of what is done in the way of tours, and addressing people in connection with the distribution of books, I have known but little of preaching the Gospel to the heathen, but in close connection with schools.

"When the mission schools at Jaffna were suspended in consequence of pecuniary embarrassments, and when it would seem that the brethren would have more time for preaching, *far less preaching was done*, actually, and I would say, *far less could be done*, than when the schools were in operation. The reasons of this will be obvious by what I have before stated.

"It has been well said, and may be clearly shown, that our Lord, in his ministry on earth, combined attention to the spiritual wants of men with a due attention to their temporal necessities. There is, probably, no way in which a missionary may imitate his Master, in this important particular, so effectually, economically, and unexceptionably, as in the establishment of schools throughout the whole field in which it is his intention to labor as a preacher of the Gospel. The gratuitous instruction of youth is charity of a high order in the estimation of the heathen. The monthly stipend of two dollars is sufficient to secure, in an important sense, to the cause of Christian instruction, the influence of one of the principal men of a village. It gives support to a family, the effects of which are felt throughout the neighborhood. The school is a key to the village. There the missionary has a friend and a home. There is a demand for school-books, and an authorized opening for the distribution of books of all kinds. The books we are desirous of placing in the hands of the children are the books which the parents can most profitably use.

"In my present situation it is my high privilege, as before mentioned, to give myself exclusively to the work of preaching the Gospel. And hence it is that I have been induced to carry the school establishment to its present extent. Any abridgment of it would, I conceive, proportionably abridge my means of access to the people for the purpose of delivering my message.

"The foregoing remarks relate to the bearings of the school establishment upon the adult population. But its bearings upon the rising generation, as furnishing the best opportunities for preaching the Gospel to them, are no less important. Even on the most unfavorable supposition, that no child is converted while a member of the school, a great work of preparation has been done to aid succeeding missionaries in preaching the Gospel to adults. The generation of heathens now coming upon the stage of life at Jaffna, or at any other place where mission schools have been long in operation, are a different race from their fathers, and fairer candidates for the eternal inheritance, by means of the Gospel now preached to them. Herein, also, is that saying verified, 'One soweth and another reapeth;' and it may not be easy to determine which of the two were the most successful preacher. Dr. Watts observed that were he to retrace his steps, as a bishop of souls, he would spend a larger portion of his time in catechetical instructions with young children. If that would have been wise in a Christian country, how vastly more important must such instructions be in heathen lands! And such instructions form a prominent feature in every well-regulated mission school. It is true there are drawbacks arising from the influence of heathen school-masters, heathen parents, and heathenism in all its dreadful forms. But this is the very nature of mission service. It is a fierce onset upon the great adversary of God and men, and a fearful struggle with him in his own strongholds."

After the observation and experience of a quarter of a century Dr. Poor recorded it as his firm conviction, that

"*A system of native free schools furnishes probably the happiest combination of influences for doing good to soul and body that can possibly be devised by the missionary. It is far more acceptable to the people of this country than the same amount of expenditure even for medical purposes.*"

In 1854 the whole number of pupils was 4206. Of these, 93 were in the seminary, 85 in the girls' boarding-school, and about 500, as usual, in the English schools, the rest being in the vernacular free schools.

The *Missionary Herald* still affirms that: "The influence of the educational labors of the mission are seen every where. . . The standard of attainment in the English schools is constantly advancing. Of the value of the education obtained in the seminary at Batticotta, and in the boarding-school at Oodooville, the eagerness of parents to place their children in these institutions is decisive proof. That the truths of Christianity are not neglected is apparent from the number of pupils who have been admitted to the household of faith." On this point it is very significant that while the whole number of living communicants is reported this year to be only 395, the number of church-members received from the seminary in all was reported last year to be 385, and from the girls' boarding-school, 136=521. After making due allowance for the number of deaths, and pupils received to the Church from the other schools, it becomes evident that the blessing of God has rested preëminently on these schools, making them the chief agency in propagating Christianity in the district of Jaffna.

1855–6.—We have traced the educational history of this mission from its origin. We have seen how the blessing of God came down upon its schools, converting the pupils and teachers, gladdening the hearts of the missionaries, and eliciting from the Board and its Committees and patrons, here at home, resolutions of commendation to those who planned and conducted these schools, and devout thanksgiving to God for his blessing upon them.

The Schools Suppressed!

And now shall we record the terrible disaster which befell this mission in 1855? Shall we describe in detail the unhappy action of the Deputation, which disbanded many of the free schools, and disallowed the Batticotta Seminary? That seminary was the brightest hope of the land, the choicest, most hopeful result of the 40 years of patient and laborious toil in that mission. In the expressive language of S. Merwin, one of its own graduates: "Jaffna is the eye of Ceylon, and *the Batticotta Seminary the pupil of that eye.*"

It had been nurtured with prayers, watered with tears and the dews of heaven's grace, and grown into the affections, loving sympathy, and confidence of praying men and women in all parts of America. Its more than 350 converts were the witness of God's approval and blessing upon it. Is it possible that upon this favored institution, the brightest light, the most effective agency of the mission, a Deputation of good men from America laid their hand, and deprived it of its power? Oh! that this action could be as if it had not been! Oh! that the lamentations of the dear fathers in this mission, as they saw this institution smitten down, could be like dreams from which there may be a pleasant awaking. But no, the action was taken, and the disaster has become a *fact* in all its stern and sorrowful reality.

We cast no reproach upon the Deputation or those who sent them; but we do pray God to forgive them, believing that they knew not what they did. Oh! that this page of missionary history could be blotted out forever, by undoing the acts. But as this can not be, may our churches and missionary societies gain from it the lessons which God would have them learn.

I would not intimate that the action suppressing these schools was in direct opposition to the views and wishes of *all* the missionaries. No. The saddest of all the results of this authoritative Deputation is to be seen in the *divided councils, and the breaches of Christian sympathy and love,* caused among brethren who had long labored and prayed together in the bonds of Christian brotherhood, breaches the healing of which will be one of the most precious triumphs of God's grace.

During both these years the customary annual committees on this mission have no reports recorded in the Annual Report of the Board, an ominous silence! The Committee, in 1855, did indeed present a report, faithfully calling in question the doings of the Deputation; but it found no place in the printed record. Why is this? Will the Prudential Committee admit no statements into their records, from their own committees even, unless they be in their praise? But let us cast a mantle of charity over their doings, though we cease not to grieve for the disaster they brought upon the missions. Against the wisdom of their action in suppressing these schools, this brief statement of Father Spaulding, our oldest living missionary on Ceylon, should be engraved as a perpetual record and testimony, till the heathen shall be all converted. This dear old missionary, speaking from the depths of his soul, and his own personal experience of nearly forty years' labor in the mission, still standing amidst the ruins of these schools, nobly testifies: "*The simple preaching of the Gospel among the people of India, when catechisms and Scripture history are not, and have not been, taught to the children, has, thus far, had very little effect.* Conversion *simply by preaching*, as the term is generally used, is yet, to a very great extent, *theory*."

Speaking of the reports prepared in the mission, under the influence of the Deputation laboring to justify the changes they dictated, Father Spaulding says: "*To restore things to their right position, I would advise the entire ignoring of the twenty-one reports.*" So deeply was he penetrated with the conviction that those reports misrepresented the honest judgment of the missionaries, and perilled the dearest interests of the mission.

The special meeting at Albany, and the appointment of a special committee of thirteen, to investigate and calm the troubled elements, show that the minds and hearts of the missionaries and many friends of the Board were deeply moved. To that committee Father Spaulding appealed as to his last hope. Their report and the action of the Board at Newark are somewhat known to the public. The action of the Deputation was slightly modified in some respects, but the restrictions resting on the Batticotta Seminary were such that it has not been reöpened by the mission. Its brightest light was put out, and this desolation was wrought, not by an enemy, but by those who claim to be the best friends of the cause.

Peruse again the history of God's blessing on these schools. Read over the repeated resolutions and records of the Board in commendation of them, and who would believe it possible that they could have come to *such* an end? When they were disbanded and restricted for want of funds in 1837, a general voice of lamentation was raised by all who loved the Board. Does not their suppression in 1855 present cause for deeper and more prolonged grief?

CHAPTER VIII.

SCHOOLS OF OUR MADURA AND MADRAS MISSIONS.

MADURA.

1834.—The Madura mission of the A.B.C.F.M. was commenced in 1834. The record is: "In July Mr. Hoisington and Mr. Todd, with three native assistants, commenced a mission here, and soon established two small schools—one for each sex."

Importance of Schools.

In 1835, "the mission was employed in establishing schools in the city and adjacent villages."

In 1836, "Oct. 30, a church was organized, with nine native members, all from Jaffna. Of 13 native helpers, 8 had been educated at Batticotta. At the close of the year, 37 schools had been opened, of which 30 were in operation—9 in Madura, and the others in the neighboring villages. They contained 1149 boys and 65 girls." *All* the teachers of these schools were *heathen* or Roman Catholics. "No others could be obtained, and even if they could be obtained, *the parents would not send their children to them.*"

The records of the mission bring to view the great difficulty of overcoming the fears and prejudices of the people, so that they might be willing to send their children to school, and expresses a very high estimate of the value of these schools. "The schools accomplish several important objects. They will raise up a numerous class of good readers. Very few of the people can now read fluently."

"Again, by means of schools we gain access to the parents of the children, and their friends. Most of the people attach some value to schools. By our giving their children an education, they see and acknowledge that we are their benefactors."

"In the city we have two schools for teaching the English language and science. The number of scholars in both is 89."

The value of these schools, in the estimation of European friends, is attested by frequent and generous donations for their support.

Three Brahman youths from the English school are mentioned as the first inquirers, and the hope expressed that they were "under the guidance of the good Spirit."

1837.—The two first converts of this mission were received into the Church the 30th of July this year; their names were Joseph and Kamache. Both had been in the employment of the mission, and thus came under the influence and teaching of the truth. It is distinctly stated that one was a *teacher*, and probably the other was also. This was the year of the terrible retrenchment for want of funds, and it pressed hard upon this as well as upon the other missions. After dismissing some of their pupils, one of the missionaries writes: "It would have awakened no slight emotion in the bosom of benevolence, to see those girls rise from their knees and go from the family altar to hide behind the pillars of our verandah, and weep. Yes, they could not refrain; and what added to my sorrow, was that our Saviour had said: 'Suffer little children to come unto me, and forbid them not, for of such is the kingdom of heaven.' His word has been confirmed by his providence and grace at Oodooville. Not one girl has ever left that institution who did not profess attachment to Jesus. And who is it that forbids these? The disciples did it before, and it was not an enemy that forbid them now, else we could have borne it. . . . If I had a voice that could reach half-way round the globe, I would cry, not only in behalf of the girls of Dindigul and Madura, but of Madras and Ceylon and Bombay and all

Asia: 'Come over and help us; send us money, if you do not wish to come yourselves.'"

In June of this year the schools had increased to 60, with 2284 scholars. "Nearly all must have been closed, had not the Madras government, learning the circumstances, made an unexpected donation of £300 sterling for their support."

"Of the school-teachers employed by the mission, two are Protestants, four Roman Catholics, and the others heathen." "We attach great importance to our schools, as means of access to the people." "We had several applications for admission to the Church from school-masters, whose minds have evidently been enlightened by the truths of the Gospel, if not their hearts converted."

1838.—April 1st, Mr. Poor writes: "The whole number of schools is 59; average of pupils, 2173." He speaks of the schools "as so many lights held out in this benighted city." Of the school-system he says: "It holds out the fairest prospect for bringing the overtures of the Gospel before the minds of the people at large. When I converse privately with our school-masters, and urge upon them the immediate claims of the Gospel, there is a response to the truth which is not witnessed in the case of the uninstructed. Thus it is, to some extent, with the monitors and children who are brought under instruction in the schools."

It is worthy of notice how closely this testimony accords with our experience in the Ahmednuggur mission, where all our best native preachers and helpers were brought under Christian instruction and converted to God, while employed as heathen teachers, or while pupils in the seminary.

In 1839 the mission reports 73 native free schools, besides English and boarding-schools at all the stations. Their estimate of the schools is clearly indicated in all their letters and reports. Of their preaching audiences they say: "They embrace about two thirds of the pupils of the English school, the school-masters of the city, persons employed in mission families, and a few occasional attendants." No *stated* attendants but those connected with the schools or families. "The obvious and substantial advantages of our schools go far towards reconciling the parents to the prominence we give to Christianity in all our printed books, and our whole course of instruction—such a prominence as would be tolerated in but few schools in Christian lands." "The scholars exhibit a deportment every way encouraging to the missionary. Some of the older boys have asked for baptism." "Boys in the boarding-school are the most attentive audience." "Were there funds at command, a blow might now be struck that would soon make heathenism ashamed. I know of no object to which I would more cheerfully contribute. To pluck these heathen youth from the paths of the destroyer, and to place them where they can be trained for doing good, instead of evil, is an object worthy of the prayers and contributions of all who love the cause of truth. Does not the finger of God point to this as the plain duty of the Church? Will it be said, the expense can not be afforded? Let the results of the Ceylon mission be compared with those of missions in India generally, and it would appear, so as not to be misunderstood, that we can not afford to do otherwise."

In view of the character and results of these schools, we do not wonder that the editor of the *Missionary Herald* remarks: "All these efforts are so directed as to have a powerful and salutary religious bearing on both pupils and teachers. *Probably in no other manner can the same number of children and youth be brought under so steady and favorable a religious influence.*"

In 1840 the mission reports 96 free schools, with 3087 pupils, and 6 boarding-schools, with 109 pupils.

This rapid enlargement in school operations shows clearly the high estimate the missionaries put upon them, and their reports and letters abound in evidence to the same effect. After stating the number and character of their schools, they add: "Thus it appears, that on our present scale of operations, we are yearly sending out into this heathen community a thousand lads, who in a short time are to take the places of their fathers, with minds somewhat enlightened, and memories stored with all the important and saving doctrines of the Bible. The great majority of these, we may safely say, but for our schools, would grow up under the most heathen and demoralizing influences, with scarcely a single counteracting good influence. The parents of the families to which these thousand boys belong, must, of necessity, listen to the recital of some gospel truth, to which, till now, they were entire strangers. It is not an uncommon thing, in passing along the streets, to be hailed by men repeating some of the simple questions and answers of our first catechism. From these facts, and many others of which we are in possession, it appears to us evident that a leaven is working, which, under the divine blessing, must eventually produce a great moral change in this mass of heathen population. This is only one view, of many which might be taken of our common free-school system. In the school-room we often find our largest and best congregations."

A Little Boy seven years old asking Baptism.

"The boarding-school contains 21 boys, most of whom are making good progress in their studies, and I have some reason to hope that a few are seeking that wisdom, the beginning of which is the fear of the Lord. One little boy seven years old, the smallest in the school, and from a heathen family, asked me some time since to baptize him. I sent him away with some slight remark, as I supposed it a mere childish notion, which had arisen from his having seen the children of the mission families baptized. After some time, he came again with the same request. I asked him why he wished to receive baptism? He replied that he was a sinner, and wished to be born again, that he might become one of God's children—with other remarks of the kind. A few days afterwards I called on him and repeated the same questions, to which he replied as before. 'You told me,' I said, 'that you wished to be baptized so that you might be born again, and become a child of God. Do you think that, by receiving baptism, you will be born again?' He replied: 'If I hate and forsake every sin, and believe in

Christ, and pray to God, and he gives me his Holy Spirit, then I shall be born again.' 'But you are a little boy, and if you become a Christian your friends may persecute you, and tell you that you must forsake the Lord Jesus Christ. What will you say when they do so?' He answered by a single but very emphatic Tamil word: 'I will not.' 'But are you able to do this by your own strength?' 'If God give me his Holy Spirit, and I pray to him, I shall have strength.' 'Do you commit sin now?' I asked. 'No, sir.' 'Do you never tell lies?' 'No, sir, not now; when I was a heathen I told lies, but none since.' 'Do you never get angry?' He hung down his head as he acknowledged that he sometimes did get angry. 'Well, do you pray?' 'Yes, sir, every day.' 'How do you pray? Do you repeat a prayer you have committed to memory?' 'I pray with my whole heart.' 'What do you ask for? What do you wish above all other things?' 'That God would give me a new heart, and make me his child.'

"After other conversations of a similar nature," says the missionary, "I kneeled down and prayed that the great Shepherd would make this dear child one of his flock. Before rising he also poured out his heart in few and simple, but most appropriate petitions that God would give him his Holy Spirit, make him his child, and finally take him to heaven. As he arose, his eyes were filled with tears, and my own thoughts were irresistibly carried back to many a happy scene in America, where I have been surrounded by a group of children pouring out their tears and their hearts before God. A few of the larger boys also are in the habit of constant prayer, not only in private but with the other boys, and I would fain hope that the Lord has begun a good work in their hearts."

With such evidence of God's blessing on these schools, we do not wonder to hear the officers of the Board say: "The time has now come for establishing a seminary in this mission, of the same general nature with that in the Ceylon mission; and the Committee expect to authorize the commencement of it as soon as the state of the funds will permit."

In proof of the happy and elevating influence of the free schools, facts and incidents crowd upon the missionaries too numerous for record. On preaching-tours, among twenty villages where the people are utterly indifferent to the truth, and know not how to read, one is found where the people crowd around the missionary, eager for books and glad to listen to his message. The reason is found to be, that in this one village, a mission school had formerly existed.

The Little Girl who would not Break the Sabbath.

"Some of the children in our schools are obtaining an amount of Scripture knowledge which is encouraging. I have just heard of a conversation which a little girl had with her mother a few days since, which will illustrate this. The mother had directed the daughter to prepare the materials for cleansing their house on the succeeding day, which was the Sabbath; against this the daughter expostulated very strongly. 'Why, mother,' she says, 'to-morrow is the Sabbath, and how can we work upon that day?' 'Then,' says the mother, 'our house will be unclean, and how can we stay in it?' 'But,' continues the daughter, 'it is God's command, mother, that we should do no work on the Sabbath, and that we should sanctify that day.' Here she repeated the fourth command; 'and besides, mother,' she says, 'if our hearts are clean, we shall not be troubled with the impurity of the house.' It is sufficient to say the house was not cleansed; and now that mother gives us some reason to hope that her heart has been changed."

Can we have more convincing proof of the blessed influence of Christian teaching on these young hearts? Take the following incident from the pen of a missionary: "A day or two since, while returning from one of the out-schools, I met some of my scholars in the north quarter of the town, and went with them to their houses. The parents seemed to welcome me cordially, and after I had looked into their houses, and made some inquiries about their domestic comforts and habits, as I was in the principal room of one of the houses, *I was asked to pray by one of the children.* I said they might call in their neighbors. They did so, and we had a very pleasing and to me novel meeting."

And is it possible that such schools are to be disallowed? The missionaries have clung to them through all the history of the Board—their letters and lives are one mass of testimony to their value. "We have *often* remarked," they write, "that our school-masters, *heathen* as they are, act for us the important part of pioneers. They open for us a door of access to the people; they do much to silence objections and to remove prejudice, and impart useful knowledge."

There were twelve additions to the churches this year, marking the more direct blessing of God upon the labors and agencies of the mission. The case of one of them, a heathen teacher, is narrated in detail, and both for the depth of his conviction and the much he had to suffer for Christ, the account awakens deep interest and sympathy.

In 1841, the whole number of pupils reported in one English school, seven boarding, and eighty-two free schools, is 3304. The missionary says: "Pupils and teachers have acquired a large amount of divine knowledge. I would fain hope and earnestly pray that it may be productive of good to their immortal spirits." "The state of religious feeling for some time past has been such as to give me much encouragement. From the middle of last year a few of the boys seemed awakened to a sense of their condition as perishing sinners. Soon afterwards three of the larger boys gave very pleasing evidence that they had been taught of the Holy Spirit. They appear to hunger and thirst after righteousness." "They were admitted to the Church last February." "A few of the other boys are seriously inclined, and feel it to be their duty to converse with their friends and others on the subject of personal religion."

"Those boys who are members of the Church give me all the evidence I could expect, and, indeed, all that I could desire, that they really love the service of the blessed Saviour. Two or three others give much reason to hope that they have chosen the Lord as their portion. Most of the boys are in the daily habit of prayer and reading the Scriptures, and I can not but hope that the Lord has still rich blessings in store for some of them, whom he will make polished shafts in his quiver."

The reports of this year mention eleven new admissions to the Church—" Three of the larger boys of the boarding-school at Tiramungulum;" three more at Sivagunga, and five at Dindigul. Both pupils and teachers were active in making known the truth to others, even while subjected to much reproach and abuse.

In 1842 the schools had so increased as to embrace 4035 pupils, 200 of whom were boarding scholars. The proposed seminary was commenced this year, September 1, with 34 pupils, 10 of whom were members of the Church. Nearly all the most cheering results and prospects of the mission are traced, as usual, to the schools. As an illustration of this fact take the following:

The Praying Girl and her Father.

" Mrs. Cherry's girls' school prospers beyond our expectation. In July the father of one of the little girls came to my study, apparently in trouble. He stood a little time, and before he had uttered his first sentence he began to weep. 'Sir,' said he, 'what can I do? My little daughter kneels down with me and my wife and repeats the Lord's prayer.' I answered: 'That is well.' Said he: 'We tried to make her stop, but she continued it, and we thought we would let her; but oh! it makes me feel so bad! I want to be a Christian.' In the evening he came with his brother, who from having oftener attended our services, knew more of divine truth. They asked for baptism. I talked with them a long time, and believe they felt earnest and honest in their wishes."

" All the girls now with us, 26 in number, are in the habit of prayer, and I am strong in the hope that they are those designated by our compassionate Lord as 'of the kingdom of heaven.'"

Special Value of Boarding-Schools.

Of his boarding-school Mr. Muzzy says: "This school has afforded us more encouragement than any other means we have been enabled to use. There has been scarcely a time for six months past that some of its members have not appeared serious, and, in some degree, anxious for the salvation of their souls; and in one or two instances, we entertain hopes that the change we see in their appearance and life is a real transformation from darkness to God's marvellous light." "I have ascertained that some of the boys in the boarding-school not only observe seasons of secret prayer themselves, but take some of the other boys apart and hold little meetings with them." "Last evening one of the boarding-school boys remained after evening service and desired conversation and prayers; he also wished to unite with the Church." "The feeling appears to be very general that the religion of this people is to be superseded by another, which is to be the only true religion."

The only additions to the churches traceable in the reports of this year are two, stated in the *Missionary Herald* of December as follows:

"Mr. Tracy mentions in his journal that two of the school-boys, who appeared to have correct views of the way of salvation, and of their own character and desert as sinners, had applied for admission to the church at Tiramungulum, and had been received."

In 1843 are reported 114 free schools, with 3353 pupils, besides 173 in select schools, 195 boarding pupils, 30 in the seminary, and 36 preparandi. "The small expense of the free schools, compared with the beneficial results which accrue, is deserving of notice. The teaching under the supervision of the Dindigul station alone, the last year, was equal to the labors of one man twenty-five years, and cost less than at the rate of $20 a year, or less than $1.50 a year for each pupil. The effect of the instruction communicated on the minds of the children, in disciplining them and qualifying them to distinguish between truth and error, and on their moral feelings, is great and salutary. 'We very much doubt,' say the missionaries, 'whether there be a child selected from our schools, after six months' or a year's training, who will admit for example the existence of more gods than one, or will reject this first element of all correct knowledge in religion.' In this manner these schools, if they do not fully supply the defect of early religious training in the family, are constantly counteracting the influence of those errors and absurdities with which heathen parents fill the minds of their children, and thus are preparing the way for them to hear intelligently the preaching of the Gospel, and to admit the truth of its doctrines."

The missionaries urge that their seminary and schools should be enlarged. Of their boarding-schools they say: "The conduct of the boys has been respectful and proper, and some of them have been serious and anxiously inquiring what they shall do to be saved." "The desire for religious conversation has been so great, that scarcely an evening has passed for weeks in which some of the boys have not come to my study for private conversation and prayer."

This quite prepares us to read: "Three boys from the English boarding-school were received to the Church." "Since my last, three from the seminary and one from the boarding-school have been received into the Church." It prepares us, also, for this summary statement in the report of the Board:

"*It is an important fact, also, that, from the pupils in the boarding-schools nearly all the* 40 *converts who have the last year been received to the mission churches, have been gathered.* A number more from among these pupils are candidates for church-fellowship."

Forty converts the harvest of this year, and "nearly all" from "the boarding schools"!

In 1814 the missionaries write: "To-day the Lord's supper has been administered, and one of the boys in the boarding-school, who has long been on trial, has been admitted to the Church; nine others are candidates for the privilege at a future time." When a "benevolent society" was formed for supporting schools and catechists, "the boys in the boarding-schools" were foremost in the work, and even ready to go "without part of a meal twice each week," to save money for the purpose. "A class six in number and all hopefully pious, graduated in February." "Of the girls in the boarding-school we hope to admit two to the Church to-morrow." "There are tokens of the Spirit's presence in the boarding-school which have encouraged our hearts." "The blessing of God has hitherto, we believe, attended our labors in the seminary. Nearly one half of the pupils are professors of religion, including the whole of the first class." "The boarding-school for boys has 41 pupils, of whom 11 are candidates for admission to the Church. In the girls' school there are 45 constant attendants. Two have been added to the Church, and there are 14 candidates for admission." "The girls' boarding-school at Madura East has 33 scholars; and it has not been without some tokens of the presence of the Holy Spirit. The preparandi class, designed to prepare school-masters and readers for the villages, is prosperous. Ten young men have been connected with it during the year. Six are candidates for admission to the Church."

1845.—This year shows an increase in the schools, the whole number of pupils being 3891. The increase was mostly in the seminary and boarding-schools. Of the former it is reported: "In May the number had risen to 61, of whom 16 were members of the Church. Of the class which finished the course of study last year, all entered into the service of the mission as helpers." "Of the progress in study, good conduct and promise of usefulness of the pupils, the missionaries speak with great encouragement." "Two or three of the students are now candidates for church membership. Many seem to feel the truth, and some are in the habit of stated private prayer. In the boarding-school "several of the boys are seriously inclined, and have asked for baptism."

Schools secure Village Congregations.

In 1846 the number of pupils in the schools had increased to 4171, and "the native churches had an accession of 97 members." These, as heretofore, were gathered in from the schools and the "Christian villages," so called, that is, villages which had placed themselves under Christian instruction for certain considerations, the most valuable of which, in their estimation, was a school. Hence the report says: "The great extension of the *school system* has resulted from the peculiar circumstances of the mission. Nearly 50 of the free schools and nearly 1000 of the pupils are in the 'Christian villages.' The least we can do for these villages, . . is to establish schools in them."

From the urgent desire of the people for education "has arisen the system of village free schools, the select schools, the boarding-schools, and the seminary."

Of the 61 students in the seminary "20 are members of the Church, 6 having been received during the year." "All the members of the first class, except two, are communicants."

Of the girls' boarding-school at East-Madura, "Nine of the pupils were admitted to the Church during the year, and six are candidates." "All the boys of the boarding-school go regularly to their closets, either in small companies or alone, to read the Scriptures and pray." "There was unusual attention to the subject of religion in the girls' boarding-school."

Of the seminary at Pasumalee it is reported: "The present number of students is 56"—"Of these 20 are members of the Church, of whom eight have been admitted to Christian fellowship within the past year." There were only "six members of the Church at P., who were not pupils of the seminary."

A good number of the heathen teachers are included among those received to the Church, and the candidates for admission.

1847 was a year of trial in this mission. An attempt to

root out caste from the native church, resulted in the separation from the mission of some 72 converts and a large number of scholars. The schools were still farther reduced for want of funds. "In consequence of a reduction in the appropriation made by the Committee for schools, the mission has reduced the number of pupils in the common schools from 3803 to 2306." This act was a painful one to the mission.

Mr. Muzzy writes of his station: "Four or five hundred scholars, who have been learning the Scriptures, who were assembled every Thursday to hear them explained, who committed to memory scriptural catechisms, and who heard the Gospel on the Sabbath and other days, are now deprived of all these privileges, and are under heathen influences entirely." The report of the mission says: "The reduction of the schools to one half the number of last year, is very sudden and great, and is calculated to shake the public confidence in the stability of the mission, and thus hinder the progress of the Gospel." The mission earnestly remonstrated against further reduction of the schools, thus attesting their high appreciation of these agencies, which is also evinced by statements like the following, showing the blessed results of these schools. "In the English school for boys, four have recently requested baptism." "At Pulney, three school-masters have expressed a desire to unite with our Church and receive baptism."

"The whole number of students who have been connected with our seminary from its commencement is 92. . . Of the whole number, 37 have been professors of religion." "Of the class which graduated in May last, nine (out of eleven) were members of the Church." "All of the class which has recently graduated, (with the exception of two, who have gone to Madras,) are in the service of the mission."

In 1848, several of the pupils became members of the Church and others were candidates. The influence of the schools in gathering "village congregations" and converts from them, is abundantly manifest. The report says: "The congregations which assembled at station churches, are composed of the free-school children, teachers, and monitors, the boarding-school boys, and the girls," "ten to fifteen strangers" being drawn in from curiosity. The adults drawn in, were for the most part "the parents of school-children," thus showing the influence of the schools in securing adult hearers.

Of the seminary the missionary writes: "The conduct of the students has been very exemplary; and several of them give me reason to hope that they have passed from death unto life. Four of them are candidates for admission to the Church."

The missionary at Dindigul writes: "Last January five persons were received into the Church—three were schoolmasters at out-stations. The other two were members of our English school." "A short time since, a lad about sixteen years old, came to me and said he formerly belonged to the English school at this place, that he now wished to be baptized and make an open profession of religion. I think it my duty to receive him into the Church."

Mr. Herrick writes: "I became much interested in a little boy ten years of age, and a member of one of these schools. The catechist pointed him out to me, saying that he regularly attended morning prayers, and often prayed himself that his parents might become worshippers of the true God. Before I left, the little boy came to me and said, with much apparent thoughtfulness: 'Sir, I have become a Christian. As I daily go to the bazaar, I meet many little boys who worship idols. What shall I say to them?' A heathen man who stood by, bore witness to the boldness with which the little fellow acknowledged Christ wherever he went."

A Revival in the Seminary.

In 1849, the whole number of pupils in the schools increased to 2560. The mission says: "We know that much good has already been accomplished by schools, in opening the way for preaching the Gospel. We believe that preaching and teaching, the pulpit and the school, the missionary and the school-master, acting conjointly, are an effectual method of propagating the Gospel." The annual report says: "The seminary was blessed with an outpouring of the Spirit, in the summer of last year. An account of the revival of religion in the seminaries among the Nestorians, excited in teachers and scholars a desire for a similar blessing among themselves. 'Several of the church members seemed to have received a new spirit of earnest, importunate prayer, and a day was subsequently set apart for special prayer and fasting. The meetings were deeply solemn, and I never witnessed more earnest prayers than were offered by some of the native members of the Church. The general feeling of solemnity was increased, and several of the most hopeless of the students were brought under conviction, and I trust were led to the foot of the cross. Nine or ten are now indulging the hope that they have been born again, and several others, with a greater or less degree of interest, are inquiring what they must do to be saved.'

"Nine of these converts were admitted to the Church at the close of the year. Several others were regarded as candidates for admission, and there were still indications of the divine presence."

Change of Policy and Retrenchment.

And yet, notwithstanding these blessed results of the schools, the same report of the Board discloses the unhappy change in the views of the Secretary and Prudential Committee in regard to them. It says: "The Prudential Committee doubt if the higher missionary schools, called seminaries, should be formed at the outset of missions, as they have often been." "The Committee express a doubt as to the propriety of the frequent employment of professedly heathen masters. They would also declare their belief, that schools are no where *necessary precursors* of the preaching of the Gospel, nor *necessary attendants* upon its merely aggressive operations in pagan communities."

Here was a manifest change of views on the part of the

executive officers. The sentiments expressed are directly in conflict with their former views, as well as with the views and practice of the missions.

The reader will bear in mind the accordant and uniform statements of the officers of the Board up to this date. In regard to these very schools with *heathen teachers*, they had repeatedly placed sentiments on record as follows : "Schools of this kind are too important an auxiliary to the missionary to be abandoned." Though their teachers are *heathen*, they "*may be an excellent channel for conveying Christian knowledge to the minds of the pupils, the teachers, the parents, and the friends of all connected with the schools.*"

What inference ought to be made from these conflicting statements? Was there a change of views, or was there not? (See Report of Deputation, p. 9.)

In 1850, the retrenchment in the schools was so great that only 1523 pupils are reported, in all, though the missionaries put on record facts, and give utterance to convictions showing the value of these agencies no less than before. Of one of the boarding-schools it is said : "Five of the girls have been received to the Church, and it is hoped that some others have been renewed." The English school is reported as "still flourishing," supported as usual, mostly by English friends, and the great value of all the schools is dwelt upon, especially in securing a large amount of Christian knowledge instilled into the minds of the pupils, and disseminated widely among the people. Mr. Muzzy writes: "I often meet, in my excursions for preaching, young men who have studied in these schools formerly ; and they uniformly, as far as I know, not only understand the most of what we say, and approve of it, but actually stand up for the truth, and argue in its defense with those who oppose it. And many of those who have been any time under instruction, and have afterwards obtained employment, either under government or rich natives, have a name for probity and uprightness which was not known in others who occupied the same places before them. The heathen notice this, and speak of it, as the 'fruit of the padres' schools.'"

Choicer fruit from these schools is reported as follows: "Early in December I had the pleasure of admitting nine of the students to the privileges of the Church; and at our last communion service, which occurred a few weeks ago, seven more were received into the fold of Christ." "Only two are now left in the seminary, who are not members of the Church; and at the close of the term, a few days since, one of these was inquiring what he should do to be saved." "I am more and more convinced, every day, that the work which has been accomplished in the seminary, has been of God, and not of man."

In 1851, the seminary "had twenty-seven pupils at the close of the year, of whom twenty were members of the Church." "Of the whole number of students from the beginning, forty-eight have been members of the Church, and eighteen are known to have engaged in missionary work." "The state of religious feeling in the seminary has been such as to afford encouragement." "The English school, still supported by the liberality of English residents, is successful." "The girls' day-schools are said to be prosperous."

In 1852, the whole number of pupils rose to 1883. "Two young men graduated from the seminary, during the year, and are usefully employed in the service of the mission." "The English school reports one hundred and sixteen pupils." "In the boarding-school at Sivagunga, an interesting state of religious feeling has existed; several of the boys, it is hoped, have been truly converted; and two have been received to the Church." In the girls' boarding-school at Madura East, "quite a number have been anxious in regard to their spiritual interests—four were received to the Church, and seven others were seeking admission."

It is well to note the gradual change in this mission in the character of the schools. For many years, all were for heathen children, and taught by heathen teachers. As converts were obtained, and became fitted to teach, they gradually supplanted the heathen teachers; and the offer of schools availing to secure "village congregations" of those who pledged themselves to forsake idolatry and thus became nominal Christians, these schools became numerous, and the schools for heathen children diminished. But it should be observed that the effective influence in obtaining these "village congregations" at first, and in giving them Christian instruction and eventually bringing individuals of them into the Church, was the schools. The report recognizes this fact, and says: "The teachers, in most cases, instruct not only the children of the schools, but the adult members of the congregations." Regular, stated, long-continued instruction in Christian truth, by means of schools, is the agency which God has preëminently blessed in this, as in all our other missions; the schools being the chief centres of influence, the nurseries especially blessed in the conversion of the pupils, and fountains whence emanated the influence which arrested attention, awakened thought, and resulted in the conversion of others. Hence we read in the frequent reports, statements like the following: "Five persons were recently admitted to the Church at Madura East, four of them being pupils in the girls' boarding-school." "A number of the girls seem to be solicitous in regard to the salvation of their souls; and six or eight are anxious to join the Church."

"After returning from the Sanitarium in October, I noticed unusual attention, on the part of the boys in our boarding-school, to the preached Gospel and to the Bible lessons. A degree of seriousness and thoughtfulness seemed to pervade the school, which I had not previously seen. I invited all who had any special desire to converse upon the subject of personal religion to call at my room. Five of the larger boys came, and said they had resolved to be Christians. A few evenings afterwards, all the boys came and declared their determination to serve the Lord. The Holy Spirit was manifestly at work."

In 1853, we find the whole number of pupils in the schools to be only 1395. The detailed reports of these schools show their high value in the estimation of the mission, and their effective influence in securing its great objects. Of the 33 pupils in the seminary, "18 are members of the Church." Of the 15 preparandi scholars, "12 are members of the Church." "The religious state of the institution is encouraging." "Ten of the pupils united with the Church during the year; and the report mentions ten or twelve, not members of the Church, who were accustomed to attend a weekly inquiry meeting, and seemed seriously desirous to know and do the will of God." "Three young men were received into the Church at our last communion season, and others are desirous of the same privilege."

The missionaries' estimate of these schools is often apparent. Mr. Muzzy, speaking of a new congregation, says: "The movement appears to have resulted from a blessing on the day-school among them." "Many of these persons have been instructed in schools, or in missionary families; and they have a much better knowledge of the Scriptures than others who have not had their privileges." Mr. Chandler says: "Our boarding-school is in a very hopeful state. Some are candidates for admission to the Church. Those received to the Church at the close of last year, have continued to adorn their profession."

In 1854, the schools report in all 1229 pupils. Of the 44 in the seminary "15 have been received into the Church." "They all seem to be walking in the fear of God. They have manifested a pleasing interest in the spiritual welfare of their impenitent companions." "Four graduated in March, and have since been profitably employed in the service of the mission," and also 14 preparandi scholars. "The English school has 137 pupils."

The annual report of this year frankly admits that "formerly those who joined the churches were generally from the schools, or the native helpers of the mission;" while it expresses gratification that now the greatest accessions come from the village congregations. But these village congregations were traceable to these same schools.

1855 commenced with 1147 pupils but closed with a diminished number. A close inspection of reports reveals the fact that two boarding-schools and the industrial school had disappeared, and also the English school with its 137 intelligent and promising young men, and instructions were given for abandoning three more of the boarding-schools at a fixed point of time.

The cause of this change of policy is found in the visit of the *Deputation.*

In connection with the suppression of *the English school* the statement is put on record that "no instance of conversion has come to our knowledge as the result of this school;" and yet in the *Missionary Herald* of July, 1848, only seven years previous, eight persons are recorded as converted in connection with the English school. They seem to have been connected with a branch of the English school, then sustained at Dindigul East, but were converted in the "English school."

1856.—The report of this year shows 996 scholars in the schools still permitted to exist. The most interesting converts are still found in connection with these schools. The report says: "Nine of the pupils (of the girls' boarding-school) have, within the year, been received to the privileges of the Church." "Ten of these (students in the seminary) have been admitted to the privileges of the Church, and several others have offered themselves as candidates for admission."

We here close this brief account of the Madura mission, with devout thanksgiving to God for his precious favor and blessing on these schools, and especially that they were not suppressed in the early years of the mission bringing upon it such a disaster as befell our more recently organized missions in Western India. The 1000 or 1200 native communicants in this mission are a living testimony to the value of these schools and the blessing of Heaven upon them.

MADRAS MISSION.

1836.—The only remaining mission in India now connected with the American Board, is at *Madras.*

This mission was commenced in August, 1836, by the Rev. Myron Winslow, D.D., who was joined the following month by Dr. Scudder.

Chief Hopes centre in the Schools.

1837.—The first annual report in 1837 reveals the policy and agencies of the mission in speaking of the press, and of 25 *schools with* 750 *pupils.* The Board made no increased allowance for these schools for want of funds, and they were nearly all closed, but such was the estimate of them by the missionaries and European Christians on the ground, that contributions came in, ($600 from one friend,) and enabled Mr. Winslow to reöpen 14 of them in October.

The importance of these schools is brought to view in the frequent and earnest pleas of the missionaries for funds to support them. In their letters to the secretaries are such statements as the following: "We regret exceedingly that the embarrassments of the Board prevent our having funds to continue and even enlarge the schools; and, as our congregations depend so much upon them, we are making an effort to acquire here the means of continuing a few." They plead for "an efficient and extensive school system; embracing a high school, boarding-school, and many native free schools. Every year's experience convinces us more and more that the great hope of missions to such idolaters as surround us, must rest on the young, and on extending to them the benefit of a thoroughly Christian education."

In 1838, the mission reports 16 schools with 500 pupils. So deeply were European Christians impressed with the value of these schools that government was induced to grant Rs. 3000, and the governor and several other gentlemen gave Rs. 100 each, to sustain them through the financial distress of the Board.

In 1839, the printing and schools went on without interruption, and one convert was received to church fellowship, of whom Dr. Scudder writes: "The man was a *school-master* named Savoyen."

In 1840, the profits of the press exceeded the expenses of the mission, and the schools were increased. The character of these schools appears from the letters of the missionaries. They say: "The school-masters are most of them heathen, but they regularly teach the lessons given from Christian books; and a good degree of faithfulness is secured by regulating their pay according to the number and progress of the pupils." "Positive good is done. Much of the seed sown may no doubt appear to be lost, and sometimes it may seem worse than lost, because the weeds in a cultivated soil will perhaps be more rank than in one wholly neglected. But there are pleasing instances of its springing up after many days. No mortal can fully appreciate the value of one important spiritual truth, lodged in the heart and conscience of an immortal being in the early stages of his existence, which may shape his character for eternity. It is a grain of mustard seed which afterwards becomes a tree." Not only are individual conversions referred to in support of this view, but the radical and thorough changes effected gradually in whole communities in India are traced directly to these schools. Another *school-master* was this year received to the Church.

In 1841, the schools and press continued to prosper, and a girls' boarding-school was added. Sixteen converts were admitted to the Church—one being a European, one or more heathen school-masters, two Romanists, and the rest of Christian parentage.

In 1842 we find 16 schools with 616 pupils. Of some of the converts admitted to the Church, it is incidentally mentioned that they were former pupils of mission schools.

In 1843 we find the schools prosperous, with some 600 pupils, and they are spoken of with much favor, and as eliciting generous contributions from European Christians.

In 1844, several pupils are spoken of as candidates for baptism. The results of the schools were such as to lead Mr. Winslow to write: "We ought to have the means of supporting three times as many schools as we now have, also an efficient high-school, and a boarding-school for girls."

In 1845 the report of the Board says: "The schools are represented as being in an encouraging state. It is the wish of the mission to give greater efficiency to this department."

In 1846, an English school for boys, and also a girls' school were established. The subscriptions of English friends on the ground amounted to some $1850. A heathen teacher and some pupils were admitted to the Church.

In 1847, the schools increased to 23 with 883 pupils. Fourteen persons were received to church fellowship. Two were a school-master and his wife, two more the father and mother of two pupils, themselves inquirers, another was a man who had been long employed as a Scripture-reader, another the eldest lad in the boarding-school; and one or two students in the English school were decoyed away and forcibly confined, after asking baptism—all showing the value of the stated teaching and influence of the schools.

A combination of the natives this year to oppose Christianity, shows their estimate of missionary efforts, and especially of the schools. "They resolved to exclude from caste any and all who send their children to a mission school." They were so excited by the baptisms of youth connected with the schools, that they got up a petition to the British government with 70,000 signatures, praying for a public school without the Bible.

In 1848, after a public examination of the schools, it is stated, the result is encouraging, as showing real progress in them all." "The foundations of heathenism are weakened by the advance of education." Rs. 2282 were liberally contributed for these schools, by European Christians at Madras, and several pupils were admitted to the Church.

In 1849, the English school had increased from some 90 to 200 pupils, and all the schools seem to have continued prosperous. "Nearly $1000 were contributed for their support by friends of the mission in Madras, so that their whole expense to the Board has scarcely exceeded $300. The schools have been instrumental in leading several of the pupils to a saving knowledge of Christ." Five accessions to the Church are mentioned as follows: "Two of the pupils have become members of our church, and we trust they are true Christians. One who was in the boys' school for a time, is now a member of a church; another [pupil] has expressed a wish to join our church." Of the whole five, four had been previously baptized and under Christian training.

In 1850, the report mentions 12 schools still supported by English friends. Their general influence and their "value in preparing the way of the Lord is certainly not small." "Many of the pupils are well acquainted with all the leading truths of Christianity, and some are so far impressed in their hearts with these truths, that but for the loss of all things, which they must incur if they profess Christ, they would ask at once to be baptized in his name."

In 1851, we find 680 pupils reported, and the contributions for their support by English residents, $1100. "The schools and congregations are in an encouraging state." The admissions to the Church in 1850 and 1851 were some 12 or 15, among whom were both teachers and pupils.

In 1852, of the more advanced pupils it is said: They are as well acquainted with Scripture truth as most lads of their age in Christian lands." Rs. 2260 were given this year at Madras, for the support of these schools.

In 1853, the high school had 200 pupils, and the number in all the schools was 665. "All the scholars attend public worship on the Sabbath, and they are also collected in classes every Sabbath morning as Sabbath-schools; so that their minds are well stored with Scripture truth." The liberal contributions of the English continued. The whole number of church members is given as 45, six of whom were added this year. Of these, two were received by letter, two were teachers in the mission, one a servant of the mission, and the other a promising pupil of the schools.

In 1854, the report gives 750 pupils in the schools, and six admissions to the church by profession, all of them young persons trained in the schools and service of the mission, two of them being monitors at the time.

In 1855, it is stated: "The number of school children may be about 350." Why this sudden falling off? It was the year of the Deputation. And yet the convictions of the missionaries are indicated by statements like the following: "Hundreds upon hundreds of children and youth of both sexes have been taught the Scriptures, of whom several, not only from the high-schools, but also from the vernacular schools, have been baptized."

In 1856 we find only two hundred and seventy-seven pupils in the schools, and though the influence of the Deputation was less felt in this than in any other of our India missions, from the fact that Dr. Winslow was there, yet it is evident the prosperity of the mission was seriously affected. May a more liberal policy soon be adopted, and the valuable schools of this mission be reëstablished and enlarged.

It is an unwelcome duty to close the sketch of each mission with such an account of schools disbanded and consequent desolation, but we can not otherwise be truthful to the facts of history.

And let us cease not to give thanks to God for his rich blessing on these effective agencies. Hundreds and thousands of the dear youth have been converted, and many thousands more have been brought to a knowledge of the truth, and the way of salvation has been made known more widely through these schools than could have been possible through any other known human instrumentalities. Let this work go on, and a Christian education be given to the children and youth of India, and her millions will soon be evangelized. The history of each mission of the Board in India furnishes the strongest possible testimony on this point.

And the same is true of every other mission of the Board. The most successful missions are those where schools have been sustained in largest numbers, and a proportionate blessing has come down upon the people. These schools have been the means of rousing and disciplining mind, and of bringing the truth of God in contact with the hearts of the people. God has honored them and will honor them till the world is evangelized.

We have thus reviewed the history of the schools in the missions of the American Board in India. The candid reader, will see that they are the agencies preëminently blessed of God in each mission, for diffusing widely a knowledge of Christian truth, for enlightening, convincing, and converting precious souls, and thus building up the Redeemer's kingdom in that land. The great fact arrived at, and the great lesson which should be forever impressed on the minds and hearts of Christians by this investigation, is involved in the results of the Ceylon Mission, which, condensed, are as follows:

Total admissions to the Church up to 1854, . . .		825
Admissions from the two seminaries, ...	537	
Heathen teachers converted and rec'd to Church,	80	
Pupils in other schools " " "	60—	677
Total conversions not *directly* traceable to schools,		148

In view of such results, is it possible that any impartial mind can hesitate as to the value of such mission schools?

I would gladly trace the history of each mission of the Board in similar detail, and educe its teaching and testimony on this point, but my limits forbid. I can only present brief notices of three or four of the remaining missions.

CHAPTER IX.

MISSIONS TO THE NORTH-AMERICAN INDIANS.

Indian Ferocity tamed by the Schools.

THE first attempts of the American Board to evangelize the aborigines of our own land, were made in behalf of the Cherokees, in 1816. The first proposition was to establish schools. Whereupon the chiefs in council replied: "We have listened to what you have said, and understand it. We are glad to see you. We wish to have the schools established, and hope they will be of great advantage to the nation." This offer of *schools* tamed their ferocity, subdued their opposition, and won them to listen to Christian teaching. Hence, the very next year, the station having been organized at Brainard, Mr. Kingsbury reports 26 boarding-pupils, and rejoices in the conversion of Catherine Brown, an interesting girl, and the first-fruit of the mission.

In 1818 the missionaries say: "We feel ourselves under renewed and increasing obligations of gratitude to the Giver of all good, for hopeful appearances among our [school] children. Several of them appear seriously and solemnly impressed with divine truth, and we have hope that two or three of them have recently been born of the Spirit."

This year the Choctaw mission was projected, and its site fixed at Elliot.

Conversion of John Arch.

In 1819 the schools were enlarged, and their influence is happily illustrated by the case of John Arch, one of the converts. Having attended school a short time in his childhood, he kept and studied his spelling-book till worn out. Hearing that a school had been established for his people at Brainard, he hastened thither, 150 miles, on foot, and sought admittance. His age (25) and wild and savage appearance were much against him, but he sold his gun, his dearest treasure, to procure decent clothing, and was so importunate that it was difficult to refuse him. He was admitted, proved diligent and earnest in study, the truth reached his heart, and he became enlightened and anxious about his soul. He was baptized, and became a helper in the mission.

The Choctaw mission school closed this year with 60 pupils, and its influence on the chiefs and people appeared in subscriptions and appropriations of $200, $600, $700, and $2000, for supporting it, and establishing other schools.

In 1820 petitions came in from Creek Path, Fort Armstrong, and other places among the Cherokees, for schools, and their establishment resulted in securing attention to Christian teaching, the conversion of precious souls, and "a great advance in civilization."

The Choctaws, too, showed increasing "zeal for the education of their children," of whom 80 were in school, and many had been refused for want of means. So much had the schools won upon the favor of the Choctaws, that they devoted their annuity of $6000 a year for the support of the mission.

Conversions in the Schools.

In 1821 the mission reports a precious revival among the Cherokees. Where did it originate? The journal of the mission says: "Early in August an uncommon degree of seriousness commenced among the older boys in the school. They soon began to hold conferences and prayer-meetings by themselves." Conversions followed, and the fire kindled and spread.

The Choctaw school at Elliot was blessed. "A general seriousness commenced among the 80 pupils in March. It continued to increase, and in a few weeks several were anxiously inquiring what they must do to be saved." "Hopes were entertained of the conversion of two of the boys," "and the spirit of inquiry was spreading and deepening in the school."

In 1822 the work prospered at Brainard, and missionary work was fairly commenced at Dwight, in Arkansas, with a school of 50 pupils. The Choctaw mission increased its schools, the chiefs and people making these the special object of their petitions. There were conversions at Elliot and Mahew, and a precious revival at Bethel.

In 1823, "at the earnest request of the people, three new stations were formed, and schools opened at all of them." At Dwight the school had 60 pupils, and "sentiments favorable to the mission, to education and good morals, were gradually gaining ground." Among the Choctaws, "the chiefs in council urged the establishment of a great number of small schools, in different parts of the nation." The Prudential Committee gladly approved this measure.

In 1824 "the schools continued to gain confidence among the people, and several new schools were opened." More than 60 converts were gathered into the churches this year.

In 1825 "the schools were improved, the Gospel was preached more extensively, and there were some instances of conversion." This year was signalized by "the translation of the New Testament from the original Greek into the Cherokee language, by a Cherokee, in an alphabet invented by another Cherokee," by the name of Guess; and also by the commencement of the first newspaper (the *Phœnix*) in their language.

In 1826 we read: "From year to year, the schools were in better order, and the pupils made better progress." "There were a few instances of conversion, and a few additions to the churches."

In 1827 "the schools were generally successful. There was some special seriousness, and some were added to the churches." The people anxiously requested more schools.

Of seven existing missions now taken under the care of the American Board, the one at Mackinaw had 112 boarding-scholars, "and there had been several interesting cases of conversion." At Maumee were 32 pupils, of whom "six gave evidence of piety."

We may not stop to trace the history of these missions through their subsequent years. Glancing on to 1843, we find such an advance in education, intelligence and good morals, that schools were highly appreciated, and the Choctaws voted an annual appropriation of $26,300 to support them. From one school "10 or 12 have been received to the Church of Christ."

Revivals in the Schools.

In 1846, reporting a blessed revival among the Choctaws, the mission says: "The revival appeared first in our school. Many of the scholars commenced prayer, and that without any particular suggestion from us." "At our communion season, 30 or more came forward bathed in tears, and asked what they must do to be saved. Some were pupils in our schools," and some were their fathers and mothers. At the next communion 21 were received, "12 of them pupils in our school."

At the close of this service, "the cloud of mercy seemed to break over us, and we all, parents and children, teachers and pupils, missionaries and people, wept over each other with joy."

"One of the most interesting features of this revival, is the fact that so many youths of the schools have been brought in. In the Wheelock school, 7 of the pupils have been admitted to the Church the past year. In the Good Water school, 24 of the pupils are church members, and six others candidates. Numbers have been received to the Church from the other schools." "At the Spencer Academy the Spirit of the Lord has wrought powerfully on the minds of many of the pupils."

In 1848 the report says: "The interest taken by the Choctaws, even from the commencement of the mission, in the intellectual advancement of the nation, has been highly praiseworthy."

"Next to the churches, the boarding-schools claim our attention, as the most striking feature of the Choctaw mission." "Religious instruction holds a much more prominent place, [in the Choctaw schools than in our common schools ;] hence the comparatively large number of pupils who have professedly become new creatures in Christ Jesus."

In 1849 we find that "these schools have prepared the way for the preaching of the Gospel in several places," and not only so, but "the pupils have attained to a saving knowledge of the plan of salvation." Of the school at Wheelock, the mission writes: "There is at the present time a most interesting state of religious feeling; and several of the older girls express a hope of having passed from death unto life. We can not but feel that the Holy Spirit is evidently operating upon the minds of not a few of the children under our care."

Two pupils had just been admitted to the Church at Wheelock, and six at Good Water, making in the latter school 26 church members.

In 1851 the report says: "The condition of the boarding-schools continues to be gratifying in a high degree," and the mission again puts on record its "high estimate of the value to be attached to these institutions." "And the Committee would report with peculiar satisfaction, that a large proportion of the scholars are hopefully pious." The missionary at Good Water writes: "We think that God has peculiarly blessed this institution from its commencement, for we have had a revival every year. Last winter almost all were affected by divine truth, and 12 have since united with the Church."

In 1852 the Committee say of the boarding-schools: "Hitherto their success has been all that the most sanguine could have anticipated. In fact, nothing is accomplishing more for the elevation of the Choctaw nation than these institutions." Mr. Kingsbury writes: "All our larger scholars are members of the Church." The great desire of the chiefs and people was for more schools. Mr. Hotchkin writes: "This is the great subject among the people. '*Schools*,' 'SCHOOLS,' 'SCHOOLS,' sound in my ear, wherever I go. 'Is the Board acquainted with our wants?' they say; 'will you not write to them to send us a *teacher?*'"

In 1854 a precious revival is reported in these schools. Mr. Kingsbury writes: "The Holy Spirit seems to be moving the hearts of some of these children, in a very remarkable manner. It is now about five weeks since the work commenced. No special efforts were used. The Spirit seemed to make effectual the ordinary means of religious instruction. We have never before seen among Choctaw children such a deep sense of sin, with such mourning and bitterness on account of it. There have been repeated instances where our pupils wished to be excused from going to their meals, saying that they wished to spend the time in prayer. The teachers have informed me that after the girls retired last night to their lodging-room, several continued in prayer until two o'clock." Mark the correspondence, in the results of these schools among the red children of our own Western forests, and the idolaters of India and Ceylon.

In 1835 another revival is reported in the boarding schools. Reporting the admission of seven pupils to the Church, Mr. Kingsbury writes: "The influence of this refreshing from the Lord seems to have been most happy on all the pupils. A quiet, subdued, teachable spirit has been generally manifested. Two have also joined the Church from the Stockbridge school."

Such has been the experience of the Board, in its mission schools among our Western Indians.

CHAPTER X.

MISSIONS AMONG THE ARMENIANS OF TURKEY.

1826.—Let us turn again to the East, and examine the history of our missionary efforts in Turkey, and especially among the Armenians. Explorations commenced in the Turkish empire as early as 1820, but no systematic and permanent labors appear till 1826. The principal scene of interest was at Beirût and vicinity, where some six free schools had been opened under hired teachers, with an average attendance of 305 pupils. The interest in the truth awakened by these schools roused the anger and opposition of the corrupt priesthood, and anathemas were read against them in both the Latin and Greek churches.

Teachers become the First Converts.

Yet "the mission rejoiced over several converts who appeared to be truly pious. Among these were two Armenians, Jacob and Dionysius, whom they called Carabet, or the Forerunner; Gregory Wotabet, an Armenian priest, engaged as a literary assistant to Mr. Goodell; Gregory's wife; her brother, Joseph Leflufy, a Greek Catholic, engaged in the autumn as an agent in establishing and superintending schools; Asaad Jacob, a Greek youth, who afterwards apostatized, [though his subsequent life was such as to furnish hope that he was a truly pious man;] and especially Asaad Shidiak," who was decoyed into the hands of the ecclesiastics, and after years of imprisonment and torture in the Monastery of Kanôbin, nobly suffered death as the first modern martyr to the faith of Jesus, in Turkey.

This Asaad Shidiak was brought under Christian influence and teaching by being employed as a *teacher*, first by Mr. King, and subsequently by Mr. Fisk, "to open a free school for teaching Arabic."

It is worthy of being noted that all these first converts were brought under the teaching of the mission, by being employed in its service, either to teach school or the missionaries, or in some employment which brought them under stated instruction. So of the next hopeful convert, Pharez, the youngest brother of Asaad, we read that he was "for some time in the service of the mission."

The Schools provoke Persecution.

In 1827 the wives of two of these converts were admitted to the Church, and the influence of the schools and Christian teaching was such as to raise a violent storm of persecution. The patriarch complained that the missionaries "have opened schools and supplied instructors at their own expense." He issued a threat of excommunication against all who should attend the schools, so that "parents dared not send their children;" and "one teacher after another received positive orders to discontinue his school, and was forced to comply, till, some time before the close of the year, not one was left."

What clearer proof can we have of the value and efficacy of such schools, than this opposition from those who hate the truth?

In 1828 we read: "The schools at Beirût were all broken up," and, as a consequent result, intercourse with the people was almost entirely cut off. Years of bitter opposition followed.

In 1831 we find Mr. King at Athens, Greece, and the first hopeful item reported is, "he soon opened a school," which prospered, and others were soon established. At Constantinople, too, "Mr. Goodell had established four Lancasterian schools for the Greeks." "Some enemy sought to crush these schools by exciting the Turkish government against them;" but the attempt failed, and Mr. G. was permitted to "establish as many schools among the Christians as he pleased." What was the result? "Towards the close of the year Mr. G. had more intercourse with the Armenians. Several young men appeared much interested in conversing on the Scriptures and religious topics; and some definite arrangements began to be made for establishing schools."

In 1832 the chief and almost only item of interest at Athens is the continuance and hopeful prospect of the schools.

So, too, at Constantinople, Mr. Goodell waited on the Armenian Patriarch, and proposed to establish Lancasterian schools among his people. The Patriarch so far listened as to appoint Boghos Fisika, alias Paul the Philosopher, "to learn the system and commence a school by way of experiment." The mission established two schools for the Greeks, employing in one of them Mr. Paspati, a Greek who had been educated at Amherst, Mass., and "a little encouragement, assistance, and advice, induced the Greeks to establish nearly thirty more, at their own expense." These schools gave the mission favor and influence of immense importance at that stage of its history.

1833.—In Greece the High-school, or Gymnasium, reports 66 scholars, and the elementary school 76. At Constantinople "the Greek schools remained as last year, and a new school was opened at Pera. The schools established last year in the Turkish barracks won favor, led the way to the establishment of others under the advice and direction of the mission, and introducing and sanctioning the books of the mission, helped to diffuse Christian truth widely among the people.

In 1834 these schools had 2000 scholars, and though supported by the people, yet, having been established by the advice and assistance of the mission, their influence was great in its favor, till the monks and priests began to preach violently against the mission and schools, "and even against the Patriarch for favoring them." But it was too late to destroy their influence. The Armenians had become roused by the spreading light. Its reflection made them conscious of their grosser ignorance and superstitions, and led to the establishment of the academy of the famous Peshtemaljan, in 1829. Hohannes, one of his pupils, and Senekerim, teacher of a school in the Patriarch's palace, became prominent actors in the movement which followed. "Hohannes began to study the English language under Mr. Dwight, and was employed to translate the Psalms," while "Senekerim was employed to open an Armenian school at Pera."

Thus it was that these youth came under Christian teaching, were hopefully converted, and prepared for the important part they subsequently acted.

This year, also, "a high-school for Armenians was opened under the instruction of Mr. Paspati, in Mr. Goodell's house." So in Syria, at Beirût, we find the progress of the mission noted by the existence of five schools; and at Broosa, a new station, Mr. Schneider had "left Hohannes to make arrangements for a school," and "notwithstanding the opposition which some of the clergy had excited, the school was commenced with 70 pupils; and in December another was opened."

In 1835 "the revival of learning and piety among the Armenians continued to advance" hand in hand. "The high-school at Pera had received its full number of scholars, (30,) and many others desired admission." "Among the Greeks better views of education were making progress, notwithstanding some opposition among the clergy. Several new schools for Greek boys were opened." At Broosa "the opposition of the clergy broke up the Armenian school," but the Greek school "continued to flourish, and another was established." "Mr. Schneider taught a few Greek boys, and his wife opened a school for girls."

At Scio Mr. Houston "established three Lancasterian schools," as his best means of winning favor with the people and disseminating Christian truth; while at Beirût it is joyfully reported that "the mission had 10 schools, containing 311 pupils," and an additional boarding-school for boys, intended to grow into a high-school, was commenced with six pupils.

At Jerusalem, Mr. Whiting "opened a school under a hired teacher, in August; but the Latin convent had influence enough to break it up." The monks endeavored to break up Mrs. Whiting's school of Mohammedan girls, but did not succeed. At Cyprus nothing so marked progress as the school with its 78 pupils.

Thus alternate success and defeat in all these missions is easily traced in the history of these schools. When opposition breaks out afresh in Greece, we at once read "the schools at Syra were broken up."

In 1836 "civilization was advancing rapidly among the Turks. The Lancasterian schools were carried on in splendid style, and with remarkable success." Though these schools were now supported by the Turks themselves, yet the missionaries had originated them, and hence their influence and success enured greatly in favor of the mission. This fact is clearly brought to view. The missionaries were invited to the public examination, "and Azim Bey publicly declared that the Turks were indebted to them for every thing of the kind. Some of the Turks hoped that such schools would soon become common throughout the empire." Those who would disparage this influence in favor of the mission, ought, in consistency, to disallow all human instrumentalities. But while the Turks were conciliated, "the Greek Patriarch at Constantinople denounced the schools in his encyclical letter." The influence of this letter extended widely. At Smyrna, Scio, Broosa, and Trebizond it broke up the mission schools and cut off almost all intercourse with the people. At Smyrna "8 schools," with 600 or 800 children, were broken up, but the cause of education had received such an impulse, that the ecclesiastical committee were obliged to carry it on themselves, compelling some of the teachers and pupils of the mission to enter their service. At Beirût "the mission schools were nearly all broken up for a time; but before the end of the year they began to revive."

At Jerusalem "the school for Mohammedan girls continued," but "encouraging attempts to establish schools in the vicinity were defeated by ecclesiastical opposition."

In 1837 "the secretary of the Patriarch resolved to break up the high-school for Armenians," and effected it principally "by compelling parents to take away their sons." This roused the Armenians so much, that another school was soon opened at Hass Koy, so enlarged as to receive 600 scholars. This was under the direction of a wealthy banker, "who in a short time expended $5000 on the school," though he kept Hohannes in it as president, and made it as evangelical as before. At Broosa opposition slackened so much that the "Greek school was again in operation," and two hopeful converts are mentioned. Who were they? Two *pupils* of Mr. Powers.

At Trebizond "the missionaries were unable, on account of opposition, to collect a school."

At Beirût "the mission seminary was doing well, with a few scholars, but was obliged to reject several applications for admission, for want of funds."

At Jerusalem "the girls' school prospered under the care of Miss Tilden." "A school for boys was opened in August, under a Greek teacher, which soon had its full number of scholars, (24,) and many applicants were refused."

In Cyprus "the high-school had seventeen, and the two Lancasterian schools had two hundred scholars;" but the threats of the patriarch availed, and all three schools were closed.

In 1838 light was evidently spreading, and a work of grace in progress among the Armenians, but as the converts were not encouraged to come out and formally join a Protestant church, its extent and results can not be distinctly traced. "The high-school at Hass Koy prospered the former part of the year," but the wealthy banker, fearing it "might attract the unfavorable notice of the Turkish government, and involve him in difficulty, withdrew his support," and the school went down.

"Several Lancasterian schools were established by the Armenians during the year, with prospects of usefulness."

At Broosa the three schools contained 220 scholars, and progress was manifest "towards truth and piety."

At Beirût the most interesting movement was among the Druzes. "They invited Mr. Thompson to visit their villages, and to open schools and places of worship among them. They applied for the admission of their sons into the seminary."

In 1839 a vigorous persecution was waged against the "Evangelicals." The two first victims seized and banished, without form of trial, were Hohannes and Boghos, who had long been teachers in the service of the mission. The Armenian patriarch was deposed, and superseded by one who would show more energy in putting down the "Evangelicals." Der Kivork, two priests, a teacher, and several others, were imprisoned, and subsequently banished."

At Broosa, too, "a vigorous attack was made on the mission. Both the Armenian and Greek bishops preached violently against schools," and pronounced anathemas on all who should favor the mission. The books and cards used in the schools were ordered to be given up, and in some cases violently seized. Teachers and assistants were compelled to leave the service of the mission.

At Erzroom the people were prohibited from patronizing the mission schools. Beirût was less affected by the threats of the ecclesiastics, and "the seminary and other schools went on as usual."

In 1840 the former patriarch, Stephen, was recalled, and some other circumstances revived the courage of the "Evangelicals," and their intercourse with the mission. "Some of them wished to place their sons in one of the mission families for education," and this led to the mission seminary at Bebek, which commenced with only three scholars. In December, however, fifteen applications for admission had been received, but the funds were sufficient for only twelve. Mr. Van Lennep commenced a boarding-seminary near Smyrna, with encouraging prospects, but the death of Mrs. Van Lennep led to its abandonment.

In 1841 the students in the seminary at Bebek had increased to twenty-four, and many were refused for want of funds. "The patriarch ordered parents to take their sons from the seminary. They obeyed, and sent them back in a few days."

The Druzes were in earnest for schools, and "Mr. Wolcott and Dr. Van Dyck removed to Deir el Kamer, and opened a school for the sons of the sheikhs." "Mr. Thompson removed to 'Ain 'Anub, to superintend the schools for the common people, of which three were soon opened in the vicinity."

The patriarch now put forth his energies anew. He "even ordered the people to rise against the missionaries, and stone them out of their villages." "The Druze sheikhs were ordered to stop the schools, and parents to remove their children. The French consul wrote to the Emir Beshir, urging him to stop these schools."

A conflict ensued between the Maronites and Druzes, in which the latter triumphed, and though the schools had been broken up, all four were soon reöpened, and petitions were sent in to the mission for four or five others. Even the Maronites sought intercourse with the mission, declaring "they wanted schools, and were determined to have them."

The Schools an Entering-Wedge.

In 1842 we find the seminary at Bebek "prospering admirably, with nineteen boarding scholars, under a constant and strong religious influence." "The Committee received so forcible an appeal in behalf of this institution that they felt constrained to make a special grant to enable the mission to place it on a broader and firmer basis." A blessed change was becoming manifest among the people, and in contrasting it with the state of things six years before, Mr. Dwight writes: "By far the greater part who [then] came to us came for the purpose of general inquiry, or to see our philosophical apparatus, or to listen to a lecture on the sciences, or on chemistry. We felt happy if by such means we could draw them to us, and make mere human knowledge the entering-wedge, by which to open a passage to their minds for that knowledge which is divine. But now how marked and how delightful the change!" Minds thus opened by the truths of science were at the same time opened to divine truth, the same result in Turkey as in India and other parts of the unevangelized world. In view of this result at Constantinople, we do not wonder that the missionaries at Trebizond write: "A good influence is exerted through some of the school-masters, and there is great need of schools." The Turkish mission, this year, reports "six free schools, with 125 pupils."

At Beirût were nine free schools, and one at Jerusalem, the ten having 287 pupils. The seminary had 44 pupils, 22 of them boarding scholars, and there were 11 boarding girls.

In 1843 the Bebek seminary had 20 students, and five free schools had 180 pupils. There were boarding scholars at Smyrna and Broosa, and an urgent appeal is made for several other schools, one argument being, that a thirst for education had become so excited that if we failed of meeting the exigency, the youth would go to the Jesuit schools, as some were actually doing.

In Syria the seminary at Beirût had 24 pupils, but for some reason was discontinued. There were 12 female boarding scholars, and twelve free schools had 279 pupils. Of the Druzes it is said: "They are as friendly as ever, and as desirous of schools." "A seminary for them is of the first importance."

In 1844 the seminary at Bebek had 26 students. Of this seminary Mr. Hamlin wrote: "Its collateral influences are becoming more obvious and important. It brings into personal intercourse with us individuals of all classes, who would otherwise have no acquaintance with us or our objects. The week-day visitors for the past month have averaged about six each day, and the Sabbath visitors, twice that number. Within a few weeks we have had calls from Nicomedia, Ada Bazer, Syria, Alexandria, Varna, Odessa, St. Petersburgh, Marsovan, Egin on the Euphrates, and Moosh. The philosophical experiments they have seen, the books they have received, and the truths they have heard, will all be topics of conversation at their respective homes, and will doubtless contribute to that general awakening of the Armenian mind which has already manifested itself at so many points. The seminary, therefore, should be considered, not simply as educating so many young men, but as a centre of influences, which are sent abroad, far and wide, into the Armenian community."

A female seminary was also resolved upon, as soon as a suitable teacher could be sent. Three common schools at Constantinople contained 100 girls, and there was a day-school at Galata, and several more at Trebizond and its vicinity. In mentioning Mr. Schaufler's school for Jewish children, the report of the Board naïvely says, "Experience shows that the effect of a school for children and youth among the Jews is, to bring adults within the reach of instruction;" quite like the experience of missionaries throughout the heathen and unevangelized world.

In Syria thirteen schools report nearly 500 pupils, and there were 11 boarding girls. "The school-houses are places for preaching, and the schools form *nuclei* for congregations, to which the Gospel may be clearly and pointedly preached."

Revivals in the Schools.

Passing to 1847 we find Bebek Seminary with 35 students, one of its graduates being ordained as a native pastor, and "several pupils hopefully converted during the year." The female seminary, with 15 pupils, was "blest with a gracious visitation from on high." "Out of 18 pupils only two remained without hope, and these two were not indifferent." The influence of this seminary is represented as "extensive and salutary on the female community." In dwelling upon its importance at some length, Mr. Goodell mentions a little girl of only four years, from one of the day-schools, and his surprise at finding she could read fluently, when he found to his greater astonishment, that the child had been the teacher of *her mother*, who had thus come to the knowledge of the truth, and was soon received to the Church. "The female seminary has much to do in keeping alive and increasing this desire for improvement."

In Syria the seminary had opened at Abeih with eight boarding pupils. Several of them were regarded as pious. The eighteen free schools of the mission report 528 pupils, and Mrs. Whiting had some boarding girls.

In 1849 we find the seminary at Bebek reduced from 47 to 28 pupils, but its "relation to the churches and the work in general is becoming more and more important." The female seminary in Pera reports 23 pupils, and a precious revival resulted in the conversion of all the unconverted pupils except five small ones. The influence of this revival extended to the other seminary, and through the Protestant community. The progress of the reformation was visible in different and distant places, but it is worthy of record, that when the conversion of a young man at Trebizond is stated, it is also mentioned that he "was for a while a member of the seminary at Bebek."

In Syria the seminary pupils increased to 16, "among whom there was at times more than ordinary attention to religion." Some twelve free schools contained 370 pupils, and a student of the seminary and a school-master were admitted to the Church. The conversion of a Greek priest is mentioned in the report, in connection with the schools, "because it seems so plainly to have resulted from the establishment of the school in his village."

In 1850 we find 24 students in the Bebek Seminary, and 23 in the Pera Seminary. Seven free schools report 112 pupils. In Syria the seminary seems to have had 20 pupils. Ten free schools report 271 scholars, and there were 20 boarding girls.

In 1851 the Bebek Seminary reports 25 pupils, and the female seminary 22, and five free schools 179. Three graduates of the seminary entered mission service. Of all the graduates 17 were in missionary work, "eleven of whom received their religious impressions in the institution. Two were pastors at Constantinople; one a pastor at Trebizond;

two licensed preachers; one a teacher in the seminary; others teachers, translators, etc. The other graduates are reported as in places of influence; four in custom-houses, two in Paris, one publishing a work on chemistry, one an interpreter of Amin Bey, one professor of the Armenian College at Paris, another of the college at Scutari, etc., filling posts of usefulness, and where their influence would be valuable to the mission.

In 1852 the report says: "It has been found impossible to restrain the number of pupils in the male seminary." Is it not a pity that the attempt was so long persevered in? The report says: "The graduates of this institution are doing much for their people." "The seminary was in a most promising state of seriousness." The female seminary reports twenty-four of whom "two or three had professedly passed from death unto life." "The influence of this institution upon the Armenian community is increasing, and there is a loud call for its enlargement. Twenty-seven have already left it with the hope that they had been born again," sixteen of whom are the wives of pious pastors and teachers.

In 1853 we are glad to find the Bebek Seminary reporting fifty students. "Its former pupils are employed as preachers, teachers, translators, and helpers in many places." Many of the students listen to the truth with interest, and "are not far from the kingdom of heaven." "Several, it is thought, have recently received the truth in love, and will carry its light to the dark places of Armenia." "A good missionary spirit prevails among the pious students." "Four spent their last vacation as colporteurs in the villages," spending days and nights in discussion and instruction. "The labors of one of them have been remarkably blessed to the conversion of a man and his wife in a remote quarter of the city."

Who would limit the numbers and usefulness of such an institution?

The female seminary reports 27 pupils. "Truth has been brought home to the hearts and consciences of the pupils," and "three or four have come to a saving knowledge of the truth as it is in Jesus." "The influence of the school on the Armenian community throughout Turkey is becoming more and more important. Its former pupils are widely scattered, and the reports of their usefulness are highly pleasing. It needs to be enlarged." 19 free schools report 451 scholars, a most desirable increase in these agencies, and to these must be added 60 children and 150 adult scholars at Aintab.

Effective Influence of the Schools.

In Syria, the female boarding-school reports 17 pupils, and its value and influence are emphatically attested by the missionaries. They say: "Our mission can present some most interesting examples of the potent influence of education and religion on the female character in Syria. The seminary for boys reports 25 students, and 20 free schools, 554 pupils. Nine teachers were members of the church, the larger portion of the teachers still being *unevangelized.*

In 1854 we find the Bebek Seminary "every way encouraging and progressive. Its number of pupils 50." "Seven of them are candidates for the ministry." The female boarding-school reports 35 boarding, and 12 day scholars. In alluding to a new class of ten, an incidental remark of the report discloses one blessed fact showing the great value of such schools. It is this: "When a child is thus given, [as a pupil,] the whole family is usually gained." Here is the secret of the very large blessing which God has bestowed on our mission schools.

At Aintab, the seminary reports 37 pupils; the boys' elementary school 100, and the girls' school 80 scholars. These and a private school of 60 girls, the missionaries say, "are doing much for Protestantism." "50 adult females have begun to learn to read during the year; more than 50 have already learned to read well, and many others are in process of learning."

This lively interest in education at Aintab prepares us for

the fact that a special blessing has rested upon that station. The whole number of free schools in the mission rose this year to 25, with 788 pupils.

In Syria, 21 free schools report 568 pupils, about half of the teachers being members of the Church. The female seminary, with twenty pupils, is more than ever appreciated, and some, when refused, besought the mission to receive their children into their families. "They blame the missionaries for not making sufficient provision for meeting the demand which they have labored to create." The seminary at Abeih reports only 18 pupils; "Mr. Calhoun and Mr. Bird call attention to the usefulness of the schools under their care, and the importance of adding to their number." "Had we the requisite funds," they say, "we could at once open several new schools, with encouraging prospects of success."

In 1855 we find the female boarding-school at Constantinople again restricted to 25, although its value is attested in the admission of six of its pupils to the Church, and increasing interest led several others to personal consecration to Christ.

In the Bebek Seminary we regret to find the Greek department suspended, and only 40 Armenian students. The prudent management of Mr. Hamlin made the institution, for a time, self-supporting. Five of the students were licensed to preach the Gospel, and went out to different posts, and others were preparing for the same service, and in the mean time doing much good as colporteurs and in other ways. "Six of the students during the year have publicly professed their faith in Christ, all of whom give promise of usefulness."

It was found impossible to supply the increasing demand for teachers and preachers from this seminary; hence the missionaries were importunate for others, and commenced one at Tokat with 12, and another at Aintab with 9 students, looking to the lower schools for future classes. The free schools increased this year to 38, and the whole number of pupils to 960.

In Syria, the mission reports 19 pupils in the seminary at

Abeih, and adds: "The fierce opposition of the Maronite hierarchy keeps many of their communion from entering the seminary who desire to do so."

"The character of the free schools is decidedly improving." These schools were found so effective in promoting the objects of the mission, that the Maronites were constrained to open schools, "to prevent all B'hamdun from becoming Protestant." "At Aleppo," too, "the Romanists were obliged to establish a school, to counteract the influence of our girls' school." Can any one desire better facts than these, to show the value of mission schools? "Urgent appeals are made," says the report, "for the multiplication of schools, but the necessary funds are wanting. The number now supported is 26, with 772 pupils, showing an advance on last year of five schools and 204 pupils."

In 1856, the Bebek Seminary reports 40 pupils, and 21 theological students were studying in other places. The female seminary had 25 pupils. A blessed revival was enjoyed in this institution, and "not one was left unconcerned." "Of a goodly number of the pupils hope is entertained that they have passed from death unto life. Six have been received to the Church within the year." The free schools were increased this year to 44, and their pupils to 1151.

In Syria, too, the seminary reports 24 pupils of much promise, and 24 free schools contain 816 pupils, showing a continued and increasing appreciation by the missionaries, of these effective agencies in making known the Gospel of Christ.

We will not pursue the history of these missions, but the following items of more recent intelligence, show the continued character and influence of the schools, and deserve a place in this connection.

Revival in Turkey.

Mr. Clark, Principal of the Bebek Seminary, writes, Dec. 24, 1858:

"We have richly enjoyed a season of refreshing from the presence of the Lord. He has indeed visited us by the wonderful power of His divine Spirit. An *eminently* spiritual work has been witnessed by us, such as I have not before known in this land; a work presenting precisely the same characteristics which belong to the great revival which God has been carrying forward during the past year in America.

"From the opening of the term, (the first of October,) an increasing spirit of prayer has been manifest. Our pious young men have been fervently praying, and meetings for prayer became more and more frequent. A deep seriousness pervaded the entire school, and we felt that the Lord was drawing nigh to bless us. This religious interest, though intense, was not attended by any marked outward manifestations, till about the middle of November. At that time, after an exhortation made to the students to pray especially for the descent of the Holy Spirit, four of the smallest pupils in the seminary commenced a daily prayer-meeting for this purpose. Not one of these four was then hopefully pious; but notwithstanding this, the Lord manifested himself immediately among them. They were at once overwhelmed with a sense of their guilt and their need of a Saviour. This little meeting rapidly increased in numbers, and within a week the place became too strait for them, and they were obliged to seek a larger room.

"It was only the fourth evening after this little meeting was established, when a student who had openly ridiculed it at its commencement, was constrained to go in for once, and see for himself. He had scarcely entered when he felt the power of the Spirit upon him. He attempted to speak, but was so deeply affected that he was unable. His distress continued for two days, and during this time, his anguish was so great that even while in his class, at recitation, with tears rolling down his cheeks, he would frequently speak to a fellow-student who sat by his side, and say: 'Oh! my sins, my sins. How can I be saved?' But Christ appeared, and his soul was filled with peace and joy. Other cases similar to this, and of an equally striking character, might be mentioned. Some were suddenly struck, as with the lightning of God's Spirit, and wept and prayed till they found peace in believing. Others could get no rest at night, but frequently rose and prayed for the pardon of their many sins. Deep conviction for sin was the striking characteristic of the work in every case.

"The effect upon the pious students has also been truly wonderful. This visitation of the Spirit has been like a fresh baptism upon them from on high. It has changed them into young converts, with all their ardor of love, their zeal and enthusiasm. They are now scattered abroad in the city and surrounding region, laboring for Christ during the vacation."

Dr. Dwight, in January adds: "The pious students, full of love and zeal, went forth among the neighboring churches, to labor chiefly among church members. One of them went to Broosa, and we learn from Mr. Barnum, who is there studying the Turkish language, that a revival has actually commenced, the church members being greatly stirred up to confess their sins and pray, and some among the impenitent being awakened. A few already, it is hoped, have given their hearts to the Saviour."

A few days later he states: "There is a wonderful revival going on here among the girls in a Jewish school, under the teaching of the Free Scotch Church missionaries. Twelve or more Jewesses have been hopefully converted, and in a most remarkable manner. . . . We have commenced a daily prayer-meeting, held at noon, in a room in Vezir Khan, not far from the bazaars. We hope that many of our brethren, who are in business, will be induced to attend."

Still Later from Constantinople.

"Shortly before the close of last year, very suddenly the Spirit of God came down upon the theological seminary of the American mission in Bebek, beginning his work of conversion with the very youngest boys, until the whole school, consisting of forty students, was turned to the Lord. Immediately after this we held our New-Year's prayer-meeting, and two days subsequently the annual prayer-meeting of all the missionaries, ministers, and Christians of different denominations in this town, at which the chief subject of comment and prayer was the outpouring of the Spirit upon this land. Then came a season of God's power in one of the American missionary families, where all the household is now safely sheltered in the fold of Christ. On the day after these last news reached us, one of the teachers in our Italian female school made cursory reference to it, to a number of girls gathered round her, before the school had commenced, and the subject of the opening prayer was a recognition of the hand of God in these recent wonderful dealings, and inquiring of the Lord whether there were no such blessings in store for us. The lesson for the day had but begun, when one of the older girls (who has been recently received by us as a boarder) came up to her teacher's side, pale and trembling, requesting permission to retire to her room to pray. Immediately after I heard the voice of one wrestling with God below my study, without knowing whose voice it was. The arrows of the Almighty had struck this soul, and her distress was intense. She passed all day in this state, praying, confessing her sins, crying for mercy, pleading the promises, and receiving direction from her teachers. Towards evening, just as the convincing power of the Lord had seized her, was she brought into the light and liberty of the children of God. She came to us, her face beaming with joy, and declared that now she had found Christ, that 'dear Jesus,' who died for her, and that now she was forever saved. Truly she now rejoiced with joy unspeakable, and was filled with peace in believing; to use her own words, she was 'full of the Spirit, quite full.' In this lively frame of spiritual joy she continues up to the present day."

"In the evening, whilst we rejoiced over her who was lost but now found, the simple question was put to our boarder, a Spanish Jewish girl of nine years, whether she did not think of seeking Christ also, or if she would be contented to remain behind, and the same moment she ran down-stairs into her room, as if struck with lightning; and the agony in which this dear child then cried to the Lord I shall not soon forget. The whole evening was spent by these two girls in prayer for one another. We likewise had a meeting for prayer among ourselves, and before the night closed upon them, the younger of the two expressed a hope that she also had been brought nigh by the blood of sprinkling, and praise and prayer were heard from their room until midnight. The elder of these, a girl of fourteen years, has since been made a great means of carrying on this work of grace in the school. She is naturally dull, and being very irregular in school, she had received little instruction, and her knowledge was very circumscribed. The change in her is therefore all the more striking, the experience and the new views of Scripture, which she pours forth like a stream, are not the *teaching of man;* and full of joy she went among the girls next morning, telling them that she had found the pearl of great price, beseeching them and praying with them to seek that dear Saviour also. On that day there was another case of a soul seeking Christ, which terminated in what we consider a decided conversion. This girl was formerly one of the worst and most troublesome of the pupils, and perhaps the last thought of in connection with the work of grace; she continued all day in prayer, and next day she received a sense of pardon; her feeling was, that 'Christ now appeared to her more beautiful than all the world beside.'

On that same morning, after the opening prayer, six girls came up to their teachers, all equally concerned, and asking permission to retire for prayer. Different rooms were given them, and nearly the whole day we heard nothing from one end of our house to the other, but the voices of these children crying to the Lord for salvation and pardon. Next day another girl was in like manner wounded by the Spirit, and so the week passed over, the most remarkable week I have been privileged to witness during the many years I have labored in this place. We have had individual conversions at different periods; we have also had times of refreshing from the Lord in our church; but on this occasion we feel as if the clouds of mercy were *resting* over us, promising greater blessings, and we feel stirred up to prayer that the windows of heaven might be opened, and a blessing poured out that there shall not be room enough to receive it. Several members of the mission have been refreshed and revived in such a manner that they feel as if they never before had known the Lord, nor enjoyed his presence and the assurance of salvation as at the present. So far as man can judge, ten girls have been accepted of the Lord; among these are a Roman Catholic and a Greek, who have shared in the blessing; seven are still anxiously seeking, while deep solemnity and a feeling of concern pervades the whole school. This week the girls have two prayer-meetings at mid-day, the elder and the younger pupils apart; we hear them singing and praying during the time of recess, and we watch these tokens with increasing interest. With startling rapidity the news reached the Jewish houses, some of the newly converted girls were so full of what they had experienced, that they openly declared to their parents that they had now looked to Christ as the Lamb of God, and were no longer Jews, but Christians. We were therefore prepared for nothing short of a complete emptying of the school, but wonderful to relate, the Lord has been greater than our fears. Nine have indeed been removed; this number includes several Spanish, and but one of the recent converts.

"It is cause of special thanksgiving, that all the other young disciples are still among us; and a most remarkable fact it is, that even *Jewish* enmity has been restrained from hindering this glorious work. This is the doing of the Lord. Is there any thing too hard for him? The one I have just mentioned, whose conversion was very marked, is in most painful circumstances. Her Bible and all her books were burnt; and she was sent to Jewish relatives in Hasskeuy. There are many other cheering circumstances which have come to our ears from the homes of these dear children. One of the converted girls gathers her younger sisters together for prayer every evening; her parents, though aware of this, do not interfere. The Greek girl mentioned before now reads and prays with her mother, and told her teachers only yesterday, that her mother has begun to search the Scriptures for herself, and to feel anxious for her soul.

"In conclusion, I can only add that there is none, either among our own number or our Christian friends, who does not deeply feel that the Lord himself is manifesting his power in the midst of us in a manner which we have never experienced before, and we all expect still fuller and richer blessings. Let the Church at home rejoice."

Who can peruse such accounts, without a deep and irrepressible conviction that these schools are God's chosen instrumentalities for disseminating the word of life, and saving precious souls?

CHAPTER XI.

MISSION TO THE SANDWICH ISLANDS.

LET us turn now to the islands of the ocean, and trace the agencies which have been most successful in bringing the Gospel to bear on *their* inhabitants.

Origin of the Mission.

The first band of missionaries sent by the ship Thaddeus to the Sandwich Islands, came in sight of them March 30, 1820. The party consisted of seventeen persons, of whom two, Messrs. Bingham and Thurston, were ordained missionaries, one a farmer, one a physician, and three were *school-masters*, thus indicating a wise forethought for schools and education. Of the rest, seven were wives of those just mentioned, and three were natives of the islands, who had been educated at the mission school at Cornwall, Connecticut. While this missionary band were on the way to the islands, a remarkable providence led the king and people to renounce idolatry and destroy their idols. They were thus found a people wonderfully prepared of the Lord for the blessed tidings of the Gospel. The missionaries found a ready welcome, but they had to deal with an ignorant people, who had no written language even, and whose hearts and lives were wholly perverted with the vices and abominations connected with their former idolatry and immoralities.

Kings, Chiefs, and People learn to read.

How did they go about their work? A brief but significant record informs us. As soon as they found lodgings, and the very day their baggage was landed, "*late in the evening the king was found busy at his book, having been engaged for two or three days in learning to read.*" Here was something which arrested and fixed his attention. The foreigners had brought a new and wonderful art, and impressed with its value, and their superior knowledge, he is ready to listen to their instruction. So jealous was the king of the advantage to be derived from this source, that he "was unwilling the common people should be taught till he had learned." "In July the king could read the New Testament intelligibly." He was willing the chiefs should be taught, and "in November the mission had four schools," and 92 scholars. This was the commencement of its labors, and wisely planned for the happiest results. The wonderful fact that thought could be expressed and communicated on paper, excited intense and wide-spread interest, and won immense favor and attention to the mission.

In 1821 George Sandwich, another native educated at Cornwall, was sent out to join the mission. The work of teaching went on successfully.

In 1822, the art of printing being introduced, a still greater impulse was given to the schools; the king and chiefs undertook in earnest to learn to read and write, and in September the mission had 500 pupils. "Delia," the first convert mentioned, "had been instructed in one of the mission families."

This special attention to education prepares us for the statement that "the strictly spiritual labors of the mission were now prosecuted to much better advantage than formerly." The spelling-book became an effective text-book for teaching Christianity.

In 1823 "Christian instruction seemed to be taking deep root." "The king, his brother, 12 chiefs, and as many distinguished women, were learning to read and write," and 200 pupils are reported in one school.

In 1824 "the schools flourished." The regents and chiefs convened the people to declare to them their own purpose "concerning *learning* and the law of Jehovah." "The people in various parts of the islands were ordered to build school-houses and receive instruction. Before the end of the year, 50 natives were employed as teachers, and at least 2000 had learned to read." Nearly *all* these teachers were still heathen. What a terrible hindrance to this mission, had our modern theory then been enforced, that none but *Christian* teachers should be employed!

With this advance of education, "the cause of religion advanced," and some were found to be "praying men."

The Rev. Mr. Ellis, of the London Missionary Society, spent some two years in joint labor with our missionaries on the islands, up to this date, and doubtless his former experience on the Society Islands proved of valuable service to our mission in its early history.

In 1825 "the schools prospered." "Every where the chiefs selected the most forward scholars, and sent them out to teach others." "40 schools were known to be in operation on Hawaii, and the number was greatly increased during the year." The number of learners was estimated at 16,000. The young princess, Nahienaena, showed her regard for learning by forbidding "any to enter her house who could not read hymns." Learning and religion were always associated, and increased attention to reading and education was followed by a revival of genuine piety, and many hopeful conversions.

In 1826 the number of pupils in some 400 schools is estimated at 25,000, and "2000 persons were known to be in the habit of family and secret prayer."

In 1827 "the number, both of schools and learners, increased greatly." "Some of the principal chiefs spent a part of their time in teaching." "The morals and customs of the people improved." Twelve were received to the Church, making the "whole number of native members 23." "Ten of these were among the highest chiefs of the islands, and other chiefs stood propounded."

Revivals in the Schools.

In 1828, on Maui and three smaller islands were found 225 schools, with 10,243 scholars, and the number soon after rose to 18,000 scholars, in a population of only 37,000 in all. The adults, as well as children, thronged the schools for instruction, and the whole number of scholars on the islands was not less than 45,000. Minds thus aroused could not neglect the higher interests of the soul. A revival followed, and the year closed with 108 communicants, and multitudes were becoming enlightened, and anxious to know what they should do to be saved.

In 1829 we find 39,208 scholars reported, and 185 communicants. The influence of the schools was felt throughout the islands in favor of Christianity, and nearly half the population was receiving instruction in them.

In 1830 there were 900 schools and 44,895 scholars. 112 were received to church fellowship.

A reïnforcement this year of four missionaries and their wives, made the whole number of laborers who had been sent out by the Board 44.

In 1831 the whole number of scholars reported is 52,882, probably more than half the entire population at that time. "The teachers, with few exceptions, were nothing but ignorant savages who had learned to read," but the schools served to arrest attention, and bring the people under Christian teaching, and did rapidly elevate them above their previous ignorance and degradation. But a higher education was desirable, and hence the mission opened the high-school at Lahaina, with 25 scholars. The year closed with 400 native communicants.

A reïnforcement of 19 persons sailed for the islands this year, of whom 7 were ordained missionaries.

In 1832 "the high-school increased to more than 60 scholars." The whole number of pupils is not reported, but the church members received from the beginning are stated to be 577.

In 1833 the young king relapsed into vice, and many of

the people followed his example. Hence "great numbers forsook the schools;" so closely did the interests of religion and learning cling together. Yet the high-school made itself felt for good, and "at nearly every station some of the missionaries or their wives engaged in teaching," and "efforts for the education of *children* were increased."

In 1834 "the *Hawaiian Seminary*, the first newspaper ever printed on the islands, was struck off." This was designed for the high-school; and another, the *Hawaiian Teacher*, was soon commenced at Honolulu for general circulation. Another reïnforcement of eight laborers was sent out this year.

In 1835 "schools were taught by the members of the mission at all the stations, and greater numbers of children were induced to attend. Hoapili ordered all children on Maui, over four years of age, to be sent to school. The high-school had 118 students. The whole number of church members from the beginning was 864.

In 1836 the schools prospered, and a revival was enjoyed, "especially in the high-school." "The first class that entered this seminary, 23 in number, completed their studies this year, and 20 or 30 of these 'graduates' were employed as school-masters, generally with good effect." 212 were received this year to the Church. A reïnforcement of 15 men (9 school-masters) and 17 women were sent to join the mission.

In 1837 "the schools improved." "Graduates from the high-school were scattered through the islands as teachers." It was sending out an increasing number every year, and "Mr. Coan had 90 teachers under his instruction," and thus better qualified teachers were being rapidly supplied.

1049 church members were reported in good standing.

In 1838 "schools were better taught, better attended, and better supported;" and "progress towards complete civilization was manifest in every department of society" but the government. A great impulse was given to the mind of the nation, rousing it to thought, and impelling to better pursuits and higher attainments. A large blessing followed the labors and prayers of this year, religion was revived at every station, and some 5000 converts were added to the churches.

In 1839 the report of the mission gives many interesting details of the station and high-schools, speaks of 200 common schools, and continues the account of the "glorious revival" in progress at the close of the previous year. This revival continued, and 10,725 were added to the churches, making the whole number in regular standing 15,915. If any one would know more particularly the influence of the schools, in preparing the way for, and carrying on this precious work of grace, let him read the following paragraph from Mr. Coan, giving account of one of them: "But the crowning blessing of all is the precious influences of the Holy Spirit in the school. These influences have continually descended in soft showers like the gentle rain and the early dew. The attention of the school can always be arrested by the subject of religion; and, when they are affectionately addressed on this subject, the fixed eye, the solemn inquisitive look, and the silent tear tell the operations of the Holy Agent within. Their consciences are already very tender, and we believe that many of their hearts have been formed into the image of Christ. Eleven of their number are members of the Church, and they have thus far adorned their profession. Others, we trust, are born again, and it may be said of all, that, so far as man can judge, their conduct is nearly unexceptionable."

The government was this year brought more under the controlling influence of the Gospel, and this resulted in a new and improved code of laws.

In 1840 "a law was enacted requiring all children over four and under fourteen years of age, to attend school five days every week." Provision was also made, assigning land for the support of the teachers. The revival continued to some extent, and 4179 were added to the churches; the whole number received from the beginning being 21,379, and 18,451 being then in good standing. Four missionaries and their wives were sent as a reïnforcement.

In 1841 the mission reports 357 common schools, with 18,034 pupils, 6 boarding-schools with 202 scholars, the seminary with 80 students, and some other schools. More than 30 school-houses were erected, and 1473 persons were received to church fellowship.

In 1842 there were 313 common schools, with 19,000 pupils, 319 boarding scholars, and 160 students in the seminary. "Of the 144 who have been connected with the seminary, 105 are usefully employed as teachers, 35 are officers of government, (8 of them teaching part of the time,) and 7 are engaged in other useful employments. Of the whole, 73 are church members in regular standing." A large portion of the boarding-pupils were hopefully pious. "A paragraph from Mr. Armstrong shows that the schools are accomplishing their great object. He writes: "The progress of the pupils is surprising. There are comparatively few children over eight years of age who can not read the Testament." Says Mr. Lyons: "I have had the most gratifying evidence of the progress made by the pupils."

It is worthy of notice that when the Papists came in and attempted to resist and supplant the Protestant missions, they at once "decried and opposed the school laws, and endeavored to counteract the chiefs in their efforts for educating the people."

During this year "the Spirit of the Lord was still poured out, sinners brought to inquiry and repentance, and the churches enlarged." The additions were 2443.

In 1843, 310 common schools report some 20,000 scholars, the boarding-schools 361, while the seminary and several select schools continued to prosper. The school for chiefs had 14 pupils. This had been in existence several years, and its influence was great and decidedly good. The missionaries say: "The cause of education is evidently advancing in these islands. An influence is going out from the seminaries to act upon the common schools, and then this influence is reflected back upon the seminaries, and in both cases the standard of education is raised."

"Christian instruction is obviously exerting an *elevating and improving influence upon the character and habits of the people.*" "Nearly all the children in the districts attend school more or less regularly." The additions to the Church this year were 5296.

In 1844 the schools continued prosperous. "Probably nearly one fifth part of the population is in one class of schools or another." The admissions to the Church are reported to be 1110.

Value of the Schools.

In the report for 1847, the missionaries give the following testimony to the value of the seminary:

"On the whole, the institution is evidently scattering blessings throughout the nation. Its graduates are every where the leading members of society, in matters civil, religious, and literary. Some of the present pious pupils are regarded as among the most promising young men in the nation." This year the government appropriated $40,000 annually for the common schools, and the Board had no longer to make provision for them. They had kindled a fire in the nation so large that it now became a self-sustaining flame.

In 1848 the Minister of Instruction says: "The number of youth in all the schools on the islands may be safely estimated at 20,000, and it is believed that in no year since the introduction of Christianity, has the cause of national education advanced more steadily and surely, not to say rapidly." "It is a cause which takes deeper and stronger hold of the national mind, and, if vigorously sustained, can not but produce the most lasting and important benefits."

Of the seminary, Mr. Alexander writes: "It is annually sending out streams of the best influence to every part of the nation. To it our churches owe much of their prosperity. It supplies many of our schools with their teachers. The good of the nation as well as the prosperity of the mission, demands that this institution be well sustained."

In the report of the Board for 1853, we find the announcement: "*The people of the Sandwich Islands are a Christian nation!* Our appropriate work on those Islands, as a Foreign Missionary Society, is completed."

"One fourth part of the inhabitants are members in regular standing of Protestant Christian churches." "The language is reduced to writing, and is read by nearly a third part of the people. The schools contain the great body of the children and youth. The annual outlay for education, chiefly by the government, exceeds $50,000."

From the first, more than 40,000 had been received to church fellowship, and 22,236 were then in regular standing, contributing more than $25,000 a year to Christian and benevolent objects.

What power effected this mighty change in a whole people in one short generation? Doubtless the Gospel and the grace and spirit of God. But what were the effective human instrumentalities in disposing the people to listen, and bringing the truth of God to bear on their minds and hearts? Let the missionaries themselves answer. Speaking of the schools in 1852 they write: "They are a leaven in the nation, which is working changes in the character of the population, slowly to be sure, but steadily, constantly, and certainly. They are doing a great and good work for the nation."

Recall the history of the mission from the landing of that first missionary band—from the moment the king was seen learning to read—trace the influence of the schools till half the population was embraced in them as learners, and the whole nation was moved—estimate their value in rousing thought and bringing the people together under stated instruction, till the focus of God's truth could be concentrated on their hearts. Oh! who can doubt the mighty and transforming influence of those schools in effecting this blessed work? What would oral preaching have availed to this day without them? We claim no undue credit for these schools. To God be all the glory for the wonders of his love and mercy to that once degraded but now evangelized people. But if we would learn to do the work of God, let us not ignore or neglect the instrumentalities on which he bestows his special blessings.

CHAPTER XII.

MISSION TO THE NESTORIANS OF PERSIA.

SHALL we examine the history and agencies of another mission among the Orientals? Let us take that to the Nestorians of Persia. Mr. Perkins, the first missionary to this people, reached Tabrez in August, 1834. He engaged Mar Yohannan as his teacher, and the first plain indication of favor to the mission appears in the fact that the patriarch, Mar Elias, "was delighted with the Syriac *spelling-book* and Scriptures, and with the prospect of printing in the language of the Nestorians." Hence he "thanked God for the commencement of the mission.

Schools are the First Effective Agency.

In 1835 we find the mission established at Ooroomiah. The bishop, Mar Yohannan, and priest Abraham, had been taken into the service of the mission, and each had "opened a school for teaching English in his native village." "A few of the boys formed the nucleus of a mission school at Ooroomiah." "It was proposed that Mr. Perkins should instruct a Lancasterian school for educating teachers." "Here one scholar from each of the thirty Nestorian villages was to be boarded and taught gratuitously, at an expense of about twenty dollars a year."

This school was so popular that the Mohammedans became jealous of the favor thus shown to the Nestorians, and the mission felt it necessary to open a school for them also.

How significant that in *every* mission, schools are the first and potent agency to win favor and arouse to thought.

In 1836 the seminary was opened and had forty-four scholars. "There were also three free schools containing ninety-three pupils, of whom eight were females." "An uncle of the King of Persia visited the mission and became acquainted with the schools, and the next day, unsolicited, sent a firman commending the mission, and commanding the governor to protect it from all evil."

In 1837, "A bishop, two priests, a deacon," and several ecclesiastics were in the service of the mission, and there was "a constant advance in promoting education and the knowledge of divine truth."

In 1838, though the financial embarrassments of the Board pressed hard upon the mission, yet the missionaries managed to avoid the necessity of suspending their schools, evidently regarding them as vital to the best interests of the mission.

Of the fifty students in the seminary "two were bishops, three priests, and four deacons. Twelve were studying English and four Hebrew." The unevangelized helpers of the mission were eight; "three bishops, two priests, and three deacons." Mar Elias, the oldest bishop in the province, was superintendent of the village schools.

In 1839 the mission had 12 free schools, with 293 pupils, 17 girls in a boarding-school, and 55 students in the seminary. Priest Dunka, one of the helpers and scholars of the mission, is the first of whom we find recorded that he "gave indications of piety."

In 1840 we find the announcement, "Preaching to the Nestorians had now fairly begun." This evidently alludes to *formal* preaching. Who can doubt that the preparatory work in the schools, and the Christian instruction thus quietly communicated, was quite as important and quite as effective as the formal preaching which now commenced? Nay, who can doubt that without this preparatory work the most eloquent formal preaching would have been in vain?

This preparatory work secured the favor of the priests

and bishops, and through them of the people. The mission, from the outset, employed the clergy as teachers and helpers. They became "the foremost students in the seminary, and the teachers of all the free schools." The mission thus availed itself of the powerful influence of the clergy in securing its great object. Its wisdom in this respect is distinctly recognized in the reports of the Board. Had the mission acted on the narrow policy now enjoined in India, and employed none but *Christian* teachers, how changed would have been its history! Thank God for the broader and wiser views which then prevailed.

In 1841 the mission had 20 free schools in as many villages, and a seminary and girls' boarding-school. The whole number of scholars was 516, taught by 19 priests and 19 deacons. Schools were requested in eight other villages, and "one of them was soon to be opened."

In 1842 we find the value of schools attested by the following report. "The seminary contains 70 pupils, and the female boarding-school 18. There are 40 free schools in 36 villages, containing 635 male, and 128 female pupils, or 763 in all. The whole number under instruction is 851." "The schools create a demand for books, furnish fresh recruits for our seminary, do away the influence of the childish and worse than unprofitable writings of many of their *melpanos*, form a taste and predilection for the Holy Scriptures, *open the door for preaching the Gospel*, and create and supply a demand for an intelligent native ministry." "The whole number of [unevangelized] teachers employed in the village schools is 56, 22 of whom are priests and 26 deacons."

"The Precious Grain shall not be Lost."

In 1843 we find 44 village free schools with 1065 pupils, and the whole number in all the schools 1142. And now for the first time, we see the seed so long, wisely and patiently sown and cultivated, springing up and bearing the first fruits of a glorious harvest. The mission was permitted "to enjoy a refreshing from the presence of the Lord, though they hardly dared to call it *a revival.* A few gave evidence of having passed from death unto life, others were serious, and many were unusually attentive to the preaching of the Gospel."

Who were the converts? The report says: "Most of the hopeful converts were young men of promise, *who had long been members of the seminary,* or in some way connected with the mission."

Patriarch and Priests oppose the Schools.

In 1844 the patriarchal family became hostile to the mission, and enlisting the inferior ecclesiastics, a storm of opposition burst upon the mission. In all such opposition why are mission schools a special object of attack? Is not the fact sufficient evidence that the enemy value rightly the influence of these schools? During this storm of opposition, the mission found it necessary to give up, for a time, *all its schools.* Many of the pupils left with tears and bitter grief, and their strong attachment to the schools did much to dispose their parents to send them back again, even in disregard of the hostile priests.

The girls' boarding-school was soon in operation again with 43 pupils, and a gracious influence was manifest among them. We read: "The female teacher of the primary department gives cheering evidence of being born again. Others in the school are in a thoughtful and serious state of mind." The boys' seminary was also resumed.

In 1845 the 2 seminaries had each 40 pupils, and 32 village schools were reöpened with 482 pupils. The report says: "As many as six of the teachers have recently become hopefully pious. The schools are lights in the villages where they exist, and it is desirable they should be multiplied."

The Secretary and Committee approve of Heathen Teachers.

In the report of this year the Prudential Committee express views in regard to the support and education of heathen as *boarding pupils,* and the employment of *heathen teach-*

ers, such as deserve the thoughtful consideration of all who are interested in the work of missions. Four unevangelized bishops were supported by this mission as *boarding pupils*, and employed, at the same time, as *native helpers.* In justifying this practice the Prudential Committee say: "It is the belief of the Committee that no part of the appropriation for educating a *native ministry* in that mission, has been more proper than this," namely, the $225 paid to those bishops as *boarding pupils.* "Why, if the mission has a seminary for training a *native ministry*, should they disregard the fact that the higher ecclesiastics of the province were ready to become their pupils?" "Supposing that none of them were pious, who could tell what the grace of God might do for them? Placing them in this connection, [boarding scholars in the seminary,] was the most appropriate means of bringing them under the power of the Gospel." The Committee go on to justify the allowance to these bishops on the ground of their influence, as leading ecclesiastics, in bringing the people into schools and under the teaching of the mission. They also justify the employment of these *unconverted* bishops as *native helpers*, and refer to our practice in India. "In the Ceylon mission," they say, "the school-masters for some time were necessarily heathens, and so they were in the Mahratta missions. In the missions in Western Asia, it has not been till of late that the teachers of the mission schools were to any great extent pious men, and really interested in the objects of the missions. Yet their services, *regarding the circumstances*, were believed to be an equivalent for what they cost." How came our Prudential Committee and their worthy Deputation wholly to discard these sentiments, in 1854, and to interdict *all heathen* teachers in *new* missions in India? In 1845 they justified the employment of *unconverted native* HELPERS even. In 1854 they interdicted unconverted *teachers*, employed only to teach secular knowledge, where schools thus gathered were the only means of obtaining a hearing for the Gospel. And was this without any change of views?

"For Grace insures the Crop."

This year witnessed a precious revival in the Nestorian mission, which deserves a special record. The first instances of conversion occurred in the *female seminary.* The religious concern soon spread to the other seminary, and "increased with great rapidity." In giving some account of this revival, Dr. Anderson says: "It began in January and was still in progress near the close of June, and has resulted in the hopeful conversion of more than 100 souls, including a number of ecclesiastics." More than 50 of these converts were in the two *seminaries.* "This outpouring of the Spirit properly dates its commencement in the two seminaries." Mr. Stocking writes: "Never, any where, have I witnessed in awakened sinners apparently more thorough convictions of sin, a deeper sense of their lost and ruined state and inability to save themselves, than was manifested in the generality of cases in the school and around us. Days and weeks together, devoted almost exclusively to religious conversation with inquirers, in various stages of interest among the pupils of this (the female) school, and with the majority of those interested in Mr. Stoddard's seminary, led me to feel that as genuine and wonderful a work of divine grace has been wrought here, as any I have ever witnessed in revivals in America." "There was great tenderness of conscience, and an uncommon disposition to spend time in prayer. During as many as sixteen hours of the twenty-four, the voice of prayer did not cease to be heard."

Speaking of the state of feeling in the seminary the missionaries say: "Though we have opened for retirement every room about the premises that can possibly be spared from other uses, such is the disposition to pray without ceasing, and so numerous are those who are awakened, that individuals are often distressed because they can find no place in which to pour out their souls to God. This evening ten of our pupils seem to be reposing their all on Christ, and are in a very interesting state of mind." The village schools also shared in this precious revival. At Geog Tapa,

John, one of the helpers, "found all the members of one school in the village weeping, and some seriously inquiring the way of life."

A young man who was to be bishop in place of Mar Elias, on the death of the latter, being among the converts in the seminary, engaged in earnest labors for the salvation of others. The people, on hearing him exhort, were overheard to say that if this new heart made such bishops as he, "they wished Mr. Stoddard had all of them in his school."

The report groups together many miscellaneous items, showing the influence and value of the schools. "Not many weeks ago," writes one of the missionaries, "every member of the seminary seemed more or less sunk in stupidity and sin. Now, besides the two teachers, 30 of the pupils are hoping that they have been washed in the blood of Christ." "We have had in the seminary to-day 25 visitors, mostly young men from the neighboring villages." "Our oldest pupils have been very prayerful and laborious in efforts to do them good, and our rooms have, from morning to night, reminded one of an inquiry-meeting. We must believe that the seminary is thus exerting a powerful influence, not only by training up young men for usefulness hereafter, but by attracting around us, at the present time, those from abroad who are in any measure awakened to the truth." "At Geog Tapa, where ten of our pupils belong, the effect of their labors has been very happy, and at the close of the vacation many of their relatives had become interested in the truth, and some hopefully converted to Christ. In the case of one young man, his father, mother, brother, and sister have all been awakened."

At Karajala "the teacher of the school" and "several of his older scholars were also awakened." At Ardishai, coming upon a gathering of people, Dr. Perkins found among them a young girl from Miss Fisk's school reading to them the *Dairyman's Daughter*, and telling the wonderful things of God.

Thus, wherever the work spread, it showed its close connection with the schools. In 1846 we find 76 pupils in the two seminaries, and 462 in the 30 village schools. "In the early part of this year the female seminary was blessed with another work of grace, and it is hoped that nine more of its pupils have been born again." "Almost all our pupils and domestics are hopeful Christians; and most of the [unevangelized] teachers who have joined us for the summer, listen with deep interest to the truth." A little girl from Hakkie had become a Christian in Miss Fisk's school. "Her father, an untamed mountaineer, soon came down to visit her. The silken cords of love were thrown around him, and on all sides he was pointed by these young disciples to the cross of Christ. He heard first with indifference, then with wonder. As his light increased, and the conviction pressed on him that he was a lost sinner, his heart rose in opposition. He struggled, though unsucessfully, with his feelings. The strong man was bowed down, and wept like a little child, and it was not long before the trembling rebel became a peaceful Christian. This man was deacon Guergis," always abundant, after his conversion, in zeal and labors for Christ, till the Lord called him home.

Eight months after the commencement of this blessed revival in the schools, the missionaries reckoned the genuine converts "at not less than 150."

In 1847 the mission reports 73 scholars in the seminaries, and 608 in 36 village schools. They value these schools as so many lights in the villages, and find urgent calls to increase their number. In 1848 the Patriarch again became hostile, and another storm of persecution burst upon the mission. The Patriarch endeavored to close all the schools, and arrest the entire missionary work among the people. But his wicked devices failed, and the storm passed over.

This year, too, the mission enjoyed another blessed revival. It commenced, as before, in the seminaries, and "all the pupils were deeply impressed by a sense of the divine presence." "The impenitent members of the seminary were powerfully wrought upon by the mighty energies of the Spirit, some of them being under very deep convictions of sin, and nearly all awakened to a sense of their dreadful depravity and their utterly lost condition."

In 1849, 32 village schools had 598 pupils, 12 of their teachers were priests, "and about half the whole number of teachers were hopefully pious." The report testifies, "these schools are a very important instrumentality," "sapping the foundations of superstition and ignorance."

Third Revival in the Schools.

The seminaries continued to prosper, and a third precious revival found its origin in these nurseries of piety. It commenced in January of 1850, and continued with remarkable power. "Scores have been bowed down under the Spirit's influence, as the trees of the wood under a rushing mighty wind." Of the work in the male seminary Mr. Cochran, after describing an evening prayer-meeting, writes: "At the close of the meeting the teachers came to my room, saying that the scholars were weeping and desired that another prayer-meeting should be held. Upon entering the school I found all with their heads bowed, and many offering ejaculatory prayer. For some time remarks were made, and prayer was offered. At length, however, the weeping became so loud and general, that I feared the result of further excitement." He therefore requested them to go to their closets.

"During the devotions of the next morning the intensity of their feelings could find vent only in sighs and audible weeping, and from that time the work advanced with great rapidity and power."

In the girls' school the work was no less extensive and searching. The older girls spent every leisure moment in prayer, several of them five hours every day. "Every day gave increasing evidence of the power of this gracious work. Up to the close of the term there was no diminution of interest." The converts were unceasing in efforts for the conversion of relatives, friends and neighbors who were still out of Christ.

The special power of this revival was seen in the seminaries, but its influence extended to some of the villages, especially Geog Tapa.

In 1850 the seminaries had 74 pupils, and thirty-five village schools had 663. Another (*fourth*) "gracious outpouring of the Holy Spirit came down upon both the seminaries in the early part of 1851. "There was every mark of a genuine revival, nor was the interest confined to the seminaries." Commencing with these favored institutions, its influence extended to other schools, and the villages where they were located.

In 1851 the mission reports 82 scholars in the seminaries, of whom 30 young men and nearly all the girls were hopefully pious. "The religious experience of many of these young men," says the mission, "is of such a character that a stranger on coming amongst them would suppose that he was in the midst of a revival." The free schools increased this year to 58, with 1023 pupils. "The increase is owing to a growing interest in education among the people, and would have been still greater but for the want of teachers and funds." In different villages 263 adults, also, were ranged in classes and learning to read. "Every school is also a nucleus for preaching."

In 1852 these village schools increased to 60, with 1038 pupils, while the male seminary had 40, and the female seminary, 50 pupils.

A *fifth* revival is reported in both seminaries, described "as unspeakably precious in quickening believers, reclaiming backsliders, and bringing a number, as is hoped, into the fold of Christ."

In 1853 there were 79 village schools, with 1334 pupils, and the two seminaries had 90. These schools were the light and joy of the mission, and its special hope for coming years. Of the 54 young men who had gone out from the seminary, 34 were "regarded as pious, many of them devotedly so." "Nine are efficient and able preachers of the Gospel, and 19 others are so far preachers that they can conduct religious meetings in the villages with great acceptance and usefulness." "Twenty-five are regular teachers in the village schools; one is superintendent of these schools; three are teachers in the seminaries; one a translator, and one a printer." Mr. Stoddard remarks: "In almost every case our scholars have joined the schools when strangers to the cross of Christ. But of those who have left us *two thirds* have gone forth the hopeful heirs of heaven; and it is delightful to feel that they preach Christ wherever they go."

Another (the *sixth*) blessed revival is reported in the two seminaries. "Many were inquiring what they should do to be saved, and many gave evidence of a saving change." The work extended to some of the villages, but its special influence was seen and felt in the schools.

In 1854, 75 free schools contained 1245 pupils, and large classes of adults, both men and women, were learning to read, and coming thus under stated Christian instruction. "In some parts of the field great enthusiasm was manifested on the subject of education." In one village 70 adults had begun to learn to read, so thoroughly were the people aroused to the advantages of education. Young men and women were going out from the seminaries and schools to remote parts of the country, increasing this enthusiasm, and diffusing light and truth wherever they went.

Opposition was attempted in some quarters. Two young men from the seminary, attempting to open a school in Khosrova, were set upon by a mob, and narrowly escaped with their lives. This opposition, as usual, was directed against the schools.

In 1855 the male seminary had 48, and the female seminary, 50 pupils. "They are felt to be sources of rich blessing to the people." "Both institutions have again been visited with the special influences of the Holy Spirit."

The agent of the Persian government, Asker Khan, showed some opposition to the mission this year, and his opposition was directed especially against the village schools. These were consequently diminished somewhat, but the fidelity of the teachers, and the interest and courage of the people kept most of them in operation, and the report mentions 60, with 1120 pupils. This (*seventh*) revival is described as one of precious and saving efficacy. "The feeling in both schools became very general and deep." "The voice of weeping and prayer was heard on every side. The prayer-closets were filled to a late hour by those who were pleading for mercy, and a large proportion of those who were not pious appeared to be seeking in earnest the narrow way." "With the exception of the youngest and most recently admitted, nearly all were indulging the hope that they had passed from death unto life."

1856.—Government opposition continued this year, especially against the village schools, so that they were reduced to 53, with 894 pupils. The thirst for education among the people was only increasing, and half the *adults* in one village were learning to read. The male seminary had 69 pupils, and the other, 40.

Another (*the eighth*) revival is reported in both seminaries. In the male seminary "most of the pupils were more or less affected, and as many as 20 gave evidence of a saving change." In the female seminary "there is good evidence that several have begun to know the Lord. The work has been characterized by great stillness and power." Of 103 who had been connected with this school, "60, or more than half, are hopefully pious, and the same may be said of three fourths of the present number." Of 150 young men who had belonged to the seminary, 91 were hopefully pious, and "a large portion of all who have left it are either preachers of the Gospel or very competent teachers of the village schools."

We pause here in the history of this favored mission. On which of its agencies has the special blessing of God rested most largely? What could its earnest and faithful laborers have accomplished without their mission schools?

Recall the facts of this and the Sandwich Islands mission, the special blessings coming down in almost continuous showers of mercy, one precious revival following closely on the former, and impressing the divine seal upon these schools in characters of living light, and can we conceive a greater calamity to either of these missions, short of their complete extinction, than an official suppression of their schools in their early history, like that which was enforced in the *new* missions of India in 1854 and 1855? May we learn wisdom both from the large blessings attending these schools, and the glorious harvests gathered in from them when allowed to prosper unrestricted, and also from the things we have suffered in their suppression.

CONCLUSION.

In closing this volume there are a few points which I desire to guard.

1. Will any fancy that my life and labors in India have been somewhat restricted to schools, and that this may have caused an undue bias in their favor? This would be a misapprehension. It is true the first duties imposed upon me by my brethren were in connection with the schools, and I always had one or more under my care, except while they were suppressed by the Deputation; but my labors and interest were never limited to them.

Before I had been at Ahmednuggur a twelvemonth the mission sent me on a preaching and exploring *tour* which extended three or four hundred miles, and occupied nearly two months. I spent from one to four months in such itineracies each year of my life in India, till the last, when health was too much broken. I have a high appreciation of this kind of labor, and if a Deputation should interdict it I should grieve for it as sincerely as I do for the schools.

I also became much interested in helping to prepare a *Christian literature.* Besides labor in Bible-translation, as one of the Committee of the "*Bombay Bible Society,*" the leisure moments, not occupied in oral preaching or the care of schools, enabled me to prepare some dozen different works in the Mahratta language, several of them original, varying from 80 to 220 pages, and the last one, a commentary on one of the Gospels, extending to over 300 pages—

all published either by the mission or "*The Bombay Tract and Book Society.*" If this department of our work were interdicted, should I not do right to grieve for it?

Nor is this all. As pastor of the dear flock at the outstations in the beautiful valley of the Godavery, and pastor for a time of the large native church at Ahmednuggur, I became deeply interested in the regular preaching and *pastoral* duties involved, and estimate their importance very highly. May we never be restricted in these labors! It is with an eye to the harmonious working of all these departments that I plead for the schools. We can not afford to be deprived of any agency that helps so effectively to win souls to Christ.

2. *My beloved brethren and associates in the missions:* Let no one infer that I am lacking in the kindest and most fraternal feelings towards them. If the views of any of them conflict with mine, they will be found to conflict quite as much with their own. I have let them speak at length in these pages, and rejoice to find my views so fully indorsed and ably sustained, not only by *all* my associates, but by *all* the officers of the Board, up to a recent date. Some of my brethren found occasion to change their former views, when the Deputation came to India; but I can not cease to love them on this account. The ties of Christian brotherhood are too sacred to be thus broken. The long years of colabor and Christian communion are linked with tender and cherished remembrances which shall not be forgotten on my part. I trust they are aware that I am always happy to be associated with each or all of them in the most intimate relations, and in all efforts by which we may save souls and advance this blessed cause of Christ.

3. *The members of the Deputation.* Have I spoken too plainly of them? I suppose God gave us speech that we might speak plainly and honestly. The *facts of history ought* to speak; its lessons *ought* to be garnered up for the benefit of the Church and of the world. I think great errors were committed; but "to err is human."

And let no one infer that I am wanting in kind and fraternal feeling towards these brethren. The memory of precious interviews for social and Christian intercourse in India, of the pleasant week spent at Roxbury since our return to America, of the delightful season with brother Thompson, whose poetic taste is not more marked than his genial social elements—that precious season when we gathered at the table of our common Lord, sharing in the sacred service; why should we not cherish such memories till we eat bread and drink wine anew in our Father's house above, where the errors of Christian men shall be all forgotten or remembered only to enhance our estimate of the wonders of redeeming love and sanctifying grace?

4. *The dear old Board.* Do I not love it? Have not the last years of my life been spent in its service? Am I not a life partner, and have I not a life-interest in it, in a higher sense than is true of any co-partners who remain here in this Christian land?

The dedication of this volume expresses the truest feelings of my heart. I have admired and loved the American Board from my earliest years. The impressions and purposes stirred in my soul by the story of Harriet Newell, and that first devoted band of young missionaries whose inextinguishable desires, prayers, and efforts resulted under God in the formation of the Board, are among my first and most cherished recollections. Our dearest friends on earth are those who have ever loved this Board and supported it largely with their prayers and their money. They love it still with an affection which no mistakes of its officers or missionaries can wholly destroy. There may be imperfections in the *organization* of the Board which give undue influence to some in its direction who love power; if so, they ought to be corrected. There may have been lacking a lively feeling of responsibility and a proper measure of watchfulness on the part of the corporate members; if so, let them be more vigilant. Errors have been committed; let them be retrieved. Restrictions have been imposed; let them be withdrawn. But let no man imagine I have become an enemy of the Board because of the errors I deprecate. I have loved it, and labored and prayed for it, too long and too earnestly for this. It is embalmed in the sweetest memories of my existence. I must be permitted to love and pray for it and rejoice in its prosperity while I live. *God bless and prosper the dear old Board forever.*

5. *The cause of missions.* Shall this volume fail of its design to help forward this glorious enterprise? Will any mind take advantage of the errors and conflicting statements of good men to disparage the work of missions? Such a mind would take advantage of the "sharp dissension" of Paul and Barnabas to disparage *their* apostolic labors; nay, it would disparage Christianity and the Bible, because of the duplicity of Abraham and the crimes of David and other good men which it faithfully records. Truth must be willing to live by truth. Christianity is *light*, loves *light*, and apart from this element she can not exist. Let not those whose business it is to spread the truth, ever be found concealing truth.

No; let the facts of these pages only inspire a higher, holier enthusiasm in this blessed work. High above all conflicting views of Boards and individuals, let the banner of our divine Redeemer wave in triumph; and while every eye is directed to that glorious inscription, "GO TEACH ALL NATIONS," let every heart be nerved with a stronger, holier purpose to do what is possible to execute this blessed commission of the Son of God, till the Gospel shall become the joyful heritage of every nation and dweller on our globe.

Too long has the Church of God rested in inglorious ease. Too long has she neglected her "*marching orders.*" For eighteen centuries she has been in possession of this divine commission to disciple all nations, but her efforts have been faint and few—not at all commensurate with the difficulty and grandeur of the work, or the priceless value of immortal souls!

There needs to be a reëxamination of the foundation-principles of this work, of the vital elements of the Gospel, divinely adapting it to all consciences, and fitting it to be aggressive in every land, subduing all hearts to Christ.

And the Church and every individual disciple of Jesus needs to be baptized with the spirit of dear old Caleb, who, conscious of the giants, and the terrible difficulties involved in the conquest of Canaan, was still able to feel that he was one of "a chosen race"—one of "a royal priesthood"—one of "a nation to whom pertained the promises"—and feeling thus, despite all the giants and the counter testimony of his timid brethren, was able to exclaim with holy enthusiasm: "Let us go up at once and possess it, for we are well able to overcome it!"

The Church needs to be more conscious of her ability, under God, to do this work. She is not to wait for some new or miraculous power to accomplish it without her, but to feel that God has intrusted it to her, and is calling upon her to put her hand and her heart to it in earnest.

I verily believe the Church of Christ is able to evangelize the heathen world in one short generation. I believe her resources, under God, are fully adequate to accomplish this work. I give utterance to this conviction, not hastily, but after mature reflection, and with a vivid impression, both of the deep depravity of the human heart, and of the terribly debasing influence of heathen rites and superstitions. Pictures of the dark debasing features of Hinduism have never been overdrawn. But sin has no forms of malignancy for which the Gospel of the Son of God has not a remedy, if timely and faithfully applied. I have a deep conviction of the inveteracy of Hindu caste and superstition, but I have a glorious conviction of the divine power of the Gospel.

The promises of God guarantee its triumph. The terms of the title-deed of Christ's inheritance are sufficiently broad and explicit. "I will give thee the heathen for thine inheritance, and the uttermost parts of the earth for thy possession." "The kingdoms of this world shall become the kingdom of our Lord and of his Christ." "Yea, all kings shall fall down before him; all nations shall serve him."

These promises shine out on almost every page of God's word, resplendent as so many stars of celestial magnitude.

God never meant that these promises, bearing the impress of his own seal and glowing with all heaven's brightness, should fall lifeless on the faith and courage of his Church. He would have them tell with their full inspiration and power. He would have the disciples of Jesus go forth to the world's conquest, not in their own name, it is true, but in the name and strength of the Lord of Hosts, and with his own pledge of certain victory. Oh! what security of triumph is here! He whose heart can faint or efforts tire, with such a divine guarantee of success, deserves no place on the battle-field.

To my brethren, then, who are waiting for the consolation and the glory of Zion in heathen lands, let me say, be strong in hope and faith. Cherish expectations of a speedy and certain victory. If you ask the grounds of my confidence that the Church is able to evangelize India, I reply, Jehovah has declared it, and his grace and truth confirm it. My assurance is based, not on the physical strength, or powerful intellects, or moral courage, or the zeal, or piety, even, of your missionaries, nor yet on the superior wisdom of your Deputations.

I expect no new invention of human wisdom for applying the truth and spirit of God to the hearts of depraved men. We rejoice in the rapid introduction of the arts and sciences to Pagan lands, and rightly too. But *railroads* have no power to effect a moral regeneration. *Magnetic telegraphs*—work by means of heaven's lightning, it is true, but they convey not heaven's grace to the heart of the unregenerate.

If the Church in America is looking to her great men and her wise men for some new appliances to carry forward the work of missions in India—if, distrusting the experience and judgment of her missionaries, who have voluntarily exiled themselves from all that is most dear in home, kindred, and native land, and who make Hindu character and superstitions constant subjects of investigation, and the most effective agencies for bringing Christian truth to bear on the understanding, consciences and hearts of the Hindus, the great object of life's study, toils, hopes and prayers—if, I say, distrusting the experience, or wisdom, or fidelity, of these first agents, whom she has commissioned and sent forth to this work, the Church now sends out Deputations destitute of any practical experience, and yet clothing them "with full power and authority" to change the plans and operations of the missions—*to suppress schools and printing-presses*, and lay restrictions on the *time*, *manner*, and *languages*, in which they shall preach Christ—I care not how wise and good the men may be who constitute such Deputations—if the Church is expecting in this way to *legislate* more rapid progress in the work of missions, she must experience still farther disappointment and defeat.

Would you commission two of your missionaries in India to go through all the missions of the Board, clothed "with full power and authority" to make such changes as they pleased? All would condemn such a proposition at once. But would not such missionaries, with twenty or thirty years' experience in India, be far better fitted for such a Deputation than two men from America, with no missionary experience at all?

And yet, count me not opposed to Deputations. If you will send us men clothed with limited power, equal only to that accorded to your missionaries, we will be thankful for their counsel, yield them all deference, and be glad of their votes on all subjects of business. We will be especially thankful for their sympathy, advice, and Christian intercourse, for our hearts often yearn for these with the longings of a thirsty soul in a parched and dreary land.

But if you clothe one or two men "with full power and authority" to change plans and agencies deliberately and prayerfully adopted by *ten*, *twenty*, or *fifty* of your missionaries, and that, too, after long years of careful observation and personal experience, while bearing the burden and heat of the day, you may expect disaster and disappointment.

And yet, even such a mistake shall not prevent the ultimate triumph of the Church in India. Mistakes may be made, but they shall all be retrieved. Defeats may be suf fered, but they shall all furnish valuable experience for the future. Neither the difficulties to be overcome, nor the magnitude of the work, nor errors in its prosecution, shall prevent our final victory. The conquest of India is sure—not because we are wise or mighty, but because "they that be for us are more than they that be against us."

The truth of God, *in its elements*, as well as in its promises, furnishes an ample guarantee on this point. Christianity has elements to subdue the world. This conviction has gathered force and strength with me every day of loneliness and toil and trial in India. The Gospel possesses both inherent vitality and aggressive power. That was no unmeaning or unphilosophical petition of our divine Redeemer when he prayed for his disciples: "Father, sanctify them through thy *truth*." Divine truth, applied by the Spirit of God, has elements to humble human pride, to alarm and subdue the sinner, to convince and convert, to sanctify and save the soul. It has done this for thousands now in glory. It is able to effect the same for every devotee of superstition in India.

As God liveth and is just, his truth shall never fail. Every enterprise for its vindication and victory shall grow, and gather strength, and finally triumph. The sympathy and efforts of those who love it, and the grace and power of Him who gave it, are a certain pledge of victory. Did not the Reformation of the sixteenth century begin with a cloistered monk? And yet it swept gloriously over Europe, and its genial vitalizing power and results still meet us on every hand. Was not Christianity itself cradled in a manger, and crucified on Calvary? And yet to-day it is fresh as the morning, and going forth in the strength of omnipotence to subdue the earth!

Oh! this mighty truth of God! Drop it into all soil; it will not be in vain. It will take root and spring up, and stretch out its arms to wrestle with the storms, and the sweet birds of heaven shall come to sing and dwell among its branches. Thank God, too, all true-hearted service in the cause of Christ is closely linked with this divine truth.

Every sincere effort to bring God's truth to bear on human hearts shall have a destiny coëval with it. Like a sweet tone of music, it vibrates in harmony with divine purposes, and its celestial melody shall be prolonged forever.

This truth of God has elements fitted to vitalize heathen hearts, and animate them with spiritual life. Not only is it pure and elevating, and just and holy, in all its requirements, but its sanctions, in their effective force on the human soul, attest its divine origin. It deals in no fancy visions of a sensual paradise, but in the glorious realities of Jehovah's unveiled presence. It portrays no fabled Sisyphus, no physical pains of purgatory, no dreams of Hindu transmigration, but God's own testimony to the reality of "the worm that never dies—the fire that is never quenched."

This truth of God, with its solemn sanctions, finds, too, an answering counterpart in man's moral nature. It is a blessed fact that man, however depraved, still retains the elements of conscience. It may be defiled—it may be seared for a time, as with a hot iron, but it still exists. Amidst the deepest moral debasement of fallen humanity, conscience still lives. Not in active power, it may be. It may lie inactive. Its voice, uniformly unheeded, may cease to be heard for years, but it still lives. It can not die. Sin can not destroy it. Death can not annihilate it. However long it may be suppressed—however deeply it may be seared and defiled, it will revive again, clothed with more terrific power for all the abuse it has suffered. From its fearful and avenging elements, have we not reason to believe it will constitute the undying worm in the world of the lost?

Yes, the Hindu has a conscience—weakened and defiled, it is true, by all the errors and superstitions of his false faith, and by all the wicked practices of his corrupt life—but it still lives, and under the influence of the word and Spirit of God it revives, and gives its powerful testimony in favor of Christianity.

The elements of God's truth concentrate their focus with peculiar brightness on the cross of Christ, or rather, they radiate from the cross, gathering their peculiar power and glory from it. Hindus, with no less scorn than Jew or Greek, reproach us with the folly of believing in a *crucified* Saviour—one who had not power, they say, to deliver himself from his enemies. They tell us that he was *betrayed and slain*—that he went down into the grave in all the weakness of human nature. The fact that he rose again in the might of deity they deny, or leave out of view. They seem at times to share in the fancied triumph of those who led him away to Calvary. But like them, too, they understand not those meaning words: "*And I, if I be lifted up, will draw all men unto me.*" Glorious prophecy! How bright and blessed the very beginning of its fulfillment! Hopeful believer, have we not here an ample guarantee that India and the world shall be Christ's? that "we are well able to overcome it"?

A *sinless Saviour* is the felt want of fallen humanity. For such a Saviour we search every system of false religion in vain. The Hindus have no such Saviour. Amidst all their fabled incarnations—amidst all their 330,000,000 of fancied gods, there is not one to whom they themselves ascribe this attribute of sinless perfection. But when slain by the law—when scourged by an accusing conscience, the trembling sinner feels the need of *such* a Saviour. The Hindu, when his intellect becomes enlightened and his conscience roused by the force of divine truth, *feels and admits* that his only hope of pardon must rest on *such* a Saviour.

Now here is the peculiar glory of the Gospel. Its divine, its joyous annunciation is: "God so loved the world as to give his only-begotten Son"—"God commendeth his love toward us in that while we were yet sinners *Christ died for us.*" Here is the crowning glory of Christianity—the element which more than all else distinguishes it from every religion of man's invention. From every fragment of that lowly tomb where lay the Son of God, flashes in heaven's own brightness the evidence, not only of man's immortality, but of God's infinite love and mercy. Around the cross of the despised Nazarene gathers a glory which shall shine with ever-increasing lustre, while God reigns and redeemed spirits strike their golden harps!

"Oh! for *such* love let rocks and hills
Their lasting silence break,
And all harmonious human tongues
The Saviour's praises speak."

Who can wonder that the early disciples made it the great burden of their preaching to bear witness to the resurrection of Christ? That Paul determined to know nothing among his hearers but Christ and him crucified? Christianity *has* become a blessed fact and power in the world. Christ *has* been lifted up. His cross has now become the centre of moral attraction for the universe. Under this banner the Church is called upon to go forth and subdue the world. Will she do it? Will the disciples of Jesus heed their glorious commission, and put their hands and their hearts to this work with resolute purpose? Will they give their sympathies, their prayers, their sons and their daughters, to carry forward this enterprise of heaven?

Oh! if Christians but knew their privilege—if they considered what is to give brightness to their crowns of rejoicing in the day of the Lord Jesus—what the peculiar glory of their heavenly inheritance—who, who would not count it all joy to bear a part in efforts to win the millions of perishing Hindus to Christ? Who would not pour out his money like water, and lay his choicest treasures, nay, even life itself, if need be, at the foot of the cross, consecrated forever to this blessed work?

Oh! that the Church of God in Christian lands would arise and shine, her light being come and the glory of the Lord being risen upon her. Why should this work be longer delayed? Why must more than 2000 precious souls continue to go down to idolaters' graves *every hour*, not knowing that Jesus has died? The truth and promises of God are not wanting. The Church of Christ is not wanting in resources. She has *men* enough to supply the heathen world with the Gospel without delay. Let political or worldly motives offer, and the sons of the Church gather by thousands. When patriotism calls them to their country's service, are they ever found wanting? When political posts require filling in Europe, Asia, or the remotest islands of the ocean, are candidates sought for in vain? When Dr. Hays calls for volunteers to penetrate the frozen regions of the polar seas, is his call unheard?

And is love to Christ and the souls of men a passion, even in sanctified hearts, less powerful than patriotism? Are worldly honors or worldly gain more attractive than the crown which filled the vision of the great Apostle, or the joy of winning the idolaters of India to Christ? I do not believe it. I do not believe there is any deficiency of pious young men and women in our American churches, ready to engage in this enterprise. I believe there are thousands who would gladly volunteer to do service for Christ in India, were the Church prepared to sustain them.

True, many missionaries have been cut down by the climate and diseases of India, and others have been sent back broken in health and disabled for life. But it was only the *traitor* spies who complained of Canaan that it was "a land which eateth up the inhabitants thereof." Are *true* soldiers any less ready to volunteer when they hear that their brethren have fallen in battle? Missionaries sicken and die in India, and for this very reason it is that the strong young men of the Church should go in larger numbers to supply their places. If the Church would show any resolute purpose to evangelize India, she must greatly increase the number of her laborers. Men laud the fearless navigator, explorer, patriot. Is it noble to encounter peril in a worldly enterprise, but madness to suffer in the cause of Christ? Is it glorious to die for one's king and country, and not glorious to die for Christ and the souls of the perishing heathen?

During the late terrific rebellion in India, Great Britain sent out some 100,000 men in a twelvemonth, to re-subjugate the Hindus. At the close of that campaign she had more than 140,000 men whom she had sent out from Europe to her service in India. Why might she not send out as many soldiers of the cross to conquer India for Christ? And then if America would add but half their number,

India would have a Christian minister to every thousand of her 200,000,000 idolaters.

Some urge that we have heathen here at home as a reason for not doing more for India. And yet statistics declare that there is one minister of the Gospel to every 900 of our population throughout the whole United States; while in New England, with a total population of only 3,000,000, are found 5000 ministers of the Gospel!—one minister to every 600 people; and these not a heathen people requiring to be evangelized for the first time, but possessing all the institutions of the Gospel, glowing with the light and love of heaven in active force among them. May I not ask, beloved brethren in America, to contrast these facts with the position of one lone missionary at Kolapoor, in a region of unbroken Hinduism, seventy miles deep in its shallowest point, and embracing millions of idolaters with no one else to care for their souls! My brethren, will you not give us more men for India?

And ye sons of the Church, looking for posts where you may endure hardness as good soldiers of Jesus Christ, where will you find a more needy or a more noble field than India? If ye seek for ease, or wealth, or literary fame, or earthly good of any kind, then rest ye on these high places of Zion. Your surroundings here will be pleasant, and many a good man has coveted them before you. But if you would seek a field in which to do much to honor God—in which to live, and toil, and *die*, in efforts to win souls to Christ—to raise the degraded and save the perishing, who but for you would never hear of Jesus—then come to India. A nobler field for Christian effort does not exist. "Let us go up at once and possess it" for Christ, for in his name and strength "we are well able to overcome it."

Do you doubt whether resources will be furnished to sustain you in this work? *The Church in America has money.* She has ample resources to evangelize India in one short generation. It was ascertained a few years ago, that of the church members who make the American Board the channel of their donations to foreign missions, each gives, on an average, *only seventy-four cents a year! about two mills a day!* Now can it be that this measures the true ability of these professing Christians? Is it in this proportion that they take shares in bank stocks, railroads, and electric telegraphs?

One cent a day from each of these church members would bring into the treasury of the Board nearly a million and a quarter of dollars every year. And then if the hundreds of thousands who now give nothing through any channel were earnestly enlisted, the present means for prosecuting this work might be at once increased ten or twenty fold. And where can the disciples of Jesus invest their funds *so safely* and with such glorious increase as in this blessed enterprise?

In one of our large cities are now the fragments of a firm, which, in 1856, found the splendid profits of their trade to be $1,300,000. The mind of the chief partner became disturbed by this rapid acquisition. Reason staggered, lost her balance, and he soon became an inmate of a mad-house. In a few months he died, leaving wealth to the amount of $2,000,000. The financial crisis followed, and the firm became insolvent! The acquisition and the insanity, the death and the insolvency, all occurred in the brief period of eighteen months. Now had love to Christ and the souls of the Hindus been strong enough in that man's heart to have drawn from him the half of his wealth as fast as acquired, who shall estimate the blessed result both to himself and to precious souls saved in heaven!

Again, think of the more than $3,000,000 annually expended in supporting the Christian institutions and home evangelizing agencies in the single State of Massachusetts; of the millions expended on the two hundred and fifteen evangelical churches in the city of New-York, and similar facts all over our Christian land; and if we acknowledge the golden rule to be our law, must not larger streams of Christian beneficence flow out to heathen lands? Must the dear children and youth who, by years of patient and persevering effort have been brought under the teaching and influence of Christian truth at such a dark point as Kolapoor, be turned out again "into the great and terrible wilderness of heathenism," and the whole mission be abandoned for the trifing sum of $2000 a year?

Let no one imagine that a missionary is disposed to complain of his brethren for expending so much in support of the Gospel and Christian institutions at home. No, support your schools and colleges, your churches, and pastors, and agencies for home evangelization. They are the glory and safeguard of your nation. Give to them—give largely. Let the munificence of your gifts attest the devotion of large, generous, noble, patriotic, and sanctified hearts. Oh! if a sincere prayer ever goes up to heaven, it is that which ascends from the heart of every American missionary in the foreign field, for blessings on "his own, his native land." A twofold motive presses upon his heart. He loves the land that gave him birth, and can not repress an intense desire to see her banners wave brightest and purest among the nations. And then just in proportion as his soul groans at sight of the corruptions and debasement of heathenism, does he long and pray for the preservation and prosperity of the "UNION," and for the purity and perpetuity of the Church and Christian institutions of America. As he longs to see healing streams flow hence more copiously to every dark land of the globe, so earnestly does he long and pray that this fountain-head may be kept pure.

But if any disciple of Jesus withholds the Gospel from India that he may give more money to the benevolent and Christian institutions of his own land, he needs to be reminded that "there is that giveth and yet increaseth," while "there is that withholdeth more than is meet, but it tendeth to poverty." The reflex influence that has come back from foreign missions into the bosom of the Church, has already repaid her in tenfold measure for all she has given and done for this cause. If the Church in America would bring upon her own land a withering curse, let her withhold her money and her Christian sympathies from the heathen.

Is it not time for those who have been bought with precious blood to mark their resolute purpose to obey the last command of their dying Lord by pouring more adequate supplies into his treasury? I believe the American churches are able to give much more largely for this work. I believe they have resources sufficient to support every missionary who will go, and every fit agency which can be pressed into this service. I have great faith in the piety and energy of our churches. If the wants and woes and claims of India were rightly understood and felt, I believe funds would flow in for this work as freely as they did of old for building the ark of God.

I have great confidence in the sympathy of sanctified hearts. The generous sympathy of unsanctified hearts are among the noblest elements of man that have survived the fall. They gush out for every bleeding Hungary and down-trodden Poland. They freight ships for famishing Ireland, and cars for suffering Kansas. Let this sympathy be baptized with the Holy Ghost and with fire, and what may it not achieve in converting the world to Christ?

Oh! if the eternal verities of God's word are not fictions, then must this Christian sympathy be an earnest, living reality. The millions of India must and will soon feel the power of this sympathy. Blest with the Christian agents and resources it will pour into her bosom, and touched with its vitalizing energy, gushing fresh from the sanctified hearts of these agents, India will soon rise redeemed, regenerated, and saved!

I would have the Church of Christ press forward in this work with the joyful assurance of a speedy victory. We may confide in the *promises of God.* They are bright as his bow in the heavens—sure as his eternal throne. We may confide in the *word and spirit* of God. Divine truth has elements to subdue all hearts to Christ.

We may confide in the *resources of the Church.* She has men and money enough to evangelize India in a single generation.

We may rejoice and thank God for what past efforts have already achieved. These efforts have been few and weak, not at all in proportion to the ability of the Church or the magnitude of the work to be accomplished. And yet results have followed, lasting as eternity, glorious as the crowns which are to adorn the brows of the redeemed.

And yet, we may not rest satisfied with these results. A mighty conflict is still before us. More glorious triumphs are still to be achieved. What are the thirty or forty thousand converts gathered into our churches in India, to the nearly 200,000,000 still held in their cruel bondage? There is *work* here for the Church!

Ye young men and women whose hearts beat with high and holy purposes to do much for Christ, there is work for *you* in India!

Ye wealthy men who hold the treasures of the Lord in stewardship, there is work here for *you!*

And *ye praying* men and women, there is work here for *you!* for the conquest of India is to be achieved, "*not by might nor by power, but by my Spirit, saith the Lord.*" Oh! if there is a man on earth who feels the need and the value of prayer which prevails with God, it is your weak missionary struggling under the ever-increasing conviction of the magnitude of this work and of his own impotence. But, thank God, Hinduism is not invincible. The hardest and most depraved heart can be brought to yield to the power of divine truth and love. Let these elements blend more sweetly and effectively in all Christian hearts—let the tide of Christian sympathy, interest, prayer, and effort in this work of God rise high enough to swallow up all petty differences of views, to remove all needless restrictions on the agencies employed—high enough to flow over all lands and submerge all hearts. Then shall India and the world be Christ's,

> "**And earth again, like Eden crowned,**
> **Bring forth the tree of life.**"

MISSION SCHOOLS IN INDIA.

WE are happy to acknowledge the very kind notices of this volume; and of the numerous commendations that have come to hand, the following will help to indicate the character of the work:

From the New-York Observer.

"MISSION SCHOOLS OF THE A.B.C.F.M. IN INDIA."

"This is a volume of 432 pages 12mo, full of stirring facts and incidents illustrating Missionary life in India, and the happy working of Mission Schools, with a neat engraving of the Mission House and City of Kolapoor. It is written in a warm, earnest, and interesting style, and will form a valuable addition to our works on Foreign Missions."

From Rev. JOHN JENKINS, D.D., Philadelphia, for several years a Missionary in India.

"I have been looking through your excellent work, and have been deeply interested in the candid history it supplies of the Missionary School system of India. My views entirely coïncide with your own as they are brought out in your work. I can not but think that the publication of the statements and opinions which you have so industriously collected, will do much to clear up the vexed question of Hindu Missionary Education. Besides this, it can not fail to excite both the gratitude and zeal of the churches of all denominations in the United States."

From Rev. SAMUEL D. BURCHARD, D.D., New-York.

"From an examination of this book, I am favorably impressed with its fidelity to facts, its value as a book of reference, and its great usefulness should it be generally circulated."

From the Rev. D. O. ALLEN, D.D., Author of "India, Ancient and Modern," and 26 years missionary of the A.B.C.F.M. in India, in the same Missions with Mr. Wilder.

"Your work, 'MISSION SCHOOLS IN INDIA,' is on a very important subject, and I am glad it has so able an advocate. Some work on this subject was much needed, and your book supplies this want better than any I have seen. I am surprised that you have been able, in your circumstances, and in so short a time, to prepare so good a book. It shows that you must have carefully examined the whole subject; that your knowledge of it must be extensive, and yet particular; that your views of the Missionary work, and of the best means to promote it, are clear and correct; and that your opinions on this whole subject have been matured by careful consideration and prayerful reflection. I hope the book will have a large circulation. I wish a copy of it could be sent to every Missionary now engaged in the cause of Foreign Missions. I am surprised at the opinions I sometimes hear, and grieved at the changes which have been made in some of our Missions. These changes appear to me as great a mistake as it would be for us in this country to dismiss our Sabbath-Schools, to discontinue our Colleges and Theological Seminaries, and determine to have, as we then should have, only an ignorant and uneducated ministry to preach the Gospel to an ignorant and depraved people."

From Rev. GEORGE POTTS, D.D., New-York.

"Your new work strikes me as a well-drawn picture of the benefits of the Christian school-system as part of the Missionary work. The details are interesting in regard to the general work also. I have read the whole book. I think it conclusive and well written."

From Rev. HOLLIS READ, late a Missionary of the A.B.C.F.M. in India, and author of "God's Hand in History," "India and its People," etc.

"A masterly argument for Mission Schools and native education, as preparatory and auxiliary to the work of preaching the Gospel. It is the work of an earnest man, who knows whereof he affirms—an able, lively, bold exposition and vindication of one of the great divisions of missionary labor. It abounds in telling statistics and documentary evidence of great value.

"The book is timely, as fitted to confirm a long-ago formed, and till recently unquestioned, high estimate of Mission Schools. It is a collection of an immense amount of information, and the presentation of an array of arguments in favor of this species of missionary labor. But it is not so much Mr. Wilder that speaks, as it is Mr. Wilder that makes every missionary in Western India speak, and every mission of the American Board. Yet the volume is any thing but a book of dry statistics and arguments. It is enlivened with incidents, anecdotes, sketches of character, and of oriental life, which commend it to the perusal of all classes of readers, as instructive as it is entertaining.

"The time has no doubt come when the different departments of the great work of Christian Missions to the heathen ought to have a more *specific* advocacy. The patrons of the work need more distinctive ideas of different fields of labor, and of the different departments of labor in the same field. Mr. Wilder has done a valuable service by his very able and exceedingly interesting exposition and defense of the *educational* department. To this department, as preparatory and auxiliary to the great work of evangelization, he has given a just yet a very high position. And he has done more. While the main object of the book is well sustained, and in this he well deserves and will receive the thanks of the many loyal friends of native education in heathen countries, its *incidental* merits are not the less to be valued. Few books on India present a more complete portraiture of the people as met in real life, of their manners, customs, superstitions, and especially of their mental and moral idiosyncrasies. Though the book appears in perilous times, it deserves, and I hope will have, a wide circulation and a great multitude of readers."

From the New-York Evangelist.

MISSION SCHOOLS IN INDIA, ETC.

"The author of this volume was for many years Missionary to India, under direction of the American Board. His connection with the Board has ceased, and yet he still intends to devote his life to the Missionary work in India. In these pages he puts forward an earnest plea in behalf of Mission Schools, especially in that country. There is much in his book which will be read with deep interest. He traces the agency of schools in preparing the way for the preaching of the Gospel to those who can be reached only through the children; and his narratives of conversions brought about through their instrumentality, are some of them deeply affecting. . . . Mr. Wilder seems to feel deeply, as he speaks strongly, and is careful to fortify his positions with documentary evidence which takes up considerable space. He gives quite fully the views of the Missionaries to India upon the subjects."

From Rev. B. C. MEIGS, forty-two years Missionary of the A.B.C.F.M. in Ceylon.

"I have read many portions of your book with great interest. You have done good service to the cause of Missions. . . . I have, for a long period of years, felt a deep interest in the cause of Christian education among the heathen children of India. You are aware I have had 42 years of experience on this subject, and I can truly say, that every year has added strength to my convictions of the importance of beginning with the children, to teach them the first principles of the Christian religion. . . . If any person has any doubt on this subject, let him spend hours, as I have done, in endeavoring to make an adult heathen, whose mind is like a field all grown over with thorns, and briers and thistles, understand the nature of repentance and faith, of heaven and hell. Let him see how he will run every Christian truth into his own heathen mold, and misunderstand and pervert every thing you can say. Then, in contrast with this, let him enjoy the privilege of preaching to an audience of young men and women who have been trained up in our village schools, and if he is not convinced of the importance and usefulness of these schools, I know not what will convince him. . . .

"I wish you much success in the sale of your book. It is a very timely and interesting volume, and appears to have been prepared with care and ability."

From the Congregationalist, of Boston.

"So far as the question of policy in regard to schools among the missions is concerned, we confess to have had from the beginning of the agitation of the subject a decided leaning to the policy which the Board and the Committee disfavor; and we find many interesting facts and testimonies in this volume looking in the same direction. We warmly wish the author well, and trust that he may be permitted, in returning to India, to demonstrate the beneficial truth of the opinions which he holds in regard to the Missionary work."

From the American Presbyterian, of Philadelphia.

"Very interesting extracts from Rev. R. G. Wilder's late work on MISSION SCHOOLS have at different times appeared in our columns; yet no extract can give a proper idea of the thoroughness and earnestness with which the author enters into the work of exhibiting the importance of this arm of missionary service, and of exposing the errors of those who have disparaged, and in part discarded it. . . He reviews the history of this branch of missionary effort in the various flourishing schools of India and Ceylon, and gives the testimony of missionaries from every country, and of intelligent English laymen, in their favor. Not content with this, he passes to the Missions among the North-American Indians, the Armenians, the Nestorians, and in the Sandwich Islands, and gathers a vast mass of facts, such as repeated revivals, important and interesting cases of individual conversions, interest excited in the minds of leading persons among the heathen, etc., which make a powerful argument in their behalf. The arbitrariness of a deputation interfering so seriously with this tried and faithful means of effort among the heathen is, in our opinion, but justly stated; while the author shows, through his whole volume, that it is not in the spirit of a mere controversialist he has written, but as an earnest friend of Christian Missions, and as a sincere well-wisher of a great institution, whose few errors by no means undermine its claims to the regard and support of the Churches. The volume is embellished with a handsome view of the Mission House and City of Kolapoor."

From Rev. E. Burgess, many years a Missionary of the A.B C.F.M., and a fellow-laborer with Mr. Wilder in India.

"I regard this book, 'MISSION SCHOOLS IN INDIA,' as one of the most valuable contributions to the literature of Missions that have ever been presented to the American public. It is intended to illustrate the importance of Schools, and to throw light on the question which has attracted so much attention since the late Deputation of the Prudential Committee of the A.B.C.F.M. returned from India. And it does throw important light on that question. It deals, not in theory merely, but in facts and their application to the work of Missions. Mr. Wilder's own experience and observation furnish many of the facts of the volume; yet some of the more important facts are derived from the history of the mission before he joined it. He gives also a record of the opinions and sayings of many missionaries, and others, on the subject. . . .

"I am glad to see this volume. It supplies a very important desideratum in the literature of Missions."

From Rev. E. S. BOYD, Professor, Monroe, Mich.

"This book is exceedingly interesting and instructive to the lover of Missions in any denomination, as it shows how much good has been done, and may yet be accomplished, by Mission Schools among the heathen."

From Rev. J. R. YOUNG, Plattsburg, N. Y.

"This book throws valuable light on the great question which has agitated the churches ever since Dr. Anderson went to India and broke up the Schools. . . . I doubt whether Mr. Wilder could have done more for the cause of Missions in any other way. I believe the Lord will bless this book and make it an instrument of great good to the Churches."

From GEORGE WASHINGTON MEARS, Esq.

"I have been reading your admirable book. I wish a copy of it were in the hands of every one who gives to the A.B.C.F.M. With such an overwhelming array of facts, the mind could not long be unconvinced of the necessity of schools in India; nay, of the utter impossibility of carrying on our Missions there without them."

From J. S. CUMMINGS, Esq.

"In my judgment this is a most timely and invaluable book. The conviction is almost irresistible that such schools are indispensable to the success of the Gospel in India. The statements of this volume will find a ready response in every unprejudiced mind; and all who pray, 'Thy kingdom come,' should wish for it a wide circulation."

From Rev. GARDINER SPRING, D.D., and others.

"We regard this book as a valuable addition to our works on Foreign Missions, especially in its bearing on the educational agencies to be employed in evangelizing the heathen."

W. J. Hoge,
Gardiner Spring,
J. H. McNeill.